RIDING FOR THE LONE STAR

RIDING FOR THE LONE STAR

Frontier Cavalry and the Texas Way of War, 1822–1865

Nathan A. Jennings

Number 2 in the American Military Studies Series

University of North Texas Press
Denton, Texas

10 9 8 7 6 5 4 3 2 1

Permissions:
University of North Texas Press
1155 Union Circle #311336
Denton, TX 76203-5017

The paper used in this book meets the minimum requirements
of the American National Standard for Permanence of Paper for
Printed Library Materials, z39.48.1984. Binding materials have
been chosen for durability.

Library of Congress Cataloging-in-Publication Data

Jennings, Nathan A. , author.
  Riding for the Lone Star : frontier cavalry and the Texas way
of war, 1822–1865 / by Nathan A. Jennings.
  American military studies ; no. 2. Denton, Texas : University of
North Texas Press, [2016]
     p. cm. -- (Number 2 in the American military studies series)
  Includes bibliographical references and index.
  ISBN 978-1-57441-635-0 (cloth : alk. paper) / ISBN 978-1-57441-
640-4 (ebook) 1. Cavalry--Texas--History--19th century. 2. Law
enforcement--Texas--History--19th century. 3. Frontier and pioneer
life--Texas. 4. Texas--History, Military--19th century. 5. Mexican War,
1846–1848--Texas--Cavalry operations. 6. Texas--History--Civil War,
1861–1865--Cavalry operations. 7. United States--History--Civil War,
1861–1865--Cavalry operations. I. Title. II. Series: American military
studies series ; no. 2.
  LCC.F391J55 2016
  355.00976409/034--dc23
                          2015040937

*Riding for the Lone Star: Frontier Cavalry and the Texas Way of War,
1822–1865* is Number 2 in American Military Studies

The electronic edition of this book was made possible by the
support of the Vick Family Foundation.

Contents

Introduction

Texans and Nineteenth-Century Warfare

The idea of Texas was forged in the crucible of frontier warfare. It emerged desperately and violently between 1822 and 1865 as Anglo-Americans encountered mounted combat north of the Rio Grande. This cavalry-centric arena, which had long been the domain of the Plains Indians and the Spanish Empire, compelled an adaptive martial tradition that shaped and informed early Lone Star culture. Beginning with initial tactical innovation as colonial militia in Spanish *Tejas* and culminating with massive mobilization of horsemen for the American Civil War, Texan society developed a distinctive way of war defined by armed horsemanship, volunteer militancy, and event-specific mobilization as it engaged both tribal and international opponents.[1]

This predilection for riding to war as frontier rangers, militia, and light cavalry—generalized in military terminology as mounted arms—developed as a nationalistic tradition against Indian, Mexican, and American enemies. Consistently characterized by tactical versatility, the association of firepower and horsemanship with masculine ideals permeated Texan society often beyond actual physical manifestation as it engaged both real and perceived threats in all directions.

1

As described by historian Robert Wooster in his seminal work, *The American Military Frontiers*, martial volunteerism allowed these men to "honor their masculinity through demonstrations of independence, civic virtue, and martial prowess" while internalizing concepts of "patriotism, community, and manhood."[2]

Texas's militarism evolved materially, with outsized cultural implications, across a broad spectrum of warfare throughout the early and mid-nineteenth century. Learned in the unforgiving academy of frontier combat, its warmaking methodologies originated in tribal clashes of colonial *Tejas*, strengthened in territorial wars of the Texas Republic, attained continental fame in the Mexican-American War, matured in border conflicts of antebellum Texas, and culminated in the cataclysmic Civil War. This march of campaigns stretched from the deserts of New Mexico to the forests of Georgia, and from the prairies of Oklahoma to the urban sprawl of Mexico City. In each conflict Texan volunteers answered the call to arms with nationalistic enthusiasm for mounted combat.

This societal approach to military affairs finds further definition in broader analytical theory associated with American history. In his foundational work of 1977, *The American Way of War*, scholar Russel F. Weigley employed German historian Hans Delbruck's binary concept to divide the United States' conflict record between strategies of annihilation and attrition. While the author asserted the former approach "seeks the overthrow of the enemy's military power," he articulated the latter is usually employed by peoples or states whose "means are not great enough to permit direct overthrow of the enemy and who therefore resorts to an indirect approach."[3]

Weigley's dichotomy finds ready applicability in Texas's early history despite its existence as an independent republic for only a decade. As a colony, nation, and state that constantly grappled with opponents both weaker and stronger than themselves, it often prosecuted tailored strategies of annihilation and attrition separately and simultaneously. If the frontier polity seemed to periodically maintain exhaustive, defensive postures against the Mexican and Union armies, it unquestionably embraced campaigns of sheer offensive destruction against tribal competitors. Stemming from seventeenth- and eighteenth-century Anglo-American traditions that "accepted, legitimized, and encouraged attacks upon and the destruction of noncombatants, villages, and agricultural resources"—as defined by historian John Grenier in *The First Way of War*—Texans, in concert with the United States Army, destroyed Indian power across the lower Great Plains by the close of the nineteenth century.[4]

Expanding beyond strategic considerations, this work additionally uses Way of War theory to interpret interrelated cultural and material aspects of Lone Star militarism. Incorporating scholar Brian Linn's definition that "encompasses tactics, operational methods, strategy, and all other factors that influence the preparation for, and conduct of, warfare," Texan warmaking is assessed as distinctive reactions to internal and external factors.[5] While a diverse threat environment, expansive frontier spaces, territorial expansion, nationalism, and constant American immigration catalyzed militancy, a combination of inadequate state revenue, minimal industrial capacity, immature fiscal systems, and aversion to standing armies compelled a volunteer-based model of frequent but limited mobilization.[6]

Sam Houston, Texas's preeminent statesman prior to the Civil War, described preference for volunteer martial service: "We are to look to the militia of our country for defense in time of trouble ... they are the men who are to form the bulwark of liberty, and to stand forth in defense of our institutions." The Victor of San Jacinto then emphasized the inherent strength of Texan methodologies when he wrote his countrymen fought with "common sympathies with the community" because they held "common interests" and "common feeling with the people."[7] Reflecting on the republic's failed attempts to maintain standing armies in 1837 and 1840 while criticizing later U.S. Army garrisons, the polemical leader elaborated: "These are the men I would depend upon. They are the men with whom I would hazard my life in full confidence."[8]

Texas's military establishment, which constantly adapted against particular foes while remaining generally consistent with preference for mounted arms, emerged along specific tactical subsets according to functional necessity. While decentralized ranger variations fought in numerous guerrilla skirmishes along expanding borders, more conventional light cavalry regiments joined infrequent contests of massed armies in the Texas Revolution, Mexican War, and Civil War. Less intensive expressions like localized militias allowed widespread but inactive mobilization at town and county echelons. While Texas did occasionally produce effective infantry, such as Houston's regiments at San Jacinto and John Bell Hood's famed "Texas Brigade" in the Army of Northern Virginia, its inclinations remained cavalry-centric until final pacification of the Indian Frontier.

Of all Texan military organizations that fought in the nineteenth century, mounted rangers emerged as the iconic manifestation of their society's way of war in form, concept, and perception. As a controversial and dynamic tradition that earned publicity for extreme lethality and brutality, the horsemen stood unique amongst contemporary military institutions in North America. This effectiveness, enabled in large measure by fortuitous adoption of revolving firearms that allowed unprecedented tactical advantage over regional competitors during the 1840s, developed in direct response to Plains Indian and Mexican enmity.[9] As noted by Nelson Lee, a Texan soldier, sailor, and ranger of the republican period: "This condition of affairs necessarily resulted in bringing into existence the Texas Rangers, a military order as peculiar as it has become famous."[10]

The advent of these fighters, which exemplified masculine ideals for broader Texan society between 1822 and 1865, came to symbolize its cultural distinctiveness both domestically and regionally. Generations of settlers militarized in tribal and nationalistic conflicts rode against territorial enemies while affiliating with the tradition. John Caperton, a former major in the Army of the Texas Republic, reflected this patriotic pride, and societal bias, after the Mexican War when he boasted rangers "were undoubtedly, as a body, the best horsemen, the best shots, and the best fighters on the American continent."[11] While contemporary nations placed their faith in professional armies, Texas relied on the versatility and spontaneity of its frontier tradition.

The rise of a distinctive Texan way of war during the nineteenth century—as defined by material and cultural implications of cavalry-centric organizations, amateur volunteerism, and event-specific mobilization—has not yet been fully captured in Texas historiography. While many studies describe relatively narrow or segmented ranger histories, conflicts of the Texas Revolution and Republic, and the multiplicity of Texan-Confederate regiments, none have yet combined the broader military experience from colonization to the Civil War into a single, interconnected narrative. This work remedies that omission by offering comprehensive analysis of the strategic, tactical, and social evolution of Texan martial traditions at varied political and military echelons with focus on manifestation across combat functions and organizational types.

Riding for the Lone Star consequently investigates several questions that have been neglected in ongoing conversations about Texas military history. The first inquiry pertains to context and formation of the Anglo-Texan martial experience. How did converging plains Indian, Spanish, and United States fighting traditions intersect to shape military cultures that evolved between the Red River and the Rio Grande? While American immigrants certainly imported weaponry and tactics from home states, especially Tennessee, that included predilections for irregular warfare and reliance on rifled musketry, they also adopted horse mobility of plains tribes and mirrored previous adaptation by Spanish presidios. Fusion of these military attributes resulted in a new type of frontier cavalry which eventually gained regional fame, and notoriety, as the Texas Rangers.

A second investigation centers on the nature of Texan mobilization throughout numerous wars and conflicts. How did centralized governments and frontier settlements prepare and generate both official and *ad hoc* military organizations as tailored responses to evolving threat environments? And why did settler militarism—often reflecting service by only a minority of the citizenry—have such profound impact on broader Lone Star culture and society? Rangers are remembered as the most visible and enduring expression, but in what ways did the larger tradition develop as Texas deployed a variety of specialized units to combat diverse foes? And how did these nationalistic mounted forces, including militia, rangers, light cavalry, federalized auxiliaries, spies, mounted rifles, minute men, brigands, and partisan horsemen, reflect both the commonality and diversity of the polity's approach to warfare?

A third aspect of inquiry incorporates military sciences and conduct that defined warfare in nineteenth century North America and influenced how Texans waged war on the periphery of Western civilization. Located at the convergence of Anglo-Germanic, Hispanic, and tribal influences, relentless raiding and intermittent battles characterized conflict across the volatile prairies and plains. Mounted skirmishing dominated this domain and Euro American colonizers, both Spanish and American, formed cavalries to counter indigenous mobility. By interpreting the embattled frontier as a defined military environment predominantly driven by asymmetric, irregular, and guerrilla warfare, the unconventional reactions that informed Texan martial development can be better interpreted.

Given this context, which military fundamentals did combatants conceptualize, and what were Texas's evolving tactical practices and strategic aims as it pursued wars of annihilation and attrition? How did Texans organize and deploy mounted units against decentralized Indian threats and massed, combined arms invasions by both Mexican and Union armies, both separately and simultaneously? And in which ways did frontier campaigns come to embrace the horror of population destruction, as opposed to Napoleonic strategies that oriented against nation-state armies? These answers allow deeper insight into the rise of Texas's way of war and offer conclusions familiar to twenty-first-century military practitioners.

In addition to comprehensively understanding Texas within the context of nineteenth century warfare, this work investigates intrinsic qualities of its individual, and often highly specialized, fighting organizations. First, it is important to recognize all manifestations of Texas mounted arms between colonization and frontier pacification as irregular and amateur in nature, as opposed to contemporary regular army institutions in the United States, Mexico, and Europe. Jefferson Davis, a veteran officer and statesman who observed both professional and volunteer forces in the Mexican War, delineated this separation when he disdainfully referred to Lone Star auxiliaries as "irregular cavalry," "irregular mounted men," and "volunteer cavalry."[12]

Differences between Texan irregulars and contemporary regulars resided in the professional continuity and institutionalized nature of the latter, and volunteerism and intermittent mobilization of the former. Even formations such as the post-independence Army of Texas and abortive 1839 Frontier Regiment, which the Texas Congress intended as permanent forces, never attained the *spirit de corps* of a nation-state service or branch. The resulting irregularity of Texan mounted arms, qualifying as frontier light horse similar to nineteenth-century European auxiliaries like Native Horse of British India and Cossacks of Russia, defined the wide range of amateur and semi-professional units that prosecuted state territorial interests until and even after Federal occupation in 1866.[13]

A second defining quality of Texas's mounted arms pertained to their civil-military context and security purpose, or absence thereof, prior to 1865. These qualities, in addition to a competitive environment that compelled constant militarization, defined continuity of military tradition. Horse formations, including rangers of the republican and antebellum periods, operated almost exclusively as military forces as opposed to lawmen policing the Old West. As late as 1859, ranger captain John Salmon Ford refused to arrest fellow Anglo-Texans in North Texas, explicitly protesting that his role was "military" and not "civil."[14] Given the nature of this self-perception, externally oriented ranging companies and battalions of early Texas remain far removed from the criminally focused ranger bureaucracies of the twentieth and twenty-first centuries.

This misperception has resulted in under-appreciation of the exclusively military orientation and cultural influence of early Texan mounted forces. Luther Giddings, an Ohio officer who observed federalized Texas Mounted Rifles in the Mexican War, described their militant stature: "Centaur-like, they seemed to live upon their horse, and under firm and prudent leaders, were efficient soldiers, especially for scouts and advanced post-service." The major then went on to note: "As a mounted soldier he has had no counterpart in any age or country. Neither Cavalier or Cossack, Mamluke nor Morstrooper are like him."[15] Not yet lawmen nor constabularies, these frontiersmen fought as functionally defined, though amateur, mounted riflemen and light cavalry in both patrolling and larger maneuvers.

A final consideration of Texas's military experience from colonization to the Civil War is perspective of the study. My intention is to understand, analyze, and explore the development of its way of war from the vantage point of Anglo-American settlers who predominantly populated and ruled the frontier polity. I will investigate the individual and collective efforts of that society, in the context of mounted warfare, as it sought regional security and pursued territorial aggrandizement. While Native American, Spanish, and United States influences on Texan martial development inform the study, complete understanding of those experiences is outside the intended scope of work.

Given focus on tactical and strategic analysis, equally important historical themes, like political, economic, cultural, gender, racial, and ethnic considerations, are included only as they shape military affairs. This mandates the absence of partisan sympathies that characterize much Texas, Native American, and *Tejano* literature concerning the period, which frequently assigns moralistic blame for ethnically disproportionate outcomes.[16] Critical contributions like Julian Samora's *Gunpowder Justice*, Gary Anderson's *The Conquest of Texas*, and Michael Collins's *Texas Devils* are incorporated, but balanced against more favorable, or at least less condemnatory, series like Robert Utley's *Lone Star Justice* and Michael Cox's *The Texas Rangers*. Moving beyond historiographical contests over memory, this work assesses values according to tactical, operational, and strategic causality with integrated assessment of societal impact.

Texan militarism prior to 1866 can be analyzed according to periods of armed conflict that demanded tailored mustering against specific challenges. From initial settlement to post-Reconstruction, with notable exceptions during larger nation-state wars in 1836, 1846, and 1861, the frontier polity rarely mobilized more than a single battalion at a given time, indicating societal impact beyond actual service. While military development during colonial, republican, and antebellum eras can be covered relatively comprehensively due to small-scale or limited mobilization, the final stage, encompassing Texas's massive effort for the Civil War, requires selection of illustrative cases to illuminate wartime involvement by the multiplicity of Texan-Confederate cavalry regiments that fought within and beyond home territory.

Beginning with the initial phases of colonization between 1822 and 1835 along the lower Colorado and Brazos rivers in Mexican *Tejas*, Anglo immigrants reacted tactically, and increasingly strategically, to varying degrees of indigenous mobility. Scattered settler militias, which gradually transitioned from localized infantry companies to expeditionary mounted battalions, shielded the establishment of new homesteads and rudimentary towns during precarious years and demanded high densities of citizen participation. The policies of *empresario* Stephen F. Austin emerged as particularly innovative when the colonists combined eastern American ranging techniques, precision marksmanship, and plains horsemanship to create a new type of frontier warrior.

The Texas Revolution of 1835 and 1836 spanned the second stage of Texan military development. Throughout the uprising, Anglo colonials united, organized, and nationalized their scattered militias for consolidated rebellion against Mexico with notable *Tejano* support. The San Jacinto Campaign, in particular, demanded the first concurrent mobilization of counter-Indian rangers and Napoleonic cavalry to simultaneously combat indigenous and Mexican opponents. This formative conflict established versatile mounted forces as the enduring instrument of Texas security. Like Austin before him, Sam Houston, as the nation's first general-in-chief and then president, proved influential in shaping war-making policy before and during national independence.

The turbulent era of the Texas Republic encompassed the third, fourth, and fifth stages of Texan military evolution. While the initial period from 1836 to 1838 reflected a basic continuation of revolutionary defenses, the middle years from 1839 to 1841 saw increased levels of settler militarization for explosive ethnic wars. As the burgeoning nation conquered new lands, militia brigades and ranging companies prosecuted regional campaigns and aggressive patrols. These efforts expanded Texan territory in all directions at the expense of Indian and Hispanic peoples even as the republic twice failed to maintain standing armies. The era concluded with a series of invasions and counter-invasions with Mexico in 1842 and the rise of an elite ranger cadre that accompanied decreased citizen participation in active service.

The sixth stage of martial development lasted from 1845 to 1860 as Texan mounted volunteers, also called irregular, auxiliary, or partisan cavalry, augmented the U.S. Army as citizens of a new American state. Federalized for service in the Mexican War, Texas regiments fought with lethal utility while earning reputations for brutality. This wartime service popularized the Texas Ranger legend and garnered them fame, and notoriety, across the continent. Throughout subsequent antebellum years, county militias and state rangers augmented flagging army garrisons in Texas against native and Mexican opponents.[17] Despite an inverse relationship between exploding population and decreasing military volunteerism, irregular cavalry continued to inform, and sometimes define, perceptions of Lone Star masculinity.

The American Civil War saw the apex of Texas's way of war as it rebelled against another distant national capital. Similar to previous wars against Mexico, the frontier polity contested the impending domination of a powerful invader: the Union Army. Between 1861 and

1865 Texans mobilized more cavalry under the Confederate banner than any other state, North or South, indicating the depth of cultural appreciation for mounted fighting in the society. This second contest for political secession compelled a return to simultaneous collisions of massed armies and guerrilla-type warfare along divergent geographic fronts as both tribal and Union forces invaded. The unprecedented scope of participation by Texan cavalry and riflemen in the Civil War, predominantly in numbered Confederate regiments, proved enduring militancy.

The following pages and chapters tell the story of Texas's expansionist origins as defined by cavalry-centric war-making on the periphery of Western civilization. It represents a confluence of historical facts and fantastical legends, a narrative replete with intrepid captains, grasping villains, and ordinary people who fought and died in a contentious environment. For Anglo-Texans who organized and militarized for nationalistic, economic, familial, and territorial interests, it reflected a deeply personal commitment to fight for kin and country. For the tribesmen, Mexicans, and *Tejanos* who fought with and against them, it became a desperate, losing struggle in the face of rising American strength. Only at the culmination of its martial tradition, in the Civil War, did Texas experience total defeat and emasculating military occupation.

These experiences combined the collision of entire peoples with the hopes and fears of individuals who shaped the frontier landscape. Cavalry cultures thrived at the center of this contest, driving and accelerating the hostility. In their own words, participants on all sides describe existence fraught with unforgiving confrontations across the lower Great Plains. Expanding beyond the narrow prism of the rangers of lore, this work explores the broader tactical evolution and societal implications of several generations of settler communities that rode for the Lone Star. Rising as the sword and shield of the idea called Texas, it is a narrative of how mobility, firepower, and adaptation influenced their destiny north of the Rio Grande.

Chapter 1

Tribal Warfare of Colonial *Tejas*, 1822–1835

The story of Texas and its dynamic martial tradition began with the challenges of American colonization between 1822 and 1835. Throughout initial settlement the settlers increasingly focused on the military use of horses as they adapted to the frontier environment of Mexican *Tejas*. The resulting transition, from woodland infantry tactics to plains cavalry techniques, developed over two stages: early militia campaigns against proximate coastal tribes, and later offensives against more distant prairie and plains peoples of central and western Texas. This steady march of conflict reflected both relentless small-unit raiding and larger expeditions in 1824, 1826, 1829, and 1835. The final campaign on the eve of revolution, comprising entire battalions of mounted men, illustrated the colonists' full emulation of Indian mobility.

In addition to tactical adaptation, colonial leaders unleashed selective hostility that reflected adept strategic exploitation of tribal power and relations. While historian Wayne Lee's thesis that Anglo colonials generally saw natives as "true barbarians, fit targets for the most extreme forms of war" is true, he is also correct that the colonists' initial decade in Texas was defined by pragmatic "graduation of intensities for particular purposes."[1] *Empresarios* like Stephen Austin swiftly recognized the population dimension as the Clausewitzian center of gravity in *Tejas* warfare, and thus identified domestic centers as both military targets and allies to be courted.[2] This calculated appreciation of the human landscape often benefited from intelligence gained from indigenous sources.

The Anglo-Texan military experience under Mexican colonial rule benefited from two further enhancements outside the tactical arena. The first was the spread of societal nationalism and political unity. Collective efforts in the face of real and perceived existential threats, in addition to feared oppression by Mexico City, directly facilitated the growth of Texan militarism and kindled the fire of Lone Star patriotism. Without the initial flowering of fundamental and democratic interdependence amongst the scattered Anglo homesteads and budding towns, the formation of a unified martial tradition would have lacked impetus and participation.

Civilian activities that inadvertently trained martial skills, specifically horsemanship, firearms marksmanship, and field subsistence, emerged as a second enhancing factor on the contested frontier. Learned from Spanish and Mexican neighbors, and also from Indian emulation, Anglo settlers gradually mastered tactical riding and equine husbandry. Cattle ranching emerged as a prime commercial influence in this regard since the necessary utilization of horses while armed during grazing and longer trail drives trained cowhands in many of the basic functions of nineteenth-century cavalrymen. These vocational skills, along with galvanized political unity, unwittingly prepared the nascent society for its formative event: The Texas Revolution.

Rising militancy and nationalism north of the Rio Grande found the Anglo-Texan colonies in a unique geographical position at the confluence of North American powers. Each of the dominant societies that bordered *Tejas* provided direct and indirect influences that enabled military adaptation. The eastern United States' tradition in ranger and militia operations bequeathed the immigrants a useful inheritance of irregular warfare expertise and familiarity with precision marksmanship. From the north and west, native peoples of the lower plains and prairies established the mobile context for conflict in *Tejas*. From the south, Spanish presidios set a precedent for Euro American adaptation to Plains Indian raiding methods. Mexicans and *Tejanos*, in particular, shaped Anglo reactions through direct cross-pollination of tactics. These factors, when contextualized against norms of contemporary cavalry conduct, deeply informed their martial inclinations.

This amalgamation consequently earned Texan frontiersmen distinction as a peculiar model of nineteenth-century mounted arms. The *Texan Democrat* later summarized the confluence of tactical abilities on September 9, 1846, when it boasted that federalized Texan horsemen—who had recently gained continental fame for their performance as scouts and assault troops in the 1846 American invasion of North Mexico—could "ride like a Mexican, trail like an Indian, shoot like a Tennessean, and fight like a devil."[3] This fusion of capabilities embraced the most effective qualities of American, native, and Spanish martial inclinations by combining mobility and firepower with desperate adaptation. The resulting tradition would inform the foundation of Texas's way of war throughout a half-century of warfare.

Initial Colonial Adaptation

The official colonization of Anglo-American Texas began in the year 1820 with Moses Austin's planned venture to establish an ambitious settlement in Spanish-governed *Tejas*. As a former resident of Spanish colonial Missouri, beginning in 1798, the enterprising pioneer enjoyed familiarity with the provincial government of New Spain. Austin's cultural ties to the United States likewise made him an ideal candidate to recruit American citizens for the Texas venture. Additionally, he boasted practical experience in settlement leadership and commercial enterprise since he had already founded a town and established a lead mine in Washington County of Missouri territory during its transition from Spanish to American rule.[4]

After agreeing to terms of settlement under the imperial administration in San Antonio de Bexar, the administrative center of *Tejas*, Austin proceeded to enlist support for Anglo colonization. The "Contract for Emigration to Texas," which he offered to potential settlers, stated they were "about to commence a settlement at the mouth of the River Colorado near the bay of San Bernardo in the province of Texas." The document also specified that the colonists would be "under the protection of the Spanish Government."[5] This promise of security, which would prove to be perilously hollow, portended dire consequences for relations between the American immigrants and Mexico City.

Stephen Austin, the son of Moses, assumed leadership as official *empresario* of the *Tejas* program upon his father's unexpected death on June 10, 1821. This title allowed him legal authority to allocate land grants to individual American colonists in the name of the Spanish government. After some hesitation, the young adventurer renewed the contract for settler recruitment, stating that he was "forming a Colony under the authorities of the Government of New Spain." He also warned each candidate to be prepared to explore "the coast, and mouths of the Rivers from Galveston to the Mouth of the Guadeloupe River," and to expect to "assist in the building of Cabbins and a Stockade." The young leader further required that each man arrive with "his own arms" and "Farming tools, Oxen, or Mules, and Provisions and Seeds."[6]

Austin would become known as the "Father of Texas" and emerged as the most influential American in Texas prior to the Texas Revolution. More significantly to the development of Texan mounted arms, his militia policies pioneered the first Anglo-Texan use of dedicated and mounted counter-guerrilla forces to "act as rangers for the common defense."[7] The Missourian's inspired recognition of the need for mobility on the frontier initiated a century of continuous and versatile service by Texan horsemen.

The turbulent secession of Mexico from Spain in the summer of 1821 forced Austin to visit Mexico City to renew his contract with the new government. The young entrepreneur then spent almost a year in the capital of the new Mexican Empire, establishing political alliances and currying favor for the *empresario* program while advocating for a broader imperial colonization act.[8] When the Mexican Federalist Party overthrew Agustin de Iturbide, the short-lived Emperor of Mexico, in the spring of 1823, Austin reported that the new "Sovereign Congress and Supreme Executive" had repealed the "Colonization law in total ... except as refers to me." The newly formed United Mexican States had fortuitously approved Austin's request as an individual agreement in the absence of comprehensive legislation. Contract in hand, the pioneer returned north to *Tejas*, leaving behind an unstable and divided Mexico.[9]

Anglo-American settlement of Texas under the Mexican banner from 1823 to 1835 reflected the general continuation of previous Spanish contracts. The subsequent series of national governments, under both liberal and conservative leadership, typically included the *empresario* territorial contracts within the newly federalized Department of *Tejas*.[10] Yet the republican change existed in name only; Anglo settlements along the Colorado and Brazos river valleys remained completely colonial. Left to construct their own towns and defenses, they developed in geographical, economic, and military isolation from Mexico City. Throughout the period the colonies retained the peculiar distinction of legal and organizational sanction by the Mexican Republic, while receiving immigration, cultural stimulation, and material provision from the United States.

Both Anglo settlers and Mexican officials in pre-revolutionary Texas emphasized the colonial status of *Tejas* in their letters. Austin, as the leading Anglo official, consistently referred to the settlement area as "the Colony" until secession in 1835.[11] Individual settlers, such as William Dewees and John Jenkins, also utilized the same term to describe the developing society. Dewees emphasized how the "Empresarios" issued land titles under "the terms of the Colonization Laws" in his letters.[12] Even Antonio Lopez de Santa Anna, the Mexican President and commander of the failed Mexican reconquest campaign in 1836, called the rebels "colonists" when describing their resistance.[13] These statements, by both leaders and settlers, indicated shared understanding of the settlements' remote position on Mexico's northern frontier.

Colonial isolation held far-reaching consequences for the future of *Tejas* as it practically placed the colonists outside the military protection of the national government. Throughout the period of Mexican sovereignty, the national government never installed federal administrators, Hispanic immigrants, or presidio soldiers directly in the Anglos' administrative center at San Felipe. Political and military instability throughout the Mexican Republic, both provincial and national, ensured *Tejas* neglect. Though Mexico eventually deployed small army garrisons to Anahuac, Velasco, and Nacogdoches to complement the Bexar presidio and enforce customs duties, settlement defense rested entirely on Anglo militia.[14] The resulting settler mobilizations, under very limited Mexican supervision, catalyzed the development of nationalistic arms to combat Indian competitors.

The movement of American settlers westward from the United States territories and states to isolated frontiers forced the pioneers to negotiate marked transitions in continental terrain. These changes generally unfolded along the ninety-eighth meridian, where the forests of eastern North America gradually ended. While the territories of western *Tejas* offered expansive plains and prairies mostly devoid of mountains, forests, and swamps, the vegetation of the eastern province provided woodlands reminiscent of the American South. Dewees, who usefully recorded his experiences as a pioneer and militiaman beginning in 1823, wrote of southeastern *Tejas* in 1830 that "the greater part of the timber is immediately on the water courses." Further west, the unfamiliarity of the Great Plains barrier, and the corresponding lack of water and construction material, convinced the immigrants to settle along fertile river systems that led to the Gulf.[15]

San Felipe de Austin emerged as the first Anglo colony and town in the new frontier. Located on the west bank of the lower Brazos River, it served as an informal capital for the network of homesteads and colonies until its destruction in the Texas Revolution. Initially a group of approximately 300 families, this center and others soon expanded under Austin's supervision to rival and surpass the preexisting Spanish and indigenous populations in number and ambition. Examination of land contract records reveals that immigrants came in order of greatest proportion from Louisiana, and then Missouri, Arkansas, and Mississippi in equal share. These frontiersmen naturally arrived familiar with rural, woodland survival in the American South.[16]

Ambitious pioneers soon emulated Austin's success in *Tejas*. Dewees again recorded that, "upon the passage of the colonization laws of Mexico and the State laws of Coahuila and Texas, the attention of many men of enterprise was directed to the example of Austin, and contracts were taken out for colonizing the whole surface of Texas." This wave of new American *empresarios* contracted land tracts across the southern and eastern portions of the province to create settlement clusters. The most successful programs included Robertson Colony, De Leon Colony, Edwards Colony, the Irish Colonies, and the later DeWitt Colony, amongst numerous unsanctioned homesteads.[17]

By 1827 a total of twenty-five Anglo colonies with a population of 8,000 had scattered throughout *Tejas*. This expanding population more than tripled in the next five years, thus establishing a capable militia reservoir to protect gains and facilitate further expansion. The resulting combination of rising American density and rapid intensification of Anglo-Indian hostility in the absence of sustained Mexican intervention compelled the settlers, according to Austin, to organize a "system of defense for this section, until the Government can adopt measures for the protection of the whole frontier of Texas."[18] The challenges of confronting native cavalry, decentralization of command, and long distances between homesteads necessitated the transition of these militias from infantry to mounted companies.

A constellation of contentious tribes surrounded the American settlement zone near the Gulf Coast and across the greater *Tejas* expanse.[19] Tribal raiding cultures created a non-linear battle zone, lacking the population density, fortifications, and combined arms armies of the eastern United States and central Mexico. Unlike the conventional focus of most idealized European conflicts, rapid raids and guerrilla warfare defined combat north of the Rio Grande.[20]

Most initial Anglo-Texan engagements oriented against the Karankawas, an aggressive coastal people that excelled in dismounted and brown-water combat in rivers and coastal waters. These warriors stood predisposed for aggression against the colonists due to past conflicts with European pirates and explorers. Since their camps were located within marching distance of San Felipe, and because the Karankawa did not use horses for tactical mobility, the first colonial skirmishes occurred as light infantry affairs.[21]

Austin stated after his first exposure to the coastal hunters that "an American population" would be "the signal of their extermination, for there will be no way of subduing them but extermination."[22] These intolerant views enhanced the intensity of Anglo retaliation and provided moral justification for territorial aggrandizement. In contrast, the less warlike Tonkawa and Tawakoni peoples further inland and near the colonial footprint, experienced mixed relations with the settlers.[23] The Tonkawa in particular would adapt to serve as valuable scouts for militia companies since the colonists lacked topographical familiarity in the early years.

Further west and north, the prairie-based Waco became the primary threat to the colony after the Karankawa. As a cavalry-centric culture, these horsemen compelled the initial mounted response from the colonists between 1824 and 1829. This tribe's use of cavalry speed and operational reach in raiding operations required the settlers to reciprocate with mobile parity for settlement defense. French observer Jean Louis Berlandier, who surveyed Mexican *Tejas* in 1830, described the Waco armament: "They have excellent horses and possess firearms, although they are very expert with the bow, the lance, and the dagger."[24] He also wrote that "travelers on the road from Bexar to the Trinity, west of Austin, are often attacked by members of this nation." Despite the Wacos' adept use of horses for transportation in warfare, they did not employ cavalry with the unrivaled skill of the feared plains peoples to the west and north.

In East Texas, the Cherokees, Caddo, Shawnee, and Choctaw tribes, some of whom were immigrants themselves, lived as more sedentary, woodland tribes. The emerging Anglo center at Nacogdoches, which usually served as the gateway for over-land immigration from the United States, coexisted uneasily with these peoples throughout the colonial period. These tribes, who often embraced farming and developed less aggressive raiding cultures, preferred infantry-centric combat methods with increased firearm use. This reliance on musketry, as opposed to horses, bows, and spears, reflected woodland hunting practices typically conducted on foot.[25]

The immigrant Cherokee people, whom Berlandier described as "well armed and fond of war, at which they are highly skilled," stood as the most powerful of the eastern tribes.[26] In 1825, as San Felipe stood beset by the surrounding peoples, Austin duly warned his colonists to maintain peace with the "Cherokee and all the Indians to the east of us," lest they "be induced to unite against the American settlements."[27] The unstable peace between Anglo colonists and the woodland tribes of *Tejas* persisted until the Wars of the Texas Republic when nationalistic Texan armies expelled the larger tribes to allow territorial acquisition.

The nomadic Comanche and Lipan Apache of the western plains proved most dangerous due to lightning raiding tactics and unique operational reach. By the time of colonial settlement in the 1820s, the more powerful Comanche had become the scourge of *Tejas* and forced the Apache south to the Rio Grande. A decade later Berlandier observed that the Plains Indians' "war against the Creoles in Mexico spread terror among the settlers up and down the border." He also noted that "their raids then became almost continuous and the garrisons were always besieged. The fields were left to run wild."[28] This assault had long stymied Spanish attempts at colonization while depopulating and destabilizing the province since the 1750s.

By the time of Texan colonization, the Comanche alliance stood dominant on the lower plains and threatened the survival of any potential settlement, Spanish or Anglo. The devastating massacre of the San Saba mission in 1758 had served bloody notice that any expansion north of Bexar would have to be highly militarized and thus not cost effective.[29] Berlandier again described the might of the twelve tribes that comprised Comancheria:

> The Comanche constitute the largest and most terrible nomadic nation anywhere in the territory of the Mexican Republic. They live in the deserts of Texas and New Mexico, being excellent

horsemen; warriors equally at home with the gun, the bow, and the lance. Many of them use the mace or the throwing axe in battle. All of them are riders of consummate skill and are equally capable of long marches on foot.

Berlandier assessed their total population at 10,000 to 12,000, with the capability of fielding up to 3,000 warriors.[30]

American observers likewise found the plains horsemen impressive. Mary Austin Holley, a relative of Stephen Austin who visited him in 1831, described Comanche combat armament and techniques: "These Indians always move on horseback. Besides the bow and arrows, the usual arms of the Indian warrior, they are armed with a long spear, having a sword blade for a point." She also wrote that "when they descry an object of attack, or pursuit, they dart forward in a column, like lightning, towards it. At a suitable distance from their prey, they divide into two squadrons, one half taking to the right, and the other to the left, and thus surround it."[31]

The success of the Comanche in frontier raiding operations emanated in part from exceptional navigational abilities that allowed deep attacks far from their own villages. This advantage is militarily defined as operational reach, which is described by twenty-first-century U.S. Army doctrine as "the distance and duration across which a unit can successfully employ military capabilities."[32] Henry Dodge, commander of the United States Regiment of Dragoons in 1833, reported the unique Plains Indian capacity for over-land navigation when a band of young Comanche traveled from Brady's Creek, Texas, to Monterrey, Mexico. Using only natural landmarks and prior verbal instructions, the natives rode over 350 miles across extremely challenging terrain and through debilitatingly arid conditions.[33]

These cavalry cultures and their unique capacity for mobile war offered an existential threat to early Anglo-Texan settlement. Due to an unrivaled ability to project force they could have easily destroyed San Felipe in its infancy. Dewees observed this strength in 1823, just as the colonial program initiated settlement, when a host of "about one thousand Comanche" rode into Bexar on a "treaty expedition." He also wrote that the warrior people "seemed to have the Mexicans under their control."[34] With this scope of raiding power threatening from the plains, it was only Austin's conciliatory policies, and the colony's remote location in southeastern *Tejas*, that prevented immediate extermination.

Raiding by indigenous competitors demanded the immediate creation of colonial militia. Austin proclaimed the need for citizen-defense in personal terms: "You are there for now called upon to protect your own homes, your own property, to shield your wives and children from the arrows of a savage and merciless enemy."[35] In response American immigrants mobilized formations on an *ad hoc*, event-oriented basis throughout the 1820s and early 1830s. Jose Trespalacios, the first Mexican governor of Coahuila and *Tejas*, officially authorized the formation of an Anglo militia on December 15, 1822. Recognizing his inability to secure the frontier, he "directed the inhabitants of the Colorado to appoint an *alcalde* of their own choice to administer justice, and to organize a militia to oppose the Karankawa or other intruders who might attack their persons or property."[36]

In early 1823, with the approval of Trespalacios, the colonists divided the Colorado and Brazos valleys into two military districts with a total of sixty effective citizen-soldiers. This organization reflected the natural settlement concentration along river systems that offered access to water, timber, and passage to the Gulf. The citizenry elected prominent leaders Robert Kuykendall and Andrew Robinson as district commanders.[37]

These first militia forces consisted primarily of government sanctioned, volunteer infantrymen who reacted to localized native attacks. They predictably imported familiar weaponry from the United States that had proved effective against woodland peoples. The ubiquitous "Kentucky" long-rifle, with its precision long barrel, served as the weapon of choice for American immigrants. As a muzzle-loading, rifled, and single-shot musket, it fired calibers between .36 and .45 that were smaller than standard military grades designed for massed volleys by less able marksmen. The rifle was also extremely accurate according to contemporary standards, especially when compared to archaic Spanish and Indian firearms.[38]

Despite advantages in marksmanship, the rifles contained a crucial limitation: they were slow to reload and unwieldy for discharge on horseback. Napoleonic general and strategist Antoine-Henri Jomini emphasized this factor in his seminal treatise, *The Art of War*, when he cautioned that there were "few marksmen who can with any accuracy fire a musket while on horseback and in rapid motion."[39] Precision fire required a stable and dismounted platform, in accordance with woodland hunting origins. In larger confrontations, the rifles often required controlled and graduated rates of fire to prevent exploitation of loading intervals by arrow flights and rapid assaults.[40]

Noah Smithwick, an Anglo-Texan ranger who participated in numerous fights during the Texas colonial and republican periods, wrote of the disparity between immigrant and indigenous weaponry:

> Primitive as the Indians' weapons were, they gave them an advantage over the old single-barreled, muzzle-loading rifle in the matter of rapid shooting, an advantage which told heavily in a charge. An Indian could discharge a dozen arrows while a man was loading a gun, and if they could manage to draw our fire all at once they had us at their mercy unless we had a safe retreat.[41]

While the cumbersome rifles and muskets remained a challenge for horsemen, colonial pistols allowed improved carrying capacity and close combat discharge. Alternately, primitive carbines and shotguns offered a compromise for mounted operations, though they retained the same reload limitations and possessed less accuracy than rifles. These weapons, along with the heavier Hawkins rifle that frontiersmen developed with a larger caliber for hunting buffalo, provided the mainstay of Texan colonial and republican arms.[42]

While Trespalacios and the settlers coordinated initial security for San Felipe, Austin simultaneously sought approval for a sanctioned militia from higher echelons in Mexico. Felipe de la Garza, the Commandant General of the Eastern Interior Provinces, approved the Missourian to create a larger and more enduring military structure. On June 16, 1823, while Austin traveled back to Texas, Garza confirmed the colony's legal right to establish a colonial levy.

The *empresario* recorded this development and his official status as senior commander: "I am fully empowered and ordered to form a Battalion of Militia in this Colony ... with the rank of Lieutenant Colonel."[43] The order sectioned the colony into two sectors along the Brazos River, two sectors along the Colorado River, and one near La Bahia, doubtlessly reflecting Austin's input. It also ensured that the colonial structure mobilized "agreeably to the Militia Law of the Mexican Nation," thus subordinating the Anglo militia firmly under the Mexican Army establishment.[44]

The formation of the San Felipe militia mirrored the earlier mobilization of Spanish settlements in northern New Spain throughout two centuries of colonization. Hispanic adaptation in southern *Tejas* historically centered on the frontier communities of Bexar and La Bahia. As a combination of presidio outposts, Catholic missions, and ranching centers, these communities, along with the outpost at Nacogdoches in eastern *Tejas*, encompassed the forward line of defense for New Spain. A professional cadre of presidio soldiers garrisoned the isolated urban centers while maintaining a tenuous grasp on security.[45]

By the mid-eighteenth century, Apache and Comanche raiding made the Spanish reliance on professional arms untenable and *rancheros* and farmers organized to augment presidio garrisons. In 1722, as the empire's ecclesiastical and economic programs in *Tejas* faltered, Catholic leaders recommended increased settler density and militia participation as a solution. As one mission leader implored that their "best defense" consisted "in seeing to it that a place is inhabited." He then noted the advantage of creating a local militia from interested stakeholders, writing that "settlers will defend their own territory."[46]

By 1779 New Spain's frontier crisis had intensified despite a limited use of citizen-soldier levies. Indian attacks frustrated hopes of revitalizing *Tejas* as officials failed to effectively manipulate the Comanche against the Apache. Appreciating the tactical situation, the Spanish Commandant-General of the Northern Provinces, Teodoro de Croix, created offensive units intended to "carry the war to the huts of the hostile Indians, dislodge those who may penetrate between the lines and punish those who attempt to introduce hostilities into the province."[47] Disinclined to commit additional royal garrisons to distant frontiers, the Spanish crown also commissioned the governors of "New Mexico, Coahuila, and Tejas to form militia in their respective provinces."[48] These directives reflected renewed focus on militarizing the empire's northern borders as lands north of Bexar became a military buffer-zone between the Plains Indians and provinces south of the Rio Grande.

The Spanish challenges in *Tejas* found marked contrast with the later successes of Anglo-American colonies. In his memoir, Smithwick offered a biased, and ethnically themed, assessment of differing colonization attempts as they faced the same native opponents:

> Before the advent of the white man the Indians held full sway. They drove out the Spanish missionaries who attempted to take possession of the country as they had done in Mexico and California, and inspired the Mexicans with such a holy horror of them that they (the Indians) went into the Mexican towns and helped themselves to whatever they wanted, no one daring to oppose them. They tried that game on the Americans, and to their dismay found it would not work.[49]

The most damaging raids for the Spanish colonial program occurred against ranching and farming enterprises that existed outside presidio protection. Season after season, merciless assaults devastated commercial ventures beyond fortified towns. In 1819 the Spanish governor of *Tejas*, Antonio Martinez, warned his superiors that "rarely a day passes that this capital is not attacked by the Indians ... Comanches or Lipanes, with various evil Spaniards, disorganized or united, are attacking our fortifications almost every night." The official then despondently predicted that "his province" would "be destroyed unwittingly by lack of inhabitants."[50]

This constant aggression predictably led to a precipitous decline in Spanish colonizers as many potential settlers sought safety south of the Rio Grande. This reduced availability of both militiamen for combat service and civilians for agricultural and ranching development.[51] Martinez again explained: "This is inevitable because no one wishes to live in the province for fear of danger and because the few inhabitants now existing are being killed gradually by the savages, and the cattle and horses as well."[52] This specter of societal annihilation informed the militant cultures of both imperialists and natives; it propelled a climate of hatred and resulted in a continuous, cyclic destruction of the human landscape.[53]

The Spanish Empire's focus on civilian augmentation in *Tejas* thus centered on the main administrative center at Bexar with its fortifications and garrison. An accounting ledger from 1785 recorded the activity of the amateur levy that complemented the presidio. It documented the quantity of "powder and bullets" discharged by the militia in "the various sorties and scouting expeditions that have been made against the hostile Indians." The report's focus on civilians conducting both raids and reconnaissance indicated the *vaqueros'* expertise with terrain, horsemanship, and frontier tactics.[54] Four decades later, when negotiating a similar onslaught of tribal raiding in 1822 and 1823, the militiamen of San Felipe would embrace an almost identical citizen service requirement.

Anglo-Indian conflict in Texas began in June of 1822 when the Karankawa attacked a colonial survey party as they explored prospective settlement sites up the Colorado River system. Then, in February of 1823, the coastal raiders struck again. This time they ambushed a convoy of supply boats moving up the Colorado River. Both incidents resulted in American deaths. Abner Kuykendall, brother of the Colorado District commander, immediately led a retaliatory attack in response to the second attack. This action set an enduring pattern of strike and counter-strike that would eventually lead to the destruction of Indian power in Texas.[55]

John Moore, one of Austin's "Three Hundred" and a significant leader in the future development of the Anglo-Texan military tradition, summarized the fight after he and a party of settlers identified the position of the raiders on a tributary called Skull Creek: "At once we returned to our company, which was commanded by Mr. Kuykendall and numbered about twenty-two men." The aggressive militiaman then narrated how they rapidly transitioned into a direct assault: "We made our way to the bottom, got between the creek and the Indians, and surprised them, driving them out into the prairie. Twenty-three were left dead, without the loss of any of the whites."[56]

Dewees likewise participated in the fight. He described the reprisal in greater detail with emphasis on the dawn approach that allowed surprise and envelopment by converging wings:

> As silently as possible, we crawled into a thicket about ten steps behind the camps, placing ourselves about four or five steps apart, in a half-circle, and completely cutting off their retreat from the swamp...We fired upon them and killed nine on the spot. The rest attempted to escape, but having no way to run, except into the open prairie, we rushed upon them, and killed all but two, who had made their escape, though wounded, after the first fire.[57]

These techniques demonstrated adept understanding of guerrilla methods from prior experiences in the United States. Also instructive, Dewees wrote that the attacking settlers rode to the suspected area of engagement and dismounted prior to the assault. This shift from mounted to infantry roles at the site of battle reflected the inherent challenges of firing single-shot, muzzle-loading muskets and rifles while astride an unsteady platform. The tactic clearly defined the early Texan militia as doctrinal mounted riflemen—similar in tactical versatility to dragoons—according to nineteenth-century military classification.[58]

Dragoon forms of horse soldiers, which generally fought with shorter-ranged carbines as opposed to longer-ranged American hunting rifles, had evolved in Europe between the sixteenth and nineteenth centuries as a response to massed infantry firepower and close-support field artillery. These technological obstacles prompted increased reliance on versatile mounted corps that could alternately fight as dismounted infantry, excel in cavalry skirmishing and reconnaissance, and charge on horseback against enemy lines if needed. Prussian statesman Otto von Bismarck reportedly described the genesis of the dragoon concept: "It being found advantageous to bring infantry quickly to any desired spot, in order thereby to effect a surprise, several divisions of the army were mounted. These mounted foot soldiers were called dragoons."[59]

European nations alternately called this kind of multi-functional cavalry *carabiniers*, guards, *hussars*, lancers, and *chasseurs*, as mounted infantry models evolved to be more flexible in armament and capability. They then transported the concept to North America where Anglo and Hispanic colonists adapted it according to New World weaponry, terrain and threats. Albert Brackett, an American cavalryman who fought in the Mexican War, wrote of the dragoons' evolution: "They were originally organized to act as either cavalry or infantry skirmishers—a sort of hybrid corps to do the duty on foot or horseback; now they are simply a body of regular cavalry soldiers, in some countries divided into heavy and light dragoons."[60] In Texas and the United States, both rangers and dragoons maintained a strong infantry emphasis until the 1840s and 1850s respectively, when adoption of revolvers facilitated sustained killing from the saddle.

While true cavalry like the Comanche and Spanish models executed primary combat functions on horseback, American dragoons and riflemen usually fought as dismounted infantry.[61] In contrast, the Spanish and Comanche cavalry traditions relied mostly on swords and lances with varying use of antiquated firearms. The plains warriors' accuracy with bows from horseback was also legendary and represented an early form of repeating weaponry. According to Dewees, the colonials employed mounted infantry tactics again a short time later to repulse another Karankawa raid near the vulnerable settlement.[62]

Ethnic violence continued that summer when an allied warband, comprised mostly of Waco warriors, invaded the settlement and killed John Tumlinson, the colony *alcalde*, or Spanish civil administrator. The attack occurred while he traveled en route to Bexar to coordinate colonial affairs with the provincial government. John Wilbarger, an amateur historian who recorded directly from participants of this fight and many others in Colonial *Tejas*, wrote that "Tumlinson was instantly killed," but another colonist, referenced only as Newman, "who was on a good horse, fled, and succeeded in escaping."[63]

When Newman reported the murder to Tumlinson's family at their homestead near San Felipe, the *alcalde's* son, John Tumlinson Jr., gathered a militia party of eleven men and pursued "thirteen Waco Indians who were discovered approaching the settlements." The angry colonials located the warriors that night in their camp on the east bank of the Colorado River, above the colony, by utilizing another of the slain official's sons, Joseph, as a forward scout. According to Wilbarger, the settlers assaulted "with such fatal effect that in a few moments twelve of the thirteen Indians soon lay dead upon the ground." The remaining native escaped "like a frightened deer" while the militiamen suffered no casualties.[64]

In the spring of 1823, in response to increased friction with the Karankawa, the colony established a fortified outpost at the mouth of the Colorado River. This plan reflected a historical predilection by American frontiersmen for placing forts or blockhouses at advantages locations to deny Indian initiative. Dewees described the peril and desperation of the early colonial existence that compelled use of forward deterrent: "we dare not go out to hunt except in companies, as we are obliged to keep on the lookout, lest the savages fall upon us." He also stated the necessity of "leaving part of the men at home to guard the settlement from the Indians, who are very hostile to us."[65]

The colonial leadership fielded the Colorado River outpost in May of 1823. Kuykendall supervised the deployment without Austin, as the *empresario* was still attempting to renew the colony's contract in Mexico City. Veteran soldier Moses Morrison commanded fourteen volunteers assigned to the unit. As a former U.S. Army officer with field experience along the Mississippi River, Morrison served as a useful tactical leader during early years of settlement.[66]

The most important development concerning the outpost was not the intended fortification and garrison but rather the more versatile augmentation that Austin proposed upon his return to San Felipe that summer. Realizing the limitations of a static garrison, he advocated that a separate "ranger" element be formed to enhance the blockhouse. This was the first Anglo-Texan conception of utilizing light and independent patrolling elements to match Indian raiders with similar speed and stealth. The documented reference to this "ranging" unit, as defined by Austin, was preserved on the back of a property deed written by the pioneer's land commissioner and mentor, Felipe Enrique Neri, also known as Baron de Bastrop.

Austin informed his fellow colonists of the plan while simultaneously announcing a recruiting initiative:

> I have determined to augment at my own private expense the company of men which was raised by the late Governor Trespalacios for the defense of the Colony against hostile Indians. I therefore by these presents give public notice that I will employ ten men in addition to those employed by the Government to act as rangers for the common defense. The said ten men will form a part of Lieut. Moses Morrison Company, and the whole will be subject to my orders.[67]

By July Kuykendall considered moving the faltering garrison to San Felipe to provide immediate security. He proposed that the company be "placed in that part of the country where they are most needed, at least for three or four months, every man in our position is essential as the upper Indians are numerous and show strong symptoms of hostility." He also described the developing Anglo-Indian enmity: "We feel it a duty we owe our countryman to revenge his blood, and the time is not far distant when we will teach those savage people better sense than to sport with the lives of our countrymen."[68] This uncertainty reflected the unpredictable nature of the frontier environment. There were no battle lines or fortified boundaries, and the colony remained vulnerable at any given point from any direction.

Despite the pressing need for security at both the settlement center and the coastal entry ways, the small defensive post proved unsustainable. Funding and logistical failures insured the demise of the colony's first attempt at forward defense. At one point Morrison wrote to Kuykendall that he had "discovered a party of Karankawa at the bay," but then complained that they had "no powder and do not feel ourselves altogether safe to attack them in our present fix." He hoped that "as soon as our powder comes we shall go and spie them out."[69] Given this failure, the combat outpost proved less consequential than Austin's innovative proposal for rangers to counter tribal mobility with reciprocal mobility.

The term "ranger," as stated in Austin's recruiting letter, was not a new concept for Anglo settlers. British colonists had employed specialized reconnaissance and strike forces with tactical success in eastern North America since the first days of New World settlement. Like the later mounted adaptation of Texan rangers, woodland rangers of British and United States frontier history developed as a reaction to superior indigenous mobility as irregular light infantry on the eastern coast. This military innovation foreshadowed and informed later reactions by Anglo colonists in *Tejas*.

One of the first documented uses of rangers occurred in New England in 1622 when Captain John Smith, an adventurous British officer, pioneered specialized woodland patrolling in America. According to his writings, the captain formed "ranging" parties from the colonial levy as he attempted to gain initiative against surrounding indigenous peoples. In this endeavor he wrote: "To range this country of New England, I had but eight, as is said, and amongst their brute conditions I met many of their encounters, and without any hurt, God be thanked." Smith also described his use of the patrol detachment: "these I would employ only in ranging the countries, and tormenting the Savages, and that they should be as a running army." The captain later requested that the southern Virginia colony provide an additional 100 men to serve as rangers.[70]

Ranging operations became more ubiquitous and successful as British population density increased along the eastern American coast. The various Anglo colonies cross-pollinated these experiences, leading to the rise of the American warrior-woodsman tradition. Later, in what became known as King Philip's War from 1675 to 1678, Puritan ranger forces under Major Benjamin Church proved instrumental in defeating the Wampanoag and Narragansett Tribes despite several damaging Indian offensives.[71]

Church's stated mission to "discover, pursue, fight, destroy or subdue our Indian enemies" embodied the aggressive and proactive patrolling concept that would later characterize ranging operations in *Tejas*. Like his predecessor Smith, he learned from his native allies, and subsequently "took care not to come too thick together." The major also criticized that the "English always kept in a heap together; that it was as easy to hit them as to hit a house," clearly emphasizing the difference between Anglo and native maneuver tactics.[72]

Charles II of England institutionalized ranging in 1679 when he authorized colonial governing bodies to enlist "soldiers to be rangers for the security of their respective countries according to such order and direction as shall be agreed upon and made by their militia officers."[73] This order, which tellingly distinguished between the rangers and militia companies, made irregular light patrolling a legitimate crown function. London authorized the first officially recognized ranger force in 1747 in Nova Scotia. Called Gorham's Rangers, the king allowed them the title of "His Majesty's First Independent Company of American Rangers."[74] These frontiersmen, and other ranging companies like them, led the Anglo advance into the North American continent throughout the early and middle years of the eighteenth century. Irregular soldiering had become an integral pattern in the fabric of British-American colonial culture.[75]

Woodland rangers assumed new importance in the Anglo-American military tradition during the Revolutionary War. From 1775 to 1781 they augmented the Continental Army with specialized capabilities unique to the eastern American landscape. As frontiersmen who were lighter, faster, and more knowledgeable of terrain, the rangers excelled at asymmetric strikes against the British Army's vulnerabilities. The withering harassment of the British column after the battles of Lexington and Concord in 1775, the capture of Vincennes by William Rogers Clark and his "Rogers Rangers" in 1779, and the unorthodox campaign waged by Francis Marion during the British Southern Campaign between 1780 and 1782 were examples of guerrilla actions by rebel fighters. Following American independence, rangers led the haphazard advance of pioneers west of the Appalachian Mountains into the heart of the continent.[76]

The resulting Anglo-American ranger legacy, though woodland-focused, heavily informed the emerging Texan way of war as it adapted to a different kind of warfare in *Tejas*. It was thus no accident that Stephen Austin imitated John Smith's initial adaptation of employing ranging units to project force beyond the settlement walls 200 years later. Both maneuvers intended to prevent unpredictable attacks while providing stand-off security for vulnerable settlements that contained women and children. Smith's and Austin's references in their letters to the concept of "ranging" were also identical, suggesting a directly connected tradition.

Frontier instability continued throughout the year 1823 as the colonists established themselves in the vicinity of San Felipe. In November of that year Austin informed the provincial government: "The roads are full of wandering thieves who are united with the Indians and without a small cavalry force to clean and protect those places where I am unable to protect, I cannot be responsible for the security of the travelers." The need for mounted interdiction forces was becoming increasingly apparent. Given the vast distances between the settlement clusters, Mexican administrative posts, and network of homesteads, route security emerged as crucial to the protection of logistical and communication lines.[77]

The failure of the forward combat outpost forced the colonists to adopt a strategy based upon an inactive military system to be deployed only when needed. Austin quickly recognized that a citizen-militia would have to defend the colony in lieu of an active garrison. By June of 1824, San Felipe contained sufficient manpower to organize the previously approved "Battalion of Militia" for "the public security," as defined by the *empresario*. The unit comprised five companies of twenty to thirty men for each and spanned the five settlement clusters along the Colorado and Brazos rivers.[78]

Even with the improved battalion organization, the combat ratio of immigrant defenders against Native American forces remained decidedly unfavorable for the colonists. Austin described their precarious position: "The Karankawa Indians were very hostile on the coast; the Waco and Tawakani were equally so in the interior, and committed constant depredations. Parties of Tonkawas, Lipans, Beedies and others were intermingled."[79] It was an environment fraught with danger for the outnumbered settlers and the potential for raiding parties from virtually any direction required constant vigilance.

The local balance of combat power in southeastern *Tejas* shifted in favor of the settlers in 1824 as new American immigrants arrived and joined the colonial militia. Austin's assessment articulated his perilous situation in 1822 and 1823, and the following policy changes in 1824:

> The Caranchua Indians (Karankawan) were very hostile on the coast; the Waco and Tehuacanies were equally so in the interior and committed constant depredations. Parties of Tonkawas, Lipans, Beedies and others were intermingled with the settlers; they were beggarly and insolent, and were only restrained the first two years by presents, forbearance and policy; there was not enough force to stop them.[80]

In the same letter, the *Empresario* explained how an influx of settlers over the next year facilitated a more aggressive posture towards previously tolerated threats. Austin wrote that "in 1824, the strength of the settlement justified a change in policy, and a party of Tonkawa were tried and whipped in the presence of their chiefs for horse stealing."[81]

The Anglo-Americans executed targeted retaliation against select Indian peoples as the colony gained in numbers and reliable commanders assumed command of militia companies. This escalation in intensity found them in direct emulation of forbearers who had previously intensified warfare against tribal networks east and then west of the Appalachian Mountains with consistent predictability.[82] Austin's policy of command delegation to subordinate officers, issued in December of 1823, allowed field leaders "to make war against the Karankawas and to raise men within his Command and attack or pursue any party of said Indians that may appear on the coast or on the river." He also prompted junior leaders to "act according to his discretion without waiting for orders from his superior officer."[83]

This delegation of combat command to actionable levels reflected Austin's understanding of the rapid tempo of tribal warfare, particularly as directed against the Karankawas. The *emprasario* himself led the expedition of October of 1823, in which he followed Tonkowa horse-thieves to their tribe's village, recovered the stolen horses, and then compelled the chief to lash his guilty warriors.

Throughout 1824 the colony focused on neutralizing the Karankawa threat. With newfound strength they intended to definitively establish Anglo dominance along the lower Brazos and Colorado river systems. That year militia leader Jesse Burnam utilized an effective river ambush to defeat a Karankawa party that had captured two American sailors. Dewees, still serving in the militia, wrote that they "secreted themselves in the bushes" along the river, with intent to strike the returning warriors in their boats. As the settlers waited silently, they watched as a "large canoe filled with Indians" soon moved up the river towards their position.[84] Burnam recalled of the attack: "I fired on them, which was intended as a signal for my men to fire. My signal shot one Indian and in less than five minutes we

had killed eight." Using tactics that maximized precision marksmanship, the militiamen killed two more natives while they attempted to
escape.[85]

Concurrent to actions like Burnam's ambush, and in accordance
with Austin's policy of balanced foreign relations, militia captain
Aylett Buckner negotiated with the Waco, Tawakoni, and Towash
peoples. The commission informed the tribesmen of Austin's intent
to "remain in perfect peace and harmony with all the tribes of
Indians" and proposed that "a clean commercial intercourse should
prevail."[86] The negotiators successfully arranged a pragmatic, if temporary, peace agreement. Buckner's treaty revealed the colony's desire
to prevent development of a second front while the Karankawa threat
remained acute.

While a tenuous peace held to the north, conflict between the
Karankawa and colonists along the coast culminated in late August.
Gibson Kuykendall remembered that "Col. Austin, in consequence of
the continual depredations of the Carancawas determined to lead an
expedition against them."[87] The campaign began on August 30 when
the *empresario* led the entire San Felipe battalion, over 100 militiamen, south to La Bahia near the Gulf Coast. As recorded in his journal,
Austin "divided the men into two divisions" and marched them down
the east and west banks of the Colorado River. He also detailed how
he "sent spies down to the mouth of the River in the night," but failed
to locate the warriors.[88]

Kuykendall, who had emerged as a leading tactical leader, assessed
that Austin soon "came to the conclusion that the enemy had gone to
the San Antonio River; but as our provision were nearly exhausted,
he determined to return to San Felipe." Once there, the colonel would
"get ample supply of provisions, increase his force, and march direct
to La Bahia." After preparing for three days the reinvigorated battalion
marched southeast towards their enemy's suspected location at the
old Spanish mission. Despite deadly intent, the colonists would again
fail to culminate their campaign. As Austin and his men approached
within fifteen miles of the town they were "met by an express from

the civil authorities," actually Spanish priests, who sought to prevent bloodshed.[89]

Dewees with the militia column watched as Catholic officials "came to mediate for the Carancawas" with Austin and his captains. The *empresario*, perhaps desiring to maintain relations with Mexican authorities, "agreed not to make war upon the Carancawas as long as they should keep this pledge."[90] The expedition returned home the next day with a temporary truce in place. The relatively large-scale nature of this deployment marked it as a significant developmental exercise that allowed valuable organizational and logistical training beyond company levels.

The Anglo colony's military focus began to shift north in fall of 1824 when a Waco party stole precious horses from the settlers, prompting immediate militia pursuit. Unlike the Karankawa and Tonkawa, the prairie horsemen compelled a similar mounted reaction by the colonists. Gibson Kuykendall, nephew of District Commander Robert Kuykendall, remembered the expedition: "We followed the thieves as far as Yegua— about fifty miles—where we lost their trail in consequence of the great number of wild horses and buffalo which then ranged through that section of the country."[91] Though demonstrative of improved capacity as horsemen and limited ability to track raiders, the mission also revealed challenges with timely interdiction. Unlike previous native threats, Waco cavalry demanded a new level of rapidity and operational reach.

Hostilities resumed in the south that September when a company under settler Randall Jones engaged Karankawa who had killed several American immigrants who were traveling en route from the United States. Wilbarger recorded the militiamen first identified and then parleyed with the warriors at the Brazos River. Disguising their true intent, the colonials left the Indians with false promises of peace. They then "attacked them the next morning, killed some of them and drove the rest away."[92]

Jones soon gained intelligence of a larger Karankawa camp, and after sending scouts to search the area, located the site. The militiamen advanced under cover of darkness and "made a vigorous charge upon the camp" as the sun rose. Wilbarger wrote that the Indians immediately "seized their arms and took shelter in the tall grass from whence they returned the fire of the whites." Unlike the first skirmish, the warriors repulsed the attackers and forced a retreat. Wilbarger attested that the colonists lost three while the coastal raiders suffered fifteen dead and more wounded.[93] The brutal war of attrition waged against the Karankawa people eventually debilitated the tribe and decreased their warrior count from over 500 in 1823 to fewer than 30 by 1836.[94] Settlers soon occupied the commercially valuable territory along the coast, despite Mexico's intent for Anglo settlement farther north.

Kuykendall and other captains retaliated against sporadic Indian attacks throughout the years 1824 and 1825 while achieving varying degrees of deterrence and pragmatic conciliation. Like Americans who previously conquered lands to the east, Austin intended to prevent unnecessary warfare on an unsustainable level by balancing tribal power. His nuanced appraisal of indigenous relations protected the colonies in their fledgling years and allowed time and space to create a military capable of challenging multiple tribes. The leader recalled the precariousness of the early days of settlement: "One imprudent step with these Indians would have destroyed the settlement, and the settlers deserve as much for their forbearance during the years 1822 and 1823, as for their fortitude."[95]

The "forbearance" praised by Austin should not be ascribed to ethical constraints, but instead to pragmatic appraisal of colonial vulnerability. He and the majority of the settlers were undeniably racist and transplanted cultural prejudice then typical in the American South. In August of 1835 Austin would write emphatically that "Texas must be a slave country. It is no longer a matter of doubt ... nothing shall daunt my courage or abate my exertions to complete the main object of my labors—to Americanize Texas."[96]

This colonist's intention to "Americanize Texas" implied an extension of the Anglo-American imperial dominance that had characterized the formation of the eastern United States, including the overt removal of Native Americans and the importation of black slavery. In

1836, as the settlers fought simultaneously against Mexico and opportunistic tribes, Austin contextualized the confrontation in racial terms as a contest between the "mongrel Spanish-Indian and negro race, against civilization and the Anglo-American race."[97]

Yet in 1825 the colonials' strategic situation remained tenuous and Austin still cautioned against "great excitement and thirst for revenge." As angry settlers called for a concerted campaign to the north he asked: "If we destroy the Waco Villages will not the other tribes consider it as a warning of the fate that must in the end befall them if the American settlements progress? Is there no danger that they may become alarmed and unite to cut us off in our infancy?" The *empresario* then answered to calm the more belligerent amongst his people: "Is it better to submit to a few insults rather than risk bringing on a war with all the northern Indians by resenting them at this time."[98] This statement revealed awareness of the perils of provoking the vast Comanche hosts to the west, which Austin desperately hoped to avoid.

By the year 1826 the rapid increase in settlers and militia recruits permitted new aggression against previously tolerated threats. The colonies postured to act more aggressively against the Waco and Tawakoni prairie tribes, while maintaining alliances with the Cherokee, Shawnee, and Delaware. Austin proclaimed the danger to the north: "The depredations of your enemies the W. and T. Indians and their hostile preparations, has driven us to the necessity of taking up arms in self defense. The frontier is menaced—the whole colony is threatened—under these circumstances it became my duty to call the militia to the frontier to repel the threatened attacks and to teach our enemies to fear and respect us."[99] This policy represented a pivotal decision to engage in northern hostilities while conciliating the east.

Anglo-Indian tensions increased in April when a party of Tonkawa warriors again invaded the colony area to steal horses and hunt enemy tribesmen according to tradition. Though not intended as a strike against the colonists, the raid nevertheless provoked a militia reaction. Captain James Ross accordingly "lost no time in sending spies to the frontier" to identify the location of the retreating warband. Once located, he led thirty-one men to interdict the warriors before they could escape. The militia caught the celebrating Tonkawa in camp, reportedly dancing amongst human scalps taken during the raid. Ross described his envelopment plan, reminiscent of Kuykendall's at Skull Creek, that surrounded the camp with converging elements:

> One party under the command of Lieutenant Rawson Alley, commenced the attack in the front, from the bank of the creek, while I took position with the others in the bottom ... this disposition had a good effect. After the first fire from Alley's party, the Indians ran for the bottom, and there received a volley from my party. Eight Indians fell dead, and five were wounded and escaped to the thicket.[100]

The victorious militia found "five fire arms, seven bows, and a considerable number of arrows and quantity of ammunition" in the camp. They also recovered one stolen horse.[101]

Ross' interdiction reflected one of the most effective militia retaliations by Anglo settlers between 1822 and 1835. Austin subsequently praised his rapid mobilization and adept use of scouts. The *empresario* reported to his Spanish superior that he "gave orders to the captains of Militia of this Colony to have their men ready at a moment's notice" and "would send spies to the Indian villages to watch their movements and ascertain their intentions."[102]

By June of 1826 the colonial network of settlements numbered over 1,800 people due to continued immigration. The prospect of land and the initial success of the settlement programs attracted new adventurers, both legal and illegal. The rapid population increase allowed the militia battalion to expand its roster to 565 citizen-soldiers, though it still suffered from the logistical and readiness challenges inherent to any amateur levy.[103]

As tribal conflict continued, and the Mexican Army refused to field a garrison on behalf of the settlers, Austin proposed to escalate the colony's deterrence with "a campaign against the Waco and

Tehuacano villages" to the north. After sending agents to the target villages disguised as traders, the *empresario* made plans "for a simultaneous attack on the three Tahuacano villages, that of the Wacoes on the Brazos and that of the Tahuiases on Red River."[104] He then exhorted the militiamen: "your decisive conduct on this first expedition will so harass our enemies that they will seek safety by humbling themselves and sue for peace...if we strike a decisive blow our future peace and security will probably be the result."[105]

Euro-Americans had long favored concepts of destroying sources of Indian power with an annihilation strategy. Elimination of domestic centers, including villages of women and children, denied enemy warriors sustenance in the unforgiving and undeveloped landscape. Nicholas de Lafora, a Spanish official who surveyed *Tejas* in 1768 with the Spanish aristocrat Marques de Rubi during a military assessment of New Spain's frontier, advocated population-centric warfare in response to rising Apache and Comanche hostility. He argued for "continuous offensive war," and stated that "by this means they (Indians) would be exterminated in short time."[106]

Manuel de Mier Y Teran, a Mexican general who assessed *Tejas* conditions in 1828 and 1829, described differing tactical methodologies between the Anglo-Texan settlements and their indigenous neighbors. Upon observing actions by Austin's San Felipe colony against the Karakawa Tribe in 1828, he reported:

> Since the North Americans understand war with the savages better than do our Mexicans, they dealt (the Indians) swift punishment, striking back ten times for every blow they received. If (the Indians) killed a settler, a large party of settlers would set out to hunt down and kill ten of the tribe, of any age or sex. By such behavior they have reduced the tribe of the Tarancahuases such that no one speaks of it, because it seems to have been exterminated.[107]

This perspective clearly identified non-combatants as targets and population attrition as a legitimate means of victory. Both Spanish and Anglo pioneers viewed camps and villages of the Karankawa as a vital component of their capacity to make war and eliminated them accordingly.

Austin launched the northern offensive under the command of veteran militia captain Aylett Buckner. He pursued this campaign while tactfully ignoring the orders of the Spanish provincial governor to desist temporarily until they could plan coordinated maneuvers. Despite the successful deployment of 185 men over 60 miles north of San Felipe, they found the villages deserted. The younger Kuykendall noted the failure: "The Waco village was on the west side of the river a little further up. We could not reach it, as the river much swollen, but ascertained that it too was uninhabited." He also recorded that "appearances indicated that the Tawacanie village had been vacated about two weeks."[108]

In the summer of 1826, in addition to sending expeditions against the Waco, the *empresario* proposed a new ranging force for settlement protection. Similar to the 1823 ranger concept, this element served as a proactive measure to counter indigenous rapidity. It also represented the colony's second employment of independent horsemen for dedicated reconnaissance and interdiction.

On August 28 Austin dutifully reported the colony's organizational actions to his Mexican superior in Bexar, Antonio Saucedo. As outlined in his letter, the *empresario* first ordered collective participation in the fielding of the new force to ensure proper contributions to collective defense: "The Commanding Officer of the Jurisdiction, having a due regard to the respective Strength of the various parties, and in conformity to the inventory of lands belonging to each person, shall assess the number of militia that each district shall supply every month."[109]

Austin then described an innovative plan that emulated inherited ranger traditions and departed from the previous San Felipe militia structure that had relied upon an inactive, reactive levy: "The object of the plan is to keep twenty or thirty mounted men continually on the frontier as spies; as well for the preventing of small parties of

Indians, as to give timely warning should they come in force to make a formal attack." The *empresario* further elaborated that "the intention of the several articles is, to compel everyone to contribute his share in the common defense in proportion to the interest he has in the Country."[110] Though the effectiveness or duration of the concept remains unknown, Austin's intention to have "one section to be sent to the frontier every month to do duty as spies, or frontier guard" demonstrated continued tactical adaptation.[111]

Another letter from Austin to Saucedo the same month, on behalf of the Nacogdoches settlement, reflected the same response to native mobility in eastern *Tejas*. Burrel Thompson's request for "authority to raise a company of mounted volunteers to assist in defending this frontier...to fight our Indian enemies," indicated a common acceptance of the fleet nature of frontier combat.[112] These proposals reflected the first instance when colonial leaders specifically ordered militia forces to be both mounted and independent.

The ranger proposal for summer of 1826 marked the stage in which the Anglo-Texans began to emulate the previous amateur cavalry adaptations of their Spanish and Mexican predecessors. Throughout the eighteenth century, the imperial forces of Spain had suffered from a disparity in capability in mounted warfare against the Apache and Comanche. Lafora described the advantages plains horsemen held over Spanish regular cavalry: "Naturally, a man whose weight, with that of offensive and defensive arms, comes to fourteen *arrobas*, and who is leading five or six horses for remounts, can never run as fast nor for so long a time as an Indian, whose arms and equipment increase his weight very little."[113] This contrast between fleet warbands and professional armored cavalry underscored the strength of irregular military cultures against typical limitations of regular armies.

As early as 1713, as presidio garrisons proved inadequate against Apache warbands, Viceroy Duque de Linares beseeched civilian communities in northern New Spain to form specialized mounted companies to assist with frontier security. Known as the *Companias Volantes*, or Flying Companies, these amateurs attained frontier expertise unknown to the Spanish professionals. When the informal Flying Company program proved successful, the Regulations of Presidios of 1772 formalized the system. These orders officially sanctioned mounted companies in each province to support the overmatched presidios. Called "Light Troops" by Spanish officials, in contrast with the heavily armed and armored Mexican cavalry, Flying Companies served as a more flexible defense in addition to static army outposts.[114]

By the early nineteenth century Spanish *Tejas* suffered from severe population reduction and economic destruction after decades of political instability and tribal raiding. Bexar, La Bahia, and Nacogdoches barely survived as forlorn outposts on the forward line and made use of irregular cavalry even more critical.[115] The Marques de Rubi assessed the ineffectiveness of the defensive presidio at San Saba, a mission north of the traditional settlement line, when he sarcastically complained that the static garrison "affords as much protection to the interests of His Majesty in new Spain as a ship anchored in mid-Atlantic would afford in preventing foreign trade with America."[116]

Despite the dismal state of the presidio system, irregular cavalry achieved some respite from native raids. In 1817 the provincial governor, Antonio Martinez, referred to the local militia of southern *Tejas* as "the most highly skilled men of this locality" when seeking to augment his professional forces with a civilian levy. These hardened frontier civilians, especially the ranching *vaqueros* who predominantly populated Spanish mounted militias, enlisted with expertise in horsemanship, land navigation, and frontier fighting. In contrast, the governor complained that professional presidio garrisons were simply "inadequate to punish the enemy."[117]

Upon transition to Mexican governance in 1824, the parsimonious government ordered the *Companias Volantes* to assume all offensive interdiction to allow presidios to focus on defensive security. Dewees later criticized that "on the frontier where standing armies are located," the Mexican garrison's "movements were slow, that they never succeed well in war, particularly with the Indians."[118] Unfortunately for Spain and then Mexico, the transference of military responsibilities to volunteers resulted in disaffected Hispanic border communities that readily joined the Texas Republic north of the Rio Grande and others that repeatedly rebelled south of the river during politically turbulent periods.

The Anglo-Texan emulation of Spanish irregular cavalry continued in January of 1827 when Austin again deployed mounted rangers to patrol forward of settlement walls. This operation developed as a secondary effect of the ill-fated Fredonian Rebellion in which Anglo settlers in Nacogdoches in East Texas attempted to detach that region from Mexican rule. Despite shared ethnic origin with the rebels, the citizenry of San Felipe declared a "Resolution of Loyalty" on January 6 that proclaimed they were "satisfied with the Government of their adoption." Austin led his militia east under the Mexican banner, in accordance with his sworn duty, to quell the rebellion.[119]

Simultaneous to the militia expedition, the *empresario* sent an economy-of-force patrol of mounted rangers to protect the colony's northern border. Gibson Kuykendall, nephew of the district commander, described the maneuver when he remembered that "so large a proportion of the men of the colony were sent on the service that Austin deemed it prudent to order my father with eight men to range the country between the Colorado and Brazos along the San Antonio road to detect any inroad of the Wacoes or other northern tribes."[120]

Kuykendall's assignment against the Waco confirmed two significant shifts in the colony's military posture by 1827. First, it revealed a second instance when Austin employed mounted forces to independently operate forward of settlement stockades. Light horse operations were attaining a higher importance in the colony's actions and he recognized the value of proactive interdiction. Second, it confirmed the Karankawa no longer provided the primary threat to the colonies. Strategic focus had definitively shifted north after the Anglos' successful attrition of the Karankawa and suppression of the Tonkawa.[121]

The San Felipe colony did not just deter native raids with patrols and retaliations as its militia gained in strength; it also negotiated with certain tribes. The settlers pursued pragmatic treaties with the Karankawa, Tawakoni, Waco, and Comanche peoples throughout 1827 as Austin balanced strategic priorities. Mexican officials assisted with diplomatic intervention, perhaps their greatest contribution to the colony's security.[122] This combination of selective aggression and conciliation ultimately reduced Anglo-Indian conflict throughout most of 1827 and 1828. The much-needed stability provided a respite from constant warfare and opportunity for the weary settlers to build towns, farms, and roads.

Despite the attempts at peace, frontier violence in colonial *Tejas* once again erupted in July of 1829. Waco and Tawakoni warriors audaciously seized and occupied a homestead at Bastrop, one of the northwestern-most settlements on the Colorado River. From his discussions with participants, Wilbarger relayed that the owner of the farm, Thomas Thompson, discovered the attack and "went below for assistance, and raising a party of ten, he returned." The vengeful militia arrived just before daylight and killed four natives while the rest fled to the woods.[123]

This aggressive action by natives did not go unpunished by the newly empowered colonials. Austin immediately raised his forces with intent to interdict the remaining tribesmen lest they regroup and strike again in another equally vulnerable location. Wilbarger recalled that the *empresario* "raised two companies of volunteers, of fifty men each...the whole force being placed under the command of Colonel Abner Kuykendall." The citizenry of Gonzales—a developing colony east of San Felipe that had also been receiving "depredations and murders by the Indians"—likewise dispatched a third company.[124]

Kuykendall soon learned through scouts that a party of Waco and Tawakoni were camped at the mouth of the San Saba River. The San Felipe and Gonzales militias, now consolidated in one of the first instances of cooperation between separate colonial contracts, "marched for that point." By the time the militiamen arrived at the camp, native scouts had forewarned the village of the battalion's approach. The chronicler reported that when "the Texans charged the camp of the enemy the found it deserted. They only killed one Indian." A mounted detachment then "pursued the Indians some distance and took from them many of their horses," offering a small consolation for the lackluster offensive.[125]

Transition to Mounted Warfare

By 1829 leading Anglo-American colonies had mastered basic organizational practices and methodologies of mounted operations on the *Tejas* frontier and were transitioning to audacious attacks against more distant tribal villages. Numerous battles against the Karankawa had trained the settlers in close combat techniques. Recent conflict with the Waco had compelled familiarity with mounted operations farther away from San Felipe. The Anglo-Texans prepared to engage in the type of expeditionary warfare that would define Anglo-Indian conflict for decades.

In August of 1829 Austin directed Abner Kuykendall to lead a task force north in retaliation against another raid by Waco horse thieves. In his orders, he emphasized not only the importance of tracking the party responsible, but also coordinated the convergence of several militia companies under Kuykendall's command. The *empresario* directed his militiamen to "pursue and kill said robbers, be they Indian or Whites, and to recover stolen property" and to "punish the robbers and afford security to our exposed and scattered settlements, by making a severe and striking example which will have the effect to prevent the repetition of similar outrages."[126]

Austin's directive reflected an increase in strategic confidence that corresponded with the colonial shift to more expansive mounted operations. He clearly intended to intimidate the tribes while shaping the tactical environment through combinations of lethal and non-lethal means. Once fearful of provoking a regional war, the colonists now operated from a position of strength against the central tribes. The reference to white offenders additionally emphasized the presence of Euro American bandits in the area, doubtless contributing to the rise in frontier tension and the militant posture of the colonials.

In accordance with Austin's instructions, Kuykendall first led a mounted company nine miles north of San Felipe where he located an allied force of "forty or fifty" Waco and Tawakana. The natives had occupied an abandoned cabin on the Colorado River but fled at the approach of the militia. Kuykendall described his pursuit and engagement: "Spurring our horses to their best speed, we intercepted them a short distance below the thicket. As we dismounted, each man dropped the coil of his tethering rope from the pommel of his saddle and charged the Indians on foot."[127] This combination of mounted movement and dismounted assault again emphasized the dragoon nature of Anglo-Texan colonial forces.

The militia attack, relying on surprise as much as audacity, shattered any semblance of indigenous resistance. The overawed Indians immediately fled the field and left six killed. Despite the colonists' initial success, they failed to capitalize with further pursuit. Kuykendall explained the reason: "As we were reduced to but nine mounted men, two of whose horses were already broken down, we were constrained to forgo the pursuit of the thieves."[128]

By September of 1829 the colony had grown sufficiently to organize two militia battalions and one mounted company. According to *The Texas Gazette*, Mexican regulation required the colony to produce militia companies of both infantry and cavalry to "sustain the independence of the nation." This focus on combined arms organization reflected the conventional European inclinations of the Mexican Army as it sought to structure auxiliary components accordingly. The law also ordered that "in the department of Texas, this force will be augmented as the *Empresarios* introduce settlers under their contracts."[129]

The new regulations further stipulated terms of civilian activation. They declared that the militiamen would be called into service by the authority of the President of Mexico and be directed by the provincial governor, similar to the 1827 colonial augmentation of the Mexican Army against the Nacogdoches rebels. This directive firmly subordinated colonial defenses under national authority.[130]

It also continued the original Spanish strategy of utilizing Anglo colonies as buffer-zones against northern Indian depredations. Despite these attempts at unity, in less than a decade the martial relationship between nation and colony would explode in rebellion.

Austin ordered Kuykendall to lead a force against a tribe near the San Saba River in central *Tejas* in the same month as the publication of the new militia regulations. He again coordinated the convergence of several militia columns that included volunteers from San Felipe and Gonzales. Though the tribe remained unspecified, it was probably the Waco due to the northwest direction of the maneuver. Confident in their numbers, the battalion assembled on the banks of the lower Colorado River and proceeded to ride north. Once in the San Saba area, northwest of San Felipe, the commander sent scouts to locate the enemy camp. The reconnaissance patrol soon identified the unsuspecting tribe near the juncture of the Colorado and San Saba Rivers.[131]

That night Kuykendall repositioned his battalion with the intent to cordon the village at dawn. He hoped to isolate the camp and then attack it from multiple sides: it was a plan designed for total destruction. In accordance with the plan, the militia rode north "over the prairie, studded with low hills" and paused in a "cedar-brake" to plan the final approach. Kuykendall next dispatched a small scout team to conduct the final reconnaissance of the objective. Despite attempts at stealth, a native party surprised the Anglos. Realizing his covert posture was compromised, Kuykendall ordered the "whole command" forward to reinforce the scouts.[132]

The militia rapidly pursued the warriors as they unwisely led the aggressors to their village. Upon arrival the colonists immediately attacked. The assault crushed any hope of organized defense and caused a scene of chaos and confusion. The surprised Native Americans fled and left behind stolen property and a small herd of horses. The militiamen killed only one warrior due to the hasty nature of the attack. According to Kuykendall, "detachments were sent in pursuit but the Indians had escaped to their mountain fastness; only a few women and children were overtaken, who were of course unmolested."[133]

Despite failure to decisively close with their enemy, this mission stood as one of the first truly successful longer-range mounted expeditions by Anglo-Texans during the colonial period. A comment from Kuykendall proved informative in his description of the approach march when he wrote that "hour after hour the long double files of horsemen followed the guide."[134] The presence of large columns of horsemen in the maneuver perhaps identified a lesson learned from the previous attack when mounted warriors had escaped and rendered victory less than complete.

In addition to the main attack on the camp, the Gonzales men simultaneously interdicted two small warbands near the main village. Kuykendall noted their reunion with the main force after the route when "a company of thirty men from Gonzales rode into camp."[135] This multi-element expedition concluded as the colonials' most complex operation to date, despite the minimal casualties inflicted by the attackers. Converging columns of mounted companies had successfully sanitized a large area containing several elusive Indian parties.

The use of indigenous agents for cultural and geographical knowledge reflected another vital counter-guerrilla principle increasingly employed by the colonial militia in the 1820s and 1830s. Attacking forces often employed either Mexican or native guides to locate tribal encampments. In Kuykendall's 1829 expeditions, the colonials carefully selected approach routes, masked movement through favorable terrain, and massed forces at the point of attack for the final surprise assault due to indigenous assistance. Kuykendall described one of his guides as a "Mexican who had once lived with the Wacos and Tawacanies."[136] Dewees, another participant in the operation, wrote that they "obtained the services of two pilots, a Mexican and an Indian, who know the route to the mouth of the San Saba river, and also where the Indians were encamped."[137]

By 1830 the expanding population of *Tejas* consisted of 15,000 residents with Anglo colonists outnumbering Mexican settlers by a factor of four to one.[138] That year, after continued territorial expansion,

Anglo-Indian conflict exploded when, according to settler John Jenkins, a party of over seventy Karankawa, including a mix of men, women, and children, "massacred the entire household" of a homestead near San Felipe.[139] The raiders killed the wife and three daughters of settler Charles Cavina, who was not present, while a fourth daughter was left for dead but survived. The coastal warriors also killed a visiting friend of the family named Elisha Flowers. The suddenness of the attack reminded the colonists that Indians could reciprocally strike at undefended and unprepared domestic sites.

Enraged settlers reacted, determined to exact revenge with little care for their own culpability in provoking ethnic strife by expanding into tribal territories. Wilbarger recorded the response that followed when he wrote that Cavina, the aggrieved widower, "raised a company of sixty men and pursued the savages. They were under the command of Captain Buckner, who had seen much service on the frontier." The militiamen then tracked the raiding party to a site where "they had taken their position on the bank of Colorado River."[140]

As the militia column approached, Buckner dispatched Moses Morrison, the veteran leader of the first outpost in 1823, to "reconnoiter their position." The former soldier "crawled up to a bank overlooking a small plateau below where the Indians had stationed themselves, but the ledge crumbled and he fell amongst the startled warriors." Morrison crashed into the midst of the raiders yet survived long enough for militia to arrive. According to Wilbarger, Buckner and his men immediately "made a charge upon them" and scattered the warband. The vengeful militia massacred forty to fifty natives, including many women and children who had accompanied the warriors. According to one participant, "the riverbanks literally ran red with blood."[141]

Given the rapid nature of this particular mobilization against an unexpected attack, Buckner's retaliation represented continued improvement in colonial military capabilities. It reflected a significant increase in readiness from the futile attempts in 1824 and 1826 when militia failed to interdict fleet attackers or track them to their source camp. The killing of so many women and children, considered beyond the bounds of civilized warfare by all Euro American societies at that time, indicated growing brutality in the attitude of the Anglos towards the indigenous peoples.

Intermittent Anglo-Indian conflict marked the years 1830 to early 1835 as colonial immigration continued and colonial territory expanded. Though sporadic violence occurred, mostly along the periphery of the main settlement zones, fighting never attained the raid and counter-raid intensity of the years 1823, 1824, 1826, and 1829. By the early 1830s the settlers had significantly depopulated, subdued, or removed the predatory tribes of Southeast and Central Texas, most notably the Karankawa and the Waco, while they enforced treaties with other tribes from a strengthened position.

Yet aggrieved and predatory Indians still sporadically inflicted horrific attacks, such as the Madden Massacre in 1832, when a Caddo raiding party assaulted the Madden homestead on the Trinity River. The raiders killed seven women and children and burned the settlement.[142] Wilbarger reported another incident in 1833 when his brother, Josiah Wilbarger, and a party "rode out in a northwest direction to look at the country" east of the future site of Austin. They were unexpectedly ambushed by a mounted force of sixty unspecified Indians, probably Comanche. The warriors killed two settlers while another two escaped. When they came upon Wilbarger, who was too wounded to walk, they "stripped him naked and tore the scalp from his head" and then left him for dead. The hardy settler amazingly survived the experience and found sanctuary at a nearby homestead.[143]

These massacres, especially attacks against defenseless women and children, produced collective, and often exaggerated, fear of widespread tribal aggression against Anglo colonies. Instances like the raid against the Cavina homestead where the men were away from the homestead during the attack created untenable scenarios in which male colonists could not leave home to hunt, farm, ranch, or travel for fear of returning to find slaughtered, or enslaved, women and children. This fear, though often hypocritical when compared to similarly brutal Anglo actions against native domestic centers, created logical impetus for preemptive strikes to eliminate possibility of tribal attacks.

Anglo-Indian conflict in *Tejas*, now called Texas by the majority Anglo population, intensified in 1835, initiating a new theater of war to the west of San Felipe. In April of that year, a warband of more than eighty Comanche ambushed and slaughtered a French merchant party near Gonzales. A nearby settler, John Castleman, observed the attack and quickly raised militia to interdict the raiders. With Captain Bartlett McClure in command, the frontiersmen tracked and pursued the warriors on horseback for three days and finally cought them by surprise at the Rio Blanco west of Bastrop. The colonists then defeated the Comanche while they attempted to retreat.[144]

Though representative of improved capacity for rapid interdiction as mounted riflemen, this incident proved ominous: it indicated that feared Penateka Comanche of the lower plains now targeted the western colonial settlements. Yet in the absence of a consolidated invasion by the tribal confederacy, these raids did not place the colonies in mortal collective danger. The increased density of the Anglo population in eastern Texas ensured that guerrilla strikes would not extinguish the settlement programs as was possible during initial years. The reckoning between the Comanche and Texans would wait until the early 1840s when the civilizations would clash in an unprecedented level of ethnic warfare.

The San Felipe colony was not the only *empresario* program that found itself tested during the 1820s. Just as in the San Felipe Colony, the DeWitt Colony contributed to the extinction of the Karankawa people. It is informative that Green DeWitt, its founder, made the same tactical deductions as Austin after his engagements in 1829. He suggested a joint effort by San Felipe and Gonzales to field a "Company of Rangers, or the public troops" for common security. This proposal offered another indication that the same broader adaptation to irregular warfare had developed amongst separate colonies in southeastern *Tejas*.[145]

The Roberts and Edwards colonies, in addition to a network of homestead clusters like Bastrop, were also programs that employed mounted militia against local threats. The resulting cumulative experience of the numerous legal and illegal Anglo settlements throughout East Texas created a large reservoir of combat experience while simultaneously degrading tribal populations.[146] Miguel Muldoon, an Irish-Mexican priest in South *Tejas*, noted with alarm the militant inclination of the colonials in 1833:

> The colonists rush out at the slightest alarm from their field labors, woods, and workshops militarily armed in such numbers and as rapidly as did the armies of old of Deucalion and Pyrro, with the advantage that of the former are mounted on great, spirited steeds that seem like large-hooved draft horses ... the rooms of the colonists do not feature saints, but their place is taken by rifles, sabers, and pistols...The Indians offend our towns but respect the Anglo Americans and dare not even tread their territory.[147]

The padre then further embellished: "Each colonist is a general in his house. All of his dependents, including the women, handle weapons with skill, and it would take an army to dislodge them."[148] Three years later, the failed Mexican reconquest of *Tejas* during the Texas Revolution proved that even an army could not accomplish that feat. Muldoon's comments described a society conditioned by continuous warfare on a violent frontier.

Conflict continued to escalate in the spring of 1835 as expanding Anglo settlements induced or drew increased friction with native peoples. In response, Colonial-Texan mounted militia responses became fully expeditionary as the settlers' transition to irregular cavalry operations attained early maturity. A large Comanche raid in April of that year against the San Felipe periphery again served notice of the potential reality of warfare with the Plains Tribes.

In July of 1835 militia commander Robert Coleman led a mounted company of twenty-five men out of Fort Parker, a fortified homestead approximately 100 miles north of Bastrop. The extreme forward position of this outpost, far beyond immediate militia support, indicated intent to deter attacks on the far northern periphery of established settlement areas. In a sign of rising Anglo military confidence, Coleman designed the campaign "for the purpose of chastising those menaces to civilized man." He accused the Indians of "wanton outrages ... not only upon our frontier, but in the midst of our settlements."[149] Coleman styled his unit "Mounted Riflemen" and prosecuted an unsuccessful campaign against the Tawakoni Indians, along with allied Caddos and Ionies near Tehuacana Springs.

The attacking company employed the proven tactic of surrounding the native camp under cover of darkness, but when they assaulted at dawn the natives repulsed the attack. Though the Texans supposedly killed a greater number of enemy, they suffered one dead, four wounded, and the larger native force compelled retreat. The captain summarized the engagement with a deceptively favorable outlook in his report: "We had a severe battle. One fourth of my men killed & wounded. We took their encampment by a charge & and the battle ended."[150] George Erath, a future Texas legislator and ranger, described what followed: "When a Colorado party under Captain Robert M. Coleman, about twenty-five in number, was repulsed at the Tehaucana village east of the Brazos, there was a call for a general campaign."[151]

The northern settlements rapidly formed a larger battalion to complete the campaign. They mobilized a force of four or five companies of rangers under command of the experienced John Moore. Edward Burleson, who would soon rise to prominence as the Texas Republic's premier field commander, was also present. A native of North Carolina with prior militia experience in Tennessee, Burleson later commanded an infantry regiment in the Texas Revolution and a battalion of Mounted Rifles in 1837. He also led the semi-professional Frontier Regiment and a full militia brigade during the 1840s. Rising as one of the most aggressive leaders of the Texas Republic, his expeditionary campaigns against Comanche and Cherokee villages between 1838 and 1842 proved devastating and set genocidal precedent.[152]

In August, Moore and his battalion rode north to Parker's Fort, which would be destroyed by Comanche in May 1836, and patrolled in search of native camps. While they managed to engage several insignificant indigenous elements, the colonists failed to locate the Tawakoni warriors or domestic sites. As Erath noted, "Texas Indians never allowed themselves to be attacked by a hundred men together; they had evacuated the village, and we had nothing to do but occupy it."[153] Like earlier evasions, natives yet retained ability to frustrate Anglo offensives through superior intelligence, mobility, and topographical knowledge.

Though the campaign ultimately proved futile, one action held tactical importance to the broader development of Texan mounted arms. It occurred when the ranging battalion located a tribal camp, which was later revealed to be abandoned, and prepared to attack. In a marked departure from previous methods, Moore deployed the battalion in line formation and charged while mounted instead of dismounting as infantry for the assault. This maneuver demonstrated increased confidence with combat on horseback and reflected a shift towards doctrinal cavalry functions.[154]

As much as the mounted attack revealed tactical progression, it also underscored the difficulties of charging with untrained volunteers. Erath narrated further: "The officers were particular to keep us in line...I was riding a young horse which had been caught a colt from the mustangs, that was fiery. When the order came to charge, it darted forward ahead of all the rest, and I found myself alone in the advance."[155] Not yet true Texas Rangers, the horsemen were nevertheless frontier cavalry in the making. The battalion essentially conducted a clearing operation along the colonial northwest border with limited deterring effects from July to September of 1835.

The Moore expedition illustrated Texan military progression on the eve of rebellion against Mexico. The deployment of Coleman's company, and then Moore's battalion, as expeditionary mounted militia in 1835 continued and expanded the raiding methodology of Kuykendall's limited offensives in 1829. As the culmination of a decade of hard-won adaptation, they proved the growing centrality of mounted operations in Anglo-Texan warfare. In a marked contrast with the early contests along the lower Colorado River against woodland and river warriors, there were no infantry involved due to long distances travelled.

While important due to its demonstration of expeditionary familiarity, Moore's campaign held legal—and eventual even cultural—implications for the nationalization of Texan militarism. In December of 1836, in the wake of revolutionary victory, the new republic passed retroactive legislation that recognized the 1835 expeditions as governmentally sanctioned mounted forces. Signifying the importance of the campaign, the act stated that "all officers and soldiers who have been actually engaged in the ranging service since July 1835, shall be included...and shall receive pay for the time he is in service."[156] This legislation effectively linked the initial development of colonial rangers to the era of the Texas Republic. Furthermore, the act established Moore's mounted battalion as the prototype for the frontier light horse that Texas would rely on over the next half century.

Texas Ranching: Preparation for Mounted Combat

Even as Anglo-Texan settlers adapted tactically and organizationally to mounted warfare in colonial and republican Texas, they also benefited from civilian activities that complemented fundamental nineteenth-century cavalry skills. The widespread use of horses in personal and commercial life on the frontier, and ranching functions in particular, enhanced the readiness of many colonists for transition to military service. The adept shift to expeditionary mounted operations demonstrated in the Kuykendall, Coleman, and Moore campaigns between 1829 and 1835 was in part facilitated by a seamless transfer of settler practices to tactical use. The functions involved in maintaining and

breeding horses while utilizing them for daily activities ensured familiarity during volunteer campaigns. This deep immersion of horsemanship into colonial life prevented some issues faced by many amateur
mobilizations, such as the volunteer Union Cavalry regiments of 1861,
when unfamiliarity with horsemanship and equine husbandry resulted
in a painful learning process under tactical stress.

Horsemanship consequently emerged as a fairly normative skill in
frontier Texas. Most early American settlers of Texas were accustomed
to riding and had only to develop unit cohesion when they formed
mounted militias. Long distances between settlements, and the much
longer eastern routes to the United States, ensured even rudimentary
skill in riding a necessary skill for effective movement rates. Later, as
Lone Star society nationalized and embraced the mounted ranging
as the prime means of border defense, the exploding cattle industry
created a reservoir of military-aged males with experience in both
complex riding maneuvers and field subsistence.

The meteoric growth of ranching in Texas held perhaps the most
important civilian shaping effect on Texan mounted arms. The rise of
a popular—and often overly romanticized—cowboy culture across the
vast environs of North, West, and South Texas coincided with, and
complemented, repeated citizen mobilization for military service. This
relationship between Anglo ranching and cavalry operations in Texas
was predated by a similar, if less successful, tradition amongst Spanish
colonizers in the eighteenth century. Decades before the onset of Anglo
immigration the maturation of the Spanish cattle industry had likewise
facilitated and enhanced the rise of the *Companias Volantes* by preparing *vaqueros* for rapid assimilation into auxiliary units. The American
settlers later benefited from the same utility of interchangeable horsemanship and combat skills.[157]

The Hispanic cattle industry in *Tejas* had evolved intermittently,
with intense concentrations along the Rio Grande, when Austin and
his settlers arrived in the 1820s. Spanish *rancheros* had introduced
cattle in 1690 as an industry to support more important mineral
extraction and religious endeavors. By 1770 the frontier settlement

of Goliad, located 92 miles southwest of Bexar, maintained over 70,000 head of cattle, with another 50 ranches in operation across the region.[158] The lack of natural predators in Texas and the vast open grazing expanses ensured favorable multiplication in the rate of cattle reproduction. Yet by 1836, due to the rapid retrenchment of Spanish colonists south of the Rio Grande due to Amerindian depredations, an estimated 300,000 abandoned and uncontrolled cattle ranged free across the countryside.[159] Aggressive Anglo pioneers benefited greatly from this reserve of unclaimed cattle when they established their own industry in the years before and after Lone Star independence.

American ranching consequently enjoyed immediate success during the first decade of colonial settlement in *Tejas*. James Taylor White, a cattleman from Louisiana, established the first recorded Anglo ranch in Texas. As an ambitious and young rancher who moved from his home state in 1828, he risked the dangers of frontier enterprise to collect a small herd of abandoned cattle in South *Tejas*. His ranch covered all of modern Chambers County along the Gulf Coast and by 1836 he had multiplied his initial investment into thousands of cattle that he later sold in New Orleans markets.[160]

White's success provided an ideal example for the early expansion of Anglo ranching in Texas. What remains unstated in the record, but implied by professional necessity, is that his team of cowhands constantly utilized horses to drive bovine stock to local foraging and along longer trail movements to Louisiana. As his herds expanded, his family and hired young men dedicated their lives to this occupation, therefore creating a small group of readily adaptable frontier cavalrymen for military activation in the wars of colonial and republican Texas.

The commercial history of rancher Sherrod Write offered another example of successful stock raising by Anglo opportunists in colonial *Tejas*. Similar to James White, he moved a small herd from Louisiana in 1832 and established sixty head of cattle in modern Jasper County in eastern Texas. By the year 1840 his stock had increased to 100 and would eventually number over 1,500. This prosperity naturally attracted investors from the United States. As early as 1831 eastern cattle merchants rode each year from New Orleans to purchase cattle from the colony of San Felipe, and in 1834 one enterprising rancher in the Galveston area drove over 1000 head to the Bayou State for an excellent profit.[161]

As the Anglo-Texan ranching economy expanded, the iconic Texas Longhorn emerged as a symbol of Texas culture. Created from the cross-breeding of imported American dairy stock and preexisting Spanish cattle, this hardy new breed attained continental importance as the immigrant ranching community assimilated and dominated the preexisting cattle industry of Texas.[162] The animal became especially prominent in the massive trail drives from the breeding grounds in the Lone Star State to northern and eastern markets, such as Chicago, in the immediate wake of the Civil War.[163]

The availability of free roaming or abandoned herds and the forceful appropriation of cattle from *Tejanos* during the colonial and republican periods explained, in large part, the rapid growth of the Anglo industry. As Anglo political and military dominance increased across East and South Texas, so did cattle and grazing land aggrandizement. Once the Texan independence had been established, vulnerable *Tejanos* in South Texas became tempting targets for criminal exploitation and brute intimidation. Political tension and military conflict with Mexico in the 1840s, particularly when many Anglos perceived that Hispanic Texans had supported the Woll invasion of 1842, enhanced rates of theft as many Texans associated *Tejanos* with Mexican nationalism.[164]

Texas ranching developed other useful skills with direct application to frontier warfare besides horsemanship. The constant threat of Amerindian raids, banditry, and poaching by commercial competitors compelled cowboys to develop familiarity with guns. Each man conducting trail drives through lawless expanses where raiding cultures preyed on any available food source unquestionably rode armed. The importance of this trait should not be understated, as it ensured that volunteers who reported to various Texas militia units had already received training in marksmanship, weapons safety, and basic mechanical understanding of firearms.

Knowledge of frontier subsistence, called "fieldcraft" in military parley, reflected another important but understated ability that pertained to driving cattle. Operating for long durations and distances on over-land cattle drives proved invaluable in later frontier conflicts, since these men enlisted in volunteer companies were already hardened to the challenges of survival on the march. Ranging units in particular needed these skills since they habitually operated outside of a garrison setting and subsisted only on carried logistics while on patrol.

Early Texan ranger units demonstrated this cross-pollination of ranching and cavalry skills during several instances during 1836 when the revolutionaries directed mounted units to drive cattle, implying an existing familiarity and capability with the task. The activities of Captain John Tumlinson's company while assigned to frontier duty near Bastrop provided a suitable example. During the Mexican attempt at reconquest they received orders to "get as many of the cattle over to the east bank as possible."[165] This directive intended to deny the invaders subsistence and retain provisions for the Texas Army. In August of the same year the new republic authorized a mounted company, under R.R. Royall, for the express purpose of collecting free-roaming cattle between the Nueces River and the Rio Grande. The action again intended to deny subsistence resources to the Mexican Army during any potential reinvasions.[166]

By the year 1835 the Anglo colonies of South and East Texas had benefited greatly from the expansion of the cattle industry. The combined growth of the cowboy population and the increased reliance on mounted patrolling resulted in a distinctly Texan culture that associated guns, horses, and tenacity with frontier masculinity; it exemplified a rough environment that created natural amateur cavalrymen. This ready-trained reserve of cowboys and horsemen provided a valuable recruiting base for mounted units as the colonies moved towards general war with Mexico, and would prove crucial during the national militia mobilizations of the Texas Republic.

By 1836 the Anglo-Texan population had increased to over 36,000 settlers with urban centers at San Felipe, San Augustine, and Nacogdoches, each surpassing the provincial capital at San Antonio de Bexar.[167] American colonists in *Tejas* now far outnumbered both the Mexicans and native residents. On the political front, this superiority resulted in awareness of the potential for political autonomy by the Anglo majority. Beginning with armed confrontations over disputed land contracts and taxation, tensions soon exploded over centralized authority and reactionary limitations on immigration. The intensification of cultural alienation and perceived unjust treatment by Mexico City, exacerbated when officials imprisoned Austin while he was on a conciliatory visit to the troubled federal capital, sparked smoldering resentment across the towns and settlements.[168]

Simultaneous to rising political unrest, the progression of reliance on armed horsemanship—as seen in the settlers' early ranging patrols of 1823 and 1827 and in the larger mounted campaigns of 1829 and 1835— emerged as a formative step in Texas's developing martial culture. The colonial evolution set the foundation for how Texans would habitually approach warmaking and initiated nearly a century of endemic border and expeditionary fighting. Tactically, the militia had achieved conditional parity with their proximate Indian foes. Strategically, they preserved a tenuous settlement foothold while aggrandizing territory. Forged in the fire of frontier combat, the rangers of colonial *Tejas* had established the genesis of Texas's way of war.

Chapter 2

The War for Texian Independence, 1835–1836

Texas's uprising against Mexico, and the associated revolutionary military structure that Anglo-Texan rebels developed through 1835 and 1836 to achieve it, represented the second formative stage in its approach to warfare. Two factors made these years distinctive in the rise of a distinctive way of war: the nationalization of volunteer horsemen as rangers and cavalrymen in organized companies and battalions, and the organizing of Texan forces to operate across a much wider spectrum of conflict than seen during the colonial period. In the case of the San Jacinto Campaign in spring of 1836, it represented the simultaneous execution of centralized, massed efforts against the Mexican Army and decentralized, irregular patrolling against tribal raiders within a comprehensive framework that centered on a concerted attrition strategy.[1]

The defense of revolutionary Texas consequently required a two-tiered military structure to negotiate the dual threat environment. Acting Governor James Robinson described the peril to Texan society—now nationalistically called Texian—with dramatic flair, proclaiming the nation stood "Surrounded on one side by hordes of merciless savages, brandishing the tomahawk and scalping knife, recently red with human gore; and on the other by the less merciful glittering spear and ruthless sword of the descendants of Cortes, and his modern Goths and Vandals."[2] Settler Noah Smithwick agreed, worrying that while "Mexico had an organized army of several thousand ... there were thousands of Indians eagerly watching for an opportunity to swoop down on us and wipe us from the face of the earth."[3]

Demands of strategic necessity thus compelled Texas to meet layered threats with tailored policies. In addition to several infantry regiments that comprised the core of revolutionary mobilization and a light cavalry battalion that supported combined arms maneuvers against Mexican invaders to the southwest, a small ranger battalion attempted to deter opportunistic raiders across the northwestern frontier. While ranging companies offered a historically proven method to conduct proactive patrols in the colonial manner, the *ad hoc* cavalry wing, aping professional European traditions, executed reconnaissance and screening for rebel infantry in larger confrontations.

The formation of these centrally commanded and democratically sanctioned formations, both north and south of San Felipe, required a challenging transition from previous colonial autonomy to sudden national unity. The specter of Mexican oppression demanded large-scale societal commitment, even as a small number of settlers remained disinterested or neutral, to risk everything in the cause of rebellion. One Texian activist, Moseley Baker, enlisted volunteers at San Felipe with a fatalistic oath: "The Texas flag shall wave triumphant, or we shall sleep in death."[4] In response to a pressing need for widespread settler participation to create a national army, the newly established Texas government consolidated mobilization, led by patriots like Baker, under the moral and legal legitimacy of republican authority.

Stephen Austin, still the most influential Anglo in Texas, proclaimed the explosion of Texian nationalism in October of 1835: "This Committee exhorts every citizen who is yet at home, to march as soon as possible to the assistance of his countrymen now in the field. The campaign is opened." Recognizing the commonality of settler origins, and doubtlessly seeking emotional relevance for armed insurrection, the former *empresario* connected Texian rebellion to the earlier American revolt against the British Empire: "You are the descendants of freemen—the descendants of brave soldiers also Americans—the blood that fills your veins has warmed the hearts of those who fought in the American Revolution and conquered the oppressors of American Liberty."[5]

Realizing the importance of galvanizing the dispersed colonists, adventurers, farmers, ranchers, and townsmen to unify against Mexico, Austin further enjoined the urgency of the moment by insisting that "Texas must be freed from military depots before it is closed."[6] Another civil leader, Branch Archer, announced the cause with passionate urgency: "War is upon us ... let us take the field. We call upon you ... in the name of everything that is dear." The firebrand then exhorted the militiamen with sentiments similar to Austin's: "You will be fighting for your wives and children, your homes and friends, for your country, for your liberty!"[7]

The resulting mobilization developed in marked contrast with the decentralized and localized reactions of mounted militia during the colonial period. As the nascent government prepared to fight for its existence, it legalized and organized mounted arms, in addition to infantry and artillery corps, as a sanctioned military function, and eventually, enduring cultural tradition. Galvanized to action, the first congress of Texas institutionalized the combined tactical experience of the thousands of veterans from numerous Anglo-Indian conflicts. The wartime contributions of these citizen-soldiers would nationalize the importance of cavalry and ranger service within the broader Texan way of war.

Bexar Campaign of 1835

The War for Texian Independence commenced on October 2, 1835, when Mexican soldiers attempted to compel the Gonzales militia to return a cannon originally loaned for defense against native raids. Asserting federal primacy, Colonel Domingo de Ugartechea, the commander of the presidio garrison at San Antonio de Bexar, ordered his subordinate, Lieutenant Francisco de Castaneda, to recover the piece. The commander intended to accomplish two objectives with the action: remove a large caliber weapon from insubordinate malcontents, and demonstrate Mexican authority over an increasingly restless colonial population.

On September 29 Castaneda led a squadron of over 200 armored and well-armed Mexican cavalrymen to Gonzales to enforce the order. After several days of inconclusive parley, the numerically inferior militia, under the leadership of the indispensable John Moore, finally engaged the Mexicans. The rebels carried a battle-standard with the words, "Come and Take It," as a reference to Spartan bravado. According to Texas lore, Moore designed the flag, which came to symbolize the burgeoning spirit of rebellion. Despite the Mexicans' ostensible advantages as professional soldiers, the militiamen repulsed them in a brief skirmish. Disinclined to escalate hostilities without clear orders or infantry support, Castaneda retreated back to Bexar.[8]

Concurrent to the contest at Gonzales, General Martín Perfecto de Cos, brother-in-law of President Santa Anna, arrived at the Catholic administrative center at Goliad in South Texas with 500 reinforcements. Once there he moved to assume leadership of the entire province at Bexar. With commencement of hostilities in the south and the demonstration of Mexican resolve with a strengthened garrison, the first military phase of the Texas Revolution had begun. In response to the confrontation in Gonzales and the subsequent call to arms by Austin, hundreds of volunteers mobilized towards the site of Moore's skirmish. On the political front, fifty-five representatives from thirteen newly organized municipalities gathered in San Felipe to plan consolidated defense and political secession.

In October of 1835, while hundreds of Texian men concentrated south against the Mexican garrison in Bexar, the Permanent Council recognized the need for a coordinated frontier guard to secure unprotected and peripheral settlements. On November 1 it proposed the historic legislation that nationalized frontier cavalry as a societal institution: "We have authorized the raising of twenty-five volunteer rangers, to range between the Colorado and Brazos, on the frontier settlements; twenty five between Brazos and Trinity Rivers, and thirty five east of the Trinity River; promising each volunteer one dollar and twenty-five cents per day."[9] In concept, function, and legislative language, this fielding held similarity to the United States' short-lived Battalion of Mounted Rangers of 1832.[10]

After coordinating initial provisions for prosecuting the war, the revolutionaries dissolved the council and elected a replacement body called the Consultation with more credible representative authority across the former colonies. On November 1 the new assembly commenced planning to establish a provisional government and coordinate military efforts. The emergent Texian infantry brigade, essentially comprising the combined colonial militias, achieved a series of surprising victories during this time. Advancing west from Gonzales they defeated the Mexican outpost at Goliad on October 10, initiated the siege of Bexar by mid-October, won a preliminary skirmish at the Battle of Concepcion on October 27, and finally seized the outpost at Lipantitlán on October 31.[11]

Austin boasted to the Consultation that the "brilliancy of the victory" accomplished by the rebels at Concepcion over the Mexicans' "overwhelming superiority" spoke "for themselves in terms too expressive to require ... any further eulogy."[12] Despite the obvious exaggeration of a relatively small skirmish, Texians had successfully displaced the forward positions of the Mexican Army in South Texas while allowing maturation for the disorganized rebels. Though achieved with inexpert and haphazard methods that reflected the amateur nature of the citizen levy, these skirmishes sparked critically needed martial confidence in the nascent polity.

The Army of Texas, first under the command of Austin and then of frontiersman Edward Burleson, soon canalized the surprisingly indecisive and much larger Mexican garrison into their defenses at Bexar while the revolution's leadership deliberated at San Felipe. The former *empresario* reported that they had taken "such a position as it will enable it to harass the enemy as much as possible," indicating his inclination for a contest of attrition in the face of Mexican combined arms superiority and entrenched defenses. He and the council agreed that any "attempt to take Bexar by storm at present" would have been "inexpedient," doubtlessly realizing the risks of launching untrained militia into such a potentially costly endeavor.[13]

Despite the fact that Cos now commanded over 1,100 men, including trained cavalry and artillery, he declined to attack the Texians during their march from Gonzales. It is likely that Mexican officers feared the famed accuracy of massed American rifles—proven when militia moving to reinforce malcontents at Anahuac defeated a Mexican force at Velasco in 1832—and opted for the protection of Bexar's fortifications. The density of the Anglo population to the east likewise dampened enthusiasm for an offensive campaign away from the Mexican logistical base. Nevertheless, Cos' hesitant posture in the fall of 1835 would contrast starkly with General Jose de Urrea's more proactive victory over Colonel James Fannin's regiment near Goliad the next year. While the former ceded military initiative, the latter maneuvered to brilliantly seize it.[14]

Cos' brigade of professional infantry, cavalry, and artillery should have ostensibly allowed him to wield combined arms superiority against undisciplined and unsophisticated militia. A statement by Mexican official Diez Noriega on the eve of the rebellion indicated appreciation of guerrilla methods associated with American rifles that may have influenced the garrison's defensive inclinations in 1835. The officer described Anglo frontiersmen's predilection for stand-off marksmanship: "To make an attack they prefer the edge of the woods, because under those conditions the best troops of the line cannot compete with marksmen who fell their enemies from behind trees, as if shooting at targets."[15] Thos Saul, a revolutionary committee member, confirmed this asymmetrical preference when he threatened to "give the enemy a specimen of their skill in rifle shooting."[16]

On November 9 the Consultation formalized the earlier acts of the Permanent Council and reemphasized reliance on irregular cavalry for frontier defense. Daniel Parker, serving as chairman, confirmed the previous authorization, purpose, and leadership for the Corps of Rangers. Seeking to expand settlement coverage, the act extended patrol sectors to fully protect the breadth of the colonies: "On the subject of a line of Rangers from the Neches River to the Colorado ... that said line of rangers be extended from the Colorado River to the Cibollo, with a company of twenty rangers under the superintendence of G.W.Davis."[17]

The chairman then coordinated to provide additional strength to his brother Silas Parker's company, indicating its sector's importance in the strategy: "From the information before your committee, they recommend that the acts of Silas M. Parker, in the organization of the company of rangers under his superintendence, before they reached the proper place of rendezvous, be recognized; and that the said S.M. Parker be authorized to add ten more men to the company, by and under the formal authority and rules."[18]

In a move that demonstrated the importance of the ranger companies, the committee established logistical provisions to facilitate success. The measure ordered each of the ranger superintendents "to be authorized to draw upon John Lott, at Washington, with whom there is a considerable quantity of ammunition deposited for ammunition sufficient to supply their several companies, or as public ammunition may be deposited."[19] This armament legislation was important because it signified the seriousness of the ranging concept in council priorities and reflected the military axiom that logistical prioritization and planning often marks the difference between effective and debilitated units.

As mobilization continued towards the south, rangers deployed to protect the strategic, and vulnerable, rear of the Mexican front. Smithwick, who immediately enlisted as a ranger, recalled the dual threat predicament: "The Indians, taking advantage of the disturbed condition of the country, were committing depredations, and the army, numbering not more than 500 or 600 men, rank and file, was preparing to invade Mexico."[20] John Salmon Ford, a South Carolina immigrant who arrived in Texas just after the revolution and would later rise as the leading ranger captain of the antebellum period, recalled the potential danger of a concerted invasion by allied tribes: "Had these Indians made war upon Texas families as they passed to the Sabine River, to escape from the hostilities of Gen. Santa Anna's army, the effects would have been terrific." The veteran fighter continued with dramatic prose: "Texas would have fallen. A scene of bloodshed, suffering and horror would have amazed the world."[21]

In order to provide consistent coverage, or at least early warning, against such a catastrophic event, the Texians divided the frontier screen into four sectors that employed the north to south rivers of southeastern Texas as boundaries. Assignments and superintendent leadership from west to east included: Captain George Davis's company to the west of the Colorado River, Captain Daniel Friar's company between the Colorado to the Brazos rivers, Captain Silas Parker's company between the Brazos to the Trinity rivers, and Captain Garrison Greenwood's company from the Trinity to the Neches rivers.[22]

The council designed these company-level sectors to secure the network of settlements along the northern periphery of the Anglo sphere. After a decade of tribal warfare, the frontiersmen well understood the value of using mobility to counter unpredictable raids. They also recognized the importance of using forward outposts, not as static garrisons like the failed 1823 Colorado River blockhouse, but rather as bases from which to patrol beyond settled areas. Parker's company utilized Fort Parker as a platform for patrolling north of San Felipe. Coleman and Moore had maneuvered their mounted riflemen from the same site earlier that year.

Parker's company activated first and soon pursued a native party that had raided a remote settlement on the new nation's northwestern border. The superintendent proudly reported this action to the council on November 2: "A large majority of the company is now in the woods pursuant to my order. I took the responsibility to instruct the officer to pursue a fresh Indian trail that had been made by late depredators." There is no record that the rangers successfully located their prey, but the mission demonstrated that the council's counter-guerrilla strategy was now at least partially in effect.[23]

Greenwood's company conducted a similar mission to that of Parker. His unit patrolled out of a forward post along the upper Trinity River, later called Fort Houston, to protect Robertson's Colony. In March the superintendent complained of "the Indians who inhabit in great numbers this part of the country" and lamented that the natives "all range through the woods and then steal horses." The company is not known to have had any significant fighting during the revolution.[24]

Unlike Parker's and Greenwood's commands, Friar's company did not utilize a frontier outpost. These rangers instead patrolled out of the settlement of Viesca north of San Felipe. These men participated in one of the few serious Anglo-Indian fights during the Texas Revolution when, as reported by officer Ennes Hardin, "Indians made the attack on us near San Gabriel."[25] The rangers retreated while suffering one horse killed, demonstrating once again indigenous ability to combine speed and surprise to defeat western technology. Friar and his men served until January while Davis's company never fully materialized due to the army concentration in his district. The presence of several infantry regiments and a light cavalry battalion essentially negated his ranging mission.

As a mutually supportive measure the council directed Parker's and Friar's commands to conduct bi-monthly meetings at the Waco village northwest of San Felipe. This command and control demonstrated basic coordination of subordinate units by the national headquarters and reflected the key element that distinguished the unified Texian government from previous colonial alliances. Of all the four authorized superintendents, Friar served as the only supervisor who doubled as tactical leader for his company. The others delegated patrol leadership to field officers and preferred to act as administrative managers.[26]

Despite the fears of men like Smithwick and Austin, the expected Indian invasions never materialized. Raiding by tribesmen, which could have devastated the preoccupied Texas nation especially if the Comanche had mobilized, did not stress the revolution throughout the Anglo conquest of San Antonio in 1835 and the San Jacinto Campaign the following year. Yet this array of legal authorizations and deployments proved consequential for both the future Texas Ranger institution and the polity's broader way of war. It represented a clear progression from the haphazard fielding of John Moore's rifleman battalion in summer of 1835 to the first continuous, organized, and synchronized deployment of volunteer mounted forces by the national government.

Texas proceeded to organize a larger military construct as the Superintendent Ranger System deployed and the rebel brigade, still relatively unorganized, invested San Antonio. On November 13 the Consultation authorized a more comprehensive—and mostly aspirational—framework of regular army, national militia, and mounted rangers. The legislation clearly emulated Westernized institutions of the United States with a distinctly Texian emphasis on frontier defense.[27] Not content to rely on fighting strength alone, the governing body likewise dispatched commissioners to attain treaties with woodland tribes in East Texas. On February 23, 1836, the rebels secured their eastern flank by agreeing to honor Cherokee territorial claims.

The provisions for a larger ranging force, in addition to European-style infantry regiments and cavalry and artillery battalions, indicated recognition of the need for a multi-faceted security posture. The council intended to deploy the new mounted command in addition to the preexisting ranger companies assigned to the river sectors, as a longer duration assignment. In this regard the act stated, "There shall be a corps of rangers under the command of a major, to consist of one hundred and fifty men, to be divided into three or more detachments." It then folded the frontier force into the broader military establishment, writing that it would "compose a battalion under the commander-in-chief, when in the field."[28] On January 21, 1836, the *Telegraph and Texas Register* published the act to assist with recruitment.

Three weeks later the General Council, which had succeeded the Consultation as a provisional governing body until a republican government could be elected, affirmed the ranger proposal. It again provided for a "Corps of Rangers" while retaining the now universally

accepted terminology Austin had used in 1823. The act established
the largest consolidated ranging force yet in Texas and stipulated that
"the whole number of rangers be one hundred and sixty-eight, and
consequently these divided into three companies of fifty-six men each,
to be commanded by one captain, and one 1st Lieutenant, and one 2nd
Lieutenant for each company." The directive organized the "whole
numbering constituting a Battalion, under the command of a Major.[29]
The council regulated pay of the men and officers and stipulated
required equipment. They additionally defined compositions for a
regiment of artillery and one regiment of infantry, and provided
limited naval provisions for presence in the Gulf.[30]

Leadership of the new ranging battalion went to a cadre of ambitious
and aggressive fighting men. For overall command the council selected Robert Williamson, a lawyer who had immigrated from Georgia. It
then chose militia veterans Isaac Burton, John Tumlinson, and William
Arrington, for subordinate company commands.[31] Tumlinson, in particular, stood well prepared for this mission given his extensive combat
experience with the San Felipe militia on the *Tejas* frontier since joining
the retaliation for his father's death in 1823.

Texian soldier John Jenkins summarized the simultaneous
mobilization of infantry and rangers to prosecute the two-front war
while focusing on Burleson and Tumlinson as popular leaders. Of the
Bexar offensive's unintended consequence he first noted that, "while
Burleson held a force at San Antonio, which was comprised mostly of
our men, our frontier was thereby left almost defenseless." The ranger
then noted the requirement to defend along the second front, writing that "the Indians were growing more and more troublesome, and
Captain John Tumlinson raised a minute company of the few men and
boys left at home. These held themselves in readiness for protecting
the homes and families of the soldiers who were doing valiant service
against Mexico."[32]

The mobilization of Williamson's battalion again embodied
the new political and geographic unity of the emerging idea called
Texas. Council leaders required control over a mobile element to

prosecute frontier duty, and if need be, support conventional infantry. Yet despite the effective nationalization of Williamson's battalion, it never adequately replaced the Superintendent structure in practice. While Tumlinson's company actively patrolled in the central area along the upper Colorado and Brazos rivers and Burton's company guarded the southeast coast only after the Battle of San Jacinto, Arrington's company never fully materialized. By war's end the battalion's mobilization would remain less than complete.[33]

Despite structural setbacks, Tumlinson's company proactively patrolled north of San Felipe where it engaged in the most significant Anglo-Indian fight during the revolution. After locating a survivor from a Comanche raid against a northern homestead, they tracked, engaged, and defeated the small raiding party near Bastrop. One of Tumilinson's younger rangers, Noah Smithwick of Moore's original ranging campaign, recorded how the native warriors were "taken completely by surprise" and then "broke for the shelter of a cedar brake, leaving everything except such weapons as they hastily snatched as they started."[34]

The young ranger provided a vivid description of the encounter that ensued that illustrated the often chaotic nature of tribal combat: "I was riding a fleet horse, which becoming excited, carried me right in among the fleeing savages, one of whom jumped behind a tree and fired on me with a musket, fortunately missing his aim." Smithwick then told how he "fired on him and had the satisfaction of seeing him fall," thereby felling the warrior before he could reload.[35]

Continuing his harrowing story, the young soldier next recounted how the fallen warrior surprisingly almost killed his commander while emphasizing how captains and soldiers alike risked death in frontier fighting. Illustrating how these engagements often devolved into hand-to-hand combat, Smithwick continued his narration: "The brave whom I shot, lay flat on the ground and loaded his gun, which he discharged at Captain Tumlinson, narrowly missing him and killing his horse." He then completed the remembrance by writing that his fellow ranger, Conrad Rohrer, "ran up and, snatching the gun from the Indian's hands, dealt him a blow on the head with it, crushing his skull.[36]

Tumlinson and his men continued to patrol the northern frontier until March of 1836, when national command redirected them to screen near Bastrop against the northern column of Santa Anna's invading army. This transition fulfilled the council's intended operational flexibility for the ranging concept.

Smithwick summarized the adroit shift from counter-guerrilla focus to conventional reconnaissance: "We were assigned to duty on the headwaters of Brushy creek, some thirty miles northwest of the site of the present capital ... we went on up to our appointed station, where we built the old Tumlinson blockhouse, making it our head-quarters till the invasion of Santa Anna necessitated our recall."[37] The company then fragmented as all Texian forces and the civilian pop-ulation retreated east in the face of the inexorable Mexican advance. Diverging sections of the unit assisted the evacuation of civilians, conducted reconnaissance for the army, and rushed to fight at San Jacinto in the decisive engagement of the war.[38]

While Tumlinson's men fought north of San Felipe before San Jacinto, Burton's company patrolled in southeastern Texas through-out the latter months of the conflict. After the Texians' improbable victory over Santa Anna in March of 1836, the national command ordered him to scour the coast from the Guadalupe to Refugio for possible Mexican amphibious invasions along the Gulf Coast. Once in position Burton placed his headquarters in a fort along the lower Sabine River.

These rangers earned peculiar fame as the "Horse Marines" when they captured three Mexican cargo ships inbound to resupply the re-treating Mexican Army. Burton and his men first captured a Mexican schooner, the *Watchman*, by signaling the crew to come ashore and then seizing the ship's captain. They then utilized that vessel to lure the commanders of two more Mexican ships, the *Comanche* and *Fanny Butler*, aboard the *Watchman* for a conference that resulted in capitu-lation of those ships as well. The seized cargo valued at over $25,000 and provided critically needed provisions for the logistically struggling Texian Army. Despite the bounty, the action had the adverse effect of straining critical peace negotiations between Texian and Mexican governments.[39]

Revolutionary militarization occurred at lower levels even as the national government marshaled resources. While the council formalized and deployed its network of ranging companies, dispersed settlement clusters simultaneously continued old colonial habits of forming localized militias for immediate defense. Smithwick remembered that the "government provided for their protection as best it could with the means at its disposal, graciously permitting the citizens to protect themselves by organizing and equipping ranging companies."[40]

One of these units, called the Houston Company, formed under ranger captain William Sadler and replaced the original Greenwood Company to protect settlements east of San Felipe. Another citizen militia, known as Robertson's Rangers, deployed to protect Robertson's colony north of San Felipe, while the Gonzales Rangers, under Lieutenant George Kimbell, reinforced the Alamo defenders at San Antonio. The latter company subsequently perished along with the entire Alamo garrison. Numerous smaller elements likewise deployed across the scattered homesteads and settlements as official ranger units expired or patrol coverage failed. This type of spontaneous Texan volunteerism at town and county levels would continue as perhaps the most consistent, and pervasive, aspect of Lone Star militarism until the 1870s.

In December of 1835, as the companies of Superintendents Parker, Greenwood, and Friar patrolled or moved towards the frontier and hundreds of remaining settlers formed *ad hoc* and inactive units for local defense, the Texian Army finally completed its investment of San Antonio. After weeks of siege operations the amateurs had almost retreated, but under the inspirational leadership of zealot Ben Milam, suddenly launched a renewed assault on the fortified Mexican positions.

The attack culminated with an explosion of urban combat. From December 5 to December 9 a Texian force of almost 500 advanced through the streets of Bexar in the face of Mexican artillery and musket fire. Town infrastructure created tactical challenges for advancing rebels as it provided defenders mutually supportive and covered positions. By the close of the second day Burleson reported that "the houses occupied by us commands [sic] some of the Cannon, or have silenced them entirely." After more brutal house-to-house fighting the rebels finally compelled the surrender of Cos and the entire garrison.[41]

Texian cavalry efforts in the Bexar Campaign unfolded with less success than their ranger counterparts to the north. While the colonials rapidly formed infantry regiments to conduct assaults on Mexican positions during the drive on San Antonio, the creation of a supporting mounted arm to support the campaign lagged behind. Small teams of horsemen provided reconnaissance as needed for Austin and Burleson but lacked structure or continuity. This organizational deficit plagued rebel commanders and illustrated the inherent militia character of Texian armies that lacked combined arms functionality and diversity.

An intrepid scout named Erastus Smith informally led most of the intelligence collection for Austin and Burleson throughout the fall of 1835. Called "Deaf Smith" due to hearing loss, he nevertheless emerged as the most effective cavalryman of the Texas Revolution. On many occasions Texian commanders relied upon his swift and accurate reports of Mexican movements to maneuver their forces. Smith's tactical prowess consequently personified the early Texas mounted arms tradition. Despite his critical contributions, the *ad hoc* brigade would not employ organized cavalry until March under the direction of Sam Houston as he endeavored to functionalize his forces according to normative nation-state standards.

In January of 1836, despite numerous organizational challenges, the rebels stood victorious in the newly conquered nation of Texas. With a small army that held more resemblance to militia than any kind of Western professional force, they had compelled the surrender of the once dominant Mexican garrisons and won *Tejas* for Anglo settlement. Seeking to preserve precarious gains with the few resources at hand, commanders garrisoned the Alamo at San Antonio and the presidio at Goliad with a few detachments of volunteer infantry. As political strife plagued the provisional government, militiamen departed to locate families and rebuild homes, and a minority of zealots even advocated invasion of Mexico proper, most Texians considered the war completed.

San Jacinto Campaign of 1836

Those who believed Texian independence to be secure could not have been more mistaken. In February of 1836 Mexico's president, Santa Anna, led a relatively large army to reconquer *Tejas*. As a hero of his nation's own war for independence from imperial rule, the veteran general ironically intended a nationalistic campaign to restore Mexican territorial integrity and political centralism. In his own words, he hoped to subordinate "those turbulent, insolent North Americans" and stated that if the colony resisted "all their property will be confiscated." The despot also threatened to "convert Texas into a desert" with connotations of a Roman-style peace.[42] The expedition comprised over 6,000 infantry, cavalry, and artillery across three primary brigades of approximately 1,500 men each. Two armored cavalry formations, one of 400 men and the other with 600, provided tactical mobility.[43]

The Mexican Army's professional and aristocratic officer corps reflected the main strength of the expeditionary force. Experience in years of independence struggles and civil war had created a cadre of elite, educated, and militarily trained officers who understood tactics and command. Many also benefited from academic studies in Napoleonic strategies and sciences at academies in Mexico and Europe. At the time of invasion, Jose Enrique de la Pena, a staff officer in army headquarters, wrote that "there were still experienced officers among the battalions and regiments, courageous and honorable and capable of leading their men to victory."[44]

Despite the benefit of many experienced officers, Santa Anna's army suffered a debilitating weakness: a high density of poorly trained and equipped conscript soldiers. The Mexican infantry—which were armed with aging flint-lock British Brown Bess smoothbore muskets that fired a sizable yet relatively inaccurate .753-caliber lead ball—debilitated the leadership advantage. Pena disparaged some of them as "companies of convicts" and claimed that others had been "snatched away from the crafts and from agricultures." In order to offset qualitative deficiencies amongst the rank-and-file, the invaders, or unifiers depending on perspective, brought twenty-one artillery pieces that included two 12-caliber and four 8-caliber guns.[45]

Despite greater quantities of infantry and significant artillery capacity, cavalry rode as Santa Anna's most effective arm in the open *Tejas* landscape and offered immense offensive potential against unfortified and untrained militia. Historian Christopher Dishman called them the "pride of the Mexican Army" with "lancers considered the elite group." The Mexican proclivity for mounted warfare with armor and edged weapons reflected Spanish heritage and ingrained aristocratic notions retained from the high medieval period. The horsemen were typically called lancers after the ubiquitous spear they carried for close combat in addition to Pagent smoothbore carbines and traditional sabers.[46]

While Anglo-American mounted arms traditions had long since eschewed body armor and spears as useless against highly mobile Indians, their Mexican counterparts yet retained proclivities that reflected knightly ideals of Iberian heritage. A town doctor serving as a scout for the Alamo garrison, Dr. John Sutherland, observed the approach of several hundred Mexican cavalry in 1836. He described them as "well mounted and equipped; their polished armor glistening in the rays of the sun as they were formed in a line between the chaparral and mesquite bushes." The Texian then observed "the commander riding along the line, waving his sword, as though he might be giving directions as to the mode of attack."[47]

As a studied general of European warfare, Santa Anna maneuvered his army according to conventional Napoleonic military practice. He elected to penetrate Texas from the south with simultaneous flying columns against San Antonio and Goliad. By March 6, at relatively high cost, he seized the Alamo by storm. Mexican cavalry proved instrumental in preventing the escape of several groups of fleeing defenders as the fort fell, again proving the utility of horsemen in West and South Texas's open terrain. In contrast, though many rebels possessed horses, they lacked cavalry cohesion and usually fought on foot with hunting rifles as light infantry.[48]

On March 20 General Jose Urrea added to the Mexican offensive's success when he defeated the rebel garrison at Goliad under command of planter and slaver James Fannin with a second flying column. Through skilled, combined arms maneuver he forced the surrender of a battalion of almost 400 Texians when he isolated them on open ground. The Mexican commander recounted how he "succeeded in cutting off their retreat with our cavalry, just as they were going to enter a heavy wood," and described how "the central column advanced in battle formation, sustaining a steady fire in order to distract the attention of the enemy while we surprised the flanks." Sanchez Navarro, a Mexican colonel, subsequently asserted that Urrea "was without doubt the General who most distinguished himself in the Texas campaign."[49] While Santa Anna achieved victory against the Alamo by costly mass assault, his subordinate utilized artful tactics to canalize and capture the Goliad defenders.

While initial Mexican victories were decisive, events that immediately followed proved more consequential. The massacres of at least 182 men at the Alamo during and after Santa Anna's final assault, and the execution of approximately 390 prisoners at Goliad, inflicted a powerful psychological effect on both Texas society and United States sympathizers. The resulting collective rage provided intense motivation for enlistment against the Mexican invasion, galvanized military resistance and gained financial, material, and volunteer support for the Texas cause from the United States. Conveniently forgetting his own campaigns of extermination against native villages, Austin called it "a war of barbarism against civilization," and claimed that the American "West and South" were "up and moving in favor of Texas." These atrocities, though claimed by Santa Anna to be legal under Mexican law as it applied to captured pirates, significantly hardened Texian rules of engagement.[50]

After investing San Antonio, the Mexican Army advanced east in three successive flying columns to locate and defeat the rebels. Santa Anna ordered his brigades to "do battle with any band of rebels that you encounter along the way," indicating his hope to clear the province in a broad linear sweep.[51] Seeking to prevent further rebellions, he also intended to occupy or destroy all significant Anglo-Texan towns. This strategy reflected the general's appreciation of population-centric warfare. From his experiences with rebellions, most recently in the Yucatan, Santa Anna fully understood that Texian nationalism could not flourish without even rudimentary urban centers.

The Mexican advance into the Texas heartland began on March 11 when a brigade under Jose de Urrea marched east from Bexar to consolidate several elements at Goliad. This maneuver secured the Mexican right flank in South Texas. The same day, a task force under General Joaquin Ramirez y Sesma moved directly towards the Texian political center, San Felipe, which obviously threatened to disembowel the rebellion. On March 24 another general, Antonio Gaona, led a third brigade northeast against Bastrop with the intention of continuing further east to occupy Nacogdoches near the Louisiana border. This march aimed to secure the Mexican left and eventually guard against United States influence. General Juan Andrade remained in Bexar with a reserve force of 1,500 men.[52]

Smithwick, then serving in the Corps of Rangers, summarized the Mexican advance from the rebel perspective: "Santa Anna, finding the Texas army in retreat, sent General Gaona across by Bastrop, and General Urrea down along the coast to sweep the country clean, while he himself hurried on after the retreating army, confident of his ability to annihilate it if only he could overtake it."[53] This offensive strategy reflected standard Napoleonic envelopment and intended to restore Mexican territorial control while clearing southern and eastern *Tejas*. If successful, the invaders would eliminate both the rebellion and Anglo-Texan presence in one fell swoop; it would turn Santa Anna's threat to "convert Texas into a desert" into brutal reality.

The Mexican attack proved initially successful, if cumbersome and lethargic, in its movement. By March 20 national forces defeated Fannin's garrison at Goliad, building on its victory in San Antonio, and total defeat seemed imminent for the rebels. This assault across the entire revolutionary front spurred mass panic, rapid civilian evacuation, and a general retreat by defenders eastward across Texas. Smithwick again recalled the peril of the strategic setbacks, lamenting that "the Alamo had fallen and its brave defenders been put to the sword. Houston was in retreat, and families fleeing for their lives." He then finished dramatically: "Here was a situation to try men's souls."[54]

Despite the Mexicans' initial success, small groups of Texians managed to slow their advance with guerrilla tactics learned through years of raiding and decentralized tribal conflict. Santa Anna, the self-styled Napoleon of the West, later emphasized the potency of rangers armed with precision rifles during his advance west from the Alamo: "The enemy, discouraged by this blow that left fateful memories, fled before our forces. Our flanks, however, were nevertheless, constantly molested by guerrilla bands." The invader then emphasized that due to "their intimate acquaintance with the country, the thickets of the woods, and the effectiveness of their rifles," the guerrillas "caused daily losses to our troops."[55]

While certainly emphasized to exaggerate military hardships that led to his eventual defeat at San Jacinto, the general's description of the colonials' fleet movement and precision fire by Kentucky Rifles revealed adept exploitation of the advancing columns' weaknesses. Efforts of these amateur soldiers ultimately allowed time and space for consolidation of the Texian army to the east. As testified by Santa Anna, guerrilla strikes against his infantry and cavalry columns ultimately allowed "the main of the enemy, now fleeing, to perfect a plan of defense."

Despite rebel harassment, the sheer weight of the Mexican advance appeared inexorable. Ranger and militia elements moved east and south to reinforce the Texian army as thousands of settlers abandoned homes to flee towards safer havens in East Texas and Louisiana. Dewees, moving to join Houston, recalled the turmoil: "After the fall of the Alamo and the massacre of Fannin's troops, the whole country was plunged into despair and dismay ... all the families west of the Colorado fled eastward with great haste." He also noted how "they went, one after another, through woods and across prairies, seeming to have nothing in view but to go eastward." This chaotic retreat became known as the Great Runaway Scrape and represented precarious times for the idea of Texas. It served as the crucible in which its society gained identity as an independent and militant people.[56]

Political and military events had continued to develop in San Felipe concurrent to the military reversals at San Antonio and Goliad. On March 2 the convention declared Texas an independent nation. On March 16 the revolutionaries adopted a republican constitution similar to that of the United States. In a fateful decision that perhaps staved off near-certain defeat, they selected Sam Houston as Commander-in-Chief of the Texian military. The council chose the polemical Tennessean due to his combat experience in the War of 1812 with the U.S. Army under Andrew Jackson and for his political gravitas as a former congressman and governor. More recently, the veteran had successfully negotiated the treaty with the Cherokee to secure Texas's eastern flank. Though Houston assumed the rank of major general, he commanded an army in name only.[57]

With the strategic situation rapidly collapsing, the council prioritized the immediate remobilization of the Army of Texas to meet the oncoming Mexican threat. Though ranging elements had continued to intermittently patrol the Indian Frontier, the main infantry regiments had generally dispersed and fragmented after taking San Antonio. Now, with Santa Anna's legions bearing down, a few ranger companies would not be sufficient for the task at hand. Facing three columns that each advanced as a combined arms threat, Texas needed infantry formations that could unleash massed firepower and wield bayonets *en masse*.

The Texian Army reflected the *ad hoc* and hurried nature of its formation, similar to the Austin's militia but better structured. As the sum of colonial militias with at least 100 U.S. Army volunteers, it comprised a volunteer brigade of amateur light infantry with extremely limited artillery and cavalry support.[58] In response to the linear Mexican offensive, Houston's men prosecuted a largely conventional campaign reminiscent of nation-state conflicts in Europe. Like all mid-nineteenth century Western armies the rebel force relied on the conventional principles of mass, maneuver, and unity of command to achieve victory. From initial mobilization in October of 1835 through the staged disbandment throughout 1837, the Army of Texas conducted offensive and defensive maneuvers with opportunistic retrograde and pursuit operations.

Though amateur, this force and its leaders consciously emulated French and British militaries that had long informed the organization and doctrine of Mexican and United States armies. To this effect, Texian soldier William Zuber wrote that "the army consisted of five classes: artillerymen, cavalry, regulars, first regiment of volunteer infantry, and second regiment of volunteer infantry." This Western European structure, and the requisite combined arms functions of a modernized army, demanded the creation of a dedicated light cavalry arm for reconnaissance and skirmishing.[59] Zuber underscored Texians' proclivity for horsemanship, even in the infantry regiments, when he wrote that Houston commanded "twenty-odd companies of volunteer infantry, with from half to three fourths of each company mounted."[60]

On March 11 Houston and a small staff arrived at Gonzales and began to assemble his regiments with only 375 men. He knew the Mexican invaders had already laid siege to the Alamo and trapped the garrison inside, but the Tennessean required more information. Like all nineteenth-century field commanders, he relied upon cavalry, covert agents, prisoners, and civilian observers to provide information concerning enemy disposition. In this situation, with the broad front of the battlefield established by Mexican initiative, Houston would call upon the most proactive of these collection assets: light horse.

On March 13 the Texian commander selected three riders as his tactical eyes and ears: Erastus "Deaf" Smith, Henry Karnes, and

Robert Handy. He then dispatched the new cavalrymen to patrol west from Gonzales to attain intelligence on the Mexican Army's advance and the fate of the Alamo.[61] Though humble in beginnings, these scouts founded the more conventional facet of Texas's martial tradition that served in nation-state wars, as opposed to ranger expressions that maintained an enduring frontier presence. The Texan light cavalry tradition would culminate during the Civil War when dozens of Lone Star mounted regiments conducted identical functions to those pursued by Deaf Smith in support of Confederate brigades and divisions.

When the Texian scouts rode west they encountered refugees from the fallen Alamo. Karnes, who had earned fame as an energetic fighter during the capture of San Antonio the previous year, immediately raced back to inform Houston of the defeat. Smith and Handy escorted the slower women and children to the army encampment. Both Karnes and Smith would later command cavalry units for the new nation. Houston wrote of the small element's reconnaissance contribution: "I received intelligence of the enemy's advance between eight and nine o'clock at night; and, before twelve, we were on the march in good order, leaving behind a number of spies."[62] In nineteenth-century terminology scouts were often called "spies" since intelligence collection or denial, rather than offensive engagement, was their primary purpose.[63]

Beginning with this first patrol, Texian light cavalry provided continuous direct support to Houston's infantry throughout the San Jacinto Campaign. As emphasized by nineteenth-century military strategist Jean Roemer, this type of mounted force, with its inherently fleet nature, served as "the illuminating torch and protective shield of the army."[64] Antoine-Henri Jomini, whose masterful treatises on the military science of early nineteenth-century warfare heavily influenced American and Mexican generalship, likewise attested that "numerous cavalry, whether regular or irregular, must have a great influence in giving a turn to the events of a war."[65]

With this dedicated, if diminutive, force now informing his maneuvers, Houston retreated further east in the face of the Mexican advance. Given his numerical inferiority he needed to continue organizing and recruiting before risking a general engagement. In addition to scouting the enemy, Karnes's squad also burned Gonzales in the beginnings of a scorched earth policy. If the defenders could not halt the invaders' advance in the south and north they would at least deprive them of resources and shelter. Cavalry mobility again proved useful in this task, allowing the slower infantry regiments to begin the retreat without risking unwanted enemy contact or worse, potential envelopment.

On March 16, as the Texian Army approached the Colorado River, Houston officially consolidated his scouts under the command of proven officer William H. Smith. This action initiated the service of Texan light cavalry as a recognized combat arm with official status. Trained in linear warfare as a U.S. Army officer during the War of 1812, Houston adhered to Roemer's declaration that "when the army, collecting its forces, either for battle or for recovery after battle, is scattered over an extended space, the cavalry must then provide for the safety of the troops."[66] Like Karnes and Deaf Smith, William Smith emerged as a founder of the Texas cavalry tradition after the revolutionary victory over Mexico. After leading his company at San Jacinto he commanded both cavalry and riflemen regiments during the republican era.

The slowly expanding Texas cavalry provided intelligence on the movement of Santa Anna's central column as the rebel army retreated east. Meanwhile in the north, Tumlinson's ranger company screened against Gaona's brigade as northern settlers fled towards Louisiana. Smithwick again recounted the rangers' supporting role: "We were called into Bastrop. Santa Anna, with a large force, was marching upon the poorly protected frontier, and all advance positions were ordered abandoned, and the forces to concentrate at Gonzales." He also wrote of their assistance to evacuating families, stating that he and his section were "ordered to cover their retreat, and afterwards join General Houston."[67]

On March 18 Tumlinson's picket identified the Mexican vanguard near Bastrop when they "woke up and saw the Mexicans, six hundred strong, on the opposite side of the river."[68] The outmatched Texians retreated southeast to join the main force, but most of them would not arrive in time to participate at the climactic battle near the San Jacinto

River. Regardless, this adept shift by frontier rangers from counter-Indian patrolling to infantry support validated the intended flexibility of the Corps of Rangers as a strategic asset. It also confirmed the successful implementation of theater-wide communication between the army headquarters and disparate elements, a significant accomplishment given the confusion that plagued the campaign. The Texian Army in the south crossed the Colorado River on the same day that Smithwick reported Mexican presence near Bastrop.

By March 20 Karnes officially assumed command of a second cavalry company and patrolled west to locate forward Mexican elements. John Sharp, one of Karnes' men, wrote of the unit's formation and task: "There was a call made for a cavalry company, who were to go back the way we had come, and see if they could find the enemy."[69] When Houston wrote to the government on March 17, "I shall raise a company of spies tomorrow to range the country from this to Gonzales. Send all the good horses you can get for the army," he referred to Karnes's new unit and the pressing requirement for steeds to allow mobility.[70]

Sharp described how the new unit advanced with stealth "some distance from the road, in the prairie, without a fire." He stated that they "took this precaution on account of the Indians, or any straggling band of Mexicans, who might have been out, like ourselves, spying." The company soon found success when it identified and attacked a Mexican patrol in an act of counter-reconnaissance. In a running battle Karnes captured one enemy scout, killed another, and wounded a third who escaped.[71] The Mexican cavalry commander, General Juan Almonte, confirmed the clash in his diary. Upon receiving intelligence of the continued Mexican advance from Karnes's prisoner, Houston resumed his retreat.

On March 21 a task force of infantry and cavalry, including Smith's and Karnes's companies, conducted a reconnaissance-in-force across the Colorado River to test the strength of the central enemy column. Zuber recalled the bold maneuver: "Our cavalry, commanded by Capt. Henry W. Karnes, crossed the river from our lower encampment at Beeson's and, under cover of timberland, marched by a circuitous

route to a point a few hundred yards from the enemy's encampment."
Then, making contact with the Mexican pickets, they "surprised
and routed" the guard force.[72] Despite the initial success, the rebels
immediately withdrew back across the water as the Mexicans "sent
their cavalry to engage them." After a scattering of musket fire, Sesma,
with approximately 700 men, elected to forego pursuit and remain
on the west bank. This hesitancy likely stemmed from Santa Anna's
habit of retaining operational decision authority for himself rather
than delegating to subordinate field officers.

On March 24 another Mexican force under General Eugenio Tolsa
reinforced Sesma's brigade and increased the central Mexican brigade
to approximately 1300 infantry, 150 cavalry, and a set of field cannon.
Sesma now substantially outmatched Houston in quantity and firepower, yet still refused to aggressively press the rebels. By March 25
the news of the destruction of the Goliad garrison had also spread
throughout the Texian ranks. The loss of so many countrymen and
relatives inflicted a severe blow on morale and deprived Houston of
much-needed reinforcements. The army resumed its retreat the next
day, catalyzing political controversy and despair amongst both the
military and political circles.[73]

The intended purpose behind Houston's long retrograde has
remained a subject of much debate. The weary commander wrote on
March 28 of his controversial decision: "I consulted none—I held no
councils of war. If I err, the blame is mine."[74] While the plan clearly
allowed him to collect reinforcements from East Texas, it is possible
that he hoped to eventually draw organized support from a sympathetic
U.S. Army brigade encamped just across the Louisiana border. Given
the nuance of his strategic victory, it is equally possible that the march
unfolded entirely calculated, as opposed to desperate, as the Texian
commander lured Santa Anna onto advantageous ground.

Despite intense pressure from impatient subordinate officers and
councilmen to make a decisive stand, Houston ordered his army east
towards the Brazos River. Throughout the retreat his infantry regiments remained completely reliant on the Corps of Cavalry to provide

intelligence on enemy movements. Zuber again described the horse-men escorting the infantry as they neared San Felipe: "Soon we saw their front guard, a small body of horsemen, emerging from the timber at the west end of the prairie ... The cavalry, being divided in to two parts, formed the flank guards on the right and left of the central column."[75] This recollection described the Corps of Texas Cavalry's transition from militia volunteers into a relatively cohesive arm of the Texian Army.

By March 28 the rebels passed through the rebellion's political center, San Felipe, as the army slowly turned north along the Brazos River. Volunteers from East Texas continued to join Houston while other soldiers deserted in despair or to locate displaced family. Like the earlier sacrifice of Gonzales, Texian forces controversially burned their unofficial capital in order to withhold sanctuary from the enemy.[76]

On March 31 Houston's army encamped at a ferry station on the west bank of the Brazos River called Groce's Landing. As the Texians continued to receive volunteers and supplies at the camp, the former Tennessean governor administered much-needed close order training in battlefield movements. The cavalry continued surveillance to the east and on April 3 reported Sesma's brigade at the Colorado River. Houston subsequently wrote of the observation, noting that his "spies returned and report the enemy only about one thousand strong on the Colorado, without pickets, and only a small campground."[77] The next day the general sent William Smith and his horsemen to picket south of the camp.

The two cavalry companies under Smith and Karnes screened to the west on April 13 while the Texian Army crossed the Brazos River. Houston then delayed with a march farther east and eventually turned south to halt north of Harrisburg. On April 14 Santa Anna impetu-ously crossed the Brazos with detachment of 750 picked soldiers in a fast-moving strike to capture the revolutionary council on the coast. On the same day the *Telegraph and Texas Register* reported that the rebel army was simultaneously "hastening down the river to stop the progress of the enemy." Four days later, the despot marched east towards New Washington on the coast, again pursuing the fleeing councilmen.[78]

Events developed rapidly when Houston's cavalry acquired key intelligence indicating that Santa Anna had divided his forces and offered a tempting target. On April 19 the Texian commanding general ordered a mobile screen for his final movement: "Captain Karnes, with his detachment of command, will remain on the east side of the bayou if he can in safety while the army will pass below, and he will then unite with the main army so as to cooperate." Houston then emphasized the covert nature of the operation and asserted that "great caution must be observed to conceal our movements from the enemy."[79]

Given the aggregate numerical differences of the armies, it remained critical that the Mexican brigades to the west were not induced to suddenly march east to reinforce the vulnerable regiment under Santa Anna, or worse, envelop the Texian army. Karnes's company accordingly picketed the Texian flank while Houston led the infantry to intercept the despot. Understanding the authoritative nature of Mexican command, Houston hoped that defeating Santa Anna would shatter resolve in his subordinate commanders and decisively end the war. In that one location, the Texian Army of approximately 900 soldiers now outnumbered Santa Anna's element of 700, allowing them temporary and isolated numerical superiority.[80]

On April 20 Karnes's riders located Santa Anna's forward elements as he returned westward from the futile raid on the coast. The Texian council had displaced before the Mexican strike force arrived and preserved the national leadership. Karnes immediately reported the intelligence to Houston, who seized opportunity to confront the president directly. After weeks of anticipation and maneuver the marches of the two armies fatefully converged near the banks of the San Jacinto River.[81]

According to Houston's official battle report, Santa Anna "took a position with his infantry, and artillery in the center, occupying an island of timber, his cavalry covering the left flank."[82] While the Mexicans established themselves, Erastus Smith and a new recruit,

Walter Lane, conducted a reconnaissance to ascertain the enemy strength. Lane recounted the exercise: "Smith pulled out this field glass, told me to hold his horse, and commenced counting tents to get an estimate of their numbers. We were three hundred yards off."[83] He then recalled that a "company of cavalry" fired upon and pursued them and compelled the scouts to hastily withdraw. Smith reported his findings directly to the commander-in-chief in another example of how mounted scouts contributed vital services to the war effort.[84]

As the two armies positioned for a general engagement, the impetuous Texian mounted arm seized the honor of initiating hostilities. In a preliminary skirmish they first attempted to occupy a tactically advantageous position in a wooded area between the two camps. The Mexican line repulsed the company with several rebel horses killed. Undaunted, the Texian cavalry reformed for a larger effort. Under the consolidated command of Colonel Sidney Sherman—an aggressive regimental commander who had criticized Houston's hesitancy to engage Santa Anna during the eastward march—they attacked again with an audacious charge.

One of the participants, infantry officer Lysander Wells, described the cavalry's objective and augmentation by volunteers from within the infantry ranks: "The field-piece of the enemy, stationed in the grove, on our right front, still kept its fire upon us, and being protected only by their cavalry, Colonel Sherman made the bold proposal to take it with his mounted men. On calling for volunteers, he succeeded in getting sixty-eight."[85] The infantryman then recounted the *ad hoc* battalion's organization as it deployed into attack formation:

We struck off at a brisk trot, and soon discovered the Mexican mounted men, sitting quietly on their horses, near a thick wood, and about half a mile from our position. When within a short distance, Colonel Sherman divided his little band into three squads, the right commanded by Captain Karnes, the center by Smith, and the left by Wells. The charge was given, and we rushed on.[86]

The hazardous nature of the attack required augmentation by inordinately aggressive riders. Mirabeau Lamar, a polemical man who would eventually become President of Texas, volunteered in this capacity. Despite the danger of attacking massed infantry and artillery, the objective of seizing the lightly guarded Mexican cannon would have upset the relative firepower capabilities of the opposing armies. This potential advantage, along with the Texian eagerness for battle after weeks of retreating, provided ample motivation for attack.

Mexican lancers interdicted the Texian charge in a chaotic collision of charging horsemen. The fight represented one of the few actions of the campaign where opposing mounted formations clashed. Santa Anna reportedly recalled the event: "Daringly the rebels threw themselves upon my cavalry ... for a moment they succeeded in throwing us into confusion."[87] This action reflected the typical skirmishing between opposing cavalries that preceded most battles in post-Napoleon Europe.

After fierce fighting in which the Texian Horse nearly captured the coveted cannon, Mexican reinforcements broke their momentum with a counter-attack. Wells narrated that after they initially "drove their cavalry nearly back to their cannon," the rebels suddenly found themselves "exposed to the incessant fire of an unequal number of cavalry, their artillery, and two hundred infantry."[88] Smith's new recruit, Lane, likewise described the unpredictable nature of cavalry engagements: "We went through them like a stroke of lightning, chased them back to their infantry, and then fell back out of their fire. They reinforced and followed us out, and challenged us again." He then finished by writing that they "charged, routed and drove them back on their infantry a second time" until "the order was given to retreat.[89]

Under tremendous pressure the Texians abandoned the field with several wounded men. Lamar earned enduring fame during the fight when he intervened to save several isolated rebels from the enemy's charge. The Georgian's inspired action, observed and applauded by hundreds of fellow Texians, provided safety for the unhorsed men until Karnes could interdict with his company. The new recruit Lane was one of these isolated men since he had lost his steed while embroiled in a hand-to-hand fight with a lancer.[90]

Though the Texian Horse failed to capture the Mexican cannon, the entire assault force, and Sherman and Lamar in particular, earned reputations for audacity. Houston later praised the action: "while advancing they received a volley from the left of the enemy's infantry, and, after a sharp reencounter with their cavalry, in which ours acted extremely well, and performed some feats of daring chivalry, they retired in good order."[91] After the skirmish the two armies retired into camps one mile apart. Many Texians suspected that Sherman had attempted to induce a general engagement with the impetuous mounted charge with the hope that Houston's infantry regiments would spontaneously join the attack.

On the morning of the next day, April 21, Cos arrived with over 500 soldiers to increase Santa Anna's total force to approximately 1,300 men. Houston's army still numbered at just over 900 soldiers. The missed opportunity of the day before, where Houston declined to attack while he held superior numbers, brought scathing criticism from his unruly officer corps. In the Texian mounted division the men elected Lamar to command the self-styled Corps of Cavalry in recognition of his intrepid performance the day prior. This rapid, and seemingly illogical, promotion from private to battalion-level command reflected the unprofessional nature of democratic command in early Texan military organizations.[92]

Erastus Smith and Karnes initiated the next round of operations with a bold and disguised infiltration of the Mexican camp to assess their increased strength. Karnes observed from a concealed position while his subordinate conducted the reconnaissance. Remarkably, Smith accomplished the feat by exploiting his linguistic ability gained as a husband to a Hispanic woman and experience as a long-time resident of San Antonio to converse with unwitting Mexican soldiers. This exploitation represented one of the enduring, and underappreciated, strengths of early rangers. They often employed familiarity with *Tejano* and Indian peoples to achieve military objectives, especially in the areas of language and cultural knowledge.[93]

Later that morning Houston dispatched his favorite scout with seven men to destroy the only viable bridge across the San Jacinto

River. Sensing an opportunity to finish the war, the commander hoped first to prevent further reinforcements from joining Santa Anna, and then to isolate the Mexican detachment in the event of a Texian victory. The mounted companies under Karnes and William Smith conducted a diversion to facilitate Deaf Smith's raid.

Scout Young Alsbury, who rode with the strike team, recalled how the "main body" of horsemen "maneuvered with the feint of an engagement." He then noted that Smith's detachment moved by a circuitous route around the Mexican pickets to "strike fire" against the wooden bridge. Once on site the squad quickly burned and hacked the bridge until it was rendered unusable. The raiders then passed through the Mexican lines to report the destruction to Houston with Smith vowing at one point, when he feared discovery and capture, "my orders are to return to camp; I will do it or die." For better or worse, the Texian Army now faced the prospect of total defeat or decisive victory with the enemy at hand.[94]

On the afternoon of the twenty-first the Army of Texas initiated a general engagement to decide the future of their nation. Under Lamar's command, the Texian cavalry formed the extreme right of the advancing line with the infantry regiments to the center and left. Smith and Karnes, now experienced cavalrymen, led their respective companies under their new commander. Houston subsequently reported the tactical purpose of his mounted men in the battle: "Our cavalry was first dispatched to the front of the enemies left, for the purpose of attracting their notice, while an island of timber afforded us an opportunity of concentrating our forces."[95] This action again reflected a standard European method of utilizing horse mobility to misdirect and probe along the dispersed points of battlefields.

Once the two infantry regiments and the artillery section advanced to their last covered position, the cannon fired to signal the general assault. As the foot soldiers overwhelmed the Mexicans' unprepared defensive positions, Lamar's mounted wing charged into the fray and engaged at close range.[96] According to Lane, the officers ordered them to "Halt, fire and charge." He also described using "guns, pistols and bowie knives" to fight, while hearing cries of "Remember the Alamo!" up and down the line.[97] Houston later reported that the battle lasted just eighteen minutes, reflecting the mutually reinforcing combination of Texian aggressiveness and the unpreparedness of the Mexican position.[98]

The Texas cavalry pursued the broken Mexican companies as they fled the field. This action fulfilled another traditional task of light horse in modernizing Western warfare: victorious pursuit. Billy Young of Smith's company recounted his experience: "We drove them into a marsh. I shot 'em till my ammunition gave out, then turned the butt end of my musket and knocked 'em in the head."[99] A band of Mexican horsemen, thought to be officers, unsuspectingly raced to escape across the destroyed bridge while Smith and Karnes rallied riders to pursue. The Texians intercepted the dismayed Mexicans, killing some and scattering the rest. Another rebel, Joseph Lawrence, recounted the final attack: "We gained on them and shot our carbines at them, dropping them off their horses."[100]

While the infantry regiments had carried the main assault, Houston acknowledged the mounted companies in his battle report. He wrote that his "cavalry had charged and routed that of the enemy upon the right, and given pursuit to the fugitives, which did not cease until they arrived at the bridge." The general also mentioned Karnes by name in the dispatch, a singular honor due in nineteenth-century warfare, by citing him as "always among the foremost in danger, commanding the pursuers."[101] These opportunistic actions prevented reconsolidation by Mexican leadership and greatly increased their casualties.

The Battle of San Jacinto—though clumsily won and enabled by Santa Anna's staggering incompetence—proved a triumphal moment for all Texians. Rifleman Robert Stevenson, who commanded Company H in the First Regiment, wrote hyperbolically of the event: "Never was there a greater victory according to the number of men engaged, and the results are glorious for the army and prospects of Texas."[102] The Mexicans lost an estimated 630 killed, 208 wounded, and 730 captured as a result of defeat. In contrast, the revolutionaries lost 11 killed and 30 wounded. The drastic differences in opposing losses indicated the measure of tactical surprise achieved by the Texians.[103]

While certainly a decisive victory, Houston's foresight and Santa Anna's overconfidence ensured a rapid translation to strategic success. Smith's destruction of the bridge, even while the main engagement had yet to be enjoined, prevented Mexican leadership from crossing the San Jacinto River to assume command of larger and unbloodied formations. Had Santa Anna united with his other brigades, the rebel victory could have proved pyrrhic given the great numerical superiority the invaders retained west of the river. Instead, a Texian patrol captured the president the next day and effectively ended all purpose and motivation behind the invasion.[104]

Because of Texian victory, and though under duress, Santa Anna officially recognized the Republic of Texas. The captured despot ordered his stalled army to immediately withdraw south across the Rio Grande. His dismayed Mexican officers, still west of the San Jacinto River, quickly agreed to retreat, reflecting the conscript nature of the *Tejas* reconquest. The failed president also signed a treaty recognizing Texas's independence, which the government in Mexico City later denied as illegitimate. As a result, the two nations would spar over territory between the Rio Grande and Nueces River, called the Nueces Strip, until ownership would be definitively decided by the Mexican-American War. Houston cleverly transferred Santa Anna to United States custody while avoiding determined calls for his execution as revenge for the Alamo and Goliad massacres.[105]

Despite the scale of victory, Texas independence remained in doubt so long as Mexican soldiers stood north of the Nueces River and held San Antonio as a potential staging point. Mindful of their good fortune, the Texian Army shadowed the retreat of the Mexican Army as Vicente Filisola, now expeditionary commander, led his brigades west across the Colorado River. Erastus Smith, ever on the move, continued his role as the revolutionary army's premier scout during the march. He observed the chaotic and demoralized Mexican withdrawal and later characterized it as "a flight—the way being strewn with wagons, artillery, horses, and baggage, abandoned by the enemy."[106]

The Texian cavalry—now the mounted arm of a nation legitimized by battlefield victory—maintained visibility on the potentially dangerous invaders throughout the retreat. Though defeated, the reconquest force yet held numerical superiority by at least 4,000 men and thus offered serious threat. Under Burleson's command, the companies of Karnes and Seguin closely monitored the withdrawal. An order from Houston to Karnes, dated May 3, outlined his intent and rules of engagement for the operation: "So long as the enemy are faithful in their retreat they will not be molested, but you are required to use utmost vigilance and not suffer a surprise nor permit an unnecessary encroachment upon them or their property."[107]

Filisola led all remaining Mexican elements across the Rio Grande and into Mexico proper by June of 1836. Walter Lane, riding with the battalion monitoring their retreat, summarized the surveillance: "We sent a detachment to follow Filasola, and see that he did not damage the settlers in this retreat. He made a strait [sic] march for the Rio Grande, via San Antonio, and never 'drew rein' till he got into Mexico."[108] After months of harrowing defeat followed by fortuitous victory, the rebels had, against all odds, achieved the impossible and gained a nation. Yet with bitter enemies threatening both from the expanse of the Indian Frontier and beyond the Rio Grande, Peace would prove illusory. The fight for political independence was over, but the Wars of the Lone Star Republic had only begun.

Chapter 3

Conflicts of the Early Texas Republic, 1836–1838

The third stage in Texas's military history spanned the initial years of the republican era as it struggled to preserve strategic gains under Houston's leadership. Beginning with the stunning victory at San Jacinto and ending with deactivation of all large-scale fighting units in 1838, this period generally continued the revolutionary framework that included a conventional brigade, at least in theory, positioned to the south, and dispersed ranger companies oriented north and west. While the Army of Texas intended to deter and counter further Mexican attempts at reconquest with Napoleonic mass, a succession of mounted riflemen regiments would follow precedent of the original Corps of Rangers in warding off Indian opponents.[1]

This choice for varied military composition—which recognized diverse threats on multiple fronts—reflected a potential inflection point in the development of Texas's way of war. On one hand the nascent polity hoped to maintain a modern, professional army comprised of infantry, artillery, and cavalry branches with a small navy to protect maritime interests on the Gulf. On the other, with much of the nation's population dispersed along expanding borders with settlement concentrations along the lower Colorado and Brazos rivers and in Nacogdoches, Texas yet required a flexible frontier guard. These two manifestations, nation-state regular army and irregular ranging forces, would present Texans with a choice: would they adopt war-making methodology along European normative standards or embrace their colonial heritage of short-duration service by volunteers?

The answer to this question would materialize over the next three years as Texas sought to maintain their tenuous position between a vengeful Mexico and the might of Comancheria. A combination of fiscal constraints, evolving threats, and inherited American aversion to long-term enlistments and standing national armies would eventually doom the reality of an enduring professional army. In its place, the embattled state embraced economized mobilization with reliance on hybrid and versatile riflemen. Years later, when Houston endorsed Texan solutions for Texas security in the U.S Senate—with naive hopes of attaining Federal funding—the statesman proclaimed: "You may withdraw every regular soldier of the artillery, infantry, and dragoons, from the border of Texas ... if you will give her but a single regiment of Texas Rangers."[2]

Strategic Security after San Jacinto

The Mexican Army's retreat across the Rio Grande in the wake of the Battle of San Jacinto left the Republic of Texas in a momentarily strong position. Beginning March of 1836 as the independence crisis militarized and exploded, the General Convention authorized an array of mounted battalions to supplement previous mobilizations. At this time companies from the original Superintendent ranging system were expiring. Williamson's Corps of Rangers actively fielded only Tumlinson's company in the Colorado River area and Burton's "Horse Marines" along the Gulf Coast. On March 10, the government again confirmed Tumlinson, Burton, and Arrington as company commanders under Major Williamson, indicating official continuation under new legislation.[3]

With volunteers streaming in from the *Tejas* countryside, and more arriving from the United States as Stephen Austin predicted, the

Texas military swelled far beyond the minimalist Corps of Rangers and combined arms brigade that defeated Santa Anna. While the Army of Texas, the successor to the revolutionary Texian Army, immediately gained newfound strength under the command of Houston's replacement, Brig. Gen. Thomas Rusk, the protection of scattered homesteads left largely undefended across the frontier remained in doubt. To remedy this omission the congress activated a steady march of light horse units throughout the next several years. The first iteration of frontier mobilizations spanned the summer and fall of 1836 and would represent the largest deployment of Texan mounted forces until the Mexican War a decade later.

The General Convention authorized the first of the supplemental ranging forces on March 3, 1836, even as Santa Anna's brigades began their advance from San Antonio. Embracing the commonly recognized ranger terminology, the legislation stated that, "Col. Jesse Benton and Lieut. Griffin Bane are hereby, authorized to raise a Regiment of rangers, the officers of which shall be commissioned by the authority of this convention."[4] The organizational chaos and recruitment requirements for countering the Mexican invasion delayed full deployment of the unit, which was actually a battalion in size, until the conclusion of the San Jacinto Campaign. Unexpectedly, the commander and a detachment marched east to establish a supply route to the United States and subsequently conducted patrols east of the Neches River.

The bulk of the regiment, now under the command of West Point graduate Lt. Col. Griffin Bayne, remained in the central theater and fought with Houston's infantry at San Jacinto. The acting commander then reformed the disparate ranger elements according to his mandate. With the Mexican Army in retreat he adopted the original rangers' mandate to patrol against opportunistic or retaliatory raids by Indians. The companies of Tumlinson and Burton reorganized under Bayne's flag, effectively replacing Williamson's old command. Burton, leader of the famed Horse Marines, eventually assumed command of the battalion.[5]

This increased focus on a cavalry-centric frontier defense reflected hard lessons learned over a decade of fiercely contested colonial settlement. William Christy, a veteran of the War of 1812 and American fundraiser for the Texas Revolution, recognized the effectiveness of mounted formations as the Anglo-Texan colonies attained independence through armed revolt. In a letter to acting-president J.W. Robinson on March 13, 1836, he attested the primacy of such forces on the Indian Frontier: "I have come to the conclusion that, an efficient & select corps of Cavalry consisting of about Two hundred men, to be placed under an Experienced Officer & Station on your frontier would be of more real service than four times their number of Infantry could be."[6]

This statement, by a confidant of Houston, precisely appreciated the unique versatility of horse soldiers in the expansive landscape north of the Rio Grande. It recognized the inherent weaknesses of static elements against fleet Comanche and the logic of countering mobility with similar, or superior, mobility. Houston emphasized the same preference for amateur riflemen as late as 1860, after years of consternation over inadequate Federal protection in Texas by infantry garrisons. Reflecting on the origins of his state's unique martial tradition, he proclaimed he had believed for decades "that mounted rangers are the only species of troops calculated to afford efficient protection against roving bands of Indians."[7]

Ethnic friction along the frontier accelerated in April and May of 1836 after cessation of combat against Mexico. As civilians and soldiers returned to abandoned settlements, many of which they had established beyond the immediate protection of the San Felipe, Gonzales, and Nacogdoches militias, hostile encounters with native competitors correspondingly intensified. The vacuum in Anglo-Texan frontier defenses that resulted from the Great Runaway Scrape had also encouraged tribal aggression. Even worse, the republic now fell under the gaze of the Comanche empire. Beginning in May of 1836 the masters of the plains repeatedly attacked the Anglo periphery, beginning a vicious cycle of retaliation between the peoples that lasted forty years.[8]

Without geographical barriers or strategic depth to shield them from the Plains Indians' exceptional operational reach, nearly every Texian homestead stood as a target to be plundered. One of the first raids spread alarm and fear on May 14 when a small war party killed two men and stole over 100 cattle near Bastrop.[9] Then, on May 19, a large Comanche warband with allied warriors destroyed the northern and exposed settlement of Fort Parker. Once protected by a dedicated ranger company, settler James Parker complacently wrote just days before the raid that "there appeared to be but little danger of an attack."[10] The ambitious frontiersman would come to regret this overconfidence.

The dramatic fall of this homestead happened quickly. After an initial attempt at deception through false truce the raiders stormed the unprepared fort directly. Revealing their society's predilection for ritual torture, they scalped, castrated, and killed five male defenders. Rachael Plummer, survivor and wife to one of the executed men, later described the Indians' "terrific yells" and wrote how "their united voices that seemed to reach the very skies, whilst they were dealing death to the inmates of the fort." The raiders captured and enslaved two women and three children though several others escaped to spread news of the attack.[11]

As a fortified settlement and patrol base for successive ranger companies throughout 1835 and 1836, many Texians believed Fort Parker impregnable. It stood as an ambitious pioneering attempt to claim and cultivate rich territory the Spanish had long forsaken while symbolizing the reach of Anglo-Texan strength. The sudden massacre and destruction of the walled homestead inflicted a severe psychological strike on the collective fears of the new republic. From a military perspective, it validated the tactical importance of fleet mounted forces in societal protection.

Indian attacks continued in June and July with small groups of settlers sporadically killed near Bastrop and throughout the upper Colorado River area. On July 4 Austin wrote to the army command describing the peril of the northern settlement zones when he stressed that "Indians have commenced active hostilities on the whole line of the frontier along the upper or San Antonio Road." As he received reports of a reinvigorated Mexican army massed in Matamoros in northern Mexico for potential retaliation, the former *empresario* worried further that "the movement of the Mexican Army into Texas again, will embolden the Indians west of the Mississippi."[12] Less than four months after the euphoria of its victory at San Jacinto, Texas again faced simultaneous threats from divergent fronts.

The Texas government increased mounted forces across the republic in response to Native American pressure. In May of that year Rusk reorganized the military structure with increased emphasis on proactive patrolling by dispersed companies of light horse. In June the Mexican expatriate Juan Seguin additionally organized two *Tejano* cavalry companies out of San Antonio with approval by Texian army command. As an irregular unit that combined Spanish martial traditions with pragmatic, and ultimately conditional, loyalty to a new capital, the Hispanic-Texan volunteers postured to conduct surveillance against potential aggression by their former sovereign to the south.

This move to integrate San Antonio citizenry, many of whom had fought under Houston at San Jacinto, reflected a pragmatic appreciation of the *Tejano* majority in the republic's southern regions—and also Seguin's position as a respected mayor of San Antonio. Rusk sought to harness the local volunteerism and communal interest in South Texas similar to the northern settlements' relationship with the ranging corps. The commanding general accordingly directed the Hispanic officer to:

> Recruit for the service of Texas a Battalion of men in whom you can place confidence ... you are particularly enjoined to be vigilant in keeping a look out upon the different roads towards the Rio Grande for the purpose ascertaining the movements of the enemy communicating fully and frequently all the information you may collect to the commandant of the army.[13]

Seguin's first attempt to establish a garrison in the south proved temporary due to an inability to recruit, and more importantly compensate, countrymen, yet the mobilization reflected the distinct continuation of frontier adaptation that had occurred over two centuries in the Spanish-Mexican community. In that respect, Seguin's intermittent military service represented the culmination of the original Spanish *Companias Volantes* who had departed San Antonio after Cos's defeat in 1835. It also illustrated *Tejano* cavalry's underappreciated tactical parity, and likely superiority, over Anglo rangers during the first years of Texas nationhood. Half a century later during the Civil War, Hispanic-Texan cavalry under Confederate leader Santos Benavides would continue this tradition with great effect.[14]

That September, in an effort to revive the southern *Tejano* garrison, the Texian government officially commissioned Seguin at the rank of Lieutenant Colonel in the national army and again directed him to form a mounted battalion. Since few Anglo-Texans yet resided in San Antonio, they appreciated that a respected leader who fought for Houston at San Jacinto held the best prospect for maintaining possession of the former provincial capital. Because Spanish, and then Mexican, border communities had long been dissatisfied due to neglect by Mexico City, they readily shifted loyalty northward. The *Tejano*s consequently secured Texas's southern border while monitoring a sizable Mexican Army contingent postured in northern Mexico until March of 1837. At that time Seguin once again dismissed his battalion due to inadequate mounts and logistical privation.

The disintegration of the Hispanic-Texan force foreshadowed the material and fiscal issues that would intermittently debilitate Lone Star units during both republican and statehood periods. The cavalry officer's final report on his belated demobilization, which stated that his men were "chiefly on foot, naked and barefoot," described the challenges of conducing military operations in South Texas without adequate supply or horse stock. Seguin also noted increased Comanche violence in his region throughout 1837 which hinted at the onset of large-scale Anglo-Indian warfare two years later. Despite the temporary nature of his command, it represented a sincere, if pragmatic, effort by the early Texas Republic to incorporate *Tejano* communities into the emergent polity.

Continued conflict in the summer of 1836 necessitated creation of a larger mounted force to patrol Texas's long and largely undefined border regions. Smithwick recalled the frontier instability of that time, writing that "Bastrop country suffered more from Indians during the year 1836 than any other year of its history." In a rare notice of how tribal warfare sometimes decimated the ranks of Anglo militia, he also lamented that he "could mention numbers of its best men who were killed during that time."[15] In response to intensifying violence, the Texian legislature planned the largest ranger formation thus far. With the company mandates of Tumlinson and Burton expiring in July and August respectively, the struggling nation required a new solution.

The Texas Congress accordingly authorized a Corps of Mounted Riflemen to serve under the popular Burleson to establish definitive security along its troubled frontiers. Intentionally departing from the European dragoon model, the regiment's method was similar to that of the short-lived United States Mounted Ranger Battalion and the later United States Regiment of Mounted Riflemen.[16] The force eventually comprised six ranging companies, exceeding all prior light horse commands. Burleson had recently led the rebel army during the capture of San Antonio in 1835 and the First Regiment of Texas Volunteers at San Jacinto and stood as the most eligible candidate for field command.[17] Years later, the ever partisan *Telegraph and Texas Register* praised him with poetic license that reflected the importance of martial leadership in Texian culture:

> Whenever an army has been gathered beneath the banner of the Lone Star, Burleson has been found amongst its leaders, and his name has been to his countrymen as a tower of strength. The Ajax Telamon of the Texian camp, his presence imparted confidence and unyielding courage to all his companions in arms. His heroic deeds have won for him the admiration of his enemies, and entitled him to the gratitude of his countrymen.[18]

Frontier mobilization quickened throughout the fall of 1836. From July to December, with varying enlistment durations for individual companies, the regiment patrolled across the expanding Texas frontier as the largest and most organized mounted force to date. With most native attacks originating from the north and west, and with the Texas Army's infantry brigade and Anglo and *Tejano* light cavalry battalions still oriented towards the Rio Grande, Burleson set is headquarters near Bastrop. This location, a historical platform for projecting ranging patrols, allowed him to orient focus and forces along the embattled northwest periphery.

The Corps of Mounted Riflemen found immediate relevance as Burleson's companies fought several warbands across the northern settlement zone. Volunteer soldier Rufus Perry recounted an interdiction patrol by one company under Captain William Hill in July of 1836: "We struck an Indian trail making towards Cole's settlements, where the town of Independence now stands." Emphasizing their mission to pursue a party of suspected raiders into the wild, he wrote that they "followed the comparatively fresh trail nearly two days and nights and overtook the Indians in thick post oak country."[19]

This manner of pursuit reflected crucial competencies that colonial mounted militia had mastered as it learned to retaliate against fleet raiders. Once Hill and his men located the natives' place of rest, Perry described how they "prepared to attack them in camp" but a "straggling warrior" sounded the alarm before they killed him. The rifleman then continued with a brief narration of how, with surprise lost, they hurtled to close with the foe: "We continued to advance, notwithstanding the fact of their being aroused to meet us. We killed three and wounded several whom we did not get … this occurred on a prong of the Yegua, twelve miles from the settlements."[20]

This account demonstrated improved capabilities of Texan horsemen in tracking indigenous raiders to their source camps. It also underscored the increased, if brutal, effectiveness of directly attacking Indian camps or villages as the preventative tactic of choice. In a bizarre addition to his narrative, Rufus then recounted a strange event that occurred after the fight:

> We were somewhat surprised and puzzled just after the fight to see a member of our company, an old backwoodsman named Dave Lawrence, step up and cut off the thigh of one of the slain Indians. I asked him what he intended to do with it. "Why," he answered, "I am going to take it along to eat. If you don't get some game before noon tomorrow we'll need it!"[21]

Though presumably not characteristic of typical subsistence methods by Texian soldiers while on campaign, this instance of possible cannibalism illustrated the extremes that some frontiersmen were driven to survive in the wild.

Burleson's regiment went into action again the next month with a larger campaign that included the companies of Jesse Billingsly, John York, and William Hill. The report did not specify the exact location of the attack, but the disparity in casualties between Anglo and native participants indicated another dawn assault against an unprepared camp.

The *Telegraph and Texas Register* reported the success of the riflemen in exuberant tones in September of 1836: "We learn with satisfaction that the companies of Billingsly, York and Hill have severally pursued and thrashed the marauding Indians; of who the first named company killed 23, the second 2, and the third 10, making in all 35, without the loss of a man on our side." The paper then stressed that "these successes have induced some of the families on the Colorado to return home and the rest will shortly follow."[22] On October 26 of that year the Texas Congress reaffirmed its pay.[23] Governmental documents confirm official continuation of the rangers' term into late 1836.

In the fall of the same year, in response to continued Anglo-Indian friction, the republic fielded two additional mounted battalions for frontier service. Smithwick, now serving in the Bastrop militia, wrote from the settlers' perspective that continued raiding necessitated mobilization: "The Indians were committing many outrages, making it again necessary to garrison the frontier."[24] These battalions, in addition to the Corps of Mounted Riflemen, indicated how serious the penurious republic considered the escalating violence on its periphery.

The first of the new units was led by Robert Coleman and was intended to replace Burleson's command along the central northern frontier.[25] Coleman had commanded the failed ranging campaign out of Fort Parker in 1835 and later served on Houston's staff during the San Jacinto Campaign. Now, commissioned as a colonel, he received orders to "raise for the term of one year three companies of mounted men for the Special Purpose of protecting the frontier inhabitants of upper Brazos-Colorado-Little River-and Guadeloupe." The directive demanded "complete protection of the inhabitants" and underscored the frustration that settlers were venting against the legislature.[26]

The *Telegraph and Texas Register* announced the new force on August 28—while conveniently avoiding issues of settler provocation and violations of treaty agreements made during the crisis of revolution—when they noted the plan to establish a forward base for patrolling:

> Col. R. M. Coleman has left this place with his men, to go and protect the inhabitants of the Colorado from the incursions of the marauding Indians, and to enable farmers to attend to their crops and to gather them. A fort will be erected in that district, probably at the three forks of the Little River, or at the foot of the mountains on the Colorado.[27]

The republic's light horse mobilization was also noted in New Orleans. As the closest major American city and port-of-call en route to Texas's Gulf Coast, it served as a frequent recruiting ground for immigrants to serve as Texian soldiers. The Bayou paper *Niles Weekly Register* wrote that "a corps of between two and three hundred cavalry is now being raised in Texas to act as independent rangers in the west."[28] This simple statement illustrated Anglo-American predilection for modifying European military norms to frontier realities. While cavalry inferred historic roles of Napoleonic mounted arms, the mention of ranging operations spoke to adaptive functions of irregular riflemen.

Coleman established his patrol base northwest of Bastrop near the site of the future state capital of Austin. The fort boasted barracks and a stockade while providing a platform for extended ranging patrols. It also served as headquarters for several other subordinate forts that formed a line intended to "give protection to the whole frontier west of the Brazos."[29] Smithwick wrote of the social composition of Coleman's command while providing insight into the demographics that comprised most republican ranging units: "Colonel Coleman's company was mostly made up of adventurers. When he built the fort a few men who had families took refuge therein and did ranging service, though not regularly enlisted."[30] This account described how early ranger companies usually incorporated unmarried young men for dangerous and often unpaid enlistments.

This more expansive outpost network significantly improved on the innovative 1835 campaign that Coleman conducted with Moore out of Fort Parker. Maximizing strengths of patrol mobility with minimalist fortifications, it set the precedent for a half-century of expanding lines of fortified outposts that intermittently screened the Colorado and Brazos river valleys against tribal incursion from the Great Plains. Smithwick again recounted the impact that proactive irregulars had on regional security when he observed that "the return of the rangers checked hostile incursions for a time, and people began to scatter out from the forts, in which they had been compelled to take refuge."[31]

With Coleman's command establishing along western frontiers, a second battalion organized for service in the forests of eastern Texas.

Sam Houston, now president, directed it to "organize the same and form them into Companies of fifty-six or more requiring from them a muster role."[32] Their specific mission was to secure eastern Texas between the Brazos and Trinity rivers while pursuing friendly relations with woodland tribes that lived amongst Anglo concentrations. Under command of Colonel James Smith, a veteran officer of the Texian Army, they eventually deployed four companies that served through the year. The battalion headquartered out of the old Fort Houston on the Trinity River.[33] This fielding along Texas's eastern regions, simultaneous to the new battalion to the west and the national army in the south, reflected the republic's precarious position within a cordon of Mexican and native opponents.

The Texas Republic had deployed at least ten ranger companies during the period of kinetic engagement with Mexico throughout late 1835 and early 1836. The young nation now buttressed this iteration with approximately thirteen companies in the summer and fall of 1836. This second phase of volunteer units provided it relatively comprehensive, mobile, and responsive defense. By stationing Burleson's, and then Coleman's, battalions along the northwestern frontier, Smith's battalion in the east, and Seguin's cavalry and the Texian Army in the south, it achieved full maturation of the original revolutionary strategy. More importantly, the activations provided a measure of interim security as the nation grappled with fiscal realities of nationhood.

This period came to reflect the diversity of early Texan mounted arms. Most volunteer companies of 1836 and 1837 served in battalions under centralized leadership, but others served by exception as independent companies, both officially and unofficially, according to local defense or expeditionary requirements. Referred to in legislation as Mounted Rifles, Mounted Rangers, Mounted Volunteers, Spies, or just Rangers, they shared an intention to proactively patrol in formations of fifteen to fifty horsemen while assigned to defined sectors. Throughout this period they displayed many iconic Texas Ranger qualities, such as independence, audacity, rapid mobility, and unflinching brutality, which would soon be tested at a far greater scale.

Failure of the National Army of Texas

While Texian mobilization increased across the volatile frontier throughout 1836, the more conventional Army of Texas in the south faced severe organizational challenges. At first, as a new wave of immigrant recruits rushed from the United States, it increased from just 350 men in June to over 2,500 in August. Fame of the improbable victory at San Jacinto and fear of renewed Mexican invasion galvanized support from interested residents, adventurous firebrands, and American relatives. Yet despite the rapid increase in manpower, only 672 of the present soldiers had fought in the San Jacinto Campaign. This differential underscored the dearth of actual combat experience in the ranks. The absence of a stalwart core of veterans who maintained discipline and fighting expertise in most armies—along with the inherently unprofessional nature of the recruits—resulted in an unreliable and ill-trained national army.[34]

Through the summer and fall of 1836 the army's light cavalry arm patrolled along the contested Nueces Strip. Representing the continuation of Houston's *ad hoc* cavalry battalion at San Jacinto, they supported the infantry corps with reconnaissance and surveillance. These actions oriented south as the Texian Army positioned at Victoria to counter yet another concentration of Mexican forces at Matamoros. Rusk explained the importance of tactical mobility: "if we have a strong force, and particularly of Cavalry, and we have our plans well laid we may annoy and cut them up in great numbers with expert horsemen."[35] This statement indicated the priority placed in mounted forces at the most senior levels of Texian command and reflected the acceptance of mounted service within the officer corps of the republic.

With such prioritization the Texas cavalry had continued to serve intact even as their ranger counterparts deployed over repeated iterations to the north. Burleson, prior to assuming command of the Corps of Mounted Riflemen, initially commanded the companies of Karnes and Smith during the initial pursuit of the Mexican Army. Sidney Sherman, who had led the opening cavalry skirmish at San Jacinto, assumed command in August during the remobilization of the national army. A third commander, Karnes, led the battalion beginning September of 1836 as it screened along the southern border. Juan Seguin and his *Tejano* horsemen likewise augmented the army in the south during this period.[36]

The Army of the Texas Republic, once the centerpiece of Texas's military framework, began to contract in the fall of 1836 following an abortive plan to invade Mexico. While some advocated for a decisive offensive south of the Rio Grande, Houston favored an economized and defensive posture buttressed by forward mobility. This relatively sparse structure reflected his preferred strategy of avoiding another general war with Mexico while seeking eventual annexation by the United States. If Houston feared they would meet catastrophe by the former, as evidenced by Texas' highly circumstantial victory in the revolution, he envisioned attaining enduring strategic security by negotiating the latter.

Texas's main infantry regiments finally began to disintegrate with the reported dispersal of the Mexican invasion force at Matamoros. Without an immediate and galvanizing threat, and given the republic's dire financial straits, there remained little perceived need in the congress for large and expensive combined arms brigades. The army's reputation was further soured by the nature of the volunteers who populated the army's ranks when they proved ill-suited to the enduring tempo of drill, guard duties, manual labor, and ceremony.

For those who championed reliance on dispersed mounted forces for national defense in the absence of a concerted invasion, the demise of the national army was viewed positively. Houston, who also adamantly opposed retaliatory invasions south of the Rio Grande, advocated a frontier focus: "It cannot be that the Army has nothing to do at home. The Colorado is swept of its inhabitants from the Frontier settlements to Moseleys Cotton Gin. The inhabitants have fled to the Brazos." In frustration with the army's seemingly unproductive activities in South Texas, he argued that "had the Army taken post on the Navidad, it could easily by throwing out its Cavalry have given protection to the inhabitants and chastised the Indians."[37]

In October of 1836, following Houston's inauguration as president, Brigadier General Felix Huston assumed command of the 2,000-strong national army now encamped at Camp Johnson on the Lavaca River. The republic also fielded smaller garrisons at Galveston and Velasco while Seguin and Karnes patrolled out of San Antonio.[38] Yet the cost of even that force proved expensive for an immature nation-state with low population, little infrastructure, and limited capital. Beginning in November the republic initiated a strategic transition to rely on a centrally controlled, yet inactive, system of national militia brigades in concert with a network of active and decentralized ranger companies.[39]

The final evolution of the revolutionary military framework consisted of two replacement mounted riflemen battalions activated respectively in spring and summer of 1837. By this point the initial battalions of the Superintendents and Williamson of 1835 had long expired and the second iteration of battalions under Burleson, Benton, Coleman, and Smith were scheduled to demobilize at the close of 1836. Anticipating reorganization over the next year, the First Congress had passed an "Act to Protect the Frontier" on December 5, 1836. They intended to reorganize Coleman's existing screen to the northwest by requiring the president "to raise, with as little delay as possible, a battalion of mounted riflemen, to consist of two hundred and eighty men, for protection of the frontier." The legislation further ordered the battalion "to be officered in like manner as the balance of the army."[40]

Moving into tactical prescription, the congress ordered construction of "block houses, forts and trading houses" in order to "prevent Indian depredations." It likewise authorized an increase to 560 men if necessary and allowed the president to attach rangers to the main army if required. These specifications firmly placed the frontier battalion of January 1837 within the broader Texian military strategy. The act then assigned riflemen to secure the new counties of Gonzales, Bastrop, and Shelby, essentially adopting Burleson's and Coleman's sectors and reflecting continued concern over rising Comanche threats.[41]

The familiar design for mounted riflemen to patrol from forward outposts demonstrated an increasing understanding of the centrality of population-centric warfare by Texas authorities on the frontier. As an assault-oriented version of the colonial ranger concept, they clearly intended to deploy mobile forces to create space between populated areas in southeastern Texas and porous borderlands. Recognizing the potential need for massed infantry in case of Mexican invasion, the congress likewise enacted provisions for an inactive, yet potentially large-scale, national militia.[42]

Texas authorities initially assigned command of the new counter-Indian organization to the experienced Coleman, but upon his sudden discharge for publicly criticizing Houston's wartime record, allocated it to Major William Smith. The veteran's successful command in the original Corps of Texas Cavalry during the San Jacinto Campaign made him an ideal candidate for the vacancy. Under Smith's leadership, and that of his successor George Jewel, the battalion deployed five companies on the frontier from January to March of 1837. The arrayed companies occupied patrol bases at the Little River Fort, Fort Milam, Fort Henderson, and Fort Colorado in clear emulation of Burleson's and Coleman's original active-barrier concepts.[43]

Throughout the spring of 1837 Smith's riflemen fought in several conflicts against tribal warriors while patrolling border areas. In October of that year, in the unit's most notable action, a company under Captain William Eastland clashed with a larger allied warband of Tawakonis, Kichais, Wacos, and Caddos along the upper Trinity River. Recalling the fight, one ranger wrote that "the Indians made a charge upon us and completely surrounded our position."[44] Though the riflemen inflicted native casualties with precision marksmanship, the clash, later called the Stone Houses Fight, cost the Texians four dead and compelled them to retreat under fire. This battle inflicted a chilling reminder that Indian mobility and superior numbers could still defeat ranger forces in open terrain.

Anglo-Indian violence continued into the summer of 1837 and instigated further Texian measures to secure vulnerable settlements.

In June, as the national army demobilized in the south, the congress authorized another act titled, "For the better protection of the northern frontier." The government ordered the creation of an additional regimental-sized "corps of mounted gun-men, consisting of six hundred mounted men" to further strengthen the republic's border defenses.[45] Reference to "mounted gun-men," similar to the previous designations of mounted riflemen, emphasized a greater role as assault troops than reconnaissance-focused rangers of the colonial period.

The new legislation divided the regiment into three battalions under direct command of the president. It assigned companies by geographic sector according to county boundaries to denote the comprehensive intent of the act. In specified allocations that emphasized the decentralized nature of the mission, the measure assigned the counties of Galveston, Harrisburg, Nacogdoches, San Augustine, Milam, Washington, Jasper, and Shelby each a single mounted company, with Red River County receiving two.[46] This proposal represented, if in concept only, the pinnacle of nationalization and organizational adaptation by the Texan mounted forces in the years following independence.

As with previous ranging legislation the act again stipulated the equipment each volunteer soldier had to provide for himself. It also directed that "if practicable, there shall be attached to each division one company of spies, composed of Shawnees, Cherokees, Delawares, or of other friendly Indians" to assist with reconnaissance and surveillance.[47] This directive for multiethnic cooperation revealed the appreciation—at the national level—of indigenous intelligence in irregular warfare. Despite comprehensive intentions, only one company of gun-men actually deployed. It patrolled under the command of John Boyer in Harrisburg County and eventually attached to Smith's existing battalion.

The Army of Texas accelerated reduction throughout 1837 as the nation became increasingly dependent upon national militia for potential operations of scale and mass. After another brief fear of a Mexican invasion in the spring of 1837, Houston finally disbanded most of the force in May. In actuality, and with acute embarrassment, the president furloughed the soldiers because the treasury could not afford to pay accrued wages. The congress officially downgraded the authorized strength of the army, now closer to a single regiment in size, to fewer than 600 men spread across small garrisons. Needless to say, this force represented a mere fraction of the opposing strength of the Mexican Army.[48]

By the fall of 1837, due to the embarrassing furlough of the central army, Texian light cavalry and mounted riflemen patrolled as the only substantial active government forces in the country. Similar to the colonial period that began its emergent way of war, Texas had once again embraced—both governmentally and unofficially across communities—a cavalry-centric tradition. The defense authorizations of December 1836 and June 1837, which established large, centrally commanded bodies of geographically decentralized light horse, reflected dynamically changing priorities. This emphasis contrasted starkly with the diminishing role of the conventional army as it emerged as less and less appropriate to the frontier setting.

The lessons of 1837 additionally taught that smaller companies of volunteer mounted soldiers offered more effective and less expensive security than large infantry garrisons. Houston and others appreciated that non-professional horsemen procured their own steeds and weapons and often served for less or even no pay. Similarly, the national militia assumed new importance for the same reasons after its reorganization in December of 1836 and expansion in December of 1837. This inactive structure, when coupled with the active mounted rifleman system, provided Texas with an economized method to mobilize larger infantry regiments and brigades only as required.[49]

Erastus Smith, the most effective scout of the revolution, participated in one of the most publicized clashes during the shift to light horse primacy. He led a cavalry company out of San Antonio from December of 1836 to March of 1837 that the congress had initially authorized under the Mounted Rifleman Act of 1836, but then attached it to Karnes's battalion in the south. With Spanish cultural familiarity and geographical knowledge of South Texas, Smith arrived ideally suited to lead in this region. By this time Texan legislators clearly associated mounted riflemen and rangers with Indian fighting along the northwestern frontier and light cavalry with conventional, nation-state warfare along the southern border.

The incident that again catapulted Smith to regional fame occurred on March 6, 1838, when his company conducted a forceful reconnaissance in the vicinity of Laredo. As a disputed border station 140 miles east of San Antonio, the Hispanic town existed nominally within Mexico's sphere of influence. The veteran scout ostensibly intended only to identify any Mexican Army activity in the area, but purportedly hoped to actually claim Laredo for the Texas Republic without Houston's approval. This intent clearly stemmed from Texas society's ambitions for expansion to the southwest.

While on patrol, the horsemen encountered a superior number of Mexican cavalry near the contested town. Despite the attempted envelopment by Mexican detachments, the Texians employed accurate rifle fire to degrade their enemy's discipline and resolve while killing ten riders. They then returned to San Antonio as heroes with twenty captured horses. The *Telegraph and Texas Register* boasted of the victory—revealing its habitual tendency to exaggerate tactical prowess—by writing that "Deaf Smith has again been at his old business. The result of this skirmish has furnished another proof to the thousands which have preceded it, that our degraded and dastard foes never make head against even half their number of the sturdy back woodsmen of the west."[50]

Despite the popularity of Smith's victory against the hated Mexican foe, the President of Texas assumed a more pragmatic view of the unproductive engagement. Not wishing to antagonize Mexico during a period of precarious relations even as his national army disintegrated, Houston admonished Karnes and Smith for the altercation. On March 31 he explained his frustration to Karnes: "I am afraid our friend Deaf Smith and his men have acted badly, if reports are true. I never ordered him to Laredo and if, my orders are not to be obeyed it is useless to give them."[51] Like his earlier opposition to the invasion of Mexican territory, the president retained the firm conviction that another general war against the far larger nation to the south could prove disastrous for Texas.

Smith's action in Laredo proved significant for an additional reason: the participation of future Texas Ranger legend John Coffee Hays in his first significant combat action. The Tennessean immigrant had first arrived in the republic in 1836 just after the Battle of San Jacinto as part of the massive wave of patriotic immigrants who arrived to join the Texas cause. Houston immediately recommended the eager recruit for cavalry service due to his previous friendship with Hays's father, Harmon Hays, and also the young ranger's namesake, Tennessee militia commander John Coffee, in the United States. The ranger's biographer summarized the older generation's relationship: "Harmon Hays served with Sam Houston in the Creek War in Alabama and was in Coffee's dragoons, becoming a second lieutenant in May, 1814. It was he who was selected to face the center of the British advance at new Orleans."[52]

With this martial lineage informing his conduct, Hays benefited greatly from serving under Smith in 1837 where he first learned tactics from the expert horseman. It was no coincidence then that after serving under the most effective scout of the Texas Revolution and then riding in Karnes' aggressive mounted companies, Hays swiftly rose to become the most famous ranger prior to the Civil War. His military service in the San Antonio area also established it as his favored sector for the balance of his career. After Smith's retirement following the Laredo fight, Karnes' untimely death in 1840, and Seguin's repatriation to Mexico in 1842, and in the absence of the old Texian Army, most Texians came to readily acknowledge Hays as the leading captain in South Texas throughout the 1840s.[53]

The initial years after San Jacinto saw the Texas government attempt to maintain a binary military division of regular and irregular forces. From October of 1835 to June of 1837 it authorized at least eight rifleman battalions and two cavalry battalions in addition to several infantry regiments and artillery batteries in the failing national army.[54] Yet by the summer of 1838, as the final ranging corps expired, the San Antonio cavalry and a few town-sponsored mounted companies patrolled as the only government-sponsored units in defense of Texas. Under extreme budgetary pressures the congress declined to reauthorize further battalion-sized frontier elements even though they had demobilized the main army the year prior. When the last company of William Smith's battalion disbanded in April of 1838, the final manifestation of the revolutionary military framework ended.

The fortunes of the struggling Texian nation thus stood precarious and uncertain in the summer of 1838. The Mexican threat simmered south of the Rio Grande and the Comanche hosts to the north and west had yet to be decisively encountered. Further conflict would prove inevitable as the polity, despite Houston's cautious warnings, transitioned from the defensive footing of the revolution to increasingly offensive postures aimed at territorial aggrandizement. Despite the intensifying contest for regional supremacy, and because of the failure of the infantry-centric national army, one dynamic emerged with certitude: Texas's way of war had been cemented with mounted arms at its core. From the rise of colonial militia to the deployment of rifleman battalions along the Indian Frontier, irregular cavalry had emerged as the shield of the Lone Star. In the near future, it would also fight as its sword.

Chapter 4

Conflicts of the Middle Texas Republic, 1838–1840

A n expanding scope of Anglo-Indian warfare defined the middle years of the Texas Republic. From 1838 to 1840 the young nation fought conflicts of territorial expansion and preservation— both state-sanctioned and unsanctioned—as it sought to establish an enduring strategic security. Texian mounted forces rode at the heart of this contest as national militia and elite rangers. Simultaneously, the explosive growth of the Anglo population from approximately 35,000 in 1836 to over 150,000 in 1845 intensified ethnic confrontation.[1] This immigration transformed the depth and reach of Lone Star military power in the wake of their hard-won independence. As thousands of adventurers, entrepreneurs, and pioneers travelled west from the United States, the phrase "Gone to Texas" became symbolic of the movement.[2]

The year 1840, in particular, saw the largest immigration wave in the republic's short history. The rapidity of population growth and increased societal militarization directly instigated among the most destructive ethnic conflicts the lower Great Plains would ever experience. As more and more ambitious Texians interjected frontier towns into the contested periphery, a reinforcing confluence of settler initiative and political encouragement attained critical mass. This pressure created a powerful impetus for aggressive settlement and a deep reserve of human capital to fight for new lands; it propelled the republic's boundaries west, north, and south with a devastating surge of violent energy.

Texas's central prairies, western plains, and Rio Grande region subsequently emerged as militarized zones of heightened conflict. The ascendancy of Mirabeau B. Lamar's imperialist presidency in December 1838 spurred aggrandizement of lands belonging to Indians, *Tejanos*, and Mexican nationals. For a struggling country lacking sophisticated infrastructure and a modernized industrial base, these acquisitions represented the true wealth to which Texian society and ambitious citizens did not hesitate to stake their claim. The construction of the new capital of Austin in 1839, deliberately postured along the Indian Frontier, represented the westward orientation and fleeting primacy of Lamar's war faction.

This expansionist spirit—and the reality of Texas's embattled and isolated position—cultivated militant nationalism amongst both new immigrants and veteran citizens. Houston, who controversially opposed ethnic provocation, nevertheless described the communal self-interest that made volunteers conditionally more effective than conscripted and professional soldiers who populated many nation-state armies: "These volunteers are the men who are to come forth from the forest in the hour of peril, and save and rescue your country. It is not a tactician, but it is a genius formed by nature that is to lead your armies to victory." The former general passionately, and naively, declared that "the call of patriotism will bring them forth from their dells, from their mountain tops, from their gorges. They will come forth as a mighty torrent to overwhelm the adversary when one shall come to our soil."[3]

Throughout its middle years the Texas Republic relied on a national system of militia brigades for decisive campaigns of scale and mass. Comprised of inactive units of mounted riflemen assigned to regional sectors, brigaded regiments offered the penurious nation a cost-effective method of countering larger incursions by Mexican divisions and consolidated tribal attacks. The success of these levies, and the numerous ranging campaigns that towns and counties produced spontaneously, would contrast starkly with the republic's second attempt at fielding a professional army in 1839. Like the previous failure of the Texas Army, the rapid demise of the vaunted Frontier Regiment would highlight the viability of a Texan way of war based in limited and volunteer service.[4]

Indian Wars of the Texas Republic

The Republic of Texas began the year 1838 with a diminishing military framework as the preponderance of frontier battalions fielded during and immediately after the revolution expired. National mobilization had temporarily spawned a professional army and a succession of irregular mounted battalions, but expenditures proved untenable. By the summer of that year the nation retained only a small light cavalry battalion in San Antonio and a few independent ranging companies that patrolled localized sectors to protect peripheral communities. Given this dearth of active fighting capacity, continued territorial competition and general regional instability necessitated the creation of a new military construct based on mobility and flexibility.

In May of 1838 the Texas Congress responded by authorizing Houston, still president, to "raise a Corps of Regular Cavalry, not exceeding two hundred and eighty ... for the purpose of protecting the Southwestern Frontier."[5] Like the earlier cavalry designations of Seguin's and Karnes's, this legislation recognized the potential for conventional conflict in the southern theater as Mexico and its former possession disputed territory between the Nueces River and Rio Grande. Despite Houston's support and the threat that remained south of the Rio Grande, slow recruitment and fiscal issues slowed the formation of the command. It belatedly provided only an interim solution for less than a year out of San Antonio and Gonzales.[6]

Anglo-Indian conflict intensified through the summer and fall of 1838 as the settler population increased and settlement zones expanded onto the central prairies. With the furlough of the original Texian Army in May of 1837 and the expiration of James Smith's Mounted Rifleman Battalion in April of 1838, the republic now relied upon a less expansive and more economized system. While cavalry in San Antonio screened against Mexico to maintain observation on any potential incursions, a geographically organized national militia maintained the broader national defense against native raids. Continuing Texas's tradition of assigning command to leaders of proven combat prowess, the industrious Henry Karnes led the Texas cavalry while Thomas Rusk commanded the larger citizen-levy.

The National Militia of 1838 and 1840 comprised four regional brigades across Central and East Texas under nominal command of a national headquarters. Each brigade included several inactive infantry regiments, which were supported by contingents of mounted rangers. In reality, most the infantry also traveled on horseback and only fought dismounted in keeping with Texas's cavalry-centric martial culture. Veteran officers and sergeants from the San Jacinto Campaign formed the hardened core of the force with the ever-aggressive Edward Burleson commanding the volatile northwestern quadrant. Once again, Bastrop served as his headquarters for western maneuvers.[7]

By this point Texas benefited more and more from internal martial traditions instead of relying purely on adopted or imported tactics and ethos from American and Spanish counterparts. Unlike in years past, Texian society now generated its own reservoir of combat veterans, officer leadership, and tactical knowledge of frontier warfare. This experiential base stimulated success for the inactive militia brigades as well as the development of elite ranging companies in 1844 and 1845. As summarized by Jose Maria Tornel, the Mexican Minister of War, "An old soldier is a treasure because he is a teacher of recruits, and because without veteran cadres, one cannot organize new corps that can be usefully employed, particularly in offensive war."[8] The national militia also benefited from the recruitment of men according to residential location that increased interest and topographical familiarity for each unit.

This methodology for galvanizing citizen participation for common defense had impacted the readiness and morale of Spanish military establishments north of the Rio Grande for centuries. Fernando Perez de Almazan, the governor of *Tejas* in 1724, had despondently noted that his presidio soldiers required inducement for service "besides their salaries, because of the resignation with which they all come to this country."[9] While the empire's professional soldiers served for pay with varying levels of interest and intensity, local *vaqueros* and townsmen fought to protect family and property with direct personal gain. For these militiamen, organizing for mutual security reflected individual investment in collective welfare along New Spain's northern frontiers.

Anglo-Texan colonists, who held the advantage of greater infusions of human capital than Spain could ever muster, later benefited from similar localized recruitment during the Texas Revolution on both Mexican and Indian fronts. When the rebel council proposed to deploy its first Corps of Rangers, they specifically intended companies to draw upon recruits from residential sectors. Acting President James Robinson emphasized this preference when he advocated enlistment "from the inhabitants of the frontier where they are designed to range." He believed, usually correctly, that localized recruitment would "increase the activity and vigilance of the corps and promote their harmony."[10]

Despite the galvanizing nature of volunteer and localized service that often accounted for Texan military successes, the enduring motivational strengths of the national militia strategy was offset by predictable weaknesses in readiness, discipline, and mobilization inefficiencies common to all citizen-levies. These issues emerged acutely when Texas, and also the United States, maintained large formations of amateur soldiers beyond short periods of immediate crisis. Theophilus Rodenbough, an officer of the 2nd U.S. Cavalry Regiment, quoted the venerable George Washington's original criticism of untrained militias:

Experience, which is the best guide for our actions, repudiates so perfectly clear and determinedly a confidence in militia, that no one who treasures order, regularity and economy, or loves his own honor, his character, and peace of soul, would risk these on the results of an undertaking with militia. Short time of service and an ill-founded confidence in the militia are the causes of all our mishaps and the growth of our debt.[11]

Yet despite these structural weaknesses—which plagued nearly all professional generals who augmented regular forces with militia or auxiliaries during the nineteenth century—Texas's perennial fiscal crises demanded enduring an reliance on amateur soldiers.

Conflict in western Texas erupted in 1838 as the militia brigades organized and ambitious settlers staked claims farther from the original colonial footprint in Southeast Texas. Henry Karnes and an independent ranger company participated in a significant battle against a Comanche warparty on August 10, 1838. The incident began when the Indians attacked the Texians as they paused to rest and water their horses while on patrol west of San Antonio near the Seco River. As reported by the *Telegraph and Texas Register*, "a party of about two hundred warriors made an attack near the Aronjo Seco, upon a company of twenty-one men, commanded by Col. Karnes."[12] The size of the Comanche force and the speed of their advance compelled the Texians into a hasty defense.

Karnes immediately fortified his outnumbered company along a defensible ridge in accordance with proven Texian methods. Understanding the limitations and strengths of his single-shot musketry, the commander dismounted his men and organized them into platoons. He then controlled rates of fire by ordering sections to discharge their rifles in alternating volleys, thereby preventing any lapse during reload cycles. Colonial settler and amateur historian John Henry Brown recorded that the rangers' "aim was deadly and warriors rapidly tumbled to the ground." Revealing patriotic bias, he called it "a gallant and successful defense against immense odds" while the *Telegraph* boasted the Indians "were completely defeated and driven from the field with the loss of several of their best warriors and a number of horses."[13]

This encounter perfectly reflected mounted infantry tactics favored by Texians that still relied upon rifled, single-shot weapons prior to adoption of Colt revolvers. Through two decades of frontier fighting they had learned to maximize precision fire from covered positions to mitigate Plains Indian superiority in mobility and hand-to-hand combat. Brown emphasized how the rangers "fired in alternate platoons, by which one-third of their guns were always loaded to meet the attack at close-quarters." He also noted that Karnes, despite boasting significant combat experience, "greatly exposed himself and was severely wounded."[14] A decade later in the American invasion of Mexico, U.S. Army officer Roswell Ripley observed similar tactics by Texan auxiliaries when he noted that "their actual services on the field are generally those of light infantry and riflemen; for, although mounted, of the duties of a dragoon as such they know nothing, and almost invariably dismount and act upon foot."[15]

The Battle at Arroyo Seco held additional significance due to the presence of young John "Jack" Coffee Hays in the Texian ranks. After serving in Deaf Smith's cavalry out of San Antonio, the scout had chosen dangerous employment as a surveyor in the region, which yielded further experienced as he gained a reputation as a competent Indian fighter. Now a volunteer rifleman with Karnes, he learned counter-guerrilla warfare from the other preeminent Texas cavalryman of the Texas Revolution. In an action that would foretell his legendary martial prowess, Hays won special distinction at Arroyo Seco by killing the chief of the warband with a critical shot that again demonstrated the conditional potency of precision rifle fire.[16]

As cavalry and ranger operations increased in South Texas, ethnic strife festered across the breadth of the republic. Tensions ran high among competing, and sometimes exploitive, tribes and communities. Enmity then exploded among Texian, Indian, and Mexican peoples during the predictable rise of the anti-Anglo conspiracy in the summer of 1838 that became known as the Cordova Rebellion. Sensing that the struggling nation could be undermined by dividing the polity along ethnic fault lines, Vicente Filisola, a former general in Santa Anna's failed reconquest and current military commander of northern Mexico, instigated a combined *Tejano* and Indian alliance to revolt against Texian sovereignty.

Julian Miracle, a cunning Mexican agent for Filisola, led the attempt to provoke an indigenous and *Tejano* uprising. Despite his leadership role, the affair was later named for his partner, Vicente Cordova, who joined the conspiracy as an angry and disenfranchised *Tejano* activist from Nacogdoches in East Texas. Throughout June and July of 1838, as they sought to instigate a general revolt of suppressed ethnic groups against the dominant Anglos, Miracle and Cordova led a combined force of over seventy Mexicans, *Tejanos*, Caddo, and Cherokee violently through Texas to arrive at a conference of eastern tribes in the Cherokee territory.[17]

The resulting alliance promised an armed rebellion by oppressed peoples against Texian rule, though the cautious and powerful Cherokee were not yet actively complicit. The ranking Texian general, Thomas Rusk, immediately led militia to intimidate the rebels and position for a larger offensive. Concurrent to the deployment of riflemen, Houston negotiated with eastern natives with hopes of separating them from Mexican instigators. Enjoying a long record of friendship with tribesmen, Houston successfully convinced most of them to remain peaceful—despite Rusk's provocative march—and the president temporarily prevented a war. Finally, on March 28, the most aggressive of the brigade commanders, Burleson, intercepted and destroyed much of the rebel leadership near Seguin east of San Antonio. Despite his defeat, Cordova escaped to Mexico to ensure future exacerbation of *Tejano*-Indian restlessness.[18]

The Cordova Rebellion, though relatively small in a military context, proved significant for two reasons. First, it expanded the scope of Texian aggression to the indigenous peoples of eastern Texas. While warfare with Penateka Comanche had been steadily intensifying since the revolution, the Cherokee, Caddo, Kickappoo, and Shawnee now became targets for justified territorial aggrandizement—often under the pretext of defensive security. Real and perceived collusion between the woodland tribes and Mexico also hardened ethnic and nationalistic attitudes across Texas's Anglo majority, thus uniting the perception of indigenous and Hispanic threats into a single foe. The seeds of distrust and fear planted by this conspiracy would manifest catastrophic consequences for the Cherokee in particular.

The second significance of the 1838 *Tejano*-Indian rebellion was the operational rehearsal it provided for Texas's mostly untested national militia system. It allowed Texian commanders and units to practice mobilization procedures, execute maneuvers on a regimental scale, implement logistical procedures, and form bonds between commanders and soldiers. The resulting familiarity enhanced readiness for the Cherokee War of 1839, the Comanche expeditions of 1840, and the formation of the more permanent Frontier Regiment. Rosters of the militia regiments mobilized were also almost entirely titled "Mounted Volunteers," "Mounted Gunmen," and "Mounted Rangers," demonstrating the Lone Star inclination for irregular cavalry service.[19]

Sporadic fighting continued across the republic through the fall of 1838 as Houston neared the end of his first presidential term and attempted to maintain peaceful relations with the larger tribes. Despite sincere efforts on his part, suspicion of Indian-Mexican conspiracy festered amongst the firebrands of the Texian military establishment. In October, because of rumored support for Cordovian rebels, Rusk opportunistically led elements of the 3rd Militia Brigade against Kickapoo north of Fort Houston. Because of hurried deployment the force comprised just two under-strength regiments totaling around 260 mounted riflemen.[20]

Despite Rusk's offensive intentions, the rebels boldly struck first. On October 16, an allied force of Mexicans, *Tejanos*, and several tribes of East Texas led by Cordova himself attacked the Texian camp, which was unwisely situated near the main Kickapoo Village. According to Rusk's report, as published in the *Telegraph and Texas Register*, "a very brisk fire was kept up on both sides for about fifteen minutes, when I ordered a portion of us to remain and protect the camp, and with the remainder charged the enemy, who precipitously fled."[21] The Texian pursuit dispersed the Cordovian threat, though not for the last time.

Throughout the remainder of 1838 the republic fielded several large militia demonstrations, again under Rusk's coordination, as Texians attacked and intimidated native peoples across Central and East Texas. Unpredictable strikes by indigenous raiders on homesteads—often unrelated to larger territorial confrontations and the Cordovian agenda—further motivated Anglo citizens to join militia regiments in their quadrant. The Edens-Madden massacre, in which Kickapoo killed ten settlers at the Eden homestead near Houston, spread exaggerated fear of a native offensive across eastern Texas. Deadly encounters with Comanche parties along the southwest frontier likewise created a perceived raiding epidemic. Strikes against Bastrop in November and Gonzales in December invited immediate reprisal expeditions by angry rangers.[22]

The *Telegraph and Texas Register* described the prevailing public sentiment in prose intentionally designed to draw an emotional response in response to Comanche raids in November of 1838 as Texas divided politically into opposing war and peace camps:

> It is useless to waste time in idle speculation, relative to the causes of war, or to declaim against those rash men who have aided in plunging the whole country into a murderous conflict in order that they might secure a few square leagues of land. Whether they or their savage opponents are to blame, is no longer of importance. The die is cast—the tomahawk is uplifted, and hundreds of helpless mothers and children call aloud for protection.[23]

This article's argument for ethnic warfare revealed the admission that territorial acquisition, by both commercial and private concerns, contributed to the destabilization of the border areas. In the end, inclinations to move past blame while embracing material and psychological imperatives to achieve victory represented the Anglo-Texan majority view.

This territorial confrontation enjoined national unity across frontier communities and the greater Texas polity. Noah Smithwick, still serving when needed as a volunteer ranger near Bastrop, described how constant raiding unified isolated and self-reliant settlers: "Our common danger was a strong tie to bind us together. No matter what our personal feelings were, when, in response to the sound of galloping hoofs, in the middle of the night, which we well knew heralded a tale of blood." Emphasizing the frightening nature of life on the periphery of western civilization, he then described how they leaped from their "beds and were at the door in anticipation of the 'hello' which prefaced the harrowing story of a slain neighbor and his family sharing his fate, or worse still, carried away into horrible captivity."[24]

The veteran ranger also provided tactical insight into the manner of the Texian response to indigenous raids when he stressed the importance of retaliating on short notice: "We hastily saddled our horses, if the Indians had not been ahead of us, and left our wives and children, to avenge the atrocious deed ... taking up the trail followed on with what speed we might, only hoping to be allowed to overtake and inflict a deadly blow upon the foe." Smithwick described the challenges of responding to highly mobile attacks with reactive militia, noting how "again and again we pursued them without success; they neither staying to eat or sleep until safe beyond pursuit."[25] With fear pervading Texian towns and homesteads, a shift towards aggressive preemptive attacks against the enemy became both predictable and inevitable.

On December 10, 1838, the Texian war faction achieved political victory in the nation's presidential election. Mirabeau Lamar, cavalry commander and hero of San Jacinto, replaced Houston as President of Texas. In contrast to his predecessor's policy of a defensive posture and conciliation, Lamar favored an overt strategy of annihilation against indigenous tribes and if need be, Mexico. The new executive's inaugural speech clearly stated his objectives for territorial and ethnic domination at Indian expense with particular focus on the Comanche and Cherokee.

With fire in his heart, Lamar summarized his uncompromising views: "As long as we continue to exhibit our mercy without showing our strength, so long will the Indians continue to bloody the tomahawk and move onward in the work of rapacity and slaughter."[26]

This proclamation foretold an unprecedentedly bloody period in Texas history. In accordance with its expansionist platform, the Lamar administration implemented a policy of aggressive and militant imperialism. Large, expensive, combined arms formations, both national militia and regular army, characterized the new president's preferred military framework. Fearful public opinion, as sensationalized in the Texas media and anecdotally recalled by citizens like Smithwick, provided a mandate for decisive presidential leadership. The resulting Texian campaigns of the years 1839, 1840, and 1841 were fought on a scale and at a duration not seen since the San Jacinto Campaign and brought destruction directly into Indian heartlands.[27]

The belligerent stance of the Texas Republic in 1839 found immediate expression in the reestablishment of a regular-type army brigade designed to place constant pressure on the hostile frontier. On December 21 the Third Congress reauthorized the spirit of the old Texian Army as a combined arms "Frontier Regiment" composed of infantry, artillery, and cavalry components. According to the legislation, they intended it to "Provide for the protection of the Northern and Western Frontier" with a more substantial line of forts. The congress also directed the regiment to construct an improved road from the Red River near the Louisiana border to the Nueces River on the Mexican border. This highway, traversing the breadth of Texas, would allow more efficient military and commercial movement between the United States and dispersed western counties.[28]

The congressional act mandated that the Frontier Regiment be comprised of 840 soldiers divided into eight "detachments" along geographically defined sectors. The existing Texas cavalry reorganized into the command to provide mobility while maintaining its historical orientation against Mexico. Burleson, still the most respected Texian field commander, assumed command of the 1st Regiment of Infantry which emerged as the core of the organization. Like his earlier Corps of Mounted Riflemen, the general headquartered out of Bastrop and oriented operations along the Comanche front.[29]

The Texas Congress next authorized the creation of a separate field regiment to provide immediate and more mobile border security. Defined as "eight Companies of Mounted Volunteers," the force enlisted for only six months as a temporary guard while the more complex and logistically demanding Frontier Regiment formed. The government approved the act on December 29 and predictably allocated command to another respected veteran: Henry Karnes of the Corps of Texas Cavalry. The congress approved the president to direct the regiment "offensively or defensively" as needed while providing an interim guard for the mobilizing republic.[30]

In addition to national-level units, communities continued the historical practices of spontaneously forming ranging companies to conduct expeditions against nearby tribal opponents. When this model of volunteerism proved effective, as it had during initial colonial settlement, the congress sanctioned an array of town and county ranger units through January and February of 1839 to secure the emergent counties of Bastrop, Robertson, Milam, San Patricio, Goliad, Refugio, and Gonzales.[31] By early 1839, with a layered system of regular army, militia, mounted riflemen, and localized ranger organizations established, the republic had postured to move aggressively against the indigenous peoples of Texas. Despite the unprecedented scale of mobilization, many new programs suffered material and manpower shortages.

The old colonial method of forming *ad hoc* units often proved most effective due to their flexibility as unofficial partisans, knowledge of terrain, and proximity to specific enemies. The resilient, and ruthless, John Moore returned to prominence in February of 1839 when he led a mounted raid against a Comanche village along the San Saba River northwest of Bastrop. His battalion consisted of three mounted "volunteer companies," meaning irregular rangers, drawn from Anglo communities on the upper Colorado River. Approximately fifty allied Apache and Tonkawa supported the settlers as scouts, agents, and fighters.[32]

Relying on intelligence from native "spies," the rangers executed the same type of dawn assault against the Comanche village that Moore had attempted with adverse results in 1835. Smithwick, who commanded one of the companies, recounted the approach: "When within a mile of the camp we dismounted and tied our horses. We then crept upon the sleeping Indians, who were not dreaming of an attack."[33] Moore described his order of battle in a later report, writing that "M. Eastland formed the right wing, the Bastrop company of Capt. Smithwick the center, and the Lipan under Castro their chief the left." He then explained that the "attack was made after day break."[34]

The hard-eyed Texians surrounded the village in the pre-dawn light and prepared to rain hell upon the unsuspecting community. Smithwick recounted the assault that followed: "As soon as daylight gave us the exact situation of the camp we made a rush for it, pouring a volley right into the lodges."[35] A young Apache warrior called Flacco also participated in the attack. This expedition provided early auxiliary training for his later work as a notable scout for Jack Hays out of San Antonio. Despite the sudden charge against their camp, Comanche defenders rallied and repulsed the attackers. The successful defense emphasized the plains warriors' continued courage and skill in close combat, which had originally propelled them to plains dominance.

The enraged tribe resolved to punish the retreating Texians for their audacity. Smithwick again recounted how "the Indians then formed in line and advanced to the attack." He stated that "after several ineffectual attempts to dislodge us, the Comanche withdrew."[36] The precariousness of Moore's position so far from Bastrop and the possibility of another Comanche counter-attack convinced him to withdraw. The rangers later lost one soldier to a mortal wound and forty-six horses to injury, indicating the Comanche intentionally targeted the larger signature of mounts. Texians claimed the Comanche lost between thirty and forty dead and sustained fifty to sixty wounded though they probably inflated these numbers to justify the lackluster raid.[37]

Like inherited colonial methodologies of proactively patrolling, the tactic of raiding vulnerable villages to eliminate indigenous threats arrived in Texas as a long-held, if brutal, Anglo-American tradition. This manner of campaign against domestic tribal centers held horrific precedence in the inexorable white settler advance west from Appalachia.[38] Long before Texian settlers like Kuykendall, Karnes, and Moore led mounted battalions of vengeful rangers against the indigenous peoples of Texas, their familial predecessors had used similar, if not identical, tactics to destroy native peoples across contested territories in the American South and Northwest.[39]

The Tennessee militia of the early nineteenth century—which conducted mounted expeditionary strikes in peripheral campaigns of the War of 1812 and the subsequent Creek War—provided an example of how American frontiersmen conducted devastating raids that directly informed later Texan maneuvers.[40] John Coffee, a senior militia commander and namesake of John Coffee Hays, led a particularly illustrative campaign in 1813 designed to provide freedom of maneuver for Andrew Jackson's army. In his battle report Coffee described how his volunteer "cavalry" and "mounted riflemen" enveloped the village at Tallushatchee, Alabama. He then explained in detail how he lured the warriors out of their houses with a decoy after the cordon was set and then suddenly ordered two wings of his hidden militia to charge.

The general's summary of the action precisely demonstrated both the maneuverability of mounted militia and the scope of wanton destruction that occurred in frontier warfare:

> The enemy retreated firing until they got around and in their buildings, where they made all the resistance that an overpowered soldier could do. They fought as long as one existed; but their destruction was very soon completed. Our men rushed up to the doors of the houses, and in a few minutes killed the last warrior of them. The enemy fought with savage fury, and met death, with all its horrors, without shrinking or complaining;

not one asked to be spared, but fought as long as they could sit or stand.

Coffee then admitted to the tragic civilian deaths that so often resulted from raiding amongst population centers, writing that "In consequence of their flying to their houses and mixing with the families, our men in killing the males, without intention killed and wounded a few of the squaws and children, which was regretted by every officer and soldier of the detachment, but which could not be avoided."[41] As noted by historian John Grenier, these "search and destroy missions" directly supported Jackson's strategic ends "as parts of an overarching strategy to destroy the Creek nation."[42]

This manner of attack, surely ranking amongst the darkest of American traditions, proved the most tactically effective method of destroying Indian power in Texas.[43] Yet while Coffee's raid proved successful and thus eliminated that particular tribe as a future threat in Alabama, Moore's failure to rout the Comanche merely provoked reprisal attacks. On February 24, enraged by the Anglo raid, warriors retaliated against several homesteads near Bastrop. Just as in the colonial period, this frontier bastion, formerly called Mina, endured the brunt of raiding warfare along the northwest periphery while serving as a platform for launching ranging expeditions.

In an act of clearly informed retaliation, the raiding party of over 100 warriors first attacked the Coleman family, of the late Colonel Robert Coleman, who had commanded ranging expeditions in 1835 and a mounted battalion in 1836. The Indians killed the colonel's wife and son and captured another son, while his two young daughters hid under cabin floorboards. The warband next struck a nearby fortified settlement called Well's Fort, but failed to penetrate the stockade without heavy weaponry like field cannon.[44]

These rapid attacks exemplified asymmetric raiding that Plains Indians historically excelled in. They also reminded Texian settlers that the horrors of population-centric warfare could impact all sides. The scattered Anglo communities along the upper Colorado River valley again realized that they offered vulnerable targets for Comanche retaliation, just as tribal domestic camps provided a lucrative opportunity for rangers. This burgeoning fear increased cycles of preemptive and retaliatory raiding that destabilized Texas's western environs for several generations.

Enraged Texans in the western counties decided the murder of the Coleman family could not go unanswered. From their narrow perspective any native attack left unanswered encouraged future assaults against equally defenseless families. Given such rationale, the men of the Bastrop area quickly gathered and readied an assault battalion. To accomplish the reprisal they raised two ranging companies, and understanding the importance of timely reaction, immediately pursued the warriors into the wilderness. Determined to exact brutal vengeance, the Texans located Comanche near Brush Creek and rushed to attack. To the surprise of the Anglos the stalwart defenders repulsed the assault.

Burleson, ever the premier field commander, soon arrived with reinforcements that included elements of the Frontier Regiment. He assumed command of the combined Texian forces and pursued the retreating warriors. In an unexpected development, the Comanche fortified themselves in what one settler designated a natural "stronghold" while rangers engaged with rifles from standoff positions. Unable or unwilling to break through the obstacles at great cost, the frontiersmen besieged the tribesmen into the night until they escaped into the darkness.[45] This clash offered one of the few instances in Texas history where Indians successfully utilized fortifications to negate Anglo firepower.

While militias in both western and eastern Texas grappled with tribal powers, intermittent guerrilla conflict between Texians and Cordovian elements continued into the summer of 1839. Then on May 17 a ranger company led by Captain James Rice intercepted and defeated Mexican agent Manuel Flores's insurgent force at the San Gabriel River near Austin. The Texians killed Flores in the fight and subsequently discovered documents that revealed an intention to undermine Texas sovereignty and conspiratorial letters to the Cherokee. This evidence, combined with other condemning papers recovered from the agent Julian Miracle, provided jingoistic imperialists Lamar and Rusk necessary justification to move aggressively against the Cherokee. Without Houston in office to mediate, war was now inevitable.[46]

While Rusk prepared for a Cherokee campaign, settler communities around Bastrop remained locked in a death struggle with the Penateka Comanche. In May of 1839 Tennessean immigrant and War of 1812 veteran John Bird led an opportunistic attack against a village to the north of Bastrop. Despite the Texians' audacity, or perhaps because of it, the angry Comanche defeated and severely punished the expedition. The defenders possessed over six times the numerical strength of their opponents, ensuring decisive victory, yet reportedly lost over forty warriors during the fight. Precision firepower and fortified positions again saved outnumbered Texians from total defeat and allowed survivors to escape.

One of Bird's men, Nathaniel Brookshire, recorded how the battle unfolded. Beginning with initial contact with the Comanche he described how "a reinforcement of about two hundred Indians came up in full view, making about two hundred and forty or fifty strong. After drawing up their lines, the war whoop from one end of their line to the other was heard." Realizing the danger of their predicament, the rangers took cover and prepared to receive the assault which turned into a "desperate charge from every point." Relying on precision marksmanship, the surrounded Texians "gave them such a warm reception that they were handsomely repulsed, though the charge continued one-half hour.[47] Bird did not survive the engagement, illustrating the perils of irregular warfare even for commanders.

Conflict with Comanche in South Texas continued the next month when Karnes, now the premier cavalry leader in Texas, led a volunteer expedition to retaliate against the nearest Comanche for attacks in the San Antonio area. Hays accompanied the colonel as a section leader while conducting reconnaissance for the main group. The young Tennessean's reputation as an inspired Indian fighter and peerless horseman had expanded under Karnes's tutelage. Hays's new position, roughly the equivalent of a junior noncommissioned officer in a professional dragoon squadron, also allowed him the opportunity to master basic tenets of tactical leadership.[48]

The Cherokee War exploded as the major military event of 1839 for the troubled republic. Exacerbated by simmering Cordovian developments that indicted the Cherokee over the summer, the Battle of the Neches and corresponding death of Chief Bowl (Duwali) unfolded as a decisive episode in the history of Anglo-Indian relations in Texas. It also provided one of the few relatively large-scale and linear battles between substantial native and Anglo forces in its history. As a strategic factor the campaign would destroy the last vestige of Indian power along the Sabine River basin and allow the polity to predominantly orient military energies west and south until the onset of the Civil War.

The Lamar administration had begun to set conditions for a deliberate move against the Cherokee since acquiring supposed evidence of that tribe's involvement with Cordovian instigators Flores and Miracle. After negotiations, perhaps disingenuous in nature, failed over the directed withdrawal of the woodland people to less arable territory north of the Red River, the republic mobilized a task force of 500 soldiers drawn from the Frontier Regiment and national militia brigades. Disinclined to withdraw, in part due to their sedentary lifestyle that contrasted with the habits of the highly mobile Comanche, the Cherokee rallied to resist the invasion. Initial skirmishing began on July 15 and the next day a "spie" company of rangers located the main Indian line under Bowl near the Neches River.

Texian assault regiments led by Burleson and Rusk vectored in on the natives and immediately attacked. Brigadier General Kelsey Douglass, the overall commander of the campaign, reported the envelopment of the final Cherokee position when "the second battalion of Rusk's regiment, under the command of Lieut. Col. James Smith, speedily reinforced the left wing and behaved handsomely." The general then concluded that "the right under Burleson was in like manner, sustained by the detachment from his command under Lieut. Col. Woodlief, when the enemy were charged and driven from their strong hold."[49]

The Cherokee line disintegrated under the weight and firepower of the Anglo assault and endured the unceremonious execution of their wounded chief. The tribesmen lost over 100 dead while Texians suffered 8 killed and 29 wounded.[50] Flush with victory, the victors destroyed the tribe's villages to deprive them of any hope of returning to their old lifestyle. Next, with the tactical portion of the campaign completed, the strategic aspirations which centered on the occupation of the valuable Cherokee lands became apparent. In his capacity as president Lamar expelled the survivors from Texas. This action set an intimidating example for other tribes and satisfied his jingoistic political supporters. While this was not the first time Anglo-Texans resorted to population-centric warfare to eliminate indigenous competitors, it stood as the most comprehensive, and destructive, removal to date.[51]

A broader program of Native American expulsion continued in the fall of 1839 as the republic definitively secured its eastern flank. Seeking to remove all Indian powers from the region, Lamar compelled the Shawnee to "return from whence they came and depart in peace from their brethren and the territory of Texas" after raising questionable disputes over the legality of their immigration.[52] He accomplished this particular deportation without overt violence in large due to the example made of the once powerful Cherokee. The administration likewise expelled the Delaware people due to alleged complicity in the Cherokee War.

By the fall of 1839 the center-piece of the Texian military structure, the Frontier Regiment, moved west to secure the new capital at Austin. Logistical and recruiting deficiencies plagued the force due to issues of combining penurious funding with regular army organization. Despite the regiment's challenges, it dispatched expeditions against Comanche encampments to clear new swaths for frontier settlement. According to the *Telegraph and Texas Register* the campaign blatantly intended to "force the Comanche from the section of country near the San Saba and to establish a line of block houses from the Colorado to the Red River." The article also promised the regiment would "remove the frontier from one to two hundred miles northward" in a clear proclamation of deliberate territorial expansion.[53]

While the Frontier Regiment oriented west, Lamar simultaneously unleashed volunteer aggression northward. In October and November the avowed imperialist deployed a temporary "Regiment of Mounted Gunmen" to clear the upper Brazos River system for uncontested Anglo occupation. The regiment consisted of five ranger companies raised from the counties that spanned from the Neches River to the Brazos River. The volunteers elected John Neill, a former company commander from Karnes' old regiment, to lead the force. The battalion rode with a single towed field cannon to allow an uncommon expansion of firepower for the expedition.[54]

The *Telegraph* praised the campaign, which reflected an improvised and fiscally economized component of Lamar's genocidal war. Displaying both tones of Texian nationalism and willful avoidance of settler causality and provocation, the editor proclaimed that it was "exceedingly gratifying" for them "to be able thus to testify the readiness with which the citizens seem disposed to obey any call that is made them to assist in driving from our borders the only enemy whom we now have to dread." The article concluded that "the troops were in fine spirits and determined to affect the objectives of the campaign."[55]

On October 25 the mounted regiment first attacked a native village in the undulating terrain of the upper Brazos River. Volunteer William Hamblem recalled that "there were about 100 wigwams and said to be about 100 warriors ... a part of two tribes, Ionis and Keechies." The resulting assault, now typical of Texian tactics, proved bloodily successful. The rangers surprised the sleeping village, killed the chief, and caused the panicked survivors to flee in chaos. Hamblem described material gains by reporting they "captured all their camp equipage and about forty Indian ponies."[56] This expedition illustrated how the steady march of Anglo attacks against indigenous centers violently eroded Native American presence in central Texas.

Engaging the Penateka Comanche

Simultaneous to Neill's campaign above the Brazos, Anglo communities in South Texas continued to grapple with the Comanche of the lower plains. In keeping with the vicious circle of raid and counter-raid that intensified ethnic hatreds, Karnes led another expedition northwest out of San Antonio. His force included mounted companies from Galveston and Gonzales and totaled 105 men. Karnes intended to destroy, or at least disrupt, Comanche threats that frequently preyed on homesteads, travelers, and commerce in the San Antonio vicinity.

This campaign again found Jack Hays's career on the rise. Once forward deployed, the young ranger was "dispatched with 3 men as spies with orders not to return until the enemy should be ferreted out," again serving in the role of junior sergeant. Karnes's habitual use of Hays for reconnaissance during advances into unknown territory offered testimony to his superior field craft. Acting on intelligence acquired by the scouts, the battalion soon attacked an unsuspecting Comanche village. Fortunately for the defenders, an astute native observer noticed the Texians just before their commencement of a planned dawn assault. As a consequence most of the Comanche escaped with homes destroyed. The Indians lost twelve dead while the Texians sustained no casualties.[57]

By the close of 1839 the Texas Republic had conducted a rigorous series of campaigns against major competing tribes, partially fulfilling Lamar's imperialistic vision and writing a terrible chapter in its history. While the National Militia and Frontier Regiment moved against the most powerful Indian peoples, volunteer mounted forces executed numerous expeditionary strikes against Indian villages. This caustic march of ethnic destruction resulted in a period of increasingly brutal raiding as opposing cultures targeted each other's most vulnerable populations. The inexorable weight of Texian enmity removed the

Cherokee, Delaware, and Shawnee, and intimidated all remaining eastern tribes. Despite strategic gains, Comanche power on the Great Plains had yet to be decisively reckoned with.[58]

The horror and inhumanity of this kind of warfare did not go unnoticed by the Texian people. Yet the acrimonious history of raid and counter-raid, along with acute personal grievances and racial antipathies, allowed emotional justifications for the atrocities. Settler and militiaman William Sadler, whose wife was killed by indigenous raiders, described a common perspective amongst his people during the collision of civilizations:

> We cannot check the Indians unless we follow them to their place of rendezvous or where they have their families and visit them with the same kind of warfare that they give us. We should spare neither age, sex, nor condition, for they do not. I know it will be said this is barbarous and too much like the savage. And it certainly is harsh, but it is the only means in my view that will put them down.[59]

This advocacy, by an admittedly biased partisan, offered ample tactical rationale for inhumane strikes by establishing moral equivalency between indigenous and Anglo atrocities. Though Sadler clearly recognized the atrocious nature of his argument, he justified brutality by placing instigating fault with the "barbarous" methods of the Indians. Unfortunately, similar ethnic and racial atrocities by Texan soldiers would also be unleashed against both Hispanics in the Mexican War and African-Americans in the Civil War.[60]

This perspective found expression in national newspapers that revealed broad acceptance of ethnic destruction amongst the white population. The *Telegraph and Texas Register*, a publication that often embraced nationalistic and racist attitudes, endorsed imperialist rationale and methodology as Texian armies collided with the Comanche Empire in 1842. The paper first explained the futility of matching native cavalry with unprepared interdiction when it explained that "these small parties of Indians are so well prepared for flight, that it would be about as useless to pursue them as it would be to pursue the wild birds in their flight to the north."

Then, in both a criticism of the continued threat from the Comanche and a plea for the government to embrace preemptive and expeditionary strikes, the paper criticized that "so little good, heretofore, has resulted from expeditions of these kinds that we have long since become convinced that some more effectual method must be adopted to check the incursions of the savages." The editor advocated that Texian forces embrace Moore's and Karne's examples "by making expeditions directly to the Indian villages and destroying them, and driving the Indian families to a distance." He concluded that "more would be affected towards affording protection to the frontier than by any other means."[61]

Tactical explanation in editorials often contextualized, rationalized, and endorsed merciless methods and ethnic competition that defined the darkest aspects of Texas's way of war. The cold logic of ethnic cleansing, or at the very least coercive population removal, stemmed from a strategic deduction that recognized the futility of defensive measures against the fleetest horse warriors in North America. The editors, and many in the general Anglo population, believed that reactive interdiction and localized patrolling were not enough; they called for the overt removal of the indigenous societies that generated lightning raids which threatened their families.

Edward Stiff, a traveler from Ohio, described the popular, and hugely exaggerated, fear of imminent Comanche devastation that pervaded Texas during this period. He believed that "were this tribe provoked to hostilities, or induced to believe that peace was not in their interest and honor, the present population of Texas would be exterminated and their homes desolate in a brief space of time."[62] The visitor continued with an overly dramatic prediction: "If these northern barbarians, like the Goths and Vandals of old, do not at some future period desolate the fair plains of Texas, she will be fortunate indeed, and the Lone Star, the emblem of the country, may

in time, shed a mild and effulgent light."[63] Adoption of this symbol in
the years after independence signified cultural militarism and rising
nationalism.

In addition to the Anglo-Indian cycles of raid and interdiction
that degraded populations, disease heavily reduced Native American
presence in Texas. This catastrophic reduction—by an opponent far
more merciless than Kentucky Rifles—severely debilitated tribal combat power. According to scholar David La Vere, throughout just the
nineteenth century over thirty generational epidemics of small pox,
measles, cholera, malaria, whooping cough, and influenza assaulted
Indians in Texas. He assessed that by 1890 "the Tonkawa had been
reduced by 97 percent, the Caddos by 94 percent, the Wichitas by
89 percent, the Lipan Apache by 43 percent, the Comanche by 77 percent,
and the Kiowas by 43 percent."[64]

Devastating diseases that Hispanic, and then Anglo, settlers
passed to tribes enabled success by frontier forces as they often
encountered severely weakened competitors. Reductions in animal
food sources, particularly buffalo, and loss of fertile agrarian lands
simultaneously contributed to decreases in native density. Adding
to calamity, merciless expeditions against the weakened indigenous centers established mutually reinforcing relationships between
disease, buffalo near-extinction, and wartime attrition. The totality
of these destructive factors and pressures of American immigration
created an untenable environment for the preservation of Indian
power north of the Rio Grande.

The beginning of the second year of the Lamar Administration coincided with renewed hostilities with the Comanche along the northwest
periphery of Anglo settlement. The Frontier Regiment now deployed
as the mainstay of Texian forces despite endemic shortages in recruits
and equipment. The struggling formation—representing an anomaly in
Texas's historical predilection for amateur and short-duration
fieldings—never counted more than 560 soldiers in its ranks and
fielded only eight of the planned fifteen companies. Despite these
challenges it established several forts up the Colorado River valley.

In late January, command passed from Burleson to Colonel William Fisher and throughout the next month the regiment transferred its equipment and supply from Houston to Austin to cement its westward orientation.[65]

By the spring of 1840 the rising scope of ethnic warfare began to take its toll on the southern Comanche. The Penateka Tribe, who had borne the brunt of Texian raiding in recent years, proposed to discuss peace. In part because of their gross overestimation of the Indians' strength, and also due to combatant fatigue amongst the settlers, the republic agreed to meet for terms. Settler Z. N. Morrell described the effects of years of mutual destruction admitting that "the Indians suffered much during these years, as well as the Texans."[66] Disease, pressure from northern tribes, and constant attrition finally persuaded the southern Comanche, once peerless masters of vast territories north of the Spanish Empire, that armistice was necessary.

On March 19 a Comanche delegation visited San Antonio to discuss terms for peace. The party included thirty-three Comanche chieftains and warriors, and thirty-two additional warriors and women in supporting functions. Despite optimistic intentions, fighting soon erupted between the visitors and Texian officers. The presence of a mutilated Anglo girl brought with the delegation prompted demands for the release of purported additional hostages. When the chiefs refused or were unable to procure immediate release of missing captives, officers attempted to take the Comanche leaders themselves as reciprocal hostages. When the fighting ended, thirty native leaders and five non-combatants lay dead while Texians suffered seven dead and eight wounded. The affair became known as the Council House Fight and would hold massively destabilizing repercussions for the republic the next summer.[67]

Militia activities continued into the summer of 1840, but without the scale or intensity of the previous year. Yet despite the receding tempo of violence the clouds of a larger war gathered on the horizon. The Comanche were assembling their strength and preparing for the greatest invasion of Texas territory since Santa Anna's march during the San Jacinto Campaign. Known as the Great Comanche Raid, the angered plains warriors planned brutal revenge for losses and perceived treachery at the Council House Fight. This event would mark the most traumatic event in a century of devastating Anglo-Comanche confrontations. It also provided another opportunity for Texan mounted arms to demonstrate its rise to frontier prominence.

The Great Comanche Raid began in the first week of August 1840. The invasion comprised over 600 warriors from various southern Comanche peoples, a detachment of Mexican supporters, and a roughly equal number of accompanying women and children. Seeking revenge, the massive raiding force attacked from the prairies of central Texas and vectored southeast into the Guadalupe valley southeast of Gonzales. The long drive ended along the Gulf Coast and culminated in a sudden and unstoppable strike against the Texian interior. An audacious chief called Buffalo Hump led the combined host.[68]

Though strategic raids of this size were not unheard of during the era of the Spanish Empire, it reflected an unprecedented maneuver by tribesmen during the years of the Texas Republic. The Comanche warhost first arrived at the town of Victoria, near the coast, on August 6 in an incredible show of force. Groups of warriors rampaged through the buildings and streets while destroying buildings and property, killing twelve people, and capturing over 1,500 valuable horses. Next, on August 8, the raiders struck the port town of Linnville. The citizenry who survived the initial assault escaped in small boats out to sea to watch their town be pillaged.

Many Texians believed that Mexican agents directed the raid towards Linnville with knowledge that the commercial port housed great quantities of finished products and goods for sale and trade. After spending the day loading plunder and destroying the town, the Comanche began their cumbersome ride north. The audacious invasion claimed the lives of at least twenty Texian civilians and captured five women and children for use as slaves. Though tragic from the perspective of western settlers, the scope of civilian casualties could have been far greater had the Comanche intended overt population sanitization, as Santa Anna had in 1836, instead of theft and intimidation. Appropriating material wealth reflected a traditional raiding objective amongst cavalry-centric Indian peoples.

Despite the immediate success of the Comanche invasion, Texians determined to prevent unmolested escape from their territory. Years of guerrilla warfare had taught militia leaders that if raiders were allowed to withdraw unpunished they would likely become emboldened and strike again. Understanding the necessity of pursuit, several ranger companies had tracked and shadowed the Comanche since August 7 under the command of revolutionary ranger captain John Tumlinson. On August 8 a combined element from Gonzales, Lavaca, and Cuero tracked the raiders' signature to Victoria where they received news of the attack taking place against Linnville. Tumlinson immediately sent messengers to inform John Moore and Edward Burleson. On August 9 the fleet rangers identified the Comanche returning from the coast and pursued them at distance.[69]

By this time the Comanche were emerging onto the central prairies but found themselves slowed by their accumulated plunder and captured horses and women. This cumbersome procession made the Texian pursuit a fairly uncomplicated task since the invading force left a massive trail of destruction, hoof tracks, and refuse in their wake. After a potentially dangerous skirmish where the rangers risked annihilation by the more numerous native cavalry, a section of the riders under Tumlinson fell back to monitor the enemy. Another section, under the leadership of future Civil War general Ben McCulloch, broke away to gather militia for a decisive engagement.[70]

While rangers trailed the Comanche host west, alarmed militiamen from all over southwestern Texas marshaled under the leadership of veteran leaders to resolve the crisis. On August 11 senior Texian officer Felix Huston established his flag twenty-five miles southeast of Austin at Plum Creek. He selected the location with hopes of intercepting the Comanche line of march while facilitating the convergence of approaching militia columns. When Burleson arrived with

Bastrop forces the small army immediately deployed into battle formation. The Texian response totaled just 200 men, reflecting hurried mobilization. Though outnumbered by a factor of three the riflemen nevertheless determined to exact vengeance.[71]

Skirmishing rapidly broke out across the front as forward ranging units engaged the Comanche rearguard. Huston initially dismounted the main battalion to defensively await an incoming militia column led by John Moore, which he considered vital. Despite sound intentions, deliberate preparation risked allowing the Comanche to escape unmolested. Burleson and McCulloch, both veteran Indian fighters, convinced their less experienced commander to charge immediately. One of Burleson's men, John Jenkins, described the attack that followed: "A double-filed line of march was formed, Burleson's forces from the Colorado marching about one hundred yards to the right of Huston's men from the Guadalupe, and in sight of the Indians."[72]

Texian soldier James Nichols offered a corresponding description of the Comanche battle line and noted how "the chiefs were running back and forth in the space between the two armies, performing such feats of horsemanship." The soldier wrote with contempt how "the line of warriors just behind these chiefs kept a continuous firing with their escopets doing no damage."[73] This ritual preparation, unfolding even as Texian companies positioned to assault with superior firepower, revealed archaic aspects of Comanche traditions that would cost them dearly.

The resulting envelopment by converging formations of vengeful frontiersmen smashed the Comanche host with an implacable and galvanizing hatred. Since most Indians were not accustomed to defensive fighting, which diverged from their accustomed mobile warfare, the battle rapidly became a rout. Ranger and militia pursuit lasted for miles as enraged Texians sought to punish their hated enemy. Huston reported—with possible exaggeration—that his men killed over eighty Comanche, including women and children while he lost only one. Nichols personally attested to the chaotic nature of the melee when he recalled accidentally killing a fleeing woman whose garb masked her gender.[74]

The Great Comanche Raid and the Battle of Plum Creek held tactical significance because they represented a series of events where both combatants exemplified fundamentals of cavalry-centric warfare in Texas. The invading Comanche first utilized long-held mastery of military horsemanship to conduct a deep, or strategic, raid with exceptional operational reach while exploiting elements of surprise and speed. The Texians then responded with reciprocal mounted skills when they tracked and intercepted the warriors' retreat. The entire episode provided a veritable display of cavalry strategy and tactics in the continental southwest. It also illustrated the sheer brutality of Texas warfare as both sides killed each others' women and children during the campaign.

The militia interdiction at Plum Creek likewise revealed the maturity of Texas's way of war by 1840. Beginning with the rangers' wherewithal to shadow the Comanche host and then excelling at rapid militia mobilization, Texan society demonstrated its ability to respond to crisis with volunteer activation. Next, as both rangers and riflemen utilized privately owned horses to deploy to the site of battle, they endorsed their nation's reliance upon mobility in warfare. Finally, when they closed with and routed the Comanche line, Texians unleashed tactical superiority—though highly conditional and often overstated—without regular army training and provision. The commanding general appreciated these feats when he reported, "I cannot speak too highly of the Colorado, Guadalupe and Lavaca militia, assembled so hastily together, and without organization."[75]

The Battle of Plum Creek also proved conspicuous for the assemblage of current and future Texas's military leaders who fought there. While revolutionary stalwarts such as Burleson and Moore led much of the mobilization and organizing, many future pillars of its martial tradition participated as junior officers or ranking militiamen. Young versions of future icons Jack Hays, Ben McCulloch, William "Big Foot" Wallace, and Mike Chevallie fought with distinction in the engagement. They would each attain fame as leading rangers and serve as volunteer officers in the Mexican War. The resulting celebration of these frontier captains—attaining impact far beyond the relatively few soldiers who fought at Plum Creek—further solidified the nationalistic importance of mounted arms in Texan society.

The western counties were not satisfied with the victory at Plum Creek and soon moved to unleash further attacks into the heart of Comancheria. After disagreement between Lamar and Huston prevented an official offensive by the National Militia and Frontier Regiment, the president authorized John Moore to lead a volunteer, and therefore politically unaccountable and financially attractive, campaign along the upper Colorado River system. According to Smithwick, Lamar designed the campaign "to find and rout them from their lair." This expedition revealed embracement by the highest levels of Texas government for economized options of activating frontiersmen, similar to Karnes's and Neill's campaigns of the previous year.[76]

The call soon went out across west Texas for recruits to join the campaign. A public announcement called for the suspension of many civil activities in Gonzales County "in order that the people may turn out *en masse* against the Indians."[77] Having arrived too late to participate in the fighting at Plum Creek, Moore was presumably eager to punish the Comanche offenders himself. It is also probable that he desired to finally conduct an expedition with decisive results after failing to achieve complete victory during similar events in 1835 and 1839.

On October 5 the expedition of 107 men, including 90 Texians and 17 allied Apache, marched north from the Austin area. They followed the Colorado River until October 23 when Apache scouts located a large Comanche village at the Red Fork. The natives had set their domestic camp about 250 miles north of Austin, marking this movement as one of the farthest Anglo expeditions to date. This long march through difficult terrain revealed that deep operational reach was no longer the exclusive domain of the Comanche.[78]

Moore proceeded to dismount his riflemen, except for a mounted detachment of fifteen horsemen, and silently approached the enemy village. The allied force arrived at dawn and occupied assault positions hoping for complete surprise. The Texian leader then "ordered a charge on the whole of their village" while sending a detachment "to act as cavalry to cut off any retreat of the enemy." This strategy emphasized both covert movement and mobile flexibility while demonstrating the effectiveness of combining infantry attack with cavalry envelopment. The deliberate nature of the attack indicated the veteran commander had internalized lessons of campaigns past where hasty and uncoordinated assaults had proved unable to overwhelm defending tribesmen.[79]

Moore led the main charge on foot while the mounted element circled to the far side of the camp. Comanche scouts noticed the attackers at the last moment but it was too late; the Texians assaulted with full momentum, according to Moore's plan, and brought destruction to the camp. According to Jenkins "the savages were completely surprised, but made some resistance as they were driven into the river, falling as they fled before the determined Texans." Moore likewise wrote of the massacre in his report: "The bodies of men, women and children were to be seen on every hand wounded, dying and dead."[80]

After years of raiding, Moore finally attained his macabre triumph. Smithwick noted that "the expedition was entirely successful" while admitting that "the camp being burned and the occupants indiscriminately slaughtered, only thirty-four women and children being spared, and they were carried into the settlements and made servants of."[81] Moore later estimated that his men killed forty-eight people in the camp and another eighty in the bordering creek. The Texians executed the operation without a single loss, again reflecting effective tactics. The frontier leader also recorded that his volunteers found "a great deal of plunder" taken by Indians during the Great Comanche Raid, ostensibly proving the culpability of this particular group in the invasion and thus allowing the rangers vengeful satisfaction.

In addition to tactical success, the raid unfolded as an effective example of Anglo-Indian cooperation against mutual enemies. Moore's report praised Apache reconnaissance in the campaign as "unsurpassed" and suggested the Texas government permanently retain their services.[82] Jenkins summarized the effect of the multiethnic campaign from his own nationalistic perspective: "The slaughter was terrible, and this raid was a considerable blow to the Comanches, the most deadly and most persistent of all our savage foes."[83] By embracing the terrible logic of war on the periphery, the attack decisively ended the future threat from that particular enemy.

The final year of the Lamar Administration in 1841 was characterized by operations on a smaller scale than the two previous years. The Frontier Regiment had not fulfilled expectations and forced the polity to fall back on traditional embracement of cavalry, volunteerism, and event-specific mobilization. Ranger and mounted militia units—best represented by the *ad hoc* regiments of Karnes, Neill, and Moore—emerged the most effective forces for achieving rapid results at minimal fiscal cost. The experiment with a revitalized professional force, largely an attempt to emulate the United States, proved that a cumbersome standing army was not the answer; irregular forces offered the solution to the Indian threat and light horse formations remained the ideal instrument. Though the Frontier Regiment managed some progress on constructing a road between Austin and the Red River, the congress starved the unit of funding through the fall of 1840 and finally deactivated it in March of 1841.[84]

Monument to *Empresario* Stephen F. Austin, the "Father of Texas," in the state capital named for him. *Courtesy of the Library of Congress.*

Sam Houston guided Texas through much of its early history as its leading general and statesman. Note the inclusion of a rifle in the photograph to imply frontier masculinity. *Courtesy of the Library of Congress.*

ERASMUS "DEAF" SMITH
CHIEF SCOUT OF HOUSTON'S ARMY

Erastus "Deaf" Smith fought as the most effective scout of the Texas
Revolution and commanded Lone Star cavalry during the republican
era. *Courtesy of the Texas State Library and Archives Commission.*

Rogers Rangers, 1758
Ranger of Rogers' Company, Summer Dress

VIII, 10

Roger's Rangers in Virginia. The Anglo-Texan concept of "ranging" stemmed directly from Atlantic martial traditions begun by earlier American frontiersmen. *Courtesy of Anne S.K. Brown Military Collection, Brown University Library.*

Genl. W. P. Lane.
A HERO, OF THREE WARS.

Walter P. Lane, veteran of the Texas Revolution, Mexican War, and Civil War, personified the Texas military tradition. *Courtesy of the Texas State Library and Archives Commission.*

Edward Burleson led *Texian* militia, mounted volunteers, and the
Frontier Regiment as one of the most effective field commanders
in Texas history. *Courtesy of the Texas State Library and Archives
Commission.*

An idealized depiction of a Comanche chief. The Comanche Empire emerged as one of Texas's most implacable and challenging territorial opponents. *Courtesy of the Library of Congress.*

A stylized depiction of Plains Indians accosting an Anglo wagon train. These sudden raids made immigration to Texas perilous until well after the Civil War. *Courtesy of the Library of Congress.*

A mounted warrior from the Kiowa people. The Plains Indians' mastery of horsemanship allowed them exceptional tactical mobility that most Anglo and Hispanic opponents were slow to match. *Courtesy of the Library of Congress.*

INDIAN WARFARE.—THE ATTACK ON THE VILLAGE.—DRAWN BY T. DE THULSTRUP.—[SEE PAGE 711.]

A late-nineteenth-century U.S. Cavalry assault on an Indian village. Texan mounted forces mastered this manner of attack in order to eliminate the source of Indian raids or aggrandize contested territory. *Courtesy of Anne S.K. Brown Military Collection, Brown University Library.*

A Frederic Remington print titled, "A Dash for the Timber." The scene aptly captures the irregular nature of Texan soldiers and their favored tactics of seeking cover to maximize the effects of precision weaponry against territorial competitors. *Courtesy of the Amon Carter Museum of American Art, Fort Worth, Texas.1961.381.*

INDIAN WARFARE—DISCOVERY OF THE VILLAGE.—DRAWN BY R. F. ZOGBAUM.—[SEE PAGE 618.]

A late nineteenth-century depiction of U.S. Cavalry officers employing allied Indian scouts to locate an unsuspecting village. Like all Anglo-American frontiersmen, Texans habitually coopted indigenous "spies" to enable preemptive raids. *Courtesy of Anne S.K. Brown Military Collection, Brown University Library.*

A Remington sketch ("We Struck Some Boggy Ground") of the Battle of Antelope Hills in 1858 when rangers and native allies under John "Rip" Salmon Ford defeated a large Comanche tribe near the Canadian River in Indian Territory. *Courtesy of the R.W. Norton Art Gallery.*

Kentucky Rifle, 1700-1900. Also called the Pennsylvania Long Rifle, this single shot, rifled, muzzle-loading weapon served as the primary hunting and combat weapon of early Texan settlers and soldiers. *Courtesy of the West Point Museum.*

Paterson Colt Revolver, 1836-1847. Texas Rangers utilized this innovative five-shot, .36 caliber, revolving pistol to gain a series of tactical victories on the Texas Frontier in the mid-1840s and during the Mexican-American War. *Courtesy of the West Point Museum.*

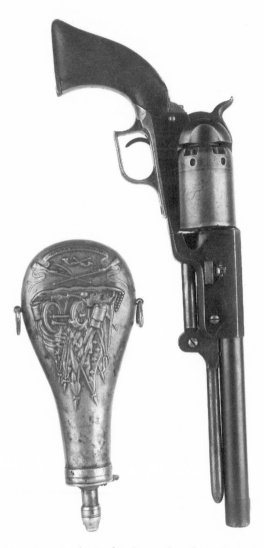

Walker Colt Revolver, 1847-1848. A wartime improvement on the Paterson model, this six-shot, .44 caliber, revolving pistol empowered Texas Mounted Volunteers during counter-guerrilla operations in Central Mexico between 1847 and 1848. *Courtesy of the West Point Museum.*

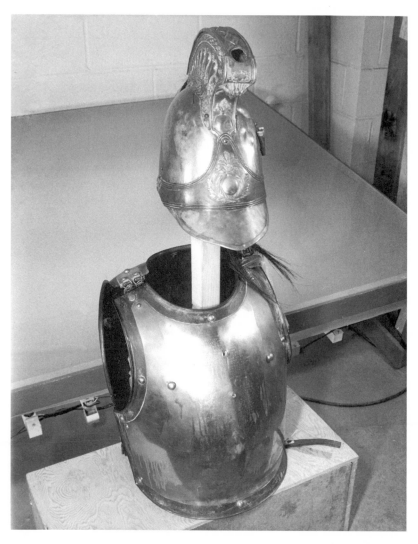

Mexican cavalry armor, mid-nineteenth century. The Mexican Army's reliance on archaic armor, edged weapons, and dated musketry proved costly against *Texian* militia armed with precision rifles at frontier engagements like the Battle of Salado Creek in 1842 and against Texan auxiliaries wielding repeating weaponry during the Mexican-American War. *Courtesy of the West Point Museum.*

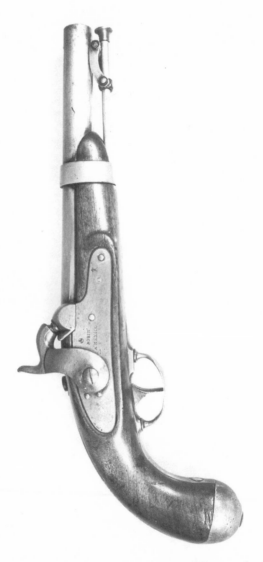

Mexican Horse Pistol, mid-nineteenth century. This single-shot firearm symbolized the tactical disparity in close-combat armament between Mexican and Texan cavalries during the late 1840s. *Courtesy of the West Point Museum.*

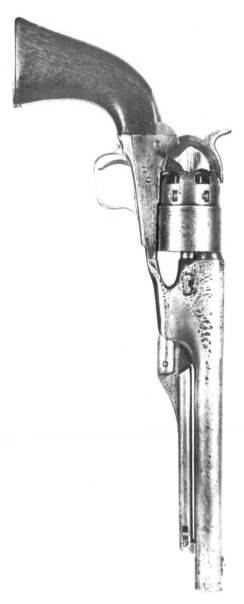

Army Colt Model 1860, 1860-1873. Texan-Confederate Cavalry relied
heavily on this weapon for reconnaissance, skirmishing, and shock
charges throughout the Civil War. *Courtesy of the West Point Museum.*

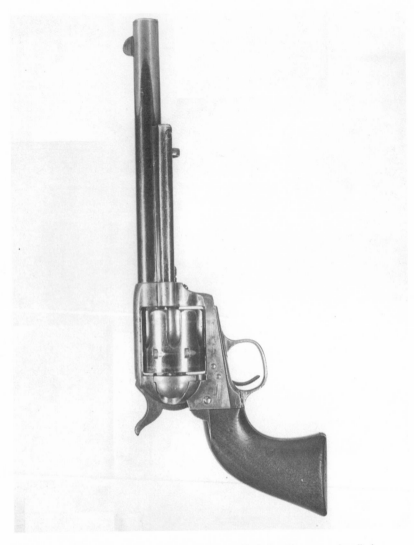

Colt Single Action Army, 1873-1892. Called the "Peacemaker," the Frontier Battalion in Texas and other Western lawmen and soldiers used this weapon to accomplish the final pacification of America's frontiers. *Courtesy of the West Point Museum.*

Texas Ranger icon John Coffee Hays. The Tennessean immigrant attained fame as Texas's most deadly partisan soldier during the era of the Lone Star Republic. *Courtesy of the Library of Congress.*

Statue of John Coffee Hays in San Marcos, Texas, commemorating his military service on behalf of Texas and the United States. Called "Devil Jack" by his Comanche enemies, Hays won peerless status as Texas's most effective ranger until the rise of the Frontier Battalion's commander, John Jones, after the Civil War. *Courtesy of the author.*

Texas Ranger Ben McCulloch. This frontier leader's remarkable military career spanned the Texas Revolution, Wars of the Texas Republic, Mexican-American War, and Civil War. *Courtesy of the Texas State Library and Archives Commission.*

COL JOHN S FORD

Texas Ranger John Salmon Ford. A veteran of the Mexican-American War, Ford attained fame as the premier ranger of the antebellum period and led the 2nd Texas Cavalry Regiment to a decisive, though inconsequential, victory at Palmetto Ranch, Texas, in the final battle of the Civil War. *Courtesy of the Texas State Library and Archives Commission.*

Samuel Walker, Texas Ranger and U.S. Mounted Rifles Captain. Walker gained national praise for his bravery as a courier and scout during the opening hostilities of the Mexican-American War on the Rio Grande. He later advised weapons manufacturer Samuel Colt on improvements to the Paterson Colt that resulted in the creation of his namesake, the Walker model. *Courtesy of the Library of Congress.*

HON. L. S. ROSS,
GOVERNOR OF TEXAS.

Lawrence Sullivan "Sul" Ross. A Texas Ranger during the antebellum period who found Comanche captive Cynthia Anne Parker during a raid, Ross later commanded a notable cavalry brigade during the Civil War and served as the 19th governor of Texas from 1887 to 1891. *Courtesy of the Texas State Library and Archives Commission.*

Mexican president and general Antonio Lopez de Santa Anna. Styled as the "Napoleon of the West," the mercurial despot failed in his attempted reconquest of *Tejas* during the Texas Revolution and later led his nation to defeat in the Mexican-American War. *Courtesy of the Library of Congress.*

EQUESTRIAN PORTRAIT OF GENERAL SANTA ANNA.

Equestrian portrait of General Santa Anna. Mastery of horsemanship remained central to masculine identity for Mexican aristocracy and military officers throughout the nineteenth century. *Courtesy of Anne S.K. Brown Military Collection, Brown University Library.*

1835; *Mexican Dragoons in Texas War.*

Depiction of a Mexican Lancer during the Texas Revolution. Note the edged weapons and European-style uniform that contrasted with the typical armament and rough dress of Texan frontiersmen. *Courtesy of Anne S.K. Brown Military Collection, Brown University Library.*

1887 Mexican Light Cavalry in Texas War

Example of a Mexican *Compania Volante*, or Flying Company, member. Hispanic volunteer cavalry proved instrumental in securing Spain's and Mexico's northern frontiers during the eighteenth and nineteenth centuries. *Courtesy of Anne S.K. Brown Military Collection, Brown University Library.*

Tejanos and other Hispanic communities across the North American Southwest earned reputations for excellent horsemanship during the nineteenth century. Many early Texas rangers learned horsemanship and tactical skills from *Tejano* associates as they adapted to frontier warfare in the continental Southwest. Remington print ("Coming to the Rodeo"). *Courtesy of the R.W. Norton Art Gallery.*

STORMING OF PALACE HILL AT THE BATTLE OF MONTEREY.

Battle of Monterrey, September 21–24, 1846. Texas Mounted Volunteers provided critical service as mounted scouts and assault troops to the United States Army prior to and during the capture of the Mexican stronghold. *Courtesy of the Library of Congress.*

The Battle of Buena Vista, February 23, 1847. Texan scouts under Ben McCulloch provided crucial intelligence of an approaching Mexican army that allowed American forces to reposition to advantageous ground and win the bloody encounter. *Courtesy of the Library of Congress.*

A watercolor portrayal by artist Bruce Marshall titled, "Charge of the Texas Rangers." The work shows Texas Mounted Volunteers under John Coffee Hays clashing with Mexican Lancers during the Mexican War. Note the disparity in opposing edged weapons and revolving firearms. *Courtesy of the University of Texas at San Antonio Libraries Special Collections and the Marshall family.*

"OLD ROUGH AND READY."

Zachary Taylor in the Mexican-American War. "Old Rough and Ready" was the first general to call for Texan auxiliaries to fight in the conflict and relied heavily on their reconnaissance contributions to inform decisions during the Monterrey Campaign. *Courtesy of Anne S.K. Brown Military Collection, Brown University Library.*

The "Alamo City Guards" of San Antonio
"Edgar's Battery," First Texas Light Battery CSA, 1862

1st Texas Light Battery in the Civil War, 1862. The Lone Star State mobilized more horsemen than any other state, North or South, for the great conflict. *Courtesy of the Anne S.K. Brown Military Collection, Brown University Library.*

A Private of the 7th Texas Cavalry Regiment. Note the deliberate inclusion of close-combat weaponry in the portrait to emphasize militancy that remained central to Anglo-Texan male identity throughout the nineteenth century. *Courtesy of the Library of Congress.*

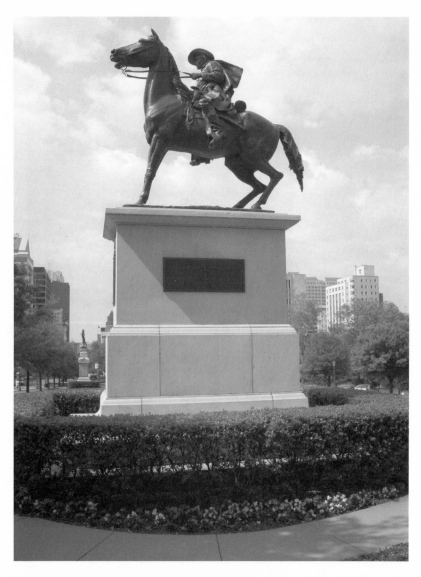

Monument to the 8th Texas Cavalry Regiment (Terry's Texas Rangers) in Austin, Texas. This unit fought across the Trans-Mississippi region and Eastern Theater during the Civil War as one of the state's most feared "charging" regiments. *Courtesy of the author.*

A Union cavalryman armed with carbine and saber. The quality of his uniform and weaponry reflects the North's logistical superiority in the Civil War. *Courtesy of the Library of Congress.*

Union cavalry slashing at fleeing Confederate infantry in the Civil War. Most Texas Cavalry eschewed traditional sabers in favor of revolvers, shot-guns, and "Bowie Knives." *Courtesy of the Library of Congress.*

Company E, Frontier Battalion. These paramilitary rangers patrolled as the final expression of Texan frontier militancy from 1874 to 1900 as they fought both external marauders and domestic brigands. *Courtesy of the Texas State Library and Archives Commission.*

Ruins of the eighteenth-century Spanish presidio at San Saba, Texas. The disrepair of the fort symbolizes Spanish and Mexican inability to colonize their northern environs while contrasting with later Anglo forts predominantly constructed of timber. *Courtesy of the author.*

Replica of Fort Parker in East-Central Texas. The destruction of this colonial fort by Comanche in 1836 ignited several generations of brutal warfare between the Comanche Empire and Texas. *Courtesy of the author.*

Replica of Fort Inglish on the Red River Frontier. Built in 1837, this fort served as a base of support for *Texian* soldiers while sheltering settlers from Indian attacks during the Texas Republic. *Courtesy of the author.*

Map 1: Colonial Tejas, 1822-1835

Courtesy of Dr. Alexander Mendoza.

Map 2: The San Jacinto Campaign, 1836

Courtesy of Dr. Alexander Mendoza.

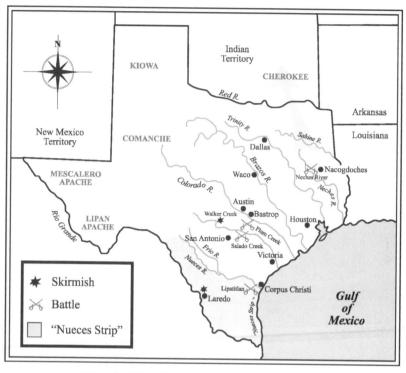

Map 3: The Texas Republic, 1836-1845

Courtesy of Dr. Alexander Mendoza.

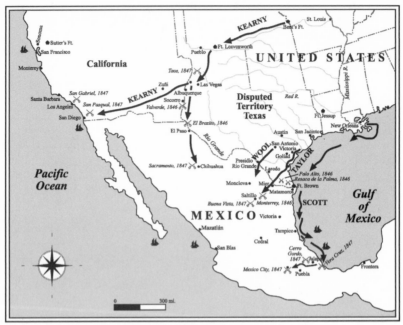

Map 4: The Mexican-American War, 1846-1848

Courtesy of Dr. Alexander Mendoza.

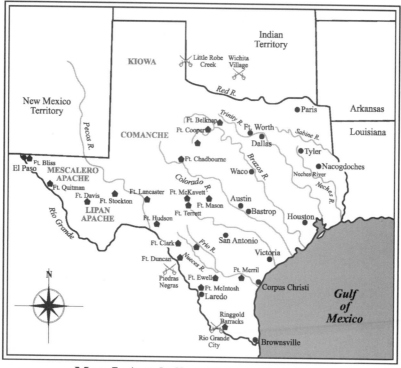

Map 5: Antebellum Texas, 1846-1861

Courtesy of Dr. Alexander Mendoza.

Map 6: Civil War Texas, 1861-1865

Courtesy of Dr. Alexander Mendoza.

Chapter 5

Conflicts of the Late Texas Republic, 1841–1845

Even as Texas conquered vast swaths of territory for Anglo settlement across the breadth of its expansive frontiers, it remained dangerous for both settler and Indian alike at the close of 1840. While Comanche, Cherokee, and other tribes had suffered greatly due to repeated militia and ranger incursions, they yet retained the capacity to strike, on a temporarily reduced scale, even as aggressive Anglo prospectors surveyed seasonal encampment and hunting grounds. That December, as the Texas Congress deliberated a replacement strategy in response to the failure of the Frontier Regiment, angry citizens cried—with willful disregard for the causality of their very presence—for military assistance: "We are exposed to a general attack, and are painfully convinced, from every appearance that we shall be overwhelmed by numbers in such an event, unless assistance is speedily sent us."[1]

As the embattled republic embraced a national militia, it simultaneously found more nuanced expression in the rise of new defenders: elite and semi-professional Texas Rangers. It was during this period—even as increasing proportions of newly immigrated Texians never saw actual combat due to the emergence of increasingly peaceful interior counties—that a specialized cadre of hardened fighters gained exceptional tactical prowess due to refinement of frontier tactics, development of hybrid equine breeds possessing both strength and endurance, and most importantly, adoption of revolving firearms with unprecedented killing effect. Under the captaincies of John Coffee Hays and other leaders, these ranging companies would patrol with outsized impact, both materially and culturally, between Texas and its enemies from 1841 to 1845.

Rangers and Economized Defense

Officials in Austin viewed funding of active ranging companies as a compromise between the prohibitively expensive Frontier Regiment and the inherently reactive National Militia. On one hand they believed major Indian threats had been thwarted, but on the other they thought they still required proactive frontier defenses. On December 26 the legislature accordingly authorized three specialized companies to patrol "as Spies upon the Western and North Western Frontier." The answer emerged as a lesser density of dispersed and decentralized ranging companies to be funded and actively maintained along strategically defined sectors. This program would ultimately allow continuity of tactical expertise while maintaining constant, albeit less dense, border presence. In short, the republic would begin the institutionalization of rangers as a famed martial order.[2]

The new mobilization's purpose was similar to the conception first offered by Stephen Austin during colonial settlement. As light horse companies they would focus on reconnaissance and interdiction rather than assault maneuvers that larger mounted riflemen corps typically pursued. Despite this objective, lethal engagements with Mexican and Indian cavalries remained perilously frequent. In a wise decision the Texian command selected Jack Hays to command one of the San Antonio companies, beginning his career as a frontier captain. Though the congress referred to them as "spies" to denote their lack of assault capacity and intent to screen for delayed militia mobilization, the horsemen now called themselves, with nationalistic pride, "Texas Rangers."[3]

Hays arrived the ideal candidate to command the San Antonio theater. Since Henry Karnes had died the previous summer of yellow fever and Deaf Smith and Juan Seguin had retired, the young Tennessean stood well positioned to assume the responsibility. Nichols, one of his rangers that year, referred to him as "a popular man and a good Indian fighter," indicating the martial respect he carried amongst peers.[4] This admiration remained crucial for legitimate leadership in the unprofessional and democratic system of command that typified Texas military units prior to the Civil War.

As with previous multiethnic cavalry efforts in South Texas, the proactive ranger concept was not just limited to Anglo participation. Antonio Perez, a Mexican expatriate who had patrolled under Juan Seguin, led another *Tejano* company out of San Antonio. The incorporation of Perez's Hispanic element into the military scheme indicated continuity of the Anglo-*Tejano* alliance in securing the Rio Grande frontier up to this point. Gaining experience for his future role in as a scout the Mexican War, firebrand John Price led the third company out of Victoria.[5] The rangers' southward orientation, in part, reflected the republic's anxiety over the political turbulence and military rebellion that was fracturing northern Mexico throughout the 1840s.

In February of 1841 the Texian Congress complemented paid ranger companies with a decentralized militia system. They authorized twenty-one counties to each raise a company of mounted volunteers to "Encourage Frontier Protection." Called "Minute Men" in the legislation, these forces allowed a legal avenue for localized defense at limited cost, or responsibility, to Austin. The title also defined the rapid reaction capability needed to protect dispersed towns and homesteads in obvious emulation of American Revolutionary heritage. The congress designed the concept to supersede, if not replace, the cumbersome National Militia brigade structure. It predictably directed that each recruit arrive with "a good substantial horse, bridle, and saddle" while specifying weapon and ammunition requirements.[6] Though not all counties formed required units, at least seventeen militia companies assembled across the republic.

Minute men companies, which were all mounted, represented the most widespread, and most underappreciated, manifestation of Texas's way of war in the early 1840s. While the handful of continuously patrolling ranger companies in the south gained the most attention for this period, county fieldings of citizen-soldiers better demonstrated the societal pervasiveness of irregular cavalry service. Hundreds, if not thousands, of Texians serving in both legislatively sanctioned militia and *ad hoc* volunteer companies gained a lesser intensity of tactical experience in the constant raiding and skirmishing that persisted throughout Texas.[7] Minute men conducted actions in almost every region of the nation during this period, including northern Texas, which rapidly developed into a new zone for contested settlement.

In April of 1841 Jack Hays led both San Antonio "Spy" companies to Laredo, southeast of San Antonio, in order to investigate reports of Mexican banditry. As a significant border town on the north side of the Rio Grande this frontier community dwelt directly in disputed territory between Texas and Mexico. As illustrated by Deaf Smith's publicized fight against Mexican cavalry near Laredo in 1837, the place remained a contentious and volatile site for clashing patrols. The small force that arrived with Hays included twelve Texians and thirteen of Perez' *Tejano* rangers.[8]

Like the earlier melded Anglo-*Tejano* Texas cavalry units of 1836 and 1837, this company embodied the fusion of Spanish, Indian, and American traditions. Unity with Hispanic-Texans in South Texas characterized Hays's tendency for combining multi-ethnic strengths. John Caperton described the distinctly *vaquero* characteristics and equipment of rangers during these years, attesting that they "were splendid riders, and used the Mexican saddle, improved somewhat by the Americans, and carried the Mexican riata, made of rawhide, and used the cabrista also, a hair rope, and the lariat, used to rope horses with."⁹ This transfer of horsemanship skills and equipment benefited from employment of both *vaqueros* and cowboys on numerous ranches.

Hays likewise routinely employed allied natives as auxiliary scouts. Years later while on campaign in Mexico, the ranger reportedly admitted that "Indians were the best spies in the world." He also said that "of all the prairie tribes" he considered "the Comanche the most superior race." This respect for indigenous tactical capabilities, and the exploitation of the historical enmity between competing plains peoples, yielded productive partnerships and explained much of Hays's success against tribal opponents. *Tejano* civilians and Indian observers also contributed to the young captain's intelligence collection as covert agents.[10]

Hays's multiethnic ranger company consequently advanced on Laredo with diverse capabilities. As they approached within ten miles of the town, a larger force of Mexican cavalry and Hispanic irregulars moved to intercept. Mexican authorities had clearly received information of Hays's march, proving the intelligence contest was reversible. Though warned of the opposition's intentions by scouts, Hays aggressively continued course with the obvious intent of forcing an engagement.

The confident Mexican patrol immediately recognized an opportunity to attain revenge for their countrymen's loss to Deaf Smith three years prior. Given such overt hostility, the two forces immediately engaged each other upon closing within firing range. At forty riders to the Texians' twenty-five, the Mexican element doubtlessly felt confident in winning the mêlée sure to unfold. The following report of the battle, likely written by Hays in third person for the benefit of publication in newspapers, detailed the encounter:

> The Mexicans charged first—they were repulsed. The Texans then charged them in return—they retreated, thus the fight continued for about an hour. The Mexicans would dismount whenever they fired & would then mount & retreat. Hays at length after

receiving & returning a fire, charged upon the Mexicans without waiting to reload, and put them to flight with pistols before the Mexicans could remount. He took possession of their horses and mounting them, pursued the flying foe; who having now lost their commander & dispossessed of their horses, surrendered; 32 in number with 8 dead on the field ... thus ended this brilliant affair.[11]

The narration recounted a particular action during the battle that further enhanced Hays's growing legend: "The Commanding officer of the Mexicans was a brave fellow, and during the last charge of Hays's men he pulled out his sword and ran at them, and Capt. Hays shot him with a pistol, about eight feet off."[12] This close combat skill marked an important aspect of Texian leadership. Like all warrior cultures, rangers and militia demanded and elected leaders who excelled in killing, displayed reliable temperament under pressure, and could endure extreme physical privation. Particular instances of martial bravado, such as Hays's victory over his Mexican counterpart, created outsized reputations that endorsed the command selection for future crises.

Hays's report of the Laredo fight, published in the *Telegraph and Texas Register*, detailed how he initially engaged the Mexicans dismounted, then remounted to regain contact, dismounted once again to fire rifles, and remounted again for a final charge. This maneuver reflected dragoon-style tactics that rangers had perfected after two decades of frontier adaptation. It maximized the precision nature of American long rifles while utilizing horses for limited and rapid advances to maintain momentum. Texian use of Colt repeating revolvers had not yet concentrated enough in 1841 to allow coordinated shock charges while mounted, though some Paterson models had matriculated into their ranks by this point.[13]

The next month Hays again patrolled west at the behest of San Antonio merchants to investigate reports of Mexican presence. In an audacious move that reflected the young captain's growing confidence, he engaged a force of Mexican lancers that outnumbered the Texians five to one. Brigadier General Rafael Vasquez, a competent Centralist leader, commanded the opposing battalion. The Mexicans were so surprised by the rapid advance they assumed Hays's company far larger than the forty he led. The audacious bluff worked and the "whole force of Vasquez was put to flight," according to the incident report."[14] The rangers doggedly pursued the Mexicans south to the Rio Grande where they broke off the chase. The captain disbanded his company upon their return to San Antonio, fulfilling the volunteer and event-specific nature of the enlistments.

Mexican regular cavalry were not the only enemy the San Antonio rangers faced in 1841. The irregular cavalrymen also proved their tactical skills against Comanche in the summer and fall of that year. In June, as ethnic hostilities continued, Hays formed a new company in San Antonio under the Minute Men provision. Though technically militia, the captain trained his men to ride and fight as well as elite rangers. Later that month sixteen Bexar County Minute Men joined twenty San Antonio *Tejanos* to retaliate against Comanche cattle thieves. Veteran officer Salvador Flores led the Hispanic volunteers.[15]

The Texians located the native village at Uvalde Canyon fifty miles west of San Antonio. Realizing his force was too small to assault the site, perhaps indicating lessons from previous failures by Moore and Karnes, Hays instead positioned to monitor the trail. The captain recorded the action that followed: "We came upon a party of Indians, on their way from the main camp of the vicinity of this town. I immediately attacked them and succeeded in killing eight, and taking the two other prisoners." As an additional benefit, they were successful in "capturing all their horses and property."[16] The ambush tactic represented yet another aspect of indigenous methods co-opted by Anglo-Texans.

Bexar Minute Men rode forth the next month to reengage the same Comanche. Hays's force of forty-three in this mission perfectly represented converging martial cultures that shaped the development of Texas mounted arms prior to the Mexican War. Comprising twenty-eight Anglos, eight *Tejanos*, and seven Apache, the company incorporated the major cultural and military influences that intersected north of the Rio Grande. Hays's trusted partner, now called Chief Flacco, led the Apache element.[17]

The Texian force first rode to the location of the last engagement near Uvalde Canyon. There they located and followed the tracks of a large hunting party. Upon finding the warriors, the rangers immediately closed with the Comanche to leverage surprise. Hays's report to Lamar, again written in third person, explained that the "battle was fought on the extreme head of the Llano. In the fight, the Indians would retreat, form a line, and prepare for battle." The energetic captain then relayed how at one point he "charged alone within a short distance of the enemy intending to discharge his piece, and retreat." Despite Hays's intention to break off, his horse instead suddenly caught its "bit in his teeth, dashed off and ran entirely through the Indian ranks."[18]

Flacco's courageous act that followed, even as Hays careened frantically into the Comanche line, revealed a depth of personal bond that occasionally developed between officer and trusted scout. The report stated the warrior, "perceiving this, followed his leader in rapid pursuit and broke thro' the lines and came off safely with his Captain." In retrospect Hays—no stranger to danger and never one to embellish reports—attested that "their escape was a miracle." A final comment indicated the nature of their relationship that belied some perceptions of universal antipathy between Texians and Indians of the era: "After the fight, Flacco remarked that he would never leave him behind."[19]

The opposing tribesmen eventually fled the battleground under the weight of Texian firepower. The Apache auxiliaries gave Hays the title, "Brave Too Much," for his reckless charge. Hays later recalled that he believed this battle had a noticeable deterring effect on Comanche raids against the San Antonio area for the remainder of the year.[20]

One of the captain's most legendary, and disputed, feats purportedly occurred in the fall of 1841. Called the Battle of Enchanted Rock, it displayed his penchant for survival against improbable odds.

According to Texan lore Hays became separated from his Bexar Company while scouting the Pedernales River west of San Antonio. A party of Comanche intercepted and pursued him to a defensive position on a prominent granite monadnock held sacred, or believed to be enchanted, by the Indians. With a rifle and two newly acquired Colt revolvers, Hays held off the gathering warband for an hour until his company rescued him. This performance, regardless of factual accuracy, further enhanced the legend of "Devil Jack" and validated his reputation for unmatched bravery and astounding luck.[21]

Continuous patrolling by San Antonio rangers and other Minute Men companies managed to establish a temporary security in South Texas by the close of 1841. Hays's fame as premier combat leader along the disputed Nueces Strip spread across the republic, and parts of northern Mexico, because of his uncanny success in irregular warfare and the Texian press's thirst for national heroes. John Ford, an unashamed admirer and friend who would command the same sector during antebellum and Civil War years, remembered the importance of the captain's efforts:

Hays had by this time gained a reputation for good management, prudence, and bravery, which made him a leader of the people. He and his men were the protectors of an immense scope of country. Under their protection the settlements were made at points hitherto considered too much exposed to risk a family to the scalping-knife of the merciless Indian. At that date there was not a single family residing on the road from San Antonio to Austin ... the whole country was beautiful, but unreclaimed wilderness.[22]

On December 8 the *Telegraph and Texas Register* provided broader, more public assessment of the Tennessean's ranging endeavors. The paper first assessed that "the spy company under Captain Hays has been very efficient and has almost completely broken up the old haunts of the Comanche in the vicinity of Bexar." Then seeking to expand his legend in accordance with the lionizing of rangers in Lone Star culture, the editor wrote that "so great has been the protection and security resulting from the active enterprise of this excellent officer that settlements are extending on every side around the city and the country is assuming the appearance of peace and prosperity that characterized it previous to the Revolution."[23]

The year 1841 proved important in the acculturation and refinement of the Texan military tradition. Hays's rise, and the aggressive actions of other new ranger captains, symbolized the passing of tactical leadership from the colonial and revolutionary generation of Burleson and Moore to a younger cadre who had gained skills and reputations in post-independence conflicts. The change simultaneously reflected a general, though not absolute, strategic and geographic shift from the Bastrop front to the San Antonio theater. In addition to Hays, other men such as Price and McCulloch established reputations as effective ranger commanders in South Texas throughout 1841.[24]

Despite idealistic and heroic images portrayed by the Texian press, ranging operations in republican Texas were extremely challenging, rigorous, and dangerous. Caperton, a contemporary ranger of Hays and McCulloch, described the living and fighting conditions of Indian fighters in the years prior to American annexation. He wrote that rangers "moved as lightly over the prairie as the Indians did, and lived as they did, without tents, with a saddle for pillow at night, blankets over them, and their feet to the fire." The major then emphasized their fleet posture: "Depending wholly on wild game for food, they of course sometimes found a scarcity of it, and suffered the privations which are known to all hunters."[25]

Caperton, who wrote as an amateur, and biased, Texas historian, also described the dangers of the assignment. Attempting to detail and even glorify hardships endured by national heroes like Hays, he wrote that "it was a life full of the most intense excitement and attended by the greatest peril. About half of the Rangers were killed off every year, and their places supplied by new men." He then noted that "fighting was their business, and they grew to like it after a time, and took all the risks."[26] This kind of attrition, and the difficult lifestyle that accompanied frontier patrolling, forged a new generation of fighters who were hardened against the roughest of campaign environments.

1842: The Year of Invasions

Lamar's imperialist presidency ended in December of 1841 with his nation flagging under war debt and its public unsatisfied with his aggressive and militant agenda. The vaunted Frontier Regiment had failed, and despite the onslaught of volunteer expeditions against the Comanche heartland—some successful and others not—the republic stood no closer to peace. Smithwick, who astutely assessed Texas's precarious position, lamented how "those were dark days for the Lone Star republic—her treasury bankrupt; without credit at home or abroad." The long serving militiaman complained that it was "racked by internal feuds and beset by cruel and savage foes without" while the "frontier was without protection."[27]

Even after the march of genocidal campaigns throughout 1839 and 1840, or perhaps because of them, the northwest frontier and Mexican border remained turbulent. Houston criticized Lamar's "extermination policy" by arguing "the country became involved in millions of debt, and the Indians of Texas were kept in constant irritation."[28] Yet despite endemic instability and insolvency, the wars yielded some strategic clarity. Native Americans of eastern Texas were generally subdued or removed and plains peoples severely punished. Decentralized ranger units and localized militia programs had also gained favor over consolidated national brigades. The collapse of the combined arms experiment, and emerging reliance upon elite ranger companies at both national and local levels, would ensure frontier cavalry remained central to Texan militancy until the 1870s.

The final stage of warfare during the era of the Texas Republic was characterized by reduced, less expensive, and more decentralized military postures as the nation staggered under more than $7,000,000 of public debt. It reflected economized and pragmatic foreign policies of the second Houston Administration and the Jones Administration between 1842 and 1845, which eschewed large-scale confrontations such as those that occurred at Plum Creek and the Neches, or general war with Mexico. The republic's new military stance, now centering firmly on localized ranger and militia companies, contrasted sharply with imperialistic policies of the Lamar regime.[29]

Zachariah Morrell, a preacher, businessman, and militiaman who settled his family in Washington-on-the-Brazos in southeastern Texas, summarized the abandonment of schemes which had attempted to extend Lone Star dominion as far west as Mexican Santa Fe: "General Houston's policy was much opposed to that adopted under the former administration. He condemned the Santa Fe expedition on the grounds that it was impossible for Texas to hold such a large territory against so many enemies." Morrell also believed the ascendant president "opposed any effort to exterminate the Indians, by following them into their territory, as utterly fruitless." He finally noted, as part of a larger conciliation strategy, that Houston "favored the establishment of trading-posts along our frontier."[30]

Differing perspectives on the propriety of aggressive strikes into native support areas—exemplified by the policies of Houston and others like Lamar, Rusk, Moore, and Karnes—reflected a polemical schism on how to negotiate Anglo-Indian contention that had periodically divided Anglo colonials since their first settlement in North America. While some appreciated indigenous tribes as sovereign peoples and sought to mitigate the effects of white expansion, others despised them as obstacles to be removed. This vacillation between conciliation and extermination, mirroring currents of previous Anglo-Germanic advances across the continent, would continue even after the Civil War as successive state governors adopted changing postures with varying degrees of Federal interference.[31]

Texas began 1842 with a limited military structure based on fewer active rangers and more inactive Minute Men. Large-scale formations like the National Militia and the Frontier Regiment were now relics of the past; it would henceforth rely on economized and volunteer mobilizations to provide regional security. Houston described fiscal challenges that compelled his nation's peculiar approach to warfare in an address to the Texas Congress on July 18, 1841, when he explained that, "for the want of means it has been impossible to sustain any efficient force, but for a few days, when emergency has called out men."

Even as the former general embraced emergency mobilizations of volunteers and militia for potential large-scale campaigns, he praised the successes of active ranging companies to the south. With Comanche raiders, Mexican Army patrols, and brigands of all ethnicities and nationalities plaguing the Rio Grande frontier, inactive militias would not be responsive enough to counter the lightning threats and the fledgling communities required proactive protection. Given these realities, the victor of San Jacinto informed the legislature that "Major Hays and Captain Menchaca" had again "received orders to raise men and act between the San Antonio river and the Rio Grande."[32]

In accordance with presidential directive, the congress continued the decentralized ranger system, albeit in a reduced form, on January 29, 1842, when it approved just "one company of mounted men, to act as Rangers on the southern frontier."[33] The concept of a semi-professional and highly specialized cavalry force had proven its value in frontier operations over the past two years and for the sake of exposed Anglo settlements it had to be continued. Dedicated ranger units possessed vigilance and expertise that militia could never attain while offering the republic a relatively inexpensive method for maintaining active fighting forces.

The Texian government naturally selected Hays to lead the new company out of San Antonio. His previous commission had expired, but no other Texian enjoyed his combination of peerless reputation, knowledge of South Texas, tactical prowess, and political favor with Houston. Caperton described the Tennessean's famed leadership: "The most remarkable thing about Hays was his capacity to control men ... being always ready to lead in everything, however dangerous or disagreeable, and doing more than his share of camp duty; and he thus won the respect and confidence of this men."[34]

Hays's newest unit reflected the coarsest aspects of Texian society while drawing on attributes that historically made his companies inordinately effective. John Forester, a recruit from Houston who served under the captain, recalled the appearance of his fellow rangers: "The men, in physical make-up, were as fine a body as I ever saw, but their uniforms were altogether new." He explained that "most of them were dressed in skins, some wearing parts of buffalo robes, deer hides, and bear skins, and some entirely naked to the waist." Referencing qualities that would soon catapult them to international fame, he also noted that "all were well armed and well mounted."[35]

Such irregularity in frontier dress often made Texian horsemen appear less like soldiers and more like the brigands they fought. Caperton likewise described the accoutrements of the new generation of Texian frontiersmen. The chronicler wrote that "each man was armed with a rifle, a pistol, and a knife, and with a Mexican blanket tied behind his saddle, and a small wallet in which he carried his salt and his ammunition."[36] The lack of uniformity described by Forester, combined with the prioritization of equipment according to utility, established enduring hallmarks of the Texas Ranger tradition. The irregularity contrasted them in form and function with contemporary American and Mexican regulars.

The frontier guard under Hays was all that stood between Mexico and a largely disarmed Texas in the spring of 1842 even as both countries disputed ownership of the Nueces Strip and towns like Laredo and Corpus Christi. Over the volatile year that followed, the militarized southern border would experience three successive Mexican invasions and occupations of South Texas and a Texian counteroffensive into northern Mexico. This series of territorial disputes commenced on March 5 when a Mexican force under command of Rafael Vasquez—the officer whom Hays had pursued to the Rio Grande in May of 1841—suddenly seized San Antonio. The invasion intended to punish Texas for Lamar's previous belligerence rather than to reconquer *Tejas.*

San Antonio, as the southernmost bastion of Texian power, served as the primary military and political center in the contested border region. The Mexican government accordingly sent a modest expedition of approximately 700 soldiers to seize their old provincial capital and demonstrate national superiority in the region. In addition to the four hundred regular lancers who comprised the core of Vasquez' task force, two companies of infantry and an artillery detachment provided combined arms firepower. A detachment of Caddo scouts and 200 *Tejano* militiamen augmented the regulars while providing regional familiarity.[37]

In addition to seizing San Antonio, separate Mexican cavalry detachments compelled surrender of Goliad and Refugio while reviving old fears of the 1836 Runaway Scrape. Texas's utter failure to resist the sudden invasion revealed astonishing military weakness. Even as Vasquez rode north from Mexico in late February and early March the defenders suspected attack was imminent. The San Antonio citizenry quickly elected Hays to command an emergency militia of eighty citizens to reinforce rangers. After losing several clumsy scouting parties to capture by the Mexican vanguard, the San Antonio citizenry panicked and voted to destroy and abandon the old town.

Vasquez's rapid approach forced Hays and his men to retreat towards the town of Seguin, east of San Antonio, where militia were gathering under John Moore. Burleson likewise collected men to the north, near Austin, for an anticipated defense of the capital in the event of a deeper invasion. Despite resounding success in capturing South Texas and doubtless satisfaction in attaining revenge against Hays for previous embarrassments, Vasquez evacuated San Antonio and marched south before the Texians could organize and counterattack. The entire operation essentially comprised an extended raid that punished the republic and frightened its people.

The unmitigated success of the Mexican incursion revealed that Texas stood utterly unprepared to withstand anything beyond raiding and skirmishing. The rapid surrender of San Antonio, Goliad, and Refugio, and the corresponding evacuation of the entire Guadalupe Valley, resulted from the immature nation's inability to maintain a nation-state standing army with combined arms and fortified defenses. Superior Mexican counter-reconnaissance also negated Hays's improvised scouting attempts and delayed formation of militia capable of defending San Antonio. In short, Mexico's initiative revealed the structural weaknesses of Houston's economy-of-force policies.

Despite recent events, the Lone Star president refused to be dissuaded from his expedient military posture. This included resisting calls for a militia build-up and counter-invasion and under Burleson, who now served as Vice President, war factions clamored to avenge Texian honor. By April the southern ranging companies again patrolled as the only security units actively fielded for Texas. Hays's riders out of San Antonio engaged Comanche when possible and fought several engagements in the spring. His Apache allies, under Flacco, remained steadfastly loyal and provided intelligence that allowed the small garrison to maximize initiative. County and town volunteers likewise served across the state when needed in both sanctioned and unsanctioned activations.

In July of 1842 Texian volunteers and the Mexican Army again clashed at the Battle of Lipantitlan, in southeastern Texas. The battle occurred when a Mexican army of 700 cavalrymen and infantry, both regular and irregular, preemptively advanced into the disputed zone and attacked a Texian volunteer buildup of 400 men near Corpus Christi. The Anglos had been postured to invade Mexico in response to the Vasquez incursion but the Mexican command moved to strike first. The hard-fought engagement, which again featured the deadly impact of American long rifles, unfolded as an inconclusive infantry fight with the larger army retreating back across the Rio Grande towards Camargo.[38]

On July 23 the Texas Congress endorsed economized ranging when it promoted Hays to the rank of major and authorized him to command "two companies to range the South-Western frontier." The legislature also approved a third company to patrol between the Trinity and Navasota rivers.[39] This act officially advanced Hays to battalion-level command with the responsibility to coordinate actions by multiple units over distance.

In fall of 1842 the Mexican Army again seized San Antonio, marking the third offensive into territory claimed by the Texas Republic in less than a year. They launched the invasion in response to their perceived failure at the Battle of Lipantitlan and continued hostility with their former colony. The New Orleans *Bulletin* dramatically emphasized the frontier polity's vulnerability:

> Never since the declaration of independence was Texas more unprepared for a vigorous contest than at this moment ... Her army is disbanded; her hopes of war lie idle at new Orleans for want of funds ... her credit is utterly prostrate, and money she has none. Still, she has brave hearts and strong ands, and, when the crisis comes, we trust she will be found equal to it.[40]

On September 11, Mexican General Adrian Woll and a robust force of 1,500 crossed the Rio Grande and occupied San Antonio with almost no resistance. The brigade consisted of over 1,000 infantry, 500 cavalry, and a set of field cannon. The density of infantry in this force, in contrast to Vasquez' mostly cavalry expedition, indicated that the French expatriate hoped to preserve gains in South Texas with a permanent, or at least longer, occupation.[41]

Hays commanded a reconnaissance by two companies, one *Tejano* and another Anglo, as the Mexicans advanced, but Hays failed to locate the invaders. Woll skillfully achieved covert movement by marching overland and avoiding the main routes while rangers patrolled the expected roads leading to San Antonio from the south and west. This represented perhaps the greatest tactical failure of Hays's career. Moving with surprising alacrity, Woll captured the town and its citizenry intact, inflicting a heavy cost for the young major's lapse.

With San Antonio once again occupied, most of South Texas was essentially lost to the republic. Realizing any stand would now be made closer to Anglo population centers, Hays and his rangers rode northeast to unite with gathering militia. Morrell, who joined the defenders, recalled the emergency mobilization: "We gathered what ammunition we could at Gonzales, and left for Seguin, with instructions that recruits coming from the east should follow our trail."

The volunteer then noted his unit's movement towards the expected site of battle, citing that "on Tuesday morning we marched on within twenty miles of San Antonio."[42]

While Texian militia marshaled to confront the invaders, Morrell transferred to join Hays's rangers now serving as mounted scouts for the riflemen corps. He described how the *ad hoc* company formed and deployed: "In a few minutes we were off, and soon men with Henry McCulloch joined us with thirteen men, swelling our numbers to twenty-seven." The militiaman also noted that "the command was organized on the spot, with Jack Hays captain, and Henry McCulloch lieutenant."[43] Now unified and democratically commanded, the scouts rode back to San Antonio and captured a Mexican soldier. They then brought the prisoner to the Texian command at Seguin where he confirmed the position and composition of Woll's army.

By September 17 the Texians had assembled just 202 men under the command of Colonel Mathew Caldwell. The Plum Creek veteran accordingly selected Salado Creek, a defensible position seven miles north of San Antonio, as a favorable site for battle. Given the numerical disparity between Mexican and Texian forces, Caldwell elected to maximize advantages in terrain and weaponry. That the defenders invited general engagement under such disproportionate circumstances indicated confidence in rifled firepower. Forty horsemen under Hays, who would prove critical in provoking the engagement on favorable terms, supported the infantry with cavalry mobility.[44]

Morrell, again riding with Hays, described how the rangers fought Mexican cavalry that night. The settler wrote that after making visual contact, "we retreated until they were drawn from the timber, when, under the order of our gallant leader, we wheeled, and forty Mexicans failed to stand the charge."[45] The Hispanic horsemen retreated without casualties on either side. This action facilitated minor, yet crucial, counter-reconnaissance that denied Woll tactical understanding of Texian numerical limitations and strengths of their defensive position. It also demonstrated ranger multi-functionality as they transitioned from habitual roles as dragoons or mounted infantry to traditional light cavalry functions.

The next day, on September 18, the Texians determined to draw a decisive engagement on advantageous terms. According to Nichols, now a veteran ranger, "Caldwell ordered Hays with his spy company to town to draw the enemy out."[46] Once in sight of San Antonio they demonstrated to entice pursuit by the occupiers. To the rangers' surprise, a force of almost 500 cavalrymen immediately thundered out of the town towards them. The rapidity of the sally indicated the Mexicans were about to commence a reconnaissance-in-force when the Texians arrived.

Hays led the Mexicans in a long, and at times desperate, chase to the militia line at Salado Creek. The fresh Mexican horses nearly caught the exhausted ranger mounts during the pursuit, revealing an unanticipated setback. Morrell offered a spirited account of the chase and a description of Hays's command presence as the company turned to face their pursuers:[47]

> The cavalry that had pursued us passed round to our rear on the prairie ... Captain Jack Hays, our intrepid leader, five feet ten inches high, weighing one hundred and sixty pounds, his black eyes flashing decision of character, from beneath a full forehead, and crowned with a beautiful jet black hair, was soon mounted on his dark bay war-horse and on the warpath. Under our chosen leader, we sallied out and skirmished with the enemy at long range, killing a number of Mexicans, and getting two of our men severely wounded. In a short time they retired, and we fell back to the main command.[47]

Once at the creek Hays and his men joined the Texian defense while the Mexicans called up larger forces under Woll. The French mercenary arrived with an assault regiment of 400 infantry and artillery regulars, a company of Cherokee auxiliaries, and 100 *Tejano* expatriates from San Antonio. He also brought two field cannon to support the final advance.

The invaders transitioned into attack formation upon arrival to the battlefield. Nichols, from his elevated vantage point in the Texian line, described the assault that Woll launched against the defenders. He recorded that "the Mexicans marched on to the crest of the hill, filed to the right, marched to the opening between the heads of the two ravines, displaying his whole force in full view of Caldwells men."[48] With a menacing line of hunting rifles aimed across the battlefield this exposure would prove a costly mistake.

The Texians, though severely outnumbered, received the engagement in high spirits. As the Mexicans deployed for a close order assault and defenders prepared to receive them, Caldwell sent a spirited call for assistance to nearby communities: "It is the most favorable opportunity I have seen. I can whip them on any ground without help, but cannot take prisoners. Why don't you come? Hurra for Texas!"[49] With so many atrocities and perceived insults to Lone Star honor to be avenged, Texians were eager to decide the issue.

Woll commenced the battle with "grape canister and round shot ... for near an hour," which proved ineffective, while his infantry marched on the elevated Texian line. This tactic represented typical cannon employment to degrade enemy readiness until the infantry ranks could make contact. Unfortunately for the Mexicans, the cannonade dispersed amongst the treeline and ridge while the Texians remained behind cover.

The resulting infantry advance proved a disaster for the invaders. Morrell observed with the riflemen line how the invaders attacked with an archaic and vulnerable approach: "The Mexicans now advanced upon us, under a splendid puff of music, the ornaments, guns, spears and swords glistening in plain view."[50] The reference to reliance on edged weapons illustrated a primary difference between the armies: while Texians relied almost exclusively on rifled firepower, with a smattering of repeating weapons, the Mexicans maintained a conservative reliance on spears, swords, and dated Brown Bess muskets.

This manner of engagement offered combat Anglo frontiersmen understood best: precision fire from protected positions. They had employed the tactic against superior Indian numbers on numerous occasions and now wielded it against conventional infantry. Kentucky

Rifles rounds cut into Mexican ranks with bloody impact as defenders unleashed precision aim. Morrell described the initial volley, explaining that "some of the Mexican infantry were within thirty feet of us before a gun was fired. At the first fire the whole of them fell to the ground." The militiaman then continued: "soon however, all that were able rose to their feet, but showed no disposition to advance further upon our line."[51]

Not only did the Texians hold advantage of engaging from steady and elevated platforms, the Mexicans' smoothbore muskets could not hope to compete with the advanced accuracy or range of American rifles. The eager defenders bloodily repulsed repeated frontal assaults by Mexican infantry as they attempted to march within firing range. Nichols, who still lay in the militia line, recounted the deadly aim of his countrymen: "We would crawl to the top of the bank and fire, and it was seldom a Texas rifle fired that there was not one seen to bite the dust."[52]

The Mexican regulars were not the only attackers who suffered during the assault. At the height of the battle, Cherokee warriors, led by troublesome agent Vincente Cordova, attacked Caldwell's flank through the woods. The auxiliaries hoped to turn the Texian line by moving against their least protected extremity. Despite the Indians' partially concealed movement, Hays and others noticed the attack. In response, volunteer Jenkins observed that "ten men, with double-barrel shot-guns, were detached, and stationed above to prevent it." The defenders repulsed the Cherokee and killed Cordova, finally eliminating an opponent who had long frustrated Texian authorities.[53]

Despite significant numerical disparity between attackers and defenders, Mexican mass could not turn or penetrate the militia line. Jenkins summarized the futility of the repeated attacks: "The Mexicans charged several times and the skirmish lasted over a half-day, but finally the Mexicans were repulsed."[54] By close of the day the invaders lost over sixty killed and many more wounded. Woll recognized the diminishing prospects of victory while taking casualties so deep in enemy territory and ignominiously retreated back to San Antonio.

The main clash at the Battle of Salado Creek ended as an unqualified success for Texas. Yet despite the improbable victory it suffered unexpected and severe defeat elsewhere. While the central clash ended near the river a separate Mexican column intercepted a Texian company of fifty-three reinforcements en route from La Grange. Nicholas Dawson, a veteran of the Texas Revolution, unwittingly led his men into an untenable situation as they neared the site of battle.[55]

The larger Mexican force, which consisted of several hundred Mexican irregulars with light cannon, immediately surrounded and overwhelmed the Texians. After suffering defeat at the main contest the invaders were in no mood to offer mercy. According to Nichols' recollection, "Dawson raised a white flag in token of his surrender and was instantly shot down."[56] Next, in the heat of battle, the Mexicans killed most Anglos who surrendered while eventually taking fifteen men as prisoners, including Morrell's son. Two rangers escaped to tell the tale of the bloody loss. Like the Alamo and Goliad executions of 1836, this action enraged all Texians and galvanized a vengeful pursuit.

On September 21 the militiamen caught up with the retreating Mexicans at the Arroyo Hondo, a small creek south of San Antonio. Woll's retreat suffered from extreme logistical privation and disarray common in defeated armies and thus provided an ideal target for retaliation. Hays and his mounted rangers, again providing reconnaissance for rifleman companies in the manner of professional light cavalry, identified the enemy rearguard on elevated ground above the creek. The Mexicans supported the picket with light cannon on the road in hopes of discouraging and delaying any Texian attack.

According to Morrell, again riding with the rangers to rescue his son, Hays determined to immediately assault the rearguard. The captain augmented his company with horsemen from Caldwell's main "line of battle" for "purpose of charging the cannon." Morrell described the audacious assault that followed:

Away went the company up a gradual ascent in quick time. In a moment the cannon roared, but according to Mexican custom overshot us. The Texan yell followed the cannon's thunder, and so excited the Mexican infantry, placed position to pour a fire down our lines, that they overshot us; and by the time the artillery hurled its canister the second time, shot-guns and pistols were freely used by the Texans. Every man at the cannon was killed, as the company passed it.[57]

Charging mounted in the face of cannon fire—a fairly unique event in Texas's military history up to that point—demonstrated how Texian mounted forces had begun to internalize the audacity and tactical skills necessary to serve as conditional shock cavalry. The mounted charge under Sherman preceding the Battle of San Jacinto provided the only precedent, but unlike that attack Hays's maneuver succeeded spectacularly.

The speed and confidence required to take the Mexican position by storm reflected basic strengths of heavy cavalry in European warfare. It represented the ultimate utility of cohesive shock horse against infantry and artillery: the psychological and physical impact of massed horsemen charging with close combat weaponry. The "shot-guns and pistols freely used" in the short melee marked the superiority of Texian firepower over archaic swords and lances.

Despite his isolated success, Hays could not retain the high ground and captured cannon. The Texian main force, under Caldwell and Ben McCulloch, failed to reinforce his position and the rangers abandoned their gains. They then stalled until morning due to indecision and disunity and allowed Woll's army to escape intact.[58] Observers, both Texian and Mexican, later agreed that had Caldwell exploited Hays's charge with a rapid general advance they would have shattered the suffering Mexican army. While volunteer Samuel Walker blamed "fickle officers" and "cowardice" for the lapse, a Mexican officer reportedly criticized those who failed to capitalize on the Hondo charge as "not fit to stand in the shoes of those who fought at the Salado."[59]

This action occurred as the first of many for a young nationalist named Samuel Walker. An immigrant from the American eastern coast and military novice during the Salado Creek campaign, he would soon have a Colt revolver model named for him and gain national attention for intrepid conduct during the Mexican War. The young firebrand rode with the men who initially discovered the corpses of Dawson's company and reported the massacre. He subsequently joined the pursuit of Woll's army to exact vengeance.

This was Walker's first experience with carnage on a military scale but it would not be his last. The famed partisan's story stands unique in that he was perhaps the only ranger of the republican period who originally immigrated from Maryland. He arrived in Texas in time to join a reinforcement company formed to fight at Salado Creek, but marched too late to join the battle. One admirer poetically wrote of the adventurer that, "war was his element, the bivouac his delight, and the battlefield his playground."[60]

Walker, Hays, and the Texian pursuit force returned to South Texas after failing to bring Woll to a second decisive engagement. In late November, after bowing to public pressure, Houston reluctantly authorized a more substantial retaliation against Mexico under command of a senior militia commander named Brigadier General Alexander Somervell. The president's order to "proceed to the most eligible point on the South Western frontier of Texas ... and if you can advance with a prospect of success into the enemy's territory, you will do forthwith," intended to demonstrate strength and resolve without engaging in a protracted invasion or occupation south of the Rio Grande. Ultimately, Houston yet hoped for annexation by the United States and the guaranteed security it would bring.[61]

The Texian expedition comprised 700 volunteers eager to avenge successive Mexican incursions against Texas sovereignty and the massacre of Dawson's men. As always, memories of the Alamo and Goliad just six years prior remained acute. Realizing that the army would need cavalry support, Houston informed Somervell that he could "rely upon the gallant Hays and his companions" and recommended the general "should obtain his services and cooperation."[62]

Hays accordingly led a mixed company of rangers and Apache scouts in support of the Texian army as it marched south. His task in the invasion, as during the earlier pursuit of Woll, was to conduct the reconnaissance and skirmishing tasks that fleet mounted forces excelled at in mid-nineteenth-century warfare. Given the indecisive and ultimately anti-climactic nature of the campaign it remains difficult to gauge ranger contributions to the invasion. However, while patrolling to the front, Hays did capture two Mexicans who provided "all necessary information," doubtlessly under duress or torture, to inform Somervell's next moves.[63]

On December 8, after enduring difficult marching conditions and internal disunity, the expedition arrived at Laredo. This border town remained a simmering point of Texan-Mexican contention due to its position along disputed territory between the Rio Grande and Nueces River. Appreciating the unexpected size of the Texian force, the smaller Hispanic garrison swiftly retreated. The aggressors immediately occupied the city and looted it in retaliation for previous despoliations of San Antonio. Simultaneous to the occupation of Laredo, Hays rode to the nearby town of Guerrero to seize money and horses.[64]

This absence of discipline reflected an inevitable manifestation of any way of war that relied upon untrained and legally ambiguous volunteers susceptible to plundering and atrocity. Somervell's logistically challenged army then fractured over diverging objectives after stripping the Laredo area of forage and valuables. While a pragmatic faction wished to return to Texas, a larger contingent of angry zealots aimed to continue the invasion. On December 10 a column of 185 men departed for home and on December 19 Somervell ordered the remaining soldiers to follow suit.

Despite the general's command, a robust splinter column of 308 men under command of William Fisher proceeded south into Mexico with the objective of capturing the larger city of Mier. Hays and McCulloch provided initial reconnaissance before wisely departing for Texas. The resulting defeat, capture, and lottery execution of militiamen involved in the Mier Expedition by a much larger Mexican army greatly contributed to Texas's desire for revenge during the Mexican War.[65] Once back in San Antonio Hays sadly discovered that his scout, Flacco, had been murdered by *vaqueros* associates to steal his horses.[66]

The invasions and counter-invasions of 1842 held great import for Texas's military tradition. Unlike most of its clashes since 1836, fighting in that year allowed mounted rangers to execute light cavalry support of infantry. Surveillance against Vasquez's and Woll's advances and reconnaissance for Somervell had trained them as conventional scouts. The charge at the Arroyo Hondo likewise reflected mastery, however limited, of the idealized Napoleonic heavy cavalry charge. These experiences prepared many of these rangers, and Hays in particular, for similar actions in 1846 and 1847 while supporting the U.S. Army in Mexico.

The Mexican offensives of 1842 held unanticipated—but tragically predictable—consequences of degrading relations between *Tejano* and Anglo communities in Texas. Men of Hispanic ancestry had previously fought bravely for the Texas Republic and contributed immensely to its military development. Juan Seguin and Antonio Perez, in particular, had commanded congressionally authorized battalions and companies. The former even served as mayor of San Antonio over a mixed Hispanic and Anglo constituency.[67] Despite these past loyalties, the enticement, or likely intimidation, of reconstituted Mexican power in South *Tejas* convinced them and many *Tejanos* to change allegiance during the crisis. This rapid shift stemmed from long-standing discontentment under Spanish, Mexican, and then Texan rule.

Much of the Anglo recrimination centered on well-known *Tejanos* who suddenly pivoted to fight against Texas in 1842. The sudden repatriation of Seguin and Perez as commissioned offers in Woll's army created symbols of Hispanic-Texan betrayal to the republic. More importantly, fighting by San Antonio *Tejanos* as Mexican irregulars at Salado Creek likewise catalyzed shift in ethnic perception amongst the larger Anglo population. Nichols' commentary argued Seguin had "turned traitor and had left Texas" while Antonio Perez "left Texas for the same purpose that Seguin did, a commission as Col. in the Mexican Army."[68]

Deterioration of the once symbiotic relationship between *Tejanos* and Anglos that had strengthened Houston's Army of Texas, the Texas cavalries of 1837 and 1838, and ranging companies of 1841 inflicted an institutional loss to Texas's martial tradition. Over the next two decades ranger companies still employed individual *Tejanos*, but Anglos increasingly populated and almost entirely led the organizations. Despite ethnic divisions resulting from the 1842 invasions and increasing aggrandizement of Hispanic-owned ranches, *Tejano* cavalry occasionally rode for Texas in future conflicts. Santos Benavides and his Rio Grande companies during the Civil War best symbolized the continuity of Hispanic-Texan militancy.[69]

The Somervell Campaign ended as the final major campaign for the Texas Republic. From 1843 to 1845 it experienced reduced scope of conflict and relied upon lesser densities of rangers for defense. The frontier nation returned to limited structures that existed under the first Houston Administration: independent, inexpensive, and proactive cavalry continuously patrolling contested spaces. In the wake of destabilizing events of 1842 it also reorganized the national militia and declared martial law in South Texas. The latter action stemmed from the enduring volatility of the Rio Grande region as fiercely contested territory.[70]

Rise of the Texas Rangers

In January of 1843 the Texas Congress again reauthorized its specialized ranger defense, albeit in smaller form, as "one company of mounted men, to act as spies on the South Western frontier."[71] While Houston refused to sign a larger militia act because of aversion to an expansive military, he agreed to authorize the "spy" company under Hays's command. Veteran ranger Big Foot Wallace served as lieutenant, or second in command, while stalwarts Chevallie and McCulloch, who had been nearly continuously on active military service since the fight at Plum Creek, also enlisted.

Hays's rangers patrolled as practically the only active government force in Texas for the entire year of 1843. Nichols, serving in the company, recalled their vigilance: "We kept out scouts all the time, when one would come in another would go out."[72] This type of proactive forward defense represented the full evolution of Stephen Austin's original intent to "keep twenty or thirty mounted men continually on the frontier as spies." It also fulfilled the colonial leader's inspired use of frontier cavalry for "the preventing of small parties of Indians" during early settlement.[73] For horsemen prosecuting Houston's vision for economized security two decades later, such methods represented the return to their favored specialty: counter-guerrilla warfare.

Even as Texian rangers rode against Indian raiders, they embraced another function that foreshadowed their primary vocation in modern memory: outlaw hunting. Given the rapid pace of banditry in frontier Texas, the irregulars' proclivity for decentralized patrolling proved especially useful against mounted and unpredictable marauders. In the summer of 1843 the outlaw Agaton Quinones and a group of *Tejano* predators, in particular, preyed upon travelers and commerce near San Antonio. Caperton described them as "guerrilla parties which were somewhat similar in their makeup and mode of operation to the Rangers, but greatly inferior in skill and fighting quality."[74] On July 12 the *Telegraph and Texas Register* likewise reported that "several bands of robbers were still roving at large."

That month, after doggedly scouring for the outlaws, the rangers caught three of Argaton's men. In a rare act of wanton murder ever attributed directly to Hays, they extracted confessions, likely through torture, and then promptly executed the prisoners. The Clarksville *Northern Standard* described the scene: "Upon interrogating the prisoners, their leader Rubio acknowledged that he and his party had, for a long time, been committing murders and stealing horses along the Colorado, the Guadalupe, and other western streams, that he killed a Texan upon the expectations of getting his horse." The paper then concluded that, "after hearing these confessions Capt. Hays immediately ordered the prisoners to be executed and they were shot forthwith."[75]

Both newspapers praised Hays's non-judicial justice, clearly reflecting the partisan nature of the publications. While the *Telegraph* argued the captain was "enforcing martial law agreeably," the *Standard* advocated that "a few such acts of retribution like this will tend more to give peace and security to the frontier than all the 'letters' the President can write during his term of office."[76] This last statement revealed less than subtle criticism of Houston's reconciliatory policies, which many opposed. Texian society's acceptance of extrajudicial execution illustrated the merciless atmosphere and racial antipathy that pervaded the frontier. More ominously, this action warned of controversial ranger policing methods to come in the late nineteenth and early twentieth centuries.

Whether fighting outlaws, Indians, or Mexicans, Hays's documented training regimen throughout 1843 explained the rangers' remarkable tactical success against their republic's enemies. The frontiersmen well understood the value of combat preparation from practical experience and hard lessons at the hands of implacable enemies. Nichols described their training priorities that year, writing how "those not on a scout were every day practicing horsemanship and marksmanship." Focus on improving riding and shooting emphasized the cavalry-centric orientation of rangers by this time.

Nichols narrated several exercises the irregulars conducted to maintain combat proficiency. In his memoir he recalled that they would "put up a post about the size of a common man, then put another about 40 yards farther on." The ranger then described the exercise that trained the horsemen as true cavalry, as opposed to mounted infantry: "We would run our horses full speed and discharge our rifles at the first post, draw our pistols and fire at the second ... there were not many men that would not put his balls in the center of the posts." Nichols also remembered another drill where the rangers, "drew a ring about the size of a man's head" and that eventually "every man could put both his balls in the circle." These events enhanced the rangers' material advantage in firepower and trained them in the smooth transition from rifle to pistol engagements while mounted.[77]

Skill in military horsemanship offered another dimension where Texian rangers typically excelled beyond professional cavalries. To improve riding abilities, Nichols wrote that Hays's men would "try riding like the Comanche Indians" who were acknowledged by many as the finest horsemen in the North America. The ranger noted how shooting and riding practice improved his company's tactical abilities: "After practicing for three or four months we became so perfect that we would run our horses half or full speed and pick up a hat, a coat ... or even a silver dollar, stand up in the saddle, throw ourselves on the side of our horses with only a foot and hand to be seen, and shoot our pistols under the horses neck."[78]

These drills proved instrumental in allowing them to achieve parity, and sometimes superiority, over Comanche and Mexican opponents. After one fight where the Texians successfully tracked, located, and defeated a band of native horse thieves, Hays summarized the training component of his extraordinary tactical success: "Boys, keep up your practicing shooting horseback. It beats the Indians at their own game."[79]

This statement revealed the conscious acknowledgment of deliberate Texan adaptation and emulation in the arena of mounted warfare by the most accomplished ranger of the era. That Hays specifically referenced training for combat actions while mounted indicates that by 1843 rangers were already shifting away from mounted infantry functions and embracing more doctrinal cavalry methods that required habitual killing from horseback instead of afoot. Even as they attained fame for martial prowess in South Texas, the frontiersmen now awaited only the proper weapon to fully dominate mounted raiding and skirmishing in the region.

This multiplier came between 1843 and early 1844—at least with impactful density—in the form of the Paterson Colt revolving pistol. Destined to revolutionize combat in North America, the advent of repeating firearms immediately empowered rangers in frontier warfare. The rapid fire capability of this .36-caliber weapon due to its five-shot rotating cylinder drastically increased lethality while mounted and allowed more aggressive close-quarters tactics. Though the Texas Navy had adopted Patersons in 1838 and individual Texian soldiers had fought with them since, Hays's rangers were the first to employ the innovative technology with concentrated and coordinated effect.[80]

Despite the Colt's superiority over competing Indian and Mexican armaments in close engagements, the revolver held one disadvantage: it had to be disassembled into several parts in order to reload spare cylinders, a difficult task while astride a horse. This practically limited a rider's reload capacity to the number of preloaded pistols that he could carry into any single engagement. Nevertheless, the ability of a ranger with two pistols to discharge the equivalent of ten times a contemporary soldier's volume of fire in moments allowed unrivaled killing capacity. In addition to advanced hand-guns, Colt repeating rifles and shotguns provided secondary and transition options to the rangers.[81]

In January of 1844 the Texas Congress renewed the ranging system once again as it further institutionalized its reliance on specialized cavalry in frontier warfare. The government authorized Hays, this time by name, to "raise a Company of Mounted Gunmen, to act as Rangers" in South Texas.[82] By defining the composition as gunmen and their purpose as rangers the act assigned historically separate assault and reconnaissance functions to fleet horseman wielding outsized firepower. While the first term stressed the killing focus of shock troops, the second referenced the functions of long-distance patrolling. Ben McCulloch was commissioned as lieutenant while Chevallie and Walker enlisted in the ranks.[83]

The depth of tactical expertise across this unit reflected an unprecedented fusion of mobility, firepower, and adaptation in their nation's short history. Hays's newest company operated more experienced and better armed than any other North American mounted forces between 1844 and 1847. Though they initially learned under veterans of the Texas Revolution like Deaf Smith, Henry Karnes, John Moore, and Edward Burleson, the new horsemen now rode as standard bearers for the ultimate fruition of Texas's way of war. They had survived a decade of harrowing combat against Comanche raiders and Mexican invaders to emerge as the primary, though numerically limited, defenders of the republic.

The rise of elite rangers—in fighting reputation if not social status—found favor in Texian society as both physical and symbolic expressions of masculinity and nationalism. The *Telegraph and Texas Register* approved and lionized Hays's rangers on April 17, 1844, as they operated at peak effectiveness:

> The company of Western Rangers, under the command of the gallant Capt. Hays, has now its full complement of men, and is now in active service on the western frontier. The main station of Capt. Hays is some distance west of Bexar. The soldiers are sent out by turns to scour the country in every direction. The men are well armed, and probably the happy, jovial and hearty set of men in all Texas.

The article also described the rangers' horses at this time, noting that they boasted "several full blooded race horses, remarkable for their fleetness, and with them they can attack, pursue, or escape from Indian or Mexican enemies at their pleasure." This emphasis on superior firearms and steeds referenced crucial material improvements that propelled tactical advances.

In June of 1844 Hays and his men fought a relatively small though historic engagement that symbolically illustrated the regional preeminence of rangers in both frontier raiding and skirmishing. At the Battle of Walker Creek, north of San Antonio, the Texians used their newfound lethality to destroy a much larger Comanche warband with unprecedented efficiency and rapidity. As stated by Jenkins, who recorded the seminal nature of the event, "here Colt's five-shooter was first used—two cylinders and both loaded."[84]

The engagement began when a party of seventy Comanche identified the rangers on patrol route. After refusing to pursue a decoy into a likely ambush, Hays maneuvered his sixteen men through masking terrain to flank the Indian position. The frontiersmen then achieved overwhelming victory when they employed repeating revolvers for the first time in coordinated volleys at close range. They fired the pistols while mounted, reflecting a distinct shift towards doctrinal cavalry techniques instead of traditional mounted infantry tactics. Participants Samuel Walker and

Ed Gillespie, in particular, enhanced their martial reputations on that day due to their aggressiveness in the running fight.

Hays's report on the battle, which emphasized the transition between long-range and short-range weaponry, rapid mounted charges, and dogged pursuit, narrated the contest. The captain wrote that "after ascertaining that they could not decoy or lead me astray, they came out boldly, formed themselves, and dared us to fight. I then ordered a charge; and, after discharging our rifles, closed in with them, hand to hand, with my five-shooting pistols, which did good execution." Hays concluded that "the fight, which was a moving one, continued to the distance of about three miles—being desperately contested by both parties. After the third round from the five-shooters, the Indians gave way."[85]

Another account of the fight, attained by Caperton directly from Hays, described the rangers' strategy of utilizing constant movement to disrupt Comanche cohesion. Relying on advanced weaponry and excellent horsemanship, the Texians "broke the Indians' line, and prevented them from reforming again, by keeping them on the move, never allowing them time to come into order again, and when the Indians charged on them they shot them down with their pistols."[86] The effect of coordinated firepower devastated the natives. Jenkins explained: "The Indians were astonished and terrified as the white men shooting their 'butcher knives' at them, and soon retreated in confusion and dismay."[87]

Late in the fight the Comanche reconsolidated for a final charge when the rangers had exhausted their revolvers. The warriors might have succeeded, but Hays identified the warband's leader and ordered Gillespie to "dismount and shoot that damn chief."[88] The young volunteer killed the chief with a precision rifle shot and the surviving warriors fled. Like the victory at Salado Creek and in numerous skirmishes across the frontier, Texian firepower won yet again over challenging odds. When the contest ended, the Indians had suffered twenty-three dead and over thirty wounded while the Anglos lost only one. The Texas Ranger ideal of superior mobility, firepower, and frontier adaptation—the tactical cornerstone of the Texan way of war—had attained full maturation.[89]

The Texas Republic's ranger system achieved organizational culmination in the spring of 1845. In February of that year the congress authorized a battalion-sized network for "Protection of the Frontier" to defend South and West Texas. The act ordered the battalion to be comprised of five "detachments of troops" with assigned sectors in Robertson, Travis, Milam, Refugio, and Bexar counties. It directed companies to "scour the frontiers of their respective counties, protect them from incursions, and when concentrated in emergencies, to be under the command of Captain Hays."[90] This measure offered the most complex responsibility to date for Hays and required increased administrative and tactical management.

In addition to Hays's unit, the government authorized a separate ranger company "for the purpose of protecting the settlements at Corpus Christi and its vicinity" under command of settler Henry Kinney.[91] Corpus Christi rangers became notable for incorporating *Tejanos* to gain local knowledge and additional skills. A sixth ranger company operated out of Fort Buckner in the Cross Timbers area of North Texas. Pioneer Jack McGarrah initially formed and led the unit in response to local threats without authorization, but later received official sanction. Activation of rangers along the northern periphery of the republic, near the future site of Dallas, revealed the broader cultural importance that military light horse had attained even on the margins of Texian society.[92]

By the summer of 1845 irregular cavalry once again patrolled across the length and breadth of Texas. The expansion of the ranging corps from Hays's original company in San Antonio to seven counties across North and South Texas demonstrated the primacy of proactive and aggressive horsemen in border conflicts on the lower Great Plains. This mobilization represented the most ambitious fielding of Texian mounted forces since the expiration of Coleman's and Burleson's regiments while emphasizing the ascendance of a new cadre of young ranger captains within Texas's social-military hierarchy.

Even as Hays adopted expanded military duties, he embraced more nuanced responsibilities befitting his status as Texas's leading tactician. Capitalizing on his deadly and outsized reputation, the republic occasionally employed him to negotiate peace with tribes. Despite, or perhaps because of, his record as the scourge of Comanche and Mexican rivals, Hays was able to approach enemies while demanding respect. The frontier commander's treaty initiatives, which were always buttressed by a realistic threat of force, partially facilitated the broader tribal conciliation programs sponsored by Houston and his successor, Anson Jones.[93]

These diplomatic initiatives found tribes of the southern plains—not to be confused with Comanche farther north that remained strong and belligerent—ready to accept peace. Houston later stated of his efforts to foster ethnic tranquility during his nation's final years: "These Indians had been our enemies; they had been exasperated by unprovoked aggressions upon them; but the proper conciliatory disposition soon won their regard and affection."[94] Though temporary and achieved through much bloodshed, the Texas Republic finally achieved a measure of territorial stability.

Noah Smithwick, looking back on the precarious expansion of his nation, wrote of the combined effects of endemic strife and renewed conciliation: "Gradually the irresistible Texans drove the Natives back till at the time of annexation, hostilities along the Colorado had ceased, the savages having transferred their operations to the southwest."[95] After two decades of brutal warfare, Anglo-Texan centers between the Colorado and Sabine river valleys were finally at peace. Yet the pause reflected only calm before a greater storm: American annexation of Texas was in the wind, and full-scale war with Mexico beckoned on the horizon.

The contentious era of the Texas Republic ended when it became an American state on December 29, 1845. Throughout a steady march of raids, skirmishes, and campaigns, its military had transitioned from a hybrid standing army to national militia to reliance on economized rangers. This organizational progression stemmed from cultural and tactical adaptations shaped through two generations of aggressive settlement. Colonial leaders like Deaf Smith, Henry Karnes, John Moore, and Edward Burleson had trained a new corps of frontier captains represented by Jack Hays, Ben McCulloch, Mike Chevallie, and John Ford. Jack Hays in particular, between 1841 and 1845, personified the fusion of colonial innovation, militant nationalism, and technological innovation into a more lethal model of frontier cavalry.

The resulting ranger ideals exemplified adaptive, and often effective, volunteer soldiers who sought to defeat the enemies of Texas through mobility and firepower. As in many early nineteenth-century societies, newspaper editorials informed the citizenry of the republic and offered insight into how Texians perceived themselves, their militarism, and their nation. *The Texas Democrat* accordingly revealed on September 9, 1846, almost a year after annexation, the deep pride of the Lone Star fighting tradition as the American state mobilized for another war against Mexico: "There is probably no set of men on earth readier for a fight, a chase, a fandango, or anything else which may come up, than the Texas Rangers."

This irregular cavalry experience, which both reflected and shaped Texan society for two decades, would soon be required again. The United States' annexation of the indebted republic led directly to a confrontation with Mexico as the dominant nations of North America collided over mastery of the middle continent. Enduring disputes over colonial *Tejas* swiftly became *casus belli* for war between America and Mexico. Caught between Anglo and Hispanic powers, Texas's future would now be decided by the clash of nation-state armies. This arena would offer new trials as the newest and westernmost American state mobilized to settle old scores with its former sovereign.

Chapter 6

The Mexican-American War, 1846–1848

The explosion of war between Mexico and the United States provided a testing ground for Texas's military strengths—and traditional weaknesses—on a continental stage. While Texan colonial, revolutionary, and republican mounted forces had attained both regional admiration and notoriety between the Rio Grande and Red River, they remained lesser known across greater North America. Deployment of rangers as auxiliary cavalry in the Mexican War would change that. As vengeful volunteers armed with rifles and revolvers augmented the U.S. Army from the initial invasion of northern Mexico to the final occupation of Mexico City, the term *Los Diablos Tejanos*, or Texas Devils, found bloody resonance across the Mexican landscape.[1]

The onset of another nation-state war again placed Texas in strategic peril. Similar to its revolution a decade prior, this conflict compelled a return to a familiar scenario: massed confrontations with Mexico to the south and ranging along its Indian Frontier. While the Mexican War years of 1846 to 1848 again demanded short-term mobilization at the regimental scale, enduring Anglo-Indian hostility compelled numerous patrols and expeditions. From Indian preserves in Oklahoma to the urban sprawl of Mexico City, Texan volunteers served as auxiliary rangers, mounted riflemen, light cavalry, and infantry as they sought conclusions to old enmities. These expeditions occurred both independent of and in direct support of the U.S. Army, an untested factor in the Rio Grande borderland.

The War in Northern Mexico

America's invasions of Mexican territory resulted from disputes over the annexation of Texas and spanned the breadth of the continent from California to Veracruz. Initially a localized border contest, the conflict rapidly expanded to decide the fate of the entire region. By January of 1846, as tensions inflamed over who would own contested lands between the Nueces River and Rio Grande, opposing nations deployed Napoleonic armies to enforce nationalistic claims. President James Polk, already intent on provoking war to maximize the opportunity for territorial gain, accordingly ordered Brig. Gen. Zachary Taylor, through the War Department, to "advance and occupy, with the troops under your command, the east bank of the Rio del Norte."[2]

The expeditionary force that marched south under Taylor comprised just 3,550 regular infantry, artillery, and dragoons. Divided into two brigades, it represented an *ad hoc* collection of regiments and companies more accustomed to fighting Native Americans. Now coalesced as a unified division, the U.S. Army postured to engage Mexico in a combined arms campaign that emphasized professional cohesion, massed firepower, and centralized command. Though Taylor's foot and cannon formations would prove victorious in costly battles to come, the opening contest between opposing cavalries found U.S. dragoons outmatched by Mexican lancers in their historical arena.[3]

Even as American soldiers gathered opposite Matamoros, the Army of Mexico moved to defend its national honor with 5,000 men. While General Mariano Arista, a veteran of the failed reconquest of *Tejas*, would soon hold overall command, aggressive cavalry officer Anastasio Torrejon, leading approximately 1,600 lancers of the

3rd Cavalry Brigade, provided battlefield mobility. The presence of so many trained cavalrymen, which more than doubled the seven companies of the 2nd U.S. Regiment of Dragoons riding with Taylor, allowed Arista an immediate advantage in preliminary skirmishing. With such strength on hand, he soon dispatched a reconnaissance-in-force to harass the *Norte Americanos*.[4]

The Mexican-American War commenced on the night of April 25 when Torrejon's cavalry intercepted and defeated two companies of U.S. dragoons on the north side of the Rio Grande. Taylor reported that "after a short affair," meaning a decisive loss, the force of sixty-three suffered sixteen casualties and were "surrounded and compelled to surrender."[5] The proud Americans, more accustomed to fighting woodland Indians and securing migrating settlers, learned with harsh effect Mexico's historical predilection for cavalry traditions. Honed through centuries of fighting with Apache and Comanche horsemen, and now riding as nationalistic Mexican lancers, they stood far more prepared than U.S. Dragoons for confrontation.

The drums of war reverberated from the Rio Grande to Washington, D.C., as the United States mobilized for a national effort. Newspapers like the Washington *Union* quickly declared "American blood has been shed on American soil" and Congress authorized volunteers to supplement its small regular army.[6] In the combat theater to the south, Taylor likewise appreciated that his flagging dragoons would be insufficient for any large-scale offensive. Like all nineteenth-century generals he relied upon horsemen for intelligence collection, counter-reconnaissance, escort duty, communications, and if need be, decisive shock charges. The resulting crisis compelled the commander to grudgingly request augmentation by a cadre of frontiersmen who had fought the Mexican Army for decades. As the closest and most experienced auxiliaries available, he called for Texan rangers.[7]

This reluctant incorporation pitted the U.S. Army's historical aversion to unreliable volunteer troops against its acute need for a larger, more capable cavalry arm. Yet Taylor could not ignore the irreplaceable role cavalry held in Western warfare. Baron Jomini, who emphasized the necessities of combined arms synergy in Napoleonic maneuver, wrote that "an army deficient in cavalry rarely obtains a great victory, and finds its retreats extremely difficult." He also recognized the importance of mobility in offensive maneuvers, attesting that "even cavalry of an inferior character," meaning irregulars, "may be so handled as to produce very great results, if set in action at proper moments."[8]

This necessity compelled Taylor, soon promoted to major general, to overcome his aversion to unreliable volunteers. After initially only requiring that Texas maintain "a few companies of rangers" for "protection of the frontier," and disdainfully noting that Jack Hays had a "reputation as a partisan," he requested two volunteer cavalry regiments, in addition to two of infantry, from the new state governor. Federalized as Texas Mounted Rifles, the 2,000 horsemen reflected a mixture of elite rangers, Texian Army veterans, and inexperienced recruits. Despite a wide variance in their actual combat experience, they all called themselves Texas Rangers. Taylor proclaimed the augmentation would allow him to "prosecute the war with energy, and carry it, as it should be, into the enemy's country."[9]

This type of augmentation—often resulting from structural mobility deficiencies in professional armies—was common in nineteenth-century warfare. Dating back to antiquity when Romans habitually recruited mounted *auxilia* to complement their invincible infantry, great powers had frequently enlisted local horsemen for specialized roles. *Silladar*, the Native Horse of British India, offered a relevant and timely counterpart to Texan partnership with the U.S. Army in Mexico. Lord William Bentinck, a commander in British-India, wrote in 1835 that "the Irregular Cavalry ... is the favorite arm of the native. It attaches him to our Service by the strong ties of interest ... if the system were sufficiently extended it would, at a trifling expense, afford us all the advantages, moral and military, which the Russians have derived from the Cossacks."[10]

Russian Cossacks in eastern Europe offered a second variation of irregular cavalry that served similarly to Texan volunteers. Robert Wilson, a contemporary British officer, observed Cossack mastery of the austere Russian environment during the Napoleonic Wars, emphasizing that "they and their horses have alike constitutions of iron temper—no toil, no weather, no privation impairs them." He further lauded the feared warriors: "the Cossacks possess an acute intelligence and capacity which belongs only to themselves ... nothing can elude his activity, escape his penetration, or surprise his vigilance."[11]

Baron Jomini likewise praised the Russian horsemen. Despite his preference for regular army discipline, he admitted that in certain operations he could not "conclude it possible for a body of light cavalry deployed as skirmishers to accomplish as much as the Cossacks or other irregular cavalry." He then explained their "habit of moving in an apparently disorderly manner, whilst they are all the time directing their individual efforts toward a common object. The most practiced hussars can never perform such service ..."[12] This reputation for tactical effectiveness, strikingly reminiscent of praise given to Texan horsemen by American officers, positioned Cossacks among the most feared fighters in Europe.

While Texan irregulars held similarities with other volunteer traditions, their regional distinctiveness and character likewise set them apart. Luther Giddings, a volunteer Ohio officer in the Mexican War, described their inherent strengths: "He is ununiformed, and undrilled, and performs his active duties thoroughly, but with little regard to order to system." The major also referenced their unique capabilities, and value to the regulars, attesting that "their knowledge of the character of the enemy and of the military frontier, acquired in their long border struggle, rendered them valuable auxiliaries in the invasion."[13]

In addition to precision and repeating firearms that allowed tactical superiority against contemporary soldiers armed with single-shot musketry and edged weapons, Texans deployed with another advantage: excellent horsemanship. In the fall of 1845, when rangers and dragoons first mingled at Taylor's staging camp near Corpus Christi, one regular observed of the rangers: "They are teaching the United States officers and soldiers how to ride. The feats of horsemanship of our frontiersmen are extraordinary."[14] Despite his men's expertise, Hays later admitted while in central Mexico, as overheard by soldier Albert Brackett, that Mexicans were often "superior to his own men in horsemanship."[15]

This tactical mobility was facilitated by superior equine breeds that Texan ranchers had developed over the previous decades. Compton Smith, a surgeon who served in the northern occupation, described the rangers' horses in 1847 as "a cross of the mustang of the Texas plains, with the Kentucky or Virginia blood-horse." He asserted that Texas stock possessed "all the fire and endurance of the one, combined with the docility, intelligence, and speed of the other." Impressed with their performance, Smith believed this strength was "perfectly developed in the half-breed horse of the Texas Ranger." This hybrid resulted in a steed that was larger and stronger than Mexican stock, but possessed endurance superior to eastern horses.[16]

A joint patrol by rangers and U.S. Dragoons in February of 1848 provided a specific comparison between western and eastern breeds ridden by Americans in the war. Hays's regimental adjutant, John Ford, observed of the Federal mounts during a long ride in Central Mexico that "some of them gave out; others were reported to have died under the saddle." In contrast, Texas horses completed the ride without faltering. After the raid Ford noted that "a good many horses of the command were tenderfooted" and the dragoons' "remounts were furnished from the captured animals."[17]

Texan regiments that rode south of the Rio Grande over the next three years with such tactical advantages would consequently achieve outsize impact on the outcome of the war. As American armies fought across Mexico to achieve national objectives, the horsemen emerged, with conditional limitations, as the most lethal and versatile fighting forces on either side. Though tactical and strategic benefit came at high cost in terms of indiscipline and excessive brutality, rangers and mounted riflemen nevertheless augmented regulars with valuable and specialized combat skills. This unique fighting capacity, so crucially needed against a larger army with more numerous cavalry, proved generally, though by no means uniformly, helpful to the American invasions and occupations of Mexico.

The first stage of Texan ranger participation in the Mexican-American War began with Taylor's initial offensive into North Mexico from April to September of 1846. The auxiliaries' expertise in mounted reconnaissance, in addition to protecting infantry columns and logistical convoys, emerged prominently as the Americans marched into unfamiliar terrain and encountered the much larger Mexican Army. Their activities during this phase reflected functions of light cavalry in traditional European warfare as the rangers explored far ahead of the main columns to identify trafficable routes, conduct counter-reconnaissance, and report enemy presence. Texans' familiarity with desert navigation and Mexican culture, in addition to their horses' acclimatized endurance, allowed them to patrol more effectively than dragoons.

This forward intelligence collection, so critically needed to maneuver cumbersome infantry and artillery regiments, made Texas auxiliaries indispensable assets during implementation of Taylor's maneuver plan. The general later reported of Ben McCulloch, who led the most impactful reconnaissance of the campaign, that "his valuable services as a partisan, and spy, were greatly needed." He went on to note—in a rare example of regular army praise for volunteers—that "services rendered by Major McCulloch and his men, particularly in reconnoitering ... were of the highest importance."[18]

Texas's military involvement began with the deployment of individual scout companies as Taylor began to realize the scope of his inadequacy in the mounted arena. From April to August of 1846, several ranger units supported the army near the Rio Grande with reconnaissance, convoy escort, and courier duty. While these *ad hoc* companies fulfilled his initial need for mobility augmentation, Taylor soon requested an entire division of Texas volunteers comprising "four regiments of volunteers, two to be mounted and two to serve as foot." This deployment would require the largest mobilization of Texan soldiers since deactivation of the Army of the Texas Republic a decade earlier. For all intents and purposes, Texas was again at war with Mexico.[19]

Captain Samuel Walker, late of Hays's San Antonio rangers and a bitter survivor of the disastrous Mier Expedition, led the first auxiliary company to serve along the Rio Grande. After beginning service with an inauspicious start when a Mexican patrol overran his forward camp on April 27, Walker gained national fame when he reestablished communications between the American main army at Fort Isabel and a forward outpost on the Rio Grande. The action required the Texans to break through a Mexican screen that had stymied Taylor's dragoons to make contact with the beleaguered battalion. Artillery officer Abner Doubleday praised the "Gallant" Walker in his journal, writing that "in spite of the dangers and obstacles, he succeeded in executing his daring project."[20]

On May 7, 1846, Taylor decisively defeated the Mexican Army at the Battle of Palo Alto and followed with another bloody victory at Resaca de la Palma the next day. He won the first through innovative positioning of "flying artillery," or mobile light cannon, along the American frontline to fire directly into massed Mexican infantry and cavalry with devastating impact. The invaders won the second clash with a series of bloody infantry attacks that hurled back the stunned defenders. While both victories were hailed as glorious achievements, the Americans suffered approximately three hundred dead between the two engagements.

These victories, representing the first Napoleonic major engagements for the U.S. Army since the War of 1812, sparked excitement across the United States and Texas. Lieutenant Napoleon Dana, who fought with the 7th U.S. Infantry, labeled Palo Alto, in particular, as both "a horrid spectacle" and "remarkable and brilliant" while recalling how "grape and canister shot had literally mowed them down."[21] Though Texan scouts left no record of action in the battles, they immediately resumed reconnaissance duties as the shattered Mexican army retreated south.

Another irregular company under Captain John Price, a respected ranger who had led patrols in South Texas between 1841 and 1845, arrived from Victoria County shortly after the twin battles. On May 19

Taylor dispatched an *ad hoc* battalion of dragoons and rangers, including both Walker's and Price's companies, to identify the course of the Mexican retreat. Captain William Henry recalled how the mixed force followed the enemy for almost sixty miles in a remarkable feat of horsemanship. Upon making contact, the Americans "fell in with the rearguard of the army, and attacked them." The scouts suffered two wounded and then returned north to report enemy positions to Taylor.[22]

While Walker and Price patrolled throughout April and May, the Texas division mobilized to join the war. The Clarksville *Northern Standard* endorsed it with nationalistic zeal: "Texans! You now have at last a glorious opportunity of retaliating on these perfidious Mexicans ... and of carrying that war into the heart of their own country." The state's first governor, James Henderson, abdicated his office to command the division advertised as "40 companies of riflemen, 60 men each, 20 of the companies to be mounted men." In reality it would comprise four regiments: three mounted and one foot. While the Texan infantry and 3rd regiment of horse never fully engaged, the 1st and 2nd Texas Mounted Rifles would prove instrumental in capturing Monterrey.[23]

The 1st Regiment, Texas Mounted Rifles—who would garner the most fame—organized out of the embattled frontier counties of western Texas. It naturally elected Jack Hays as its colonel and voted Walker and veteran ranger Mike Chevallie as majors. Walter Lane of San Jacinto fame served as a junior officer while McCulloch commanded a company. McCulloch's unit deployed early to join Walker's and Price's units near Fort Brown on the Rio Grande and arrived ahead of the division. The 1st Texas eventually comprised over 1,000 men across ten companies.[24]

The second regiment gathered concurrent to recruitment of its western counterpart. It likewise organized ten companies out of counties across East Texas where the men elected George Wood, a wealthy plantation owner, to command. Though still inordinately lethal compared to regulars under certain conditions, the 2nd Texas never possessed the frontier edge that the 1st Texas enjoyed from recruitment amongst western communities that had borne the brunt of the state's Indian Wars.

In addition to mounted units, the Texan infantry, called the 1st Regiment of Texas Rifles, likewise formed ten companies. They elected former Texian general and Secretary of War Albert Sidney Johnston as colonel.[25] A veteran of the 2nd U.S. Infantry Regiment and the Black Hawk War prior to immigration to Texas in 1834, the Kentuckian's long military career generally belied—except for brief command of the 2nd U.S. Cavalry in 1856—the mounted arms focus of Texan peers. Johnston would later command Federal forces in the "Utah War" and, most notably, the Confederacy's Western Military Department until his death at Shiloh.

By late June the 2nd Texas had formed, marched south by grouped companies, and passed through Corpus Christi. In early August it briefly halted in Matamoros on the Rio Grande, rode west to consolidate with the army at Camargo, and arrived on August 15. The Texan division staff, led by Henderson, joined Taylor's camp a week later. The eight deploying companies of the 1st Texas with Hays lagged behind, having to travel farther from West Texas.[26]

Events continued to develop south of the Rio Grande while Texas mobilized. Taylor had already advanced west from Matamoros through-out the first and second weeks of June. McCulloch joined the main army on May 23 to provide the expedition a third company of scouts. The rangers joined Walker's and Price's men in a camp that Samuel Reid, a lawyer in McCulloch's company, compared to "a Hottentot hamlet" and an "Indian Village." On June 5 the general dispatched Price to assist the 1st U.S. Infantry Regiment's march to Reynosa sixty miles up the Rio Grande. He specifically ordered them to "escort the train on its return," again indicating reliance on auxiliaries to conduct typical dragoon duties.[27]

On June 12 McCulloch's rangers conducted a longer patrol southeast towards Linares in order to, as reported by Reid, "gain information touching the number and disposition of the enemy."

They also hoped to identify a southern approach to Monterrey that could support "the line of march for a large division, with its artillery and wagons." Wary of observation by "Mexican Spies," the rangers feinted towards Reynosa and then cut cross-country to the Linares road after night fall. After exploring routes in front of the army and finding their intended directions impassable, the scouts returned to report findings. They then set camp near the 1st U.S. Infantry at Reynosa.[28]

Taylor's use of rangers for critically important tasks indicated clear recognition of their singular capacity for forward patrolling. In one instance that revealed the advantages of regional experience that regulars lacked, McCulloch's party unexpectedly encountered a Mexican patrol. The officer deceived the enemy by greeting his opponents in Spanish before opening fire and subsequently captured a mail carrier. The rangers then read a captured Mexican map and conversed with local Mexican civilians, which provided critical knowledge concerning lack of water and forage ahead. This conversancy with the Spanish language and culture illustrated how Texans arrived with specialized skills that most regular army counterparts lacked.[29]

The army continued its march west along the Rio Grande towards Camargo, Mier, and Monterrey through early July with McCulloch's rangers diligently patrolling ahead of the vanguard. The ten companies of the 2nd Texas followed the column's trail and passed Reyonsa on July 24 while the 1st Texas continued its march from southern Texas towards Matamoros. McCulloch again provided valuable reconnaissance, this time focusing on the China Road, which offered a northern approach to Monterrey. When the rangers disqualified the road due to trafficability issues for logistical and artillery trains, Taylor reported they had "given valuable information touching on one of the routes to Monterrey."[30]

In late August the main army divisions, McCulloch's scout company, the 1st Texas Foot, and the 2nd Texas Horse consolidated around Camargo. This placed the united expedition approximately half-way to Monterrey, the provincial capital. Taylor then employed McCulloch to assess the next route, this time to Mier and Cerravlo, while reporting that the 2nd Texas were "rendering useful service as escorts." The Texas Infantry's enlistment ended while in Camargo, where Taylor disbanded the regiment. This unit's lackluster service in the war underscored Texan societal preference for mounted service over fighting afoot. McCulloch's company officially reorganized into Hays's command during this period.[31]

While the 2nd Texas supported the regular infantry with escort duty, Taylor reported the 1st Texas was "on its march from Matamoros, having taken San Fernando in its route, which passed through a part of the country not before examined." A New Orleans *Picayune* reporter traveling with Hays wrote the regiment would "take up the line of march again tomorrow and move for a town called China, about one hundred and fifty miles from this place." He also predicted that, "at China the regiment will probably join the main body of the army." Reid simply called the maneuver a "long scout." This sweep cleared a large swath of territory of enemy raiders while preventing a surprise attack against Taylor's extended southern flank.[32]

On August 19 the Americans turned southwest away from the Rio Grande and oriented on the prize of Monterrey. With two full-sized irregular cavalry regiments available, Taylor possessed the means to fully secure and scout his southwest line of march and thus move more aggressively. The general accordingly employed Hays and Woods to patrol along both sides of the army's axis of advance. He then ordered them to reunite with the army at Marin, an ideal consolidation point before attacking Monterrey.[33]

While the 1st and 2nd Texas patrolled his flanks, Taylor detached McCulloch's and Captain G.A. Gillespie's companies to explore the army's remaining route to Monterrey, again eschewing professional dragoons. The rangers patrolled southwest and arrived at the town of Cerralvo on September 5 with the lead infantry regiments close behind. American foot and cannon columns soon marched in behind the Texans and established camp. The 1st Texas skirmished against Mexican guerrillas to the south during this period. While they lost three men in the fighting, the western rangers fulfilled their guard mission.[34]

On September 15 the twin Texan regiments consolidated under Henderson as a complete volunteer division and rode to converge with the main army column at Marin. Holland recalled that "Col Hay's with about 100 men were ordered in advance as spies," indicating the elite status that the western rangers held amongst their countrymen.[35] McCulloch and Gillespie remained detached from the Texas division to directly support Taylor's advance. As the commander's trusted scouts, they patrolled ahead to meet their parent division in Marin where he would issue the final order of battle for the great assault.[36]

On September 14, while leading the American advance, McCulloch's rangers fought off a larger Mexican Lancer detachment near Marin. Reid described how the Mexicans "opened fire with their escopetas, or carbines, which was returned by our boys in a most spirited manner." He then wrote that "the Mexicans staggered under our fire and retreated into the town in the greatest confusion." As previously proven in frontier towns like Laredo on the Texas frontier, Mexican carbines and sabers proved grossly inferior to Patersons and precision rifles. With the enemy pickets now in retreat, the rangers advanced to occupy the town only twenty-five miles from Monterrey. Though just a skirmish, the engagement illustrated the Texans' firepower advantage over Mexican counterparts.[37]

The main column arrived in Marin by brigade over the next few days while Taylor once again employed trusted rangers to scout ahead, this time as his personal escort. Dana remembered that "as soon as General Taylor arrived at his camp, he and an escort of dragoons and two companies of Texan rangers went to reconnoiter the enemy's positions."[38] On September 18 Henderson's volunteer regiments arrived at the staging ground to bring Taylor's army of invasion to full strength at just over 6,000 men. For the first time in the war all twenty Texan companies rested together in one location.

The consolidated American force began its final march south towards Monterrey on September 19. Taylor ordered the "Texas mounted troops" to "form the advance ... except for two companies to compose the rearguard." This directive efficiently preserved the regulars from advance and rearguard duties and thus retained them in close readiness for the battle to come. The Texan order of march, as the army's vanguard, comprised Gillespie's company, McCulloch's company, the 1st Texas, and then the 2nd Texas. Taylor followed with a procession of professional and then volunteer infantry regiments.[39]

The consolidated weight of the invaders now advanced inexorably towards their target. As remembered by Walter Lane, the army marched "as if it were like the ocean's swell" and "formed a noble and imposing pageantry." All present were eager to participate in what they believed would be the decisive event of the war. Reid, now riding with the 1st Texas, recounted how Mexican cavalry "in proud array, with lances bright" contested the Texans' advance. Hays's regiment was soon "charging at full gallop," and the enemy was "seen to wheel and retreat towards the city."[40] When it reached the crest of a hill overlooking the city, the mounted division halted to allow engineers a final assessment of the daunting fortifications. The main column then deployed from line of march into attack formation in preparation for brigade maneuvers.

The final advance on Monterrey completed the reconnaissance phase of the rangers' role in the campaign. From Point Isabel to Monterrey, the volunteers had led the American march through 200 miles of unfamiliar and challenging terrain. They excelled at both route reconnaissance to inform the main army's advance and larger clearing patrols to protect its extended flanks. Texan horse also executed effective counter-reconnaissance by defeating lancers in forward skirmishes to deny the enemy information while preserving Taylor's options. Now, as the Americans positioned directly north of Monterrey, the irregulars prepared to demonstrate another ability. The whole army knew rangers could scout; soon they would realize Texans could also fight.

The second stage of Texan ranger operations in North Mexico encompassed the American expedition's attack against the strategic capital of Monterrey. This combined arms assault against a massively

fortified bastion illustrated the Texan volunteers' second specialized ability: close combat as both shock cavalry and infantry. While
reconnaissance and screening had required mobility, endurance,
navigation competency, and timely reporting, defeating massed
formations while mounted or afoot required lethality, audacity, and
aggression. Hays of the 1st Texas confirmed this proficiency when he
assessed rangers "as well calculated for street fighting as any body of
troops could be."[41]

The Battle of Monterrey unfolded according to a sophisticated
envelopment plan as the culmination of the 1846 invasion. When
Taylor and his engineers surveyed the Mexican defenses on September 19 and 20, they found the city well defended and fortified.
A Mexican garrison of 7,000 regulars and 3,000 militia under command of General Pedro de Ampudia held three strong points that
anchored the city's walled perimeter. In the east stood the fortified
Bishop's Palace on Independence Hill and two elevated positions
on Federacion Hill. In the north, directly in front of the American
advance, was the vaunted citadel called the Black Fort. The Santa
Catarina River protected the Mexicans' southern perimeter along
the edge of the city. Dana with the infantry called the place a "second
West Point in strength," while Doubleday in the artillery predicted
that it "must be stormed at a heavy sacrifice."[42]

Taylor chose to envelop the city from the west and east by
dividing the army, and his volunteer cavalry, into converging wings.
The 1st Texas would support Brig. Gen. William Worth's division in
a circuitous attack against the enemy's rear flank from the southwest,
while the 2nd Texas would support Brig. Gen. David Twiggs's division against the enemy's extreme right from the north. In a hazardous
strategy, Taylor intended Twiggs to distract and fix the Mexican
defense on one side while Worth penetrated and seized the city plaza
from the other. Doubleday, who marched with Worth, worried that "in
case of defeat the disaster would be overwhelming," as they "ran the
risk of being sacrificed" in detail.[43]

Worth initiated his long flank attack on the afternoon of
September 20 with the 1st Texas moving predictably as the vanguard.

Lane remembered that after hours of marching and attempting to remain outside of the range of the Black Fort, the Americans "got in the rear of the bishop's palace and camped that night." The division halted at a site called Walnut Springs and uneasily awaited the trial to come. The Mexican garrison easily observed the march and reinforced their eastern redoubts accordingly.[44]

Worth's men resumed thier march, with Hays still in the lead, at sunrise next morning. After almost two miles of marching south through undulating terrain, Reid wrote that the Texans "received a rattling fire of scopets from about five hundred of the enemy's cavalry, who had suddenly come upon us, and had taken position on the point of a hill near by." As described by Lane, "The Mexicans formed in gallant style and attacked us, under command of one of the most distinguished cavalry officers." Despite the lancers' bravery, Texan precision firepower proved too much. The frontiersmen "gave them a withering fire, emptying many a saddle, when our infantry and artillery opened on them, and in five minutes there were no Mexicans to be seen." Reid also recalled that "unerring rifles poured on them a most destructive fire," stressing the impact of superior firepower.[45]

This skirmish opened the way for a direct attack on Federacion Hill, situated at the extreme southwest of the city. Despite the facts that Texans were cavalrymen and Worth possessed two professional and several volunteer infantry regiments, he ordered the rangers to dismount and lead the assault against the heights. Accepting their new role, the volunteers set their horses aside and deployed with the 5th U.S. Infantry Regiment in support. Reid recalled the subsequent charge across the Santa Catarina River in the face of the Mexican batteries: "On we pressed, towards their murderous artillery, until we gained the bank of the rapid stream ... a terrific storm of shot and grape was now poured into our ranks."[46]

Mexican soldiers reinforced the battlements while Americans rushed upwards, making the battle a contest to gain critical mass first. Worth, sensing victory, dispatched the 7th U.S. Infantry Regiment to buttress the advance. Dana recalled the combined charge by volunteers and regulars, "Up the hill we went with a rush, the Texans ahead like devils." Reid concurrently described how "the Texians, who commenced ascending the steep and rocky cliffs" were "pouring into the enemy the fire of their deadly rifles ... as we drove back the retreating foe." He wrote that "inch by inch they disputed our ascent, until at last they gave way under our terrible fire ... we carried the height with shouts of victory."[47] Despite the success, the assault carried only the first layer of defenses: "the main work was yet to be done ... another bloody fight and more difficult and hazardous awaited them on the early morrow."[48]

The Americans cleared Federacion Hill and oriented the captured cannon against the Bishop's Palace to the north. Simultaneously, Twiggs's division attacked northeastern parts of the city on September 21. This audacious offensive required advances directly into deadly cannonade from the Black Fort. Though the costly assault failed to gain a significant foothold in the city, it did distract Ampudia's attention away from Worth's effort in the west. Holland remembered that the 2nd Texas conducted security patrols to prevent attacks by "Rancheros and Lancers" against the American rear during the first day of attacks.[49]

Worth commenced his attack against the vaunted Bishop's Palace on September 22 with a predawn assault. All involved understood that possession of this fortress would position the invaders to move against the city proper. As before, Texans and U.S. Infantry assaulted together. American firepower and bayonets then shattered a Mexican line that defended forward of the castle, while artillery pounded the fort at close range. Lane described the culminating moment that followed: "After a few discharges we made a breach in the walls, charged through, and took the palace in gallant style. The enemy retreated down to the city."[50]

The contest for Monterrey climaxed on September 23 with Americans assaulting its interior from the west and northeast. The fighting that followed was characterized by house-to-house and alley-to-alley fighting. At this time in United States history, veterans of the wars of the Texas Republic possessed more experience in urban combat than any other American demographic. While the U.S. Army had been predominantly preoccupied since the War of 1812 with woodland Indians in forested places like Florida, Alabama, and the Old Northwest, Texans had fought the Mexican Army for control of border towns like San Antonio and Laredo for decades.[51]

The Lone Star regiments attacked in the vanguard of the final American assault, marking the third offensive in which they joined lead infantry companies on foot. During the night both divisions managed to gain footholds on the city periphery by occupying abandoned houses as Mexican soldiers and civilians retreated inwards. In the morning, at first light, both wings began a vicious advance through the inner streets. Competition between Worth and Twiggs to first occupy the city plaza—and therefore reap glory in the American press—further galvanized the attack.

The climactic assault was truly terrible. American soldier T. B. Thorp observed the 2nd Texas during the battle, attesting that "it was a terrible sight, even compared to the two days of sanguinary battle of Monterrey, to witness the Texians; adopting their own mode of fighting, they soon broke into the shut up houses, scaled walls, and appeared on the housetops." He then described how they wielded "heavy axes" to break through house walls and doors to avoid "enfilading fire" and "barricades of solid masonry." With such tactics Texans inexorably fought "towards the center of the city." Thorpe also emphasized their firepower, hyperbolically claiming that "wherever a Mexican displayed himself, the deadly fire of the rifle brought him down." He comparatively assessed that "the escopet gave way before the rifle, whose unerring aim brought death on every side."[52]

A simililarly bloody advance occurred in the city's western precincts where the 1st Texas fought through urban density with similar tactics. Lane narrated his regiment's actions: "Our force, under Gen. Worth, charged down the main street, on our side, but the fire being so heavy behind the barricades they had thrown up across the street, and from the house-tops." The San Jacinto veteran then continued: "we had to take the houses on each side and go through them. Col. Hays went down the right hand, and Col. Walker on the left of the streets, fighting from house to house, and dislodging the Mexicans as we went."

Taylor's gradual envelopment proved inexorable as dispirited Mexicans gave way to the onslaught. Lane stated that "by nightfall, we had got within fifty yards of the main plaza, which was filled with their troops." After spending an uneasy night in seized positions the invaders commenced their attacks again in the morning "from the housetops, on both sides of the street, firing on them." The Mexican command finally capitulated when Twiggs's artillery began firing mortars into the congested plaza, making organized defense untenable.[53]

Texan actions in support of Taylor's assault on Monterrey perfectly illustrated the strengths of their society's way of war. The rangers' contributions during the culminating battle, learned in the brutal academy of frontier conflict, rested upon three factors: audacity, tactics, and technology. While adept maneuvering certainly facilitated rapid advancement under enemy fire, repeating revolvers and precision rifles allowed an irresistible advantage over the Mexican Army's dated musketry and blades. Memories of mass executions at the Alamo and Goliad in 1836 and Mier in 1842 then galvanized the aggressive use of these technologies. Napoleon Dana later summarized these effects when he simply stated that "our Texan riflemen told well upon the enemy."[54]

The final stage of Texan ranger service in northern Mexico reflected the U.S. Army's transition to occupation duty across a large expanse of newly conquered territory. With little hope of repelling the invaders through decisive confrontations, Mexican leadership resorted to a relentless, brutal, and highly effective guerrilla campaign. As vulnerable American convoys, outposts, and patrols came under sudden attack by patriots, partisans, and brigands, Taylor complained bitterly of widespread "murder and pillage."

In March of 1847, as violence escalated, the commander proclaimed his disgust to the Mexican people. Frustrated by an intensifying resistance, Taylor complained in a public letter that "the citizens of the country, instead of pursuing their avocations quietly at home, have in armed bands waylaid the roads, and under the direction and with the support of government troops, have destroyed trains and murdered drivers, under circumstances of atrocity which disgrace humanity." In exasperation, he called the attacks "atrocious barbarism unprecedented in the existing war" and appealed directly to "all good citizens to remain absolutely neutral."[55]

Decentralized, mobile, and unpredictable raiding challenged the U.S. Army as it assumed its foreign governance role in conquered territories. While it had excelled in linear contests against the organized Mexican Army, the raiding and harassment by partisan cavalry that predictably followed conventional victory proved almost impossible for regular, and largely infantry-centric, garrisons to quell. The asymmetric nature of these attacks demanded that irregular methods be countered by irregular soldiers. In this task, highly mobile and well armed Texan horsemen arrived well suited to counter the guerrillas.

The northern zone of occupation had expanded throughout the invasion as Taylor extended his line of march west from Matamoros to Monterrey. The rolling conquest placed numerous villages and several major towns under American military governance. The resulting requirement to pacify resistant populations and maintain constantly extending lines of communication and logistics to the United States required soldiers to implement both security and civil programs in dispersed urban centers. Governance responsibility then expanded when Taylor extended the occupation beyond Monterrey to Saltillo, another large Mexican city seventy miles to the southwest.

Following the victory at Monterrey, Taylor dismissed his two regiments of Texas Mounted Rifles. Both he and they believed the war for northern Mexico was won and volunteer augmentation no longer required. Yet in January of 1847, again lacking proficient scouts, the general reenlisted McCulloch's company to provide surveillance to the south. Throughout the next month they patrolled for the army and reported critical intelligence on the approach of a large retaliatory army under Mexico's president, Antonio Lopez de Santa Anna.

On February 22 and 23 the American force of 5,000 repelled the Mexican army of 16,000 in a costly engagement. Called the Battle of Buena Vista, McCulloch's rangers performed traditional light cavalry functions before, during, and after the engagement while earning special praise from the general.[56] Ohio officer Luther Giddings later credited "that trusty and accomplished scout, Captain McCulloch" for allowing Taylor to reposition to advantageous and defendable terrain prior to Santa Anna's arrival.[57]

After Buena Vista the occupiers' focus shifted firmly to countering Mexican guerrillas. With Santa Anna's army shattered, local leaders turned towards decentralized resistance that maximized familiarity of home ground while minimizing American superiority in firepower. Roemer evaluated such resistance from a nineteenth-century European perspective when he argued "the irregularity of the guerrilla party consists in its origin, for it is either self-constituted or constituted by the call of a single leader, not according to the general law of levy, conscription, or volunteering." The officer then emphasized that "it consists in its disconnection to the army as to its pay, provisions and movements, and it is irregular as to the permanency of the band, which may be dismissed or called together at any time."[58]

Guerrilla resistance in North Mexico culminated in February 1847 when raiders devastated a train of 200 wagons and its infantry escort. The attackers killed and mutilated almost 100 local teamsters to make clear the price of collaboration with the invaders. Compton Smith, serving along Taylor's line of communication, described the U.S. Army's challenges:

> The guerrillas had become numerous; every rancho and village contributing men to swell their ranks. Our trains were liable at any moment, while in transit, to be attacked by them. They had adopted a system of annoyances, that required the utmost vigilance of our troops, escorting them, to guard against. They had hidden rendezvous all along the road, form Camargo to Monterrey; and had spies at every rancho near the route.[59]

The frequency of sudden strikes from Saltillo to Matamoros compelled Taylor to again request Texan auxiliaries to supplement his flagging garrisons. Volunteers responded quickly, though mostly in *ad hoc* and improvised companies this time. Chevallie's Battalion emerged as the largest when it mustered three companies in Monterrey on April 25, 1847. By June the battalion owned five companies of over 100 rangers each serving across the northern theater. In accordance with decentralized counter-guerrilla assignments, they both patrolled and escorted convoys to allow both proactive and defensive protection. Mike Chevallie, late of the 1st Texas, served as nominal commander.[60]

This stage of the campaign found the Irishman Walter Lane again rising to prominence. Recently of the 1st Texas, he commanded Company A of the Texan battalion in the Saltillo and Monterrey areas. His memoir described how the federalized rangers countered enemy partisans, nationalists, and brigands in the most wantonly destructive phase of the war. One instance in particular, while Lane was working directly for Taylor out of Monterrey, revealed how the hardened partisans raided, with often indiscriminate effects, amongst the Mexican population to eliminate indigenous resistance.[61]

The mission began when Lane received orders to "go down to Ceralvo and capture or kill a band of guerrillas there, under Juan Flores." The ranger captain noted that the "guerrilla chief" had "captured several of our trains and perpetrated the most atrocious cruelties on our teamsters; and after killing them, he would have their hearts cut out and placed on their breast." Long accustomed to fighting in his state's border wars and thus trained in mounted patrolling, Lane immediately "scouted around the neighborhood of that bandit" and "found some thirty of them encamped."

The Texans immediately executed a surprise assault, reminiscent of their favored methods of destroying unsuspecting indigenous villages in Texas. Wasting no time, the rangers "charged into them" with revolvers blazing and killed eight while scattering the rest. Lane personally pursued Flores through the chaos into the town and then employed Mexican informants to track the evasive leader to his sanctuary. The attackers then cordoned the house, charged inside, and captured the elusive leader. Army authorities executed Flores at noon the next day as a deterring example to other malcontents.[62]

While American military governors sought to deter insurgency through punitive example, the Mexican resistance likewise conducted their own coercion. The brutality of nationalistic partisans like Canales and Flores warned any Mexicans inclined to assist the invaders. They knew that the isolated army required immense logistical support and hoped to starve it of civilian workers and supplies. Compton Smith accordingly emphasized that the partisans "much preferred to waylay the mule trains; as these were attended and managed by Mexican *arrieros*, who were readily intimidated."[63]

Unfortunately for the populace of northern Mexico, vengeful Texans often responded with reciprocal or instigating brutality that extended to noncombatants. Their reputation for extreme brutality and excess soon found merit and Taylor complained that "the mounted men of Texas have scarcely made one expedition without unwarrantedly killing a Mexican." He also reported, while demonstrating an understanding of the critical role of civilian populations in counter-insurgency strategy, that "there is scarcely a form of crime that has not been reported to me as committed by them ... were it possible to rouse the Mexican people to resistance, no more effectual plan could be devised than the very one pursued by some of our volunteer regiments."[64]

Already predisposed to disdain volunteers, Taylor declared the "companies of Texas horse" were the worst behaved of all American volunteers. Eventually their actions reached unmanageable violence and the frustrated general ordered that "no more troops be sent to this column by the State of Texas."[65] This decision reflected an attempt to achieve balance between security and stability so necessary for successful foreign pacification. Simply stated, Taylor valued the Texans' skills in combat, but could not afford the instability they engendered after.

Compton Smith, who observed ranger units in Mexico before and after the drive on Monterrey, made an insightful distinction between the first iteration of Texas Mounted Rifles and the volunteers who replaced them after Buena Vista. He described the first group as "genuine, brave, and hardy pioneers" who "measured arms with the Mexicans and had a just appreciation of them," while castigating the later "so-called Texas Rangers" as "adventurers and vagabonds who's object was plunder."[66]

This difference in quality was, in large part, explained by the organizational natures of different units. While the 1846 auxiliaries served in relatively centralized regiments, later Texans patrolled along geographically dispersed sectors that allowed less command supervision. Personalized leadership influence was an important factor in the discipline of various companies. Commanders like Jack Hays deployed to Mexico with significant supervisory experience on the Texas frontier, while most of the later counter-insurgency leaders had only served as militia volunteers and low-ranking rangers. In terms of sheer lethality, Smith stated that all rangers were the "very devils incarnate."[67]

The controversial Texans departed the northern theater of occupation in the summer of 1848. Despite Taylor's wish to be rid of troublesome rangers, the battalion, now under Lane's nominal command, remained in service till close of the war. This final period coincided with a similar counter-guerrilla campaign by a new regiment under Hays in Central Mexico. The resulting service, though highly destructive to civilians and property, assisted the U.S. Army in forcing advantageous terms on the defeated Mexican government.[68] With the fate of Texas decided, and a massive annexation of land by the United States from Texas to California enforced, the Mexican War was over.

Lane's auxiliary cavalry supplanted U.S. dragoons one last time before departing for Texas. As American regiments under Taylor's replacement, Brig. Gen. John Wool, evacuated Saltillo and Monterrey to conduct long marches home, he ordered rangers to occupy "the post of honor, to bring up the rear." As the most viable mounted force at hand, the general required the Texans to "send in all stragglers" while guarding infantry and supply columns against opportunistic attacks.[69]

American occupation forces concentrated at Camargo to gain ship transport to the coast as they streamed in from the Mexican interior. While there Lane attended a final officer banquet aboard a steamship, where Wool surprised all present by toasting the ranger's health and thanking him for services "rendered to Gen. Taylor and himself." The commander praised the Texans' unique ability to rapidly deploy, in particular, stating they were "in the saddle en route" within forty minutes of receiving any order.[70] Such public praise from a "strict martinet" of the regular army to rough volunteers offered a fitting conclusion for their tour in northern Mexico. With their obligations complete, the Texans mustered out of active service on June 29 and 30 and headed for home.[71]

The War in Central Mexico

The Mexico City Campaign offered further opportunity for Texas to fight in a confrontation of much larger scope than previously experienced. It also allowed the auxiliaries to again prove their tactical effectiveness in direct contrast with both American dragoons and Mexican lancers. This volunteer mobilization, similar to those in North Mexico, was necessitated by the U.S. Army's deficiency in battlefield mobility. The need for augmentation arose in the spring of 1847, at the height of the conflict, when Lt. Gen. Winfield Scott led an invasion of the heart of Mexico. Not content with limited victories in northern provinces, Polk hoped an offensive into the Mexican interior would compel territorial concessions.

Despite a dearth of dragoons, the initial invasion went very well for the invaders. On April 18, after seizing the Atlantic port of Veracruz and then marching inland, the expedition won a decisive victory at the Battle of Cerro Gordo.[72] With superior cannon and infantry, Scott shattered another national army led by Santa Anna. Despite the strategic triumph, the general soon complained from his forward outpost at Jalapa, a town along the road to Mexico City, of "bands of exasperated rancheros" fomenting decentralized resistance. A veteran of many wars, the sixty-one-year-old officer speculated that Mexicans were resorting to "the guerrilla plan."[73]

Scott's fears proved correct as the defeated Mexican elite embraced the timeless resistance strategy of all occupied societies: guerrilla warfare. Pedro Maria Anaya, now substitute president in Mexico City, swiftly recognized that the U.S. Army's vulnerability lay in the unconventional arena. On April 28 he accordingly decreed the creation of a decentralized, national system of partisan resistance. Santa Anna confirmed this strategy when he declared intent to "harass the enemy's rear in a sensible manner."[74] If Mexico could not win through decisive confrontation, it would isolate and destroy the American army with patriotic savagery.[75]

The resulting resistance perfectly exploited the invaders' geographical and structural weaknesses. Expanding distances between the American logistical center at Veracruz, interspaced garrisons, and the army's forward line of march provided an ideal opportunity to attack and punish the foreigners in detail. While Scott possessed well-trained infantry and artillery arms for set-piece battles, he lacked adequate cavalry to protect critical supply and reinforcement columns marching west from Veracruz.

Mexican aristocrats enthusiastically embraced the call for guerrilla resistance as war progressed throughout spring of 1847. As noted by Pennsylvanian John Jacob Oswandel in his journal, General Jose Marion Solas announced an official "Guerrilla Corps" to "attack and destroy the Yankee's invading army in every way imaginable." Officially designated the Light Corps for its light cavalry composition, the mobilization comprised localized formations riding against isolated American garrisons and columns. Mexican nationalists, who took up the battle-cry "War without Pity," unleashed the same merciless raiding that won independence from Imperial Spain just two-score years prior.[76]

By the fall of 1847 Scott's vulnerability and occupation challenges more than doubled with his inexorable westward march and stunning capture of Mexico City. The strained American army of nearly 24,000 now relied upon an embattled chain of fortified outposts, stretching 260 miles from capital to coast. As Washington and exiled Mexican officials failed to negotiate an armistice, the resistance gained momentum and threatened to reverse the United States' strategic gains. To remedy this untenable scenario, Scott, like Taylor before him, called for specialized fighters to counter the Light Corps. For the bloody task at hand, he needed rangers.[77]

The pivotal summer of 1847 thus provided an opportunity for Texan frontier cavalry to again gain national recognition. Even as Texas suffered raids by Comanche to the west, the U.S. Army struggled with protracted occupations across the Monterrey and Mexico City regions. The overwhelmed U.S. Dragoons divided between Taylor and Scott could not hope to match the superior quantity and quality of Indian and Mexican cavalry arrayed against them. Caperton lamented the ensuing instability, noting that "Mexican guerrillas were very active in robbing, murdering and committing depredations of various kinds." With security unraveling across the massive American front, it became apparent that Texas auxiliaries would again have to make the difference.[78]

The War Department in Washington, D.C. responded to the crisis. It authorized the Lone Star State, with its readily available reservoir of frontier veterans, to raise another "Regiment of Texas Mounted Volunteers for twelve months and during the war."[79] Jack Hays was naturally selected to command the ten companies as colonel. Peter Bell, a ranger who would supervise Texas's Indian Frontier during the war, signed on as executive officer. Taylor, who yet commanded in the northern theater, ordered Hays to "leave such a force as the Governor of Texas may deem necessary for protection of the frontier" under Bell, and then to "proceed with the remainder of his command (say five companies) to Mier."[80] With irregulars deploying north and south, the American leadership hoped to increase security on both the Indian and Mexican fronts.[81]

The new regiment departed from San Antonio on August 12, 1847, to serve in Mexico. Hays led half of the regiment, consisting of five robust companies and officially designated the 1st Regiment of Texas Mounted Volunteers. He originally intended to reinforce Taylor along the Rio Grande, but the guerrilla crisis in Central Mexico compelled the War Department to redirect him to Scott. The Secretary of War, under pressure from Scott for assistance, ordered Hays to "proceed to Vera Cruz with such of his command as can be spared, for the purpose of dispersing the guerrillas which infest the line between that place and the interior of Mexico."[82]

The men who rode south under Hays comprised rangers from South Texas, veterans from the old Texian army and militia, and auxiliaries from the recent Monterrey Campaign. His ranks also included inexperienced recruits who required training in military cohesion and discipline. Composed of 110 to 130 men each, the companies held letter designations of E, F, G, I, and K, and hailed predominantly from Shelby, La Grange, Washington, Rusk, Dallas, and Fannin counties. Captains Alfred Truett, Jacob Roberts, G. M. Armstrong, Isaac Ferguson, and Stephen Kinsey served as commanders. Hays and a small staff that included an adjutant, surgeon, and later an executive officer, provided a skeletal regimental headquarters.[83]

One of Hays's staff officers, in particular, emerged historically important for documenting ranger contributions to the Mexico City Campaign. John Salmon Ford, who served as adjutant throughout the deployment, provided the most comprehensive, if overly favorable, memoir about the regiment's patrolling and raiding across the central Mexican plateau. His position directly under Hays, while coordinating the five companies, allowed an ideal vantage to observe both commander and subordinates in action.[84]

Throughout August and September the volunteers rode south through Laredo, crossed the Rio Grande, passed through Mier, and camped near Matamoros. After waiting eight days for naval transport, they moved to Point Isabel on the Gulf Coast for embarkation. The regiment then shipped out by individual company at the port of Brazos de Santiago between October 5 and 17. Ford remembered that some worried apprehensively of challenges ahead. The adjutant, who had previously worked as a newspaper editor, wrote that "they presented the dangers of campaigning in the interior of Mexico as very numerous" and worried that "the valleys of Mexico were little better than graveyards."[85]

Hays sailed with the final transport after ensuring each company had departed for the combat theater. The volunteers paused in Louisiana en route to their final destination of Veracruz on the Mexican Atlantic seaboard. As the Texans passed through a neighboring state that had long held sympathies for the cause of Texas, the New Orleans *Picayune* approved of mobilization: "The Rangers are the very men for these guerrillas ... Jack Hays is a remarkable man, as useful to his country as he is modest and independent." The paper also attested—while revealing how rangers had gained fame, and in some circles notoriety, beyond Texas—that the volunteers were "worth four times their number of any other mounted men" that the writer had seen.[86]

The regiment arrived at Veracruz by company, with captains Ferguson and Truitt in the lead. According to Ford, who shipped with the advance, the rangers encamped at the village of Vergara "three miles from Vera Cruz on the road to Jalapa," which positioned them dangerously forward of the protection of the walled city. He then explained that "the Mexican guerrilla bands were giving considerable trouble outside the walls of Veracruz." This constant harassment around Central Mexico's primary port made any westward march by reinforcement columns extremely hazardous. With Texas partisans on site, renewed enmity between the former colony and empire was now imminent.[87]

The Texans viewed this asymmetric raiding with naked contempt after encountering it for decades on their frontiers. Caperton, who heard of the campaign directly from Hays, endorsed their perspective with clear ethnic bias when he wrote of Mexicans: "a more depraved, unprincipled and unfeeling set of men were never banded together." He also disdainfully claimed they "were destitute of courage," revealing typical

Texan condescension. In reality, the Mexican resistance emerged as a haphazard endeavor that included both state-sanctioned cavalry and opportunistic brigands, often blurring lines between patriotic raiding and marauding theft. Despite the rangers' contempt, guerrillas often fought with exceptional bravery and usually suffered only from inferior weaponry.[88]

Brigadier General Robert Patterson, ranking American officer on the coast, immediately launched the Texans to fulfill their purpose of enlistment. He informed the eager rangers of a "place of resort for the irregular forces of Mexico" at the "hacienda of San Juan" located about thirty miles from the city. The frustrated commander complained that guerrillas under command of a leader known as Colonel Zenobia had been "particularly troublesome." Without adequate mounted support, Americans in Veracruz had been forced to endure Zenobia's harassment.[89]

The next day, despite Patterson's skepticism concerning their ability to "penetrate the country and do effective service," the Texans tracked and attacked the guerrillas at their ranch. Just as in Texas, revolving pistols allowed deadly overmatch against opponents armed with archaic muskets and swords. Ford recorded that "two or three of the guerrillas were killed" while admitting "the balance escaped."[90] The Texans then burned the establishment, but not before "some nice things were taken from Colonel Zenobia's house." After returning to Veracruz, during which "other little affairs occurred" that included killing a Mexican officer, they proudly boasted "credit of having marched sixty miles that day."[91]

This action set precedent for the human and infrastructure destruction that would make Texan volunteers notorious across Central Mexico. Ford remembered that Patterson advised them "they might have trouble over the house burning," fearing a violation of Scott's pacification policy.[92] This warning recognized the commanding general's relatively sophisticated occupation strategy that appreciated Mexican civilians as an element to be courted and mollified. While he intended to defeat the national army and guerrillas to force terms on the ruling class, the veteran strategist, who studied Napoleon Bonaparte's difficulties with military occupation in Spain, hoped to gain support, or at least exploit the apathy, of Mexican churches and commoners.[93]

Scott summarized anxiety about the effect volunteer soldiers, including rangers, would have on the occupation:

> With steady troops, I should not doubt the result; but the great danger lies in the want of that quality on the part of the new reinforcements, including the recruits of the old regiments. The average number of disorders and crimes, always committed by undisciplined men, with inexperienced officers, may destroy the best concerted plans, by exasperating the inhabitants, and rendering the war, on their part, national, interminable, and desperate.[94]

Despite hopes for conciliation, the general also understood the core of the Mexican resistance, the Light Corps, could only be countered through reciprocal violence. This was where rangers complemented the strategic equation: the regular army would garrison urban centers along the Veracruz Road with a focus on governance, while Texans would counter guerrillas with merciless savagery. Scott accordingly ordered Hays to "give attention to these guerrillas ... fighting them whenever he could find them and keeping the roads clear of them." This plan held the added advantage of freeing dragoons for escort duties.[95]

As Taylor had learned in the north, any strategy that incorporated partisans held great risks. In hi memoirs, Scott recalled "wild volunteers" who committed "all sorts of atrocities on the persons and property of Mexicans" in the northern theater. As exemplified by their first raid at Veracruz, the question remained: would rangers defeat the guerrillas at the cost of catalyzing popular support for the resistance? The answer would unfold over the coming months as they executed punitive aspects of Scott's nuanced occupation plan.[96]

By late October Hays and the entire regiment had arrived at Veracruz. After advance companies drove away the local resistance, the regiment received a marked upgrade in weaponry from the U.S. Army Ordinance Department. They drew 280 Walker Colt revolvers in two consignments to augment the Patersons that many possessed. Acquisition of these much more powerful .44 caliber hand-guns—which had been jointly designed by ranger Samuel Walker and manufacturer Samuel Colt after the Monterrey Campaign—reflected one of the first instances of fielding new technology to an ongoing American war.[97]

The unlikely collaboration resulted in the Model 1847 Army Pistol. Unlike the Paterson, it required just a cylinder exchange to reload instead of complete disassembly and consequently allowed rapid reloading while mounted. Ford wrote that in a "trial between the Mississippi rifle and the six-shooter," the Walker Colt "threw the ball a greater distance than the rifle." He also attested that "with the improved revolvers we felt confident we could beat any number the enemy could bring to bear upon us," offering an explanation for extremely aggressive tactics that would have placed conventionally armed cavalry in untenable danger.[98]

The new revolvers allowed Hays's men a superiority of lethality over all other soldiers in the Mexican-American War, save for Walker's company of U.S. Mounted Rifles who also received an allocation. Walker boasted that "there is not an officer who has seen them but what speaks in the highest terms of them," and attested that "all of the Cavalry officer are determined to get them if possible." He further declared that with such an arsenal he could "soon clear the Road of all these bands between this and Vera Cruz."[99] The differential in repeating capacity practically allowed a single Texan with two revolvers to discharge the firing volume of ten soldiers. Albert Brackett of the 4th Indiana Volunteer Regiment attested that "a hundred of them could discharge a thousand shots in two minutes."[100]

On November 2 the Texas Mounted Volunteers, now 580 strong with new revolvers and better horses, moved west into the Mexican interior while securing a large reinforcement column. They soon passed the famous National Bridge and arrived in Jalapa, one of Scott's outposts. Soldier John Oswandel in the town garrison observed the

Texans' arrival with the brigade: "next came Col. Jack Hays with five companies of mounted Texan rangers, and we gave him three good cheers." He also praised their horses and weapons, stating "they are a fine body of men and well mounted, with six-shooting rifles."[101]

This praise indicated that the rangers' reputation preceded them. Daniel Harvey Hill of the 4th U.S. Artillery at Puebla agreed in his journal on November 14 when he assessed that "the Guerrilleros have pretty much abandoned the road frightened by the knowledge of the arrival of Col. Hays' Regiment of Texas Rangers." The lieutenant further explained that "a private carriage reached here two days ago all the way from Vera Cruz having come through without the slightest interruption." In a comment that revealed how costly the insurgency had become, Hill noted how it was "considered a wonderful feat."[102]

Hays continued west with two companies while the rest of the regiment remained at Jalapa under his second-in-command, Chevallie. He soon arrived in Puebla, the occupied city approximately half-way between capital and coast. The other companies remained in the vicinity of Jalapa to clear the area of guerrillas. In this decentralized setting, their inordinately large rosters proved extremely beneficial by allowing each unit to patrol independently, buttressed by outsized firepower, while covering more ground.

The American occupation of Puebla had proved tenuous in recent months. According to Brackett, the isolated garrison had "been besieged for a long time by the Mexicans" and "was in a famishing condition." Loss of this outpost would have severed Scott's line of communication and supply with Veracruz, hence Santa Anna's determination to seize it. With the garrison near defeat, a reinforcement brigade rushed from Veracruz to relieve Puebla and soundly defeated Santa Anna on October 9 at the Battle of Huamantla.[103] Americans under the command of Brig. Gen. Joseph Lane subsequently destroyed the town and accosted civilians in retribution for the death of Samuel Walker who fell leading the U.S. Mounted Rifles. Daniel Hill of the 4th U.S. Artillery Regiment condemned the lawlessness: "'Twas then I saw and felt how perfectly unmanageable were volunteers and how much harm they did."[104]

The relief column that won at Huamantla emerged as an independent counter-guerrilla brigade which Scott unleashed to secure his line of communication. When Hays arrived in Puebla he naturally joined Lane to allow it unprecedented speed and lethality. This merge would terrorize Mexican partisans, and civilians, through the occupation. As remembered by Brackett, the task force initially comprised "five companies of Texas Rangers, Lewis' company of Louisiana cavalry, the 4th Ohio, and 4th Indiana Volunteers." Because of mobility requirements to pursue mounted lancers, the unit later shifted to a purely mounted regiment and left its infantry to guard occupied towns along the Veracruz Road.[105]

Hays and Lane quickly formed an effective partnership. On November 20 they moved to strike a guerrilla encampment at the town of Izucar de Matamoros, which reportedly held American captives. Brackett explained that the enemy's "numbers were considerable" and that they "continued to infest the neighborhood ... frequently killing our soldiers." Leaving an infantry regiment to secure Puebla, Lane led a mounted battalion of rangers, riflemen, and dragoons for the attack. Brackett, who remained in Puebla, claimed the force was "all well mounted" and contained 160 men. Lane towed light cannon to increase firepower.[106]

The Americans rode through the night to reach the enemy stronghold by morning. Brackett recorded "a sudden and rapid charge was made into the town" immediately upon arrival.[107] Ford recounted the bloody clash that followed when "a heavy forced march carried them upon the enemy at daylight. A fight came off, and the Americans were victorious. They killed a good many Mexicans, captured artillery, small arms, and ammunition." More importantly, they "recaptured fifteen American prisoners."[108] The raiders reportedly killed or wounded "sixty or eighty of the enemy" while "capturing three pieces of artillery."[109]

Despite the battalion's successful attack, the return march proved more challenging. They had seized military equipment and supplies from the town and were thus slowed from their normally swift gait. According to Lane's report on the affair, as preserved by Brackett, a Light Corps regiment seized the opportunity to attack the smaller American column when "the train was considerably extended" in a "long mountain pass." Since Texans were the most heavily armed soldiers present, Hays and his men quickly rode ahead to ward off the attack.[110]

The rangers immediately "charged the enemy to the teeth" with revolvers blazing. They engaged 200 Mexican lancers in a running fight that led to an ambush by another 300 guerrillas. Severely outnumbered, the Texans expended their remaining ammunition as they held their ground until Lane could move field cannon up to disperse the enemy.[111] Brackett recounted that "a few rounds poured into the head of the Mexican column of lancers, changed their direction very suddenly and relieved the brave Texans from imminent danger."[112] Lane subsequently praised Hays in his report to Scott, writing that "never did any officer act with more gallantry than Colonel Hays in this affair."[113]

Aggressive patrolling by rangers soon brought the resistance in the Puebla and Jalapa areas to manageable levels for local garrisons. Their initial purpose fulfilled, Scott ordered Hays to join him in Mexico City. Guerrilla bands were severely disrupting the capital region, and given his dearth of mounted companies, the general required augmentation by fleet forces. With victories and a growing reputation in hand, the Texans followed the Veracruz road west to offer service in the capital district. Throughout the march they continued to secure Patterson's volunteer infantry column.

The Texas Mounted Volunteers arrived in Mexico City on December 6, 1847, causing "a sensation among the inhabitants." The capital had thus far uneasily accommodated occupation by American regulars and volunteers, but had yet to encounter the feared rangers. Upon their arrival Ford recalled how fascinated Mexican citizens "thronged the streets along which we passed," and that "the greatest curiosity prevailed to get a sight of 'Los Diablos Tejanos,' the Texas Devils."[114] One newspaper correspondent, according to Caperton, called their arrival the "greatest of American curiosities that have as yet entered the City of the Aztecs."[115]

The Texans' exotic appearance bolstered their fearsome reputation. The reporter described "old-fashioned maple stock rifles lying across their saddles, the butts of two large pistols sticking out of the holsters, and a pair of Colt's six-shooters belted round their waists," allowing ready armament of "fifteen shots per man." Another account, by an unnamed reporter, explained how "they rode some sideways, some standing upright, some by the reverse flank, some faced to the rear, some on horses, some on asses, some on mustangs, some on mules." This ostentatious display, obviously intended to intimidate and impress, revealed the psychological aspects of the Texans' success. According to Caperton, they aimed to "prove to the world at a glance that they are neither regulars nor volunteers, but Texas Rangers."[116]

Despite the novelty of seeing outlandish Texans up close, curiosity soon turned to terror. Ford recalled an incident where a ranger killed a Mexican civilian for hitting him with a small rock. The Texan shot the man with a rapid draw of his pistol and caused a "stampede" of the crowd where more civilians were injured and died. For men who had lost relatives and friends in Santa Anna's massacres at the Alamo, Goliad, and Mier, and doubtlessly embraced racial antipathy towards Hispanics, there was little compunction with killing enemy civilians and combatants alike.[117]

The longer Texans resided in the sprawling city, the more residents died from ranger brutality. Ford remembered that every morning "three to five Americans were found dead in the streets of a morning" due to "assassin's knife," indicating simmering discontentment in the capital. The casualty count then exploded when a "murderous crowd" killed Adam Allsens, a ranger who had strayed alone into precincts inhabited by "lower orders." Ford reported the Texans' "outburst of revenge" resulted in "more than eighty bodies lying in the morgue." With tensions rising in the capital, it was past time for the volatile auxiliaries to refocus on hunting fleet guerrillas. Ever mindful of his conciliation policy, Scott hoped they would cause less harm away from urban centers.[118]

Despite Lane and Hays's earlier successes, Mexican resistance gained intensity along the American line as the New Year approached. On December 12, 1847, Scott proclaimed that "the highways of Mexico, used or about to be used by the American troops" were "still infested in many parts by those atrocious bands called Guerrillas and Rancheros." He accused "late Mexican authorities" of promoting violence that continued to "violate every rule of warfare observed by civilized nations." Seeking to adopt a more proactive posture, the jaded general resolutely ordered his dispersed garrisons to "daily push detachments or patrols as far as practicable, to disinfest the neighborhood, its roads and places of concealment."[119]

This directive indicated that instability across the central plateau had become critical, while revealing the command's rising frustration. The resistance now forced the army to dedicate over 25 percent of its strength solely to counter-guerrilla and convoy escort duties. Over the next six weeks the Texas Mounted Volunteers accordingly pursued known partisan leaders farther into their support areas. This mission drew upon strengths unique to rangers since they alone possessed specialized horsemanship and firepower required to locate and defeat resistance captains in remote haunts.

Hays first pursued a Catholic padre named Celedonia de Jarauta who had risen as a popular and inspirational guerrilla commander. The rangers followed him to San Juan Teotihuacan just twelve miles from the capital. Upon arrival they immediately attacked the padre with a company at the town center. Ford remembered the audacious Mexican counter-attack that followed: "the cavalry probably seventy-strong, charged across the plaza upon on our quarters." The lancers hit the Texans with several charges in the city plaza, but as in previous engagements, superior firepower won the day. Hays also used men with precision rifles on rooftops to attrite Mexican riders. The cross-fire by cavalry and snipers killed fifteen and wounded five, yet the "priest-general," as referred to by Ford, escaped with wounds.[120]

The militant padre's reputation grew the longer he fought as a patriot against foreign occupation. On January 13, in a message to the War Department, Scott described the "guerrilla priest, Jarauta, at the head of a small band that has long been the terror of all peaceable Mexicans within his reach … he has frequently had skirmishes with our detachments." The frustrated general also noted that "Colonel Hays, with a detachment of Texan rangers" had returned from their recent foray against the "robber priest." The fact that Scott cited both Jarauta and Hays in official reports indicated how seriously he perceived guerrilla menace—and means to counter it—as factors in his occupation designs.[121]

On January 18 the Texans again united with Lane's command to pursue enemy leaders. The Americans again aimed to neutralize Jarauta and another partisan, General Mariano Paredes, who were "in charge of guerrilla forces and giving trouble." According to Caperton, Lane intended to "pursue these guerrillas in the mountains, attack them in their own retreats and strongholds where they lived with their families and their plunder, and to break them up if possible."[122] The *ad hoc* regiment comprised over a 1,000 men, including 250 rangers, 130 dragoons, and an allied "Mexican Lancer Regiment." Inclusion of Hispanic "contra-guerrillas" revealed an adept and pragmatic integration of indigenous fighters to enhance the foreigners' lack of geographical and cultural familiarity.[123]

The hunters arrived at the target city of Tulancingo at dawn, reflecting their preference for night marches to gain surprise. Ford recorded that "at an early hour in the morning the Americans dashed into Tulancingo, and were directed to the house of Paredes." A dragoon officer immediately demanded that a civilian show him the home of the general. Once located, a man thought to be Paredes, who was actually the chief's brother, distracted the Americans while the real patriot escaped. As so often happens in foreign invasions and occupations, indigenous wile had again defeated military might.[124]

Santa Anna, former president and perennial enemy of all Texans, offered the next target. The Americans first moved east to Puebla to resupply and then rode forty miles to Tehuacan, where they narrowly missed him. The potential apprehension or death of this man offered an especially gratifying objective for rangers who blamed him for massacres of their countrymen at the Alamo, Goliad, and Mier. Brackett described how the raiders cordoned and cleared the town:

As the command came to the entrance of the town, the dragoons and rifles dashed to the right and left, and in a few minutes every outlet was stopped; and the Texan rangers galloped ahead toward the plaza, with their revolvers cocked, glancing warily on every side, with the belief and hope that the enemy was on the house-tops. The rangers in the plaza formed into squads, and galloped through every street, but no enemy was found.[125]

The efficiency by which the task force isolated and cleared Tehuacan reflected the internal coordination they had achieved after months of patrolling. Still hopeful, the regiment rode next to another suspected hide-out at Orizaba, but again failed to capture Santa Anna. The Americans occupied the city for a week while they flushed out another guerrilla leader, Manuel Falcon, at the town of San Juan de Teotihuacan. Yet the Americans missed him too, further illustrating the difficulties of locating partisans amongst sympathetic populations.[126]

The frustrated hunters returned to Mexico City to resupply. On February 17 they launched another raid against Mariano Paredes and Padre Jarauta. Relying on informants, the Americans rode hard for seventy-five miles to reach the city of Tulancingo northeast of Mexico City. Lane attempted to avoid previous mistakes during the final approach by dispatching "rapid movement of a small portion of my force, to surprise the town." Upon arrival, the advance element, naturally led by Hays, learned that Jarauta had been absent for two days and Paredes had just escaped.[127]

The relentless horsemen pursued the wily padre to Sequalteplan, a town seventy-five miles north of Tulancingo, on the advice of a local turncoat. Riding through the night, the dragoons and rangers arrived at dawn the next morning with exhausted horses. Lane reported the tactical sequence that immediately unfolded: "With the Texas rangers in advance, I marched my force with a rapid charge upon the town." The veteran commander countered "a heavy fire" from a housing area with one company, while sending another to engage enemy in the town plaza.[128]

The attacking companies initially became separated between buildings, but according to Lane, soon managed to break opposing Mexican lancers and infantry with a charge "gallantly led by the officers." He emphasized the "fatal effect" of the Texans' "unerring rifles" while describing how at one point the contest was fought at a distance of thirty feet, or "muzzle to muzzle," until it "became necessary to make a charge."[129] Ford attested they killed over 150 enemy soldiers and captured another 50. Jarauta once again escaped but "did not recover from his defeat at Zacualtipan sufficiently to give the Americans much trouble during the continuance of hostilities." Ford praised him as "brave and energetic."[130]

This battle ended as the Texas Mounted Volunteers' last significant fight in Mexico. Like previous victories, success stemmed from superior firepower and relentless audacity. After consolidating their wounded the raiders reported to Mexico City to receive instructions and resupply. Each man carried a captured lance as they rode through the capital streets in a visible demonstration of martial prowess. Over the past six weeks the rangers had spent five on patrol while riding more than 900 miles, a remarkable feat for horsemen of any era.[131]

By spring of 1848, due to a combination of Scott's nuanced policies and the reestablishment of a provisional Mexican government, guerrilla attacks lessened against American garrisons. Diplomacy had taken center stage and combatants on both sides understood the invader's exit was now inevitable. The Texas Mounted Volunteers completed their duty in Mexico with a final patrol down the Veracruz road to ensure a safe withdrawal for the garrisons. This task, usually the domain of professional cavalry in Western warfare, revealed the degree which frontier auxiliaries had supplanted U.S. Dragoons in Scott's operations.

The Texan regiment participated in a final incident, largely anecdotal, before departing for home. On March 28, 1848, the rangers encountered their hated enemy, Santa Anna, while he and his wife conducted a sanctioned exit from Mexico. A tense moment occurred when Hays and the self-styled "Napoleon of the West" met at a dinner party in Jalapa, where Santa Anna traveled under American protection. According to the escort officer, Major John Kenly, the failed president's "whole appearance and demeanor changed" and he kept "his gaze on the table" when confronted with the famed colonel who had become the scourge of Mexico.[132]

Tensions continued later that night when Santa Anna left in a carriage for the coast and exile. Ford restrained his men from killing the despot who had, as claimed by the adjutant, "waged an inhuman and un-Christian war upon the people of Texas" and "murdered prisoners of war in cold blood." The rangers instead lined the road to silently glare while Hays personally escorted the party to ensure none under his command would "dishonor Texas." Their last duty complete, the Texans mustered out in Veracruz and shipped for home. After seven months of rigorous combat the controversial volunteers had completed their mission in Central Mexico.[133]

Texan Auxiliaries: A Double-Edged Sword

Texas emerged from the Mexican-American War in the summer of 1848 with one of the most effective martial traditions in North America. After two decades of tactical evolution that emphasized short-term mobilization and interested volunteerism— and despite a proportional decline in citizen participation when compared to colonial and revolutionary mobilizations—its inspired way of war achieved full maturity. With unmatched firepower and expert horsemanship, Texans demonstrated unique tactical versatility across diverse landscapes. Building on tactical achievements at places like Plum Creek, Salado Creek, Walker Creek, and Monterrey, the string of ranger victories in Central Mexico culminated years of frontier development.

This combat record earned the volunteers grudging respect even from the regular army establishment. Caperton recorded that Scott "regarded Col. Hays and his men as invaluable" and "gave them great credit for their active and efficient services in suppressing the guerrillas."[134] Without specialized counter-guerrilla capabilities stemming from advanced firepower and mobility, Mexican resistance may have degraded the U.S. Army in the interior and ultimately weakened the American diplomatic position. From Veracruz to Mexico City, and across northern environs, federalized rangers held an important role in achieving strategic victory.

These wartime contributions resulted in two profound legacies that shaped the enduring Texas Ranger tradition. The first reflected their enviable fighting reputation amongst militaries in North America. Caperton emphasized this tactical prowess, with embellishment, when he boasted they could "run on foot like deer for long distances, and could fight equally well on foot or on horseback, and in either case could discharge their weapons while going at full speed, and with good effect."[135] Giddings, an outside observer, described Texans as "chivalrous, bold and impetuous in action. ... yet wary and calculating, always impatient of restraint, and sometimes unscrupulous and unmerciful." The Ohioan further praised the individual Texan volunteer as "an excellent rider and a dead shot," while noting that their arms were "a rifle, Colt's revolving pistol and a knife."[136]

While partisans like Caperton and Sam Houston certainly held a cultural bias and professional interest towards inflating Texan military skills—a common inclination across Lone Star society—documented military successes since Hays's 1844 victory at Walker Creek endorsed tactical effectiveness more objectively. Largely due to fortuitous adoption of innovative repeating firearms before and during the Mexican-American War, Lone Star horsemen had countered the Comanche, bested the Mexican Light Corps, and habitually supplanted U.S. Dragoons. The *Hartford Daily Times* endorsed this tactical superiority, if only conditionally, when it referred to rangers as the "best light troops in the world" while praising Hays's leadership.[137]

Declarations of exceptional military ability, though highly conditional, rested upon comparative tactical achievements in Mexico. When Taylor needed critical reconnaissance, he repeatedly sent Texan scouts forward. When Worth called for troops to assault Monterrey, Texan regiments led the crucial advance. And finally, when military occupation required counter-guerrilla expertise, commanding generals unleashed Texan irregulars in separate theaters. In each instance, frontier auxiliaries replaced or augmented professionals to provide crucial service. Volunteer James Holland, riding with the 2nd Texas during the march on Monterrey, described this reliance succinctly: "Texas went ahead today—now that danger is expected old Taylor has put us in front."[138]

The second legacy of Texas's wartime contributions reflected darker aspects of its culture, and by extension, its way of war. Recognizing the extreme brutality, even Caperton admitted that "rangers were the terror of the Mexicans *all* throughout the war."[139] As he watched Hays's and Wood's regiments depart Monterrey Giddings denounced their "lawless and vindictive spirit" and sympathetically hoped that "all honest Mexicans were at a safe distance from their path."[140] Hill likewise noticed Texan proclivity for violence against noncombatants. Before ever meeting Hays's men on the Veracruz road, the lieutenant "heard dreadful stories of their excesses on the road." The future Confederate general later attested that "atrocities" in the central theater were committed "principally by Col. Hays' Regiment of Texans" and accused them of "murder, rape and robbery" in the "broad light of day."[141]

Senior commanders who requested ranger augmentation echoed this criticism. As Texan regiments discharged Federal service after seizing Monterrey, Taylor hoped that "with their departure we may look for a restoration of quiet and order." As the exasperated general sought to stabilize relations with local Mexicans he lamented the "shameful atrocities" counterproductively "perpetuated by them since the capitulation of the town."[142] Scott likewise personally admonished Hays for the chaos his men caused in Mexico City.[143] Unfortunately, this ethnic and racial violence would continue over coming decades with the despoliation of natives and *Tejanos* across Texas, and most notoriously, in the execution of hundreds of captured black Union soldiers during the Civil War.[144]

In the final assessment, considering all the bravado and recriminations, Texas's military involvement in the Mexican War remains controversial. Like all advances in the unforgiving academy of warfare, *Diablos Tejanos* emerged as a double-edged sword to bring both tactical value and lamentable brutality to American victory. As mounted auxiliaries they contributed specialized mobility and firepower to the cumbersome and slow U.S. Army. As partisans they accosted Mexican soldiers, guerrillas, and civilians with a terrible vengeance. Perhaps Taylor, as the first commander to call for rangers, summarized this duality best: "On the day of battle I am glad to have Texas soldiers with me for they are brave and gallant, but I never want to see them before or afterwards, for they are too hard to control."[145]

Chapter 7

Conflicts of
Antebellum Texas,
1846–1861

Texas fought along its historical Indian Frontier throughout and after the Mexican-American War. From American annexation in 1846 to secession in 1861, the new state intermittently deployed rangers and militia to augment newly arrived, and often inadequate, Federal garrisons.[1] Explosive population growth and territorial expansion—which actually resulted in a proportional decrease in military participation by state residents—ensured further friction with *Tejanos* and natives. John Salmon Ford, who would replace Jack Hays as the preeminent frontier captain, described the border volatility from a predictably biased perspective: "The war waged upon Texians, by Indians, upon the inhabitants of Texas was cruel and barbarous." Looking south, he also lamented they were "constantly subjected to a war of the butcher knife and the lasso" by Mexican marauders along the perennially troubled Rio Grande.[2]

Such exaggeration belied the incredible attraction Texas held for American immigration after achieving statehood. Population density during antebellum years rose from 154,431 Anglos and 58,161 black slaves in 1850 to 421,294 Anglos and 182,921 black slaves by 1860.[3] Over the same period, the state benefited from

approximately $10,000,000 in Federal stimulus—mostly in support of
U.S. Army garrisons—totaling 4 percent of Texas's value growth.[4] This
economic expansion, and the territorial aggrandizement that it inevi-
tably spurred, demanded limited but repeated mobilization of government sanctioned, nominally unsanctioned, and even illegal rangers to
preserve and enhance territorial gains. Even though many new residents avoided actual combat, militant traditions continued to define
Lone Star culture.

With the U.S. Army now holding constitutional primacy, partisans
like Sam Houston advocated Texan answers for Texas problems. After
grappling with Comanche and Mexican foes for decades he believed
that irregular combat required specialized and interested volunteers.
Simultaneously, the former president and many Texans retained a
deeply American mistrust of standing armies controlled by distant
national capitals. With equal measures of old Texian bravado and
naive patriotism, the statesman proclaimed: "Give us rangers in Texas.
I ask you to give us one regiment of rangers, and you many withdraw
your regular troops." He then qualified his criticism of regulars—with
some truthfulness—by complaining that, "they have not that efficiency
which is necessary for frontier service."[5]

These statements, however aspirational, were echoed by congressional delegations from other border states like Missouri and Indiana
and created dilemmas for Texas officials. They preferred locally recruited
and controlled rangers over Federal troops to protect peripheral settlements, especially in the western plains, central prairies, Red River
borderlands, and Nueces Strip, but could not afford the cost. The state
remained penurious after decades of constant warfare and was thus
fiscally, and also constitutionally, compelled to rely upon the national
army for defense. Tensions were then exacerbated when the U.S. Army
proved institutionally unsuitable, at least initially, to combat the dynamic
raiding cultures that permeated the Great Plains.

The resulting partnership between state and Federal militaries
in Texas, sometimes symbiotic and often contentious, was characterized by fluctuating army concentrations with intermittent volunteer

augmentation. While the state never attained a permanently funded mounted regiment prior to the Civil War, dozens of ranging companies and militia detachments, in addition to a few short-duration battalions, served under both Federal and state sanction during crises. In both form and function they operated similarly to the mounted rifleman regiments of 1836 and 1837, Jack Hays's companies that patrolled South Texas between 1841 and 1845, and the plethora of inactive militia units that had flourished since colonial settlement.

The requirement for continued Texan militarization during the antebellum years emanated primarily from Federal inability to adapt to the plains raiding environment and largely stemmed from fiscal, and thus structural, limitations. The *Texas State Gazette* lambasted the U.S. Army's economized infantry-centric approach as early as 1849, as the War Department assumed frontier responsibility, when it criticized that "the idea of repelling mounted Indians, the most expert horsemen in the world, with a force of foot soldiers, is here looked upon as exceedingly ridiculous." The paper conversely, and hyperbolically, assessed that "the only effective resistance now on our frontier, extending well-nigh a distance of two thousand miles is, therefore, the five mounted companies consisting of probably 250 men."[6]

Despite constant criticism levied against Washington, D.C. by Texans over inadequate defenses that ranged from accusations of intentional negligence to sheer incompetence, department commanders fully appreciated the pressing need for mounted forces on the Great Plains. While Brevet Major General Brooke, who commanded the Texas Frontier from 1849 to 1851, was "perfectly convinced that dragoons or mounted men" were "the only troops capable of proper action against these Indians," his successor, Brevet Major General Persifor Smith, likewise assessed there was "no corps in the army calculated to be so eminently useful on this western frontier as one of mounted riflemen."[7]

Moving beyond interested reports by field commanders, senior officers in the distant national capital also admitted to systemic deficiencies in frontier garrisons. In 1850 the General-in-Chief of the Army,

Winfield Scott, officially requested funding for "two additional regiments of horse (dragoons or mounted riflemen)" due to the "great extent
of our frontiers" and the "peculiar character of the service devolving on
our troops." The aging commander, whose victory in Central Mexico had
earned him a peerless reputation as a strategist and tactician, justified
the requirement by noting how due to "the want of regular cavalry, the
commanding general in Texas has been compelled to call out, at great
expense, a considerable body of volunteer horse."[8] Despite tactical
necessities that compelled state augmentation, Brooke, like Taylor in his
previous hesitancy in Mexico, initially objected to "placing rangers in
immediate contact with the Indians" lest they "bring about what we wish
to avoid—a general war."[9]

While the regular army establishment usually viewed security in
places like Texas operationally, national politicians typically assessed
Anglo-Indian conflict through a different lens: fiscal prioritization.
A quartermaster assessment in 1865—an admittedly inexact reference due to the implications of the massive Civil War mobilization—
estimated that the annual operating costs of a cavalry regiment,
precluding the initial purchases of horses and equipment, doubled
that of an infantry regiment, approximately $600,000 to $300,000.[10]
With such a disparity in cost the U.S. Congress habitually resisted
mounted arms expansion in favor of more foot soldiers. The creation
of two new cavalry regiments in 1855, in large part due to lobbying
efforts by Jefferson Davis, stood as notable exceptions to trends in
War Department funding.[11]

In addition to sincere demands for protection, much of Texas's
desire for increased War Department investment stemmed from the
ancillary benefit of economic stimulus. U.S. Army garrisons offered
potential market improvement for proximate communities and regional
commerce. Direct injection of Federal cash into the state's relatively
unsophisticated and austere economy—especially beyond the few urban
centers like Austin and Houston—incentivized their inflation of security requirements to justify an expanded army presence. Since cavalry
regiments required more logistical support, increases in mounted units

naturally provided greater stimulus. Throughout the antebellum period the U.S. Army spent over $1,000,000 on animal forage alone, much of it through local purchase.[12]

Disparity in military spending between Washington, D.C. and Austin revealed both the importance of Federal stimulus to Texan prosperity and the state's inability to resource its own enduring military structures. Between 1852 and 1855 the U.S. Army spent $3,600,000 at 6 percent of its total budget for defense of the state with another $5,700,000 spent between 1856 and 1861. In contrast, the Texas Congress allocated just $95,000 and $375,000 during the respective periods to fund ranger and militia organizations. Across all antebellum years the national government spent over $1,000,000 on civilian employees, $812,000 on transportation costs, almost $200,000 on building programs, and approximately $150,000 on rents.[13]

Despite this unprecedented military and economic investment, Texas governors comprehensively lambasted Federal defense efforts until secession.[14] In addition to criticizing the overreliance on infantry, they routinely mocked army strategies of constructing static fortifications as linear barriers against tribal incursions. Houston exasperatedly explained that "the Indians can go around their forts, and unless there is continual vigilance kept up along the border you cannot protect the frontiers by regulars." He further believed "there is no sense in saying that a fortification gives protection to the people when an Indian can go within a mile of it and pass down and butcher the inhabitants. Then you start and run after the Indian, but he laughs at you."[15]

These tactics, advocated by frontiersmen who had acquired bloody education from Comanche warriors, reflected raiding dynamics that stymied most efforts of the U.S. Army until its return to the Great Plains after the Civil War. Like Spanish presidio soldiers of previous centuries, American regulars rapidly learned that infantry outposts could not hope to deter the fleetest cavalry in North America. Even when Federal commanders called for shifts to offensive mindsets, exemplified by Brooke's proposal in July 1850 for the Fort Graham, Fredericksburg, and Fort Inge garrisons to attack "simultaneously and in concert," the dearth of combat power and mobility retarded success. According to frontier historian Robert Wooster, the garrisons simply "lacked the manpower to launch the offensives Texans so badly wanted."[16]

After years of inadequate defense a few U.S. Army units began to emulate Texan techniques of proactive patrolling and expeditionary strikes. The elite 2nd U.S. Cavalry Regiment—which conducted 36 percent all army combat actions in Texas between 1849 and 1861—perfectly illustrated learned tactical improvement. Just as Anglo-Texans had absorbed hard lessons of irregular mounted warfare in previous years, Federal cavalry on the western frontier eventually adapted to Comanche and Mexican methods while achieving temporary regional security. As praised by Mexican-American War veteran Robert E. Lee, then leading the 2nd U.S. Cavalry in Texas, "the energy and determination evinced in bringing them to battle merits high commendation."[17]

Despite highly conditional improvements, Federal protection remained comprehensively inadequate to protect rapidly expanding settlements lines and left ambitious pioneers to grapple with ethnic competitors, victims, and opportunists. While many Texans found tension between the desire for autonomy and the need for military and economic investment, the *Texas State Gazette* criticized the perceived lack of national prioritization for Texas in 1852—with typical misunderstanding of the U.S. Army's disproportionately large investment in their state—by dramatically proclaiming that "blood is daily spilt by the marauding Indian and Mexican, hundreds of valuable lives have already been lost on our frontier." The paper then complained that "these are treated far more lightly than some squabble about fishing smak in the northern waters."

This security lapse, even though often exaggerated by settlers, politicians, and editors alike, ensured that Texas's way of war remained relevant. A new generation of energetic horsemen rode and fought for communal and individual territorial interests even as they unleashed cultural influence far beyond their relatively few numbers. The Lone Star military tradition, which could have potentially elapsed had the

U.S. Army managed to pacify volatile border regions, was sustained and validated by continuous border warfare. As a result, Texas again called citizens to militarize against the chaos of its volatile position between competing tribes, lawless marauders, and an unstable Mexico.

Patrolling the Indian Frontier

The military partnership between Texas and the United States began in 1846 concurrent to American mobilization for the Mexican-American War. While the preponderance of American combat forces and Texan auxiliaries marched south to occupy disputed territory, the Comanche threat, among others, remained acute. This division of opponents across vast geographic distances demanded a return to a strategic posture similar that which revolutionary Texas had adopted in 1836: regiments and brigades would deploy south to face the nation-state threat, while decentralized ranger companies guarded against native raiders across vulnerable settlement regions north and west.[18]

The new state first recognized a need for home auxiliaries in the summer of 1846 as conflict erupted between the U.S. Army and Mexican forces along the Rio Grande. While Taylor's army concentrated towards Matamoros near the border, Colonel William Harney, a career cavalry officer who was notable for his harsh discipline and methods, remained in Central Texas with just three companies of the 2nd U.S. Dragoons. The small garrison, which reflected both the War Department's underestimation of the Indian threat and dearth of available expeditionary units, was divided between Austin and San Antonio in a vain attempt to protect the troubled region.[19]

It did not take long for tribal raiders to sense the opportunity for material gain. Pressured by a spate of attacks, settlements along the northwest periphery petitioned their new government at state and national echelons for authorization and funding to raise ranging companies. Bereft of thousands of fighters who enlisted in the Texas Division for the Monterrey campaign, the frontier counties now lacked many of the adventurers and "young bloods" that typically volunteered first for hazardous duty.[20]

Albert Horton, serving as the acting governor in the absence of Henderson, wrote to President Polk requesting authorization for "five companies of volunteers" for "protection of the frontier." He qualified the need for experienced Texans by emphasizing that U.S. Army officers were "strangers to this country and its citizens, as well as to the Indians themselves."[21] Horton likewise appealed directly to Harney at San Antonio.

Texas's frontiers fell under Zachary Taylor's broader responsibility due to their proximity to the contest in Mexico. As the commanding general's deputy north of the Rio Grande, Harney quickly approved state requests to form ranger companies for six-month enlistments. The colonel, who was a veteran horse soldier and understood the value of mounted protection, wrote to Horton from San Antonio that "a company on the Trinity is no doubt of great importance, and I will receive it." Continuing the geographic assessment, he considered "companies at the following places equally important to give perfect protection to this exposed frontier: one on the Brazos River, one on Little River, one at or near Castroville, and one at or near this place."[22]

Harney then revealed his strategic intent: "This will form a complete chain of posts from Fort Washita to Castroville, and if the officers will do their duty, the settlements will be completely protected."[23] Similar to the Superintendent Corps of Rangers deployed during the Texas Revolution, he planned to screen along interlocking sectors. The companies organized with "fifty privates and the usual complement of Officers & Non commissioned Officers." As wartime volunteers, they would receive army pay but were required to join with horses and weapons. Harney then asserted Federal authority by stating the rangers "should be informed that although assigned to particular stations, they are no less liable at any time to be called to any part of the country."[24]

Horton immediately assigned captains to lead the five companies, indicating a peculiar sharing of military responsibility between army officers and state officials. Though the national president, and by extension his assigned theater commander, retained the ultimate authority to mobilize Federal volunteers for the Mexican contest, wartime rangers activated for home defense effectively served under gubernatorial direction. As late as the 1870s governors usually selected and commissioned respected men from local communities to lead due to better familiarity with available candidates.

Horton soon identified settlers and frontiersmen with the requisite experience to fill command billets. He assigned Tennessean John Grumbles to lead a company out of Austin, settler Andrew Stapp to form a company on the Trinity River, and veteran ranger John Conner to command a third out of San Antonio. He also directed Shapley Ross, a Waco pioneer and former member of Jack Hays's San Antonio company, to patrol between the Little and San Gabriel rivers in the north, and Salado Creek veteran Thomas Smith to command an outfit along the upper Brazos River.[25]

Despite reports of Comanche raiding and corresponding urgency to mobilize the frontier network, bureaucratic obstacles delayed official sanction. Harney then retarded activation further when he suddenly deployed south with his dragoons and eight volunteer companies of the 1st Texas Mounted Rifles without informing his successor, Colonel Thomas Fauntleroy, about plans for state protection. Taylor, who viewed undisciplined volunteers with a disdain then typical amongst regulars, finally, and flatly, disapproved the activation of state forces. He naively believed that Brigadier General John Wool's western maneuvers, oriented on Saltillo, would clear the frontier and obviate the need for northern auxiliaries.[26] This cancellation reflected obvious, or willful, geographical misunderstanding of the scope and reach of the Indian threat.

Despite "Old Rough and Ready's" official primacy in the chain of command, he held little practical authority in Texas. Horton simply disregarded the general and continued ranger deployments while placing public approval over tenuous Federal authority. He also bypassed Taylor and wrote directly to the Secretary of War for approval: "The Comanche, and other tribes, bordering upon this State, when they see that there is no armed force upon the frontier, to restrain their lawless propensities, will not be able to withstand the temptation thus afforded, of gratifying them." He then offered a subtle incentive for Federal action, stating that if the army failed to act, "the citizens of the frontier will protect themselves, and retaliate whenever the occasion occurs."[27]

Taylor responded to further state requests to federalize rangers by ordering Wool to simply discharge any mobilized Texans. Like many veteran officers of the War of 1812, he held volunteers and militia in low esteem due to their propensity for lawlessness and erratic behavior. The general accordingly wrote that it was "not supposed that it will be necessary to retain any of the companies called out by Colonel Harney."[28] Despite Taylor's orders, the governor maintained the rangers on frontier duty under his own authority for three months until receiving delayed approval and funding from Washington, D.C.

In September and October, with an overriding mandate from the War Department, Wool discharged, and immediately reenlisted, the companies of Grumbles, Conner, and Ross for terms of twelve months each. Smith's and Stapp's commands continued under their original enlistments until term completion. After months of indecision, a responsive, though spare and dispersed, ranger system again guarded the state's contentious borderlands.[29]

In April of 1847 the Texas governor centralized his auxiliaries when he administratively united the disparate ranger companies into a single, though small, regiment. To accomplish the consolidation, which resulted in a loosely coordinated battalion in actuality, he combined existing the companies of Grumbles, Ross, and Connor with additional units under Henry McCulloch and E. S. Wyman into a larger force under command of Salado Creek veteran Thomas Smith. This formation now resembled the second Corps of Rangers from the Texas Revolution as well as Coleman's and Burleson's mounted rifleman corps of 1837.

Centrally commanded yet still operationally dispersed regiments of active rangers like Smith's would offer the preferred military structure for Texas governors until the Civil War. This conceptual ideal, emulative of American or European regular cavalry but decentralized according to tactical necessity, would be rarely achieved and never sustained. Failure to permanently consolidate frontier defenses—mostly due to lack of funding and Federal insistence on the primacy of regulars—continued the intermittent and unprofessional nature of its way of war.

In the summer of 1847 a Virginian immigrant named Peter Bell, who would soon be elected governor, assumed command of a larger ranging organization. The new regiment included Smith's battalion, two detached companies from Hays's Regiment of Mounted Volunteers, and several unattached ranger companies. Colonel Bell, who emerged as an ambitious leader, had first learned mounted tactics in Henry Karney's light cavalry at the Battle of San Jacinto and won further distinction as an Indian Fighter under Jack Hays in 1840 and as a U.S. Army officer in the initial campaign of the Mexican-American War. Captain Samuel Highsmith and Captain Big Foot Wallace commanded two of the new companies.

Bell positioned his men along a more comprehensive line of patrol stations designed to counter Comanche raids. *The Texas Democrat* reported the mobilization: "They have taken the field to settle old scores with the Red man if the chance presents." It also emphasized "scouting" to underscore light and fast skirmishing capability.[30] The network extended from Dallas, south to Fredericksburg, south to San Antonio, southwest to Laredo, and east to Corpus Christi. This chained defense, which allowed proactive interdiction, created two axes of protection: one stretching from central Texas to the northern Indian Frontier, and another from southern Texas towards Mexico. Bell's concept would set immediate precedent for the U.S. Army's postwar posture in the troubled state.

The rangers' use of fortified outposts differed from historical American military strategies in the east where defenses often centered on the fortifications themselves. For Texans, they served merely as forward bases to facilitate patrolling by small and fast companies. John Ford described deployment of state troops concurrent to the Mexican-American War "on a line near the upper edge of the settlements" and recalled that "they were required to send out scouts, in each direction, daily. The guard detachments from each company were to meet those of another company, and pass the night together, and return to their respective camps the next day, unless they struck an Indian trail, and followed it."[31]

This tactical posture typified Texan reliance upon active-defense that had characterized most previous frontier screens. Focus on constant patrolling, reminiscent of Jack Hays's earlier ranging companies, minimized the native cavalry's advantage in raiding initiative. The requirement for mutual support between companies resulted in inter-locking sectors that aimed to deprive the warriors of likely approaches. This system would contrast with later U.S. Army forts in Texas that were predominantly manned by infantry and accounted for stark differences in interdiction success between the state and Federal soldiers.

In March of 1848 Highsmith and his company experienced one of the few recorded skirmishes for Bell's command. Acting on orders to conduct a reconnaissance of the San Saba Valley to locate a warband that had killed a German settler, the captain led two lieutenants, forty-three privates, an interpreter, and a doctor to scour the area. The rangers departed from their camp at the Enchanted Rock on March 13 and discovered a native village on the Llano River two days later. Highsmith described their eagerness to attack with macabre enthusiasm: "We immediately prepared for action and every eye flashed with animation at the prospect of inflicting merited chastisement on this lawless band, whose hands were yet warm with the settler's blood."[32]

The rangers immediately "dashed down upon them" but unexpectedly encountered friendly Apache near the village. After allowing the allies to depart, Highsmith spoke with the chief of the targeted Wichita and Waco to ascertain their identity and purpose. The warriors attempted to retreat during the parley, and the captain, ostensibly assuming duplicity, killed the warband's leader while the rest of the company engaged fleeing tribesmen. Highsmith later reported that his men had "done their work with dispatch, and in the most satisfactory manner." He concluded that "the party numbered 35 or 40—but few escaped." The Apache later confirmed, with suspect veracity, that the slain chief had murdered several Texan citizens.[33]

Texas's frontier defense during the Mexican-American War eventually comprised thirteen companies. As in years past, ranger service against perceived savages found nationalistic and racial approval with the state's media and Anglo population. The *Victoria Advocate* lionized Bell's horsemen in November of 1848: "We are much pleased. We know they are true men; and they know exactly what they are about. With many of them Indian and Mexican fighting has been their trade for years." The paper then advocated: "that they may be permanently retained in the service on our frontier is extremely desirable; and we cannot permit ourselves to doubt that such will be the case."[34]

Though it remains unknown how many Anglo-Indian engagements like Highsmith's in the San Saba Valley occurred between 1846 and 1848, the mere presence of so many partisan horsemen along the frontier presumably allowed some deterrence. McCulloch's company reported only one skirmish as they patrolled northwest of Austin, but the "constant scouting and watchfulness" recalled by fellow ranger John Brown clearly described proactive and energetic patrol methods.[35] The ranger system served into the spring of 1849 when most of them demobilized due to the cessation of the Mexican-American War and corresponding Federal funding for auxiliary troops.

In addition to fielding irregular cavalry battalions, wartime Texas pursued a new, and ultimately more effective, round of conciliatory treaties with reconcilable tribes. As a presumably impartial arbiter, the national government often assumed the lead in negotiations while hoping to offer new beginnings to historically bitter Anglo-Indian relations. While most Texans viewed obstinate tribes as obstacles to be overcome, the U.S. Interior Department and its subordinate agency, the Office of Indian Affairs, usually maintained a more balanced approach. This difference in perspectives would severely complicate efforts to achieve ethnic tranquility as Federal officials and Texan partisans often pursued differing agendas through different means.

In May of 1846 U.S. Commissioners P.M. Butler and M. G. Lewis facilitated an important Anglo-Indian agreement when they met with chiefs from the Comanche, Ioni, Anadarko, Caddo, Lipan, Longwa, Keechi, Tawakoni, Tonkawa, Wichita, and Waco peoples. The treaty explicitly placed the tribes "under the protection of the United States, and of no other power, state, or sovereignty," while implying protection from Texan imperialists and explicitly proscribing murder and robbery. It also agreed to place "trading houses, agencies, and posts" at tribal borders in the hopes of establishing civilizing commerce. Despite the well-intended agreement, renegades and aggrandizers from all sides would repeatedly violate the terms.[36]

While Indian Agents and some state officials sincerely desired peace, treaties sometimes reflected pragmatic, and sometimes knowingly temporary, attempts to prevent consolidated attacks by opportunistic tribes while so many U.S. Army soldiers and Texan volunteers fought in Mexico. Appreciating his vulnerability, the governor ordered Thomas Smith, an envoy with fighting credibility, to focus "attention to those tribes most likely to commit hostilities upon the frontier or join the Mexicans against the United States."[37] This conciliation represented a return to the nuanced policies of Stephen Austin and Sam Houston that strove to forestall unmanageable warfare across too many fronts during colonial and republican crisis periods.

American pursuit of Anglo-Indian coexistence in Texas proved relatively successful during the Mexican War years but would ultimately, and dramatically, fail over the next half-century. Vengeful rangers, ambitious settlers, and aggressive army officers occasionally embraced the brutal methods of population-centric warfare. Renegade warbands likewise attacked settlements and travelers, thereby damning entire tribes from the vantage point of many Texans. Refusal by Austin to permanently allocate productive land within their borders for permanent and inviolable Indian settlement further complicated enduring peace and eventually compelled Federal departments to move many tribes beyond the Red River to less arable lands in Oklahoma.[38]

Constant settlement expansion from Central Texas to northern and western expanses provided a final catalyst that ensured continued Anglo-Indian friction. As hardy pioneers marched north and west to explore and claim new lands they routinely exceeded fixed military defenses and treaty boundaries. Army garrisons and rangers then repositioned farther out to protect burgeoning settlement areas, thereby engendering cycles of constant pressure and hostile contact with tribes. While the southern Comanche had long fought Texans, waves of Anglo expansion created new friction with the powerful Noconi, Kotsoteka, and Yamparikas peoples of middle and northern Comancheria.[39] In 1849, as the victorious American army repositioned from Mexico to the Texan frontier, territorial warfare in Texas was far from over.

The first postwar iteration of ranger service lasted from 1849 to 1851 as newly arrived Federal garrisons failed to comprehensively secure Texas's long borders and frontiers. This strategic lapse necessitated continued augmentation by irregular cavalry and provided the impetus for revitalized Lone Star militancy. It also heralded the passing of many military icons of the Texas Republic, most notably Jack Hays and Edward Burleson, away from tactical leadership and resulted in the ascent of new ranger captains. Hays's adjutant from the Mexican-American War, John Ford, would soon rise to prominence as the most visible of the antebellum state officers.

By the time Texas joined America in 1846 its western settlements had expanded to encompass the future counties of Cooke, Denton, Tarrant, Ellis, Navarro, McLennan, Bell, Williamson, Travis, Blanco, Gillespie, Kendall, Bexar, and Medina. Areas substantially populated by civilians were no longer just concentrated along the southeastern river systems, but had sprung onto the open prairies, north to the Red River, and southwest to Laredo. This rapid migration created new corridors of vulnerable homesteads for ethnic confrontation. Alarmed pioneers soon beseeched their government, and by extension the U.S. Army, for protection from both retaliatory and opportunistic tribal attacks.[40]

Like the early Texas Republic's predilection for forward outposts, the U.S. Army chose to establish a chain of forts along the western and southern periphery of emerging settlement belts. But unlike earlier Texan use of blockhouses to facilitate ranger patrolling, Federal troops employed the sites as the centerpiece of their predominantly static defense. From north to south the First Federal Line included Fort Worth near Dallas; Fort Graham on the upper Brazos River; Fort Gates to the south of Fort Graham; Fort Croghan to the northwest of Austin; Fort Martin Scott to the west of Austin; Fort Lincoln to the west of San Antonio; Forts Lincoln, Inage, and Duncan to the southwest of San Antonio; Fort McIntosh and the Brownsville installation along the Rio Grande; and Corpus Christi on the coast.[41]

Brevet Maj. Gen, George Brooke, commander of the expansive Eighth Military District that included Texas, intended the north-south and northwest-southeast axes to separate Anglo settlements from the Comanche Empire. Despite supportive concepts, his 1,400 soldiers proved grossly inadequate for screening against rapid Indian and Mexican incursions and fought in only three engagements throughout 1849. Of the twenty-two companies stationed in Texas—which comprised 14 percent of the entire national army—sixteen were infantry, indicating a reliance on relatively unresponsive defenses. Like past Spanish presidios, Federal garrisons immediately found themselves unable to anticipate, interdict, or effectively pursue fleeter native cavalry.[42]

In August of 1849, with security diminishing along the Federal line, tribal attacks forced Brooke to grudgingly request augmentation by Texan auxiliaries. As reported in the *Texas Gazette* on August 25, the new governor, George Wood of the 2nd Texas Mounted Rifles in the 1846 Monterrey Campaign, agreed to limited mobilization immediately ordered "three mounted companies of Rangers, 78 strong in the aggregate" to take the field. As department commander, Brooke ordered the irregular cavalry to "operate through the Southwestern frontier ... from Goliad to Corpus Christi, and thence to the Rio Grande, ranging the whole country."

Wood assigned company commands to John Ford, late of the 1st Texas Mounted Rifles, and John Grumbles and Henry McCulloch of Bell's more recent regiment. Brooke then requested two more volunteer companies, indicating that he found value in the augmentation. Big Foot Wallace, who had survived the notorious Black Bean Episode during captivity after suffering defeat at the Battle of Mier in 1842, assumed command of one of the additional units.[43] All five captains arrived as experienced tactical leaders. Ford, Wallace, and McCulloch, in particular, stood well prepared, as each had patrolled under Jack Hays. Brooke wrote with surprising approval of the auxiliaries, noting they applied "energy and perseverance in the most active scouting and pursuit of the savages, with a perfect obedience in the execution of all orders."[44]

Ford, an educated and versatile man who had worked as a doctor, legislator, newspaper editor, and soldier, was the first captain to lead the newest ranger iteration into action. He had recently led an unofficial volunteer company out of Austin to patrol from Corpus Christi to Laredo and had gained attention as a competent leader. As noted in the *Texas Gazette*, Ford and his "company of Mounted Rangers," now patrolling under an official mandate, quickly moved to secure their assigned sector "between Corpus Christi and the Rio Grande."[45]

The most memorable Texan-Indian engagement of 1850 occurred when Ford's company fought a Comanche warband in May of that year while en route to Fort Merrill near Corpus Christi. The ranger intended to draw an allotment of Colt pistols for his men from the army quartermaster there, indicating the scarcity of revolving weapons following the Mexican War. He described the mission as "a scout ... to scour the country above Laredo, then move across country in the direction of San Antonio, turn to the right, make Corpus Christi." Once at Fort Merrill, he would acquire "better pistols and return to San Antonio Viejo."[46]

Ford divided his forty-man company into two platoons to clear more ground. His section discovered an Indian trail and soon closed within visual range of the unsuspecting natives. According to the captain, they "followed, marching as much as possible over low grounds, galloping when practicable, doing all they could to force a fight." The Texans soon closed with the Comanche and the two forces prepared for battle. Ford recorded opposing composition and armaments: "each commander had sixteen men. The Indian had his bow, his arrows, his lance. The rangers were armed with Mississippi rifles—muzzle loaders. The Captain and Sergeant alone had revolvers."[47]

According to the captain's account, he immediately rode forth alone to engage the Comanche leader. Ford killed the hapless chief with his revolver and the rangers charged the native formation. The Comanche soon broke and fled with Texans in close pursuit. The ranger remembered how "the Indians, seeing the day was going against them, being demoralized by the fierce onset and the damage they had suffered, left the prairie, entered a wooded country, and managed to outrun their inveterate and dreaded foes." He also wrote that the "skirmish covered a line of four or five miles," emphasizing how fights between cavalries often became running engagements.[48]

Ford expressed surprise at the decisiveness of his victory. After relying on revolvers with Hays in Mexico to win numerous clashes, he was impressed that his men had fought effectively with single-shot rifles while mounted. He wrote of the battle with the dramatic flair of a former news editor: "A running fight has seldom been made by men armed with muzzle-loading guns and no pistols, inflicting such heavy loss upon their opponents."[49] *The Nueces Valley* newspaper attributed success to superior equine stock when it described "the Rangers being mounted on better horses than the Indians," while noting how the Texans "soon dashed in among them."[50] Despite boastful reports, the Comanche suffered just four men killed and seven wounded.

This skirmish represented typical skirmishing that ranger companies engaged in between 1849 and 1851. The days of large-scale invasions by Comanche warhosts lay in the past, if only temporarily; indigenous plains cavalry now raided in smaller and fleeter parties. While unable to overwhelm fortified garrisons and larger settlements, small-unit attacks allowed greater rapidity and stealth, perhaps explaining the cumbersome Federal army's failures with interdiction. It also facilitated traditional Indian objectives of opportunistic thievery that usually aimed for the capture of horses, captives, and finished goods instead of winning decisive military victories.

The five ranger companies rode throughout South Texas through the rest of the year and into the spring of 1851. In March of that year the original auxiliary authorization expired, but several captains, including Ford and Wallace, reenlisted their companies for a second term. Ford's men continue to support the First Federal Line with much needed patrolling expertise until their second and final discharge in September of 1851.

The U.S. Army—and the 2nd U.S. Dragoons in particular—fought eighteen skirmishes in Texas in 1850 but surprisingly recorded none in 1851.[51] Given such an erratic combat record, the Texan public preferred its own rangers who often proved more aggressive, responsive, and interested. Numerous citizen complaints and newspaper editorials indicated dissatisfaction with the army garrisons while frontier communities praised irregular cavalry as ideal for Indian deterrence. An article in the *San Antonio Ledger*, which the *Texas State Gazette* reprinted on October 11, declared unequivocal preference for ranger protection when Ford's term expired:

> Now that the company is disbanded, the Indians, who have so much dreaded its presence … can again carry devastation and death, with little dread of molestation from the Nueces to the Rio Grande … it is hoped that Governor Bell will redeem his promise to give the frontier protection. The ranging companies have done the State good service, and the roads have been freed from danger to the traveler and merchant. We hope Governor Bell will recall them immediately to protect the frontier, or it will be again devastated and destroyed.[52]

The same article also offered insight into differences between rangers and U.S. Dragoons then serving on the same volatile frontiers.

When recounting the impact Ford's company provided South Texas, the editor wrote that "the citizens of Laredo, in particular, fell a daily prey to marauding bands of Indians until Capt. Ford's company of Rangers was stationed within striking distance of the town." The paper then assessed that in a "short period afterwards—a very brief one indeed, a rapid succession of bloody and victorious encounters with the Indians soon taught them that Rangers could ride, shoot and maneuver rather differently from mounted infantry."

This statement, by observers on the front lines of Anglo-Indian and Anglo-Mexican conflict, gauged the rangers' distinct and seemingly irreplaceable role in combating raiders. First, the unstated fact that a Federal company had been stationed in the area before Ford's arrival indicated the regulars' impotence against tribal initiative. Despite the U.S. Army's protection Indians had inflicted "cattle steeling and scalping forays along the whole line of settlements from the farms and ranches above Laredo, to Davis's ranch, and from thence across the country to Corpus Christi." In contrast, once Ford proactively patrolled the Nueces Strip the native cavalry found themselves stymied by a motivated force with similar mobility.[53]

Houston, with years of combat experience in both American and Texian armies, summarized differences between proactive ranger patrols and often passive regular army garrisons. Exasperated with War Department policy, he argued: "Texas wants a regiment of rangers that she can rely upon; she does not want a force that will be inert and inactive until depredations are committed." The statesmen then complained how, "when the people get to a fort at some distance and give information that such and such depredations have been committed, some infantry, or perhaps some dragoons or cavalry, are sent out on the march; but by that time the Indians are far in advance of them."[54]

This perennial desire for the national government to fund state supervised, and presumably more responsive, military forces found direct conflict with both War Department and congressional priorities. Predictably centering on fiscal concerns, the professional military establishment had long critiqued volunteers and militia not only as undisciplined and ineffective, but as far more expensive than regulars. The sudden conversion of the short-lived and irregular Battalion of Mounted Rangers into a professional dragoon regiment back in 1833 had perfectly illustrated this preference. Secretary of War Lewis Cass, a predictable champion of prioritizing expansion of professional components, justified the reorganization by citing an annual ranger cost of $297,530 compared to just $143,598 to maintaining comparable dragoons.[55]

Both Secretary of War Jefferson Davis's annual report in 1854 and an army quartermaster report in 1857 claimed that over the previous two decades the government might have saved over $30,000,000 by relying on regulars instead of volunteers. While Davis cited "property destroyed, compensations to suffering inhabitants, and on account of pensions and bounty lands" for the differential, the latter officer's calculations were based, in part, on an 1838 Paymaster General report that ascribed disproportionate volunteer costs to, "expenses for traveling," the "hire, maintenance, and indemnity for horses," and "supply of clothing." In a critique that proved prophetic in the Mexican-American War, the paymaster likewise critiqued auxiliaries for "comparative loss and destruction of military stores and public property." He finished, less convincingly, by professing concern for the "great inconvenience" that activation inflicted on citizen-soldiers and the "heavy tax imposed on their patriotism."[56]

While presumably resting on sound statistics, fiscal justifications for reliance on regulars generalized data from American conflicts that included a wide variety of volunteers from dozens of states and perhaps held less applicability in Texas. In accordance with colonial and republican traditions, antebellum Texans almost invariably enlisted with their own horses, clothing, and except for a few revolver consignments, weaponry. While charges of indiscipline and wanton destruction certainly held merit—as exemplified by Texan behavior in the Mexican-American War—rangers conversely incurred minimal transportation and pay costs since they usually served locally and in smaller companies than regular dragoons. Furthermore, War Department ment arguments must be viewed with skepticism as an institution justifying organizational expansion while warding off rival funding recipients.

Despite commendations by both civilians and officials alike the ranger companies all expired by the close of 1851. By this time John Ford had risen as the most publicized and tactically effective ranger captain, largely replacing Jack Hays as a popular, and culturally influential, frontier icon. Like the prior service of Texan volunteers in the Mexican-American War, irregular cavalry augmentation of the U.S. Army along the First Federal Line provided mobility and aggressiveness to overmatched and under-resourced regulars. Texas's amateur based and event-specific methodology, stemming from three decades of frontier adaptation, remained relevant even under a new national flag.

The next iteration of Texas auxiliary service lasted from 1852 to 1853 as the U.S. Army altered its strategy. The new commander of Texas, Bvt. Maj. Gen. Persifor Smith, surveyed the existing forts and garrisons and decided to counter native mobility with a defense-in-depth. The new system, later called the Second Federal Line, established a second chain of forts 150 miles to the west of the original network and essentially created inner and outer perimeters around Central and East Texas. While cavalry would hold the inner line, infantry would garrison the outer chain to the west.[57] The Texas Congress spent just 6 percent of its budget on state troops over this period as it sought to reap benefits of statehood even as it criticized Federal inadequacy.[58]

The improved fort system spanned the vast expanses of the western plains and prairies and encompassed a staggering endeavor. The fortified stations, often isolated in hostile territory, included Forts Belknap and Phantom Hill to the west of Dallas; Fort Chadbourne to the west of Waco; Forts Mckavett, Terret, and Mason to the west of Austin; and Fort Clark to the west of San Antonio, in addition to many of the previous outposts retained from the First Federal Line.[59]

As new forts established presence in unsettled areas, settlers followed, often without sanction, to claim adjacent properties. This new influx ensured a fresh continuation of Anglo-Indian conflict despite the intended purpose of the buffer zone.

The War Department also addressed manpower issues. In addition to creating the second line, the U.S. Army increased its strength in Texas to 3,600 troops across forty-eight companies with a marked increase in mounted capacity. The professional garrison now comprised six companies of the 2nd U.S. Dragoons, eight companies of the 1st U.S. Mounted Rifles, four companies of the 4th U.S. Artillery, and a combined total of thirty-two companies from the 1st, 5th, 7th, and 8th U.S. Infantry regiments. This buildup stationed almost 25 percent of the U.S. Army in Texas at an annual cost of $6,000,000.[60]

Despite increases in mounted units, the heavy proportion of infantrymen and fact that cumbersome dragoons remained far slower than Indian cavalry ensured continued mobility limitations. Astoundingly, throughout 1852 and 1853 the entire garrison in Texas only recorded a single engagement across the long chain of forts.[61] William Cushney, editor of the *Texas State Gazette*, exclaimed with combination of exasperation and exaggeration:

> Nothing but mounted troops will do for this country. Infantry will be a dead-expense for this country, and by sending them here, the Government is guilty of a capital military blunder ... The enemy we have to contend with can only be reached with the sabre and the rifle. Two regiments of mounted riflemen would, in one year, bring all these Indians to a permanent peace, while ten infantry regiments could not accomplish it in twenty years.[62]

The strategy behind the two-tiered system rested on mutually supportive efforts between infantry and cavalry. Smith intended foot companies, which were often newly situated in hotly contested territory, to identify, slow, and report raiding parties. Horsemen would then attack from the inner cordon to destroy any tribesmen that bypassed the infantry. The inner location of the mounted troops likewise enjoyed logistical benefits of closer proximity to fodder and supply depots in Central and East Texas. In practice, the strategy proved untenable. As before, foot soldiers could not compete in a mobile arena and the second line could not respond with rapidity. As before, the state would again have to mobilize rangers to fill the security gap.[63]

The year 1853 initially proved relatively calm as the Federal government—in large part due to advocacy by Secretary of War Jefferson Davis—attempted to ease tensions by placing elements of the Caddo, Anadarko, Waco, Kichai, Tawakoni, Delaware, Tonkawa, and Penateka Comanche on reservations in Central Texas. Despite attempted pacification, by 1854 bands of dissatisfied tribesmen, both on and off reservations and often in response to settler provocations, again raided homesteads and settlements.[64] In desperation, Smith beseeched the state capital to mobilize a new iteration of "Texas Mounted Volunteers" to patrol as auxiliaries.

Little is known of these rangers' service record. With six full companies the force comprised a small and decentralized regiment, or perhaps a large battalion, but never operated consolidated. All the companies remained active throughout the first term as they reinforced the Federal Line along dispersed patrol sectors. Smith then retained three for a second enlistment—again validating the utility of light horse augmentation. One company under command of Virginian William Henry, grandson to the famed American patriot, served out of Fort Clark to the west of San Antonio. Ford remembered the fellow Mexican-American War veteran as "brave" and "possessing merit" but "difficult to control." The Texans' co-use of the army fort demonstrated a potential for symbiotic relationships between regulars and auxiliaries. Smith discharged all the ranger companies by April of 1855.[65]

Transition to Expeditionary Strikes

Native American attacks, in concert with cross-border marauding by Mexican elements, rose sharply in the summer of 1855. Guadalupe and Bexar counties in South Texas bore the brunt of the raiding. Even as the U.S. Army remained stretched across expansive fortification lines it reported only six Indian engagements in 1854, and tellingly, just two the next year. In frustration the governor authorized Georgian immigrant James Callahan, a popular veteran, rancher, and farmer who held singular status as the sole remaining survivor of the 1836 Goliad massacre, to form a special command of "Mounted Volunteers" to seek out and destroy both Indian and Hispanic offenders.[66] Given his harrowing experiences in the Texas Revolution and service as a militia officer in the Texan-Mexican invasions of 1842, the captain held a long-standing and deeply ingrained ethnic hatred for Mexicans.

The governor's orders emphasized proactive interdiction and rapid pursuit while implicitly criticizing the army's more passive posture: "It is expected that you will be actively engaged in ranging in their vicinity unless it may become necessary to pursue any marauding parties of Indians that may be found in the neighborhood, in which case you are authorized to follow them up and chastise them wherever they may be found."[67] State fiscal prioritization would rise to match gubernatorial rhetoric as the Texas Congress expanded military-related expenditures to a shocking 24 percent of its entire budget over the next six years.[68]

Callahan swiftly recruited a small battalion of three companies. He distributed company commands to himself, the energetic William Henry, and San Jacinto veteran Nathaniel "Nat" Benton for a total strength of 111 men. This event-specific and short-term mobilization reflected a return to the volunteer, and extremely partisan, activations favored by Henry Karnes and John Moore during the genocidal campaigns of the Texas Republic. It also represented the largest instance where multiple ranging companies fought consolidated, as opposed to geographically dispersed, since deactivation of the Mexican War regiments.[69]

Disregarding international treaty stipulations, on October 1 the rangers followed suspected tribal marauders south into Mexico in order to eliminate the threat. Then, on October 3, they clashed with a surprisingly large force of 600 allied Mexicans and Indians. The engagement began when a detachment of 200 warriors attempted to draw the

Anglos into a prepared ambush. Callahan sensed deception, refused to charge, and instead established a dismounted line that would favor American long rifles. John Samson, a volunteer in the ranks, recalled the enemy response: "We had no sooner placed ourselves in battle array than, to our surprise and dismay 600-700 armed Mexicans and Indians climbed up the bank and formed in line parallel with the stream."[70]

Severely outnumbered and potentially outflanked, Callahan embraced the tried and true Texian tactic of unleashing coordinated rifle volleys from behind cover to attrite enemy ranks and resolve. Sensing a shift in momentum as marksmen peppered the advancing lines, he then remounted the portion of his men that possessed Colt revolvers and charged straight into the weakened Indian component. Samson again narrated: "We followed, charging at full speed, and when our guns were emptied, using their butts as cudgels on such of the enemy as dared to await our approach."[71] The speed and audacity of the assault shattered the warband and caused it to break and flee. The Mexican companies likewise withdrew in haste, clearly hesitant to engage Texan firepower at close range. The retreating Natives set fire to the field to obscure their escape.[72]

The rangers lost four men killed and seven wounded while the opposing allies reportedly suffered at least thirty dead. Requiring shelter and a defensible position to regroup, the Texans occupied the nearby Mexican town of Piedras Negras. The next morning Callahan learned that an even larger and better organized Mexican counter-attack was coming. Exhausted and constrained by wounds, the invaders finally retreated back north. They attempted to create their own smoke screen to facilitate escape, but inadvertently, if not intentionally, destroyed most of the town when the flames spread. This act would prove diplomatically controversial as the Mexicans claimed that the action was wanton and purposeful.[73]

The rangers re-crossed the Rio Grande into American territory on October 9 while leaving an international uproar in their wake. Governor Pease applauded the pursuit into Mexico and commended the victory, but censured Callahan, however superficially, for the destruction of

Piedras Negras. The governor ultimately justified the expedition to General Smith, writing that he had "made no objection to his pursuit of the Indians across the Rio Grande" but "only objected to his occupation of the Territory of Mexico after the termination of his engagement with the Indians."[74] Despite the controversy, Mexican forays into South Texas decreased over the next year.

Texas experienced a reduction of Federal troops in 1857 as national priorities shifted. By end of year the War Department reduced total army presence to 31companies to defend the state's 1,300 mile frontier.[75] Despite reductions in mobility capacity that included the departure of the 1st U.S. Mounted Rifles for New Mexico Territory to counter Apaches, the elite and newly formed 2nd U.S. Cavalry Regiment had assumed responsibility for volatile sections of the frontier two years prior. This regiment's impact was immediate, bloody, and tangible as total U.S. Army engagements had spiked to fourteen in 1856 and nineteen the next year.[76]

Anglo-Indian fighting—in addition to rising Anglo and *Tejano* criminality—increased again even as the U.S. Army shifted its posture. Ford described how throughout "the winter of 1857–1858 murders and robberies were regular occurrences on the whole line of the frontier from the Red River to El Paso and from El Paso to the mouth of the Rio Grande."[77] He then recalled popular criticism, as editorialized in the *Texas State Gazette*, which claimed that "Texas, with little or no federal patronage, is left by the Federal Government to protect herself from the savage foe, or to heedlessly stand by and witness the daily and brutal murder of our people."[78] This feeling of national neglect, though naive and often overstated given Texas's generous share of Federal investment and concurrent provocation of Indian wrath, would fire its enthusiasm for secession in 1861.

The new Texas governor, Hardin Runnels, addressed the state senate in January of 1858 to gain political support for expanded military funding. He first reminded the legislature that they now had "four Companies of Rangers on the frontier, three of 20 men each and one of 30 ... stationed on the head waters of the Guadalupe, on the Colorado, and two on the waters of the Brazos." The governor then complained that these detachments were "insufficient for the protection of the frontier." Finally, in an obvious attempt to deflect political blame, Runnels criticized Washington, D.C. for security lapses while promoting a tactical solution:

> It is the duty of the Federal Government to afford the protection required ... from the great extent of the frontier exposed nothing short of a permanent mounted force of several hundred men will be anything like adequate to the object, unless an expedition be authorized to follow the Indians to their places of retreat, break up their lodges and execute on them that summary vengeance which along can give permanent peace.[79]

This genocidal prescription echoed brutal patterns of ethnic elimination that had characterized Texan solutions to Indian problems during previous periods. The governor's intent emulated the aggressive and nakedly imperialist policies of the Lamar administration, in particular, during the height of the Texas Republic's assault against the Cherokee and Comanche. Frustrated and intensely biased, many Texans again concluded that offensive campaigns would achieve greater success than defensive interdiction could ever hope for.

On January 27, 1858, the Texas Congress accordingly approved "an Act for the better protection of the frontier" to counter the feared, and perennially exaggerated, threat of the Comanche Empire. The legislation, largely sponsored by colonial ranger and antebellum legislator George Erath, authorized an expeditionary force of 100 men to enlist for six months. It allocated $70,000 to fund the deployment. The act also directed the company be discharged if replaced by Federal troops, offering subtle invitation for the army to assume a similarly aggressive posture or be supplanted, and thus embarrassed, by state initiative.[80]

The *Texas State Gazette* reported the predictable selection of a highly respected and experienced ranger to lead the company: "Gov. Runnels has appointed Capt. John S. Ford to the command of the frontier troops, with the rank of Senior Captain." The paper endorsed the appointment when it attested that the popular frontiersman was "an old Indian fighter, and we predict that he will rid the frontier of all annoyances in the first campaign."[81] Like his one-time mentor Jack Hays, Ford had now fully assumed the role of preeminent tactical leader in Texas.

On January 28 Runnels empowered the senior captain with clear and specific orders: "I impress upon you the necessity of energy and action. Follow any and all trails of hostile or suspected hostile Indians you may discover, and if possible, overtake and chastise them, if unfriendly."[82] In accordance with his mandate, Ford formed an inordinately large company comprised of four lieutenants, four sergeants, four corporals, one hundred and eight privates, and two buglers. This organization reflected his appreciation for defined military structure gained while on campaign with the 1st Texas Mounted Rifles in Mexico.

Edward Burleson Jr., son of the former Texian general and vice president, joined as senior lieutenant for the company. As the off-spring of one of the most capable and ruthless militia commanders in Anglo-American history, the younger Burleson represented another generational shift within the state's martial tradition. He personified the first generation of Texans that grew to adulthood as frontier residents, thereby fully absorbing militant culture that flourished in the western counties. In Burleson's case, the son who had grown to adulthood watching his father lead mounted regiments for the republic out of Bastrop now led his own irregular cavalrymen to fight for Texas.[83]

In late February Ford launched the campaign from Austin with a northern sweep of the Colorado River and Pecan Bayou valleys. The company rode in four detachments moving along parallel axes that maximized ground cleared. He simultaneously dispatched an advance party to establish a base in North Texas for the Comanche expedition. Named Camp Runnels, the crude station was situated near Fort Belknap. After clearing the valleys, Ford was "satisfied that there are no Mounted Indians in the regions," he consolidated the rangers at the forward camp.[84]

The location of Fort Runnels positioned the Texans to aggressively clear the prairies of northern Texas, and if necessary, attack into Indian Territory north of the Red River. While in camp the senior captain revealed another quality learned under Hays: appreciation of disciplined and realistic tactical training. Ford described how he accordingly prepared his men for action: "Drilling was done daily. The Indian drill was not neglected. Firing at targets on horseback at all gaits was practiced." The men also boasted a greater density of Colt revolvers by this time, reflecting much improved armament from the years immediately following the Mexican War. The Colt Model 1851 Navy, which contained six cylinders at .36 caliber, offered a popular option for the horsemen.[85]

The rangers marched north on April 22 with 102 well-armed and well-mounted Texans. In a brilliant act of tactical multiplication, Ford enlisted 113 friendly Caddo, Waco, Shawnee, Delaware, Tawakoni, and Tonkawa from the Brazos Reservation to support the campaign. This augmentation hinted at previous, and common sense, colonial and republican methods of co-opting indigenous knowledge to assist reconnaissance and navigation. After recruiting auxiliaries the captain stated his pleasure with the alliance: "When we take up the line of march we shall feel assured of being able to direct our course upon the Comanche camp." With such diverse capabilities Ford now felt "sanguine of success."[86]

The task force rode up the Red River and soon crossed into Indian Territory. Throughout the advance the senior captain recalled how "Indian scouts and spies made reconnaissance in every direction." This division of duty maximized the natives' fleeter horsemanship while preserving the Anglo riflemen platoons for potential assault. On May 11 allied warriors identified a band of Kotsoteka Comanche chasing buffalo and surmised a large camp or domestic village stood close by. The Texans trailed the hunters with the intention of organizing a dawn strike but lost them in the undulating terrain. Despite the setback, scouts located a small village on the Little Robe Creek a short time later.

Ford described the delayed assault that followed: "Our plan was now frustrated, since the sun was coming up: we were compelled to march upon the foe in open day." He explained that "at 7 o'clock A.M. a small camp of five lodges was discovered and taken. The Tonks remained, demolished the camp, took some prisoners, and mounted their footmen." Hoping for a more decisive victory, the rangers pursued as the "Comanche fled towards the Canadian." They then "followed at full gallop, knowing that they were hurrying to inform their people" of the Texans' approach.[87]

The allied task force pursued the fleeing Indians and came upon "a large encampment" three miles away on the north bank of the Canadian River. A canny veteran of many battles, Ford first sent his auxiliaries ahead to deceive the Comanche as to the true size of his multi-ethnic battalion and presence of well-armed soldiers. In an effective example of how all sides employed deception ploys in frontier warfare, he hoped the defenders would believe that "they had only Indians and bows and arrows to contend with."

The Comanche war chief, conspicuously clad in an ancient coat of Spanish chain-mail, immediately rallied his warriors to face the invading tribesmen. He realized too late that Ford had armed his Indians with "Mississippi rifles and six-shooters" and the chief was immediately struck down. The Texan main force then advanced and charged the main camp, where according to the captain, the Comanche "intended to make a stand." The weight of the combined assault soon routed the defenders. Ford remembered that "Indians fled in every direction" while his rangers "moved straight through the camp and poured in a galling fire upon the retreating enemy."[88]

The Texan platoons dispersed to give chase as the Comanche fled the scene. Ford called it "a series of single combats" as "squads of rangers and Indians were pursuing the enemy in every direction." Though seemingly unorganized and chaotic, decentralization actually allowed more thorough engagement of enemy warriors. Had the rangers remained consolidated in a single body, the majority of the Comanche would have escaped in smaller, elusive elements. The resulting fight, really a series of skirmishes, unfolded over "a circuit of six miles in length and more than three in breadth" as the aggressors pursued on horseback. The Texans reconsolidated at mid-day and permanently destroyed the village.[89]

Despite the unqualified victory, the day's fighting was far from over. Comanche from "a large encampment three or four miles above the Canadian" had heard of the attack and mobilized to counter the invaders. The allied Indians, fired by age-old hatred of the Comanche Empire, requested the honor of engaging first. Yet they pragmatically requested that Ford "keep his rangers in line to support them, if necessary." The Texan commander mocked the ritual demonstrations that followed between opposing Indians: "A scene was now enacted beggaring description. It reminded one of the rude and chivalrous days of knight-errantry." Growing impatient, Ford eventually sent rangers to force the confrontation and the Comanche began to retreat.[90]

The gunmen charged forward after the Indians in hopes of achieving a third victory in one day. Ford recalled how his men advanced "not with the precision of practiced veterans, yet with as much coolness and bravery." They attempted to envelop the Comanche before they could escape, but the "untimely arrival of the Tonkawa Indians" complicated the plan and thus "prevented the complete success of the maneuver." The rangers pursued their enemy for two miles before halting the chase. Ford recalled that with "jaded horses" the exhausted men finally returned to the first Comanche village.[91]

Called the Battle of Antelope Hills, the raid proved a bloody tactical success with limited strategic impact. According to the battle report, which reflected probable exaggeration, the Comanche suffered at least seventy-six killed and "a great many wounded" while Texans lost only two killed and three wounded. After destroying the enemy villages the expeditionary force returned to Camp Runnels on May 21 having fulfilled the governor's intent.[92] Ford later attested that "the conduct of the men of my command was characterized by obedience, patience, and perseverance. They behaved, while under fire, in a gallant and soldier like manner and I think that they have fully vindicated their right to be recognized as Texas Rangers of the old stamp."[93]

This reference to the Lone Star martial tradition unfortunately invoked barbarity reminiscent of atrocities during the Mexican War and hundreds of years of tribal genocides before that. Ford's attack into Comanche territory emulated the brutal raiding patterns that had plagued the region for centuries. Like Apache, Comanche, Spanish, and Texians before them, rangers of American Texas utilized preemptive strikes against domestic centers to eliminate the enemy's capacity for war. This strategy followed merciless frontier logic acculturated, if not institutionalized, by leaders like Stephen Austin, John Moore, Henry Karnes, Edward Burleson, and John Hays. Moving beyond morality and entirely willing to justify ruthless means for strategic ends, it represented a return to the most insidious form of North American warfare.

In September of 1858 the 2nd U.S. Cavalry conducted a long-distance raid emulative of Ford's expedition. The sheer audacity of the attack indicated marked tactical adaptation and conscious internalizing of Texan methods. Under command of Major Earl Van Dorn—a West Point graduate and future Confederate major general—the northern garrison launched an audacious expedition to also strike Comanche north of the Red River. The mission included companies A, F, H, and K from the 2nd U.S. Cavalry with detachments from the 1st U.S. Infantry in support. Like his state counterparts, Van Dorn recruited natives from the Brazos Reservation to provide reconnaissance. The task force totaled 225 soldiers and 135 tribesmen in one of the larger expeditions of the antebellum period.[94]

In what eventually became known as the Wichita Expedition, the *ad hoc* battalion attacked a village of approximately 500 Comanche at Rush Springs in the Wichita Mountains. They adopted the proven Anglo-Texan tactic of striking the village at dawn, which was actually inherited from eastern American frontiersmen, and the fight quickly devolved into a chaotic melee that lasted for almost an hour.

The attackers destroyed 120 lodges, killed 56 men and 2 women, and captured 300 horses. Van Dorn callously boasted of the victory in his report: "nothing was left to mark the site of their camp, but the ashes and the dead."[95]

The decisiveness of the Wichita raid—despite the fact that it occurred as only one of three total engagements by the U.S. Army in Texas that year—created the template for tactical, if not strategic, success for Federal forces after a decade of failing to effectively counter or eliminate Indian threats.[96] In May of 1859 Van Dorn consequently repeated the maneuver with a larger raid on a Penateka Comanche camp in Kansas Territory near Crooked Creek. This assault force included companies A, B, C, F, G, and H of the 2nd U.S. Cavalry for a total of 427 soldiers with 58 native horsemen in support. Completely mounted, the small regiment deployed as an extremely mobile formation with exceptional operational reach.[97]

The raiders located the target village on May 13. Because of the mountainous nature of the terrain, Van Dorn elected to approach mounted but then assault on foot. The soldiers found the Indians unprepared and the attack commenced as planned. Despite their tactical disadvantage and the presence of many women and children, the warriors resisted stubbornly and desperately. When the battle, or more aptly described massacre, ended, the Comanche had lost forty-nine men and eight women killed. The attackers suffered two soldiers and two native auxiliaries dead, and another thirteen wounded.[98]

The expeditionary strikes of the 2nd U.S. Cavalry in 1858 and 1859, however brutal, illustrated the belated tactical adaptation by the U.S. Army on western frontiers. In contrast with the historical American dragoon model, Secretary of War Jefferson Davis had personally designed, equipped, and manned the elite regiment to fight and ride more aggressively with better weaponry and equine stock.[99] The resulting victories by the regiment in Texas, which ironically emulated ranger strengths even as Davis despised the rough auxiliaries, maximized the twin enablers of mobility and firepower to achieve operational success on the Great Plains.

This gradual reaction to Indian initiative followed the precedent for Euro-American adaptation established initially by Spanish *compañies volantes* and later by Texian rangers. Each nationalistic military had responded to the same guerrilla challenges in Texas with nearly identical answers: mounted forces to counter fleet threats. For the newly empowered American army in Texas, increased willingness to attack preemptively at a distance now allowed them to execute Brevet Major General David Twiggs's exasperated directive to "follow up the Comanche to the residence of their families."[100] After years of struggle, the Federal army in the Lone Star State now embraced the familiar horror of population-centric warfare.

The final ranger events of 1858 again involved Ford, now unquestionably the most respected ranger captain in the state. In November the governor authorized him to raise "a company of Rangers to serve for six months." Despite initial successes by Texas's reservation program, which had settled an array of amenable tribes on territories near the upper Brazos River, a flurry of raids by renegades, Anglo imposters, and northern Comanche again accosted "exposed settlements" on the state's periphery.[101]

In response, Runnels authorized additional village-oriented campaigns to eliminate the source of the raids. He then issued the following directive to Ford:

> You will take measures to render your Campaign effective, defensively and offensively. Should the good of your service, and the danger to the border settlements from Indian incursions, require the organization to move against the Comanche in their own haunts, you are fully authorized and empowered to muster the requisite number of men into State service to accomplish the object.[102]

Like the Lamar Administration almost ten years before, the Texan executive now fully embraced ethnic destruction as a legitimate policy to stabilize borders. Capitalizing on recent successes, Ford formed a larger command: a battalion of four mounted companies. Despite the offensive's intended scope it failed to attain a decisive victory as before due to its inability to locate targets. The true import of the mission was that it revealed the methodical acceptance of tribal elimination by officials in Austin.

Ford's rangers were involved in an event of cultural importance to Texas's way of war that occurred in January of 1859. On December 27 a group of vigilante Anglo settlers led by zealot Peter Garland murdered seven innocent Caddo women and children from the Brazos Reservation. They attacked as retaliation for the reported murder and rape of two Anglo women and molestation of two Anglo girls. Under pressure from the Federal government, state authorities ordered Ford to arrest seventeen men purportedly involved in the slaughter. The ranger refused, stating he would facilitate the writ only "under the direction of a civil officer." He then questioned the propriety of using a "military officer to arrest citizens."[103] More pragmatically, Ford also worried about fighting between the arresting rangers and local militia if he prosecuted the warrant.

This incident held importance to the development and inherent nature of Lone Star militarism because it revealed the exclusive military orientation of rangers prior to Reconstruction. Ford, in his own words, viewed his purpose as purely "military" and not "civil." He offered to "assist" the arrest under judicial orders, but would not command the operation. While frontier cavalrymen like Hays had occasionally hunted outlaws in the past, exemplified by the hunt for Agaton Quinones near San Antonio in 1843, early rangers considered themselves a defined military arm.[104] The institution's adoption of the police function, even in its volatile and capricious frontier forms, would not emerge until well after the Civil War.

The First Cortina War

The U.S. Army and rangers' focus shifted south in the summer of 1859 in what became known as the First Cortina War. Tensions between *Tejano* and Anglo setters in South Texas, which exacerbated centuries of discontentment amongst Rio Grande border communities, had inflamed as Anglo merchants, ranchers, and settlers seized lucrative properties and resources from Hispanic owners. The rapid transfer of local political power to Anglos in South Texas, begun in earnest following the perceived treachery of San Antonio *Tejanos* during the Woll Invasion of 1842, catalyzed the social discontentment necessary for armed rebellion.

Hispanic militancy exploded on July 13, 1859, when Juan Nepomuceno Cortina, a prominent rancher and Mexican Army veteran of the twin battles of Palo Alto and Resaca de la Palma, killed a Brownsville constable who was subjecting one of Cortina's former employees to harsh treatment. Cortina escaped to Matamoros and *Tejanos* and Mexicans along the Rio Grande hailed him as a hero. Ford later complimented the revolutionary leader as "fearless, self-possessed, and cunning," and wrote that he often "acted decisively and promptly."[105] The popular rebel would frustrate both rangers and regulars alike for a score of years while demonstrating his remarkable ability to combine guerrilla and conventional tactics.

On September 28 Cortina exacted revenge on the town that had spurned him. He led a force of over seventy-five riders, largely gathered from supporters in Mexico, to attack Brownsville directly. Cortina's prime objective was the execution of the town marshal and a former business partner, Adolphus Clavaecke, in addition to rescuing several *Tejano* prisoners. With surprise and shock the raiders "killed whomever they wished, robbed whomever they pleased" as they occupied the town, according to Ford. Two days later Cortina set camp seven miles away and repulsed an ill-advised counter-attack by militia called the "Brownsville Tigers" on October 24. The rebel's legend was expanding across the disenfranchised *Tejano* communities and the rangers had found a new enemy.[106]

Runnels responded to the crisis by immediately authorizing an improvised expedition of mounted riflemen to counter the Cortina militants. The governor selected veteran ranger William Tobin for command and the company rode south to Brownsville, which effectively stood under siege. On November 20 Cortina's force defeated a detachment of Tobin's rangers and killed three of them. When Tobin found the bodies they had been mutilated and left to rot in the sun. The fight was now personal for the discovering Texans, who yet retained ethnic enmity over atrocities of earlier wars.[107]

Skirmishing continued over the next two weeks as both sides mustered additional fighters to their side. By mid-December the U.S. Army joined Tobin's rangers in Brownsville under the command of Major Samuel Heintzelman. Adopting an offensive mindset, the infantry officer led an *ad hoc* battalion comprising two infantry companies, one artillery company, one cavalry company, and attached rangers as mounted auxiliaries against Cortina on December 14. He brought two 24-pound howitzers to provide mobile fire support.[108]

The American task force of 165 regulars and 125 irregulars marched down the Laredo Road with "Rangers in advance & on the flanks," meaning they were reconnoitering as light cavalry, according to Heintzelman's journal. The advance scouts soon discovered Cortina had evacuated camp and established a fortified position supported by captured cannon in a "dense chaparral" farther down the road. Upon making contact, Heintzelman neutralized Cortina's cannon with his own and then charged the position with several companies. When the Americans arrived they discovered that the slippery Cortina had displaced again.[109]

Mounted rangers and cavalry pursued the *Tejano* rebels along parallel roads with the Texans making first contact. They discovered that Cortina had left a rear guard in a dense brush, allowing the leader to again escape. Tobin dismounted his Texans and cleared the position with intense close-quarters fighting. Heintzelman—who held volunteers in low regard like most regular officers—offered rare praise when he admitted that "the Rangers, supported by the foot, soon routed them again." Despite the commendation, later reports by Tobin and the major conflicted on who owned fault for allowing the rebels to withdraw. In actuality a combination of indecision and challenging terrain conspired to retard the American advance. Cortina, ever the elusive guerrilla, escaped to fight another day.[110]

Simultaneous to the escalation at Brownsville, the governor had dispatched Ford with another company of fifty-three rangers as reinforcements. Ford wrote that his men "reached Major Heintzelman's regulars shortly after they had driven Cortina from the field" and that "the two commands went into camp." Much to Tobin's disappointment, Runnells had also appointed Ford commander of all state troops at the rank of major.[111] Though modest, this promotion represented Texas's highest active auxiliary rank since the Mexican War.

On December 20, after several days of reconnaissance patrols by rangers and collaborative planning between Ford and Heintzelman, the improvised battalion marched west towards Rio Grande City. Cortina had established a defensive position in the town with approximately 600 revolutionaries. Though ill-trained and newly formed, the rebels' impressive numbers, firepower, and fortification would require a set-piece attack by the Americans.[112] Ford, now in command of all volunteers, described the advance:

> About the twentieth of December a forward movement was made. The main body consisted of regular infantry, cavalry, and artillery. Tobin's and Tomlinson's companies followed the road leading from Brownsville to Rio Grande City ... the third day's march brought to light many acts of vandalism. Houses had been robbed and fired, fences burned, property destroyed or carried into Mexico ... Cortina had committed these outrages upon citizens of the United States regardless of race and upon Mexicans suspected of being friendly to the Americans.[113]

The Americans halted on December 26, eighteen miles from the town, to plan their final approach.

Heintzelman elected to attack with an ambitions envelopment strategy designed to definitively end the uprising and kill Cortina. After conducting night reconnaissance of the disposition of Cortina's defensive positions, Ford discovered that the Mexican position was sound: Cortina's right was protected by the river, the center by two infantry companies and cannon along the road, and the left by men and cannon in a cemetery. The veteran soldier held cavalry in reserve. Despite the *Tejanos'* readiness, and similar to the American strategy used to capture Monterrey on a far larger scale, the Texans led the American assault with simultaneous attacks against the Mexican center and left at daybreak.[114]

The rangers rapidly made contact with Cortina's lines and commenced a dismounted assault against both fronts. After taking "terrific fire," Ford's men outflanked the central cannon and routed the rebel infantry. The Texan commander recalled how they utilized horses to quicken the infantry-style assault: "Our mounted men advanced at a brisk gallop, and left the road by an inclination to the right at less than a hundred yards from the enemy artillery. Cavalry halted, dismounted about forty yards from the cannon, and opened fire. I now instructed them to advance under cover of chaparral and take the pieces in flank."[115]

Cortina launched infantry, and then riders, to repulse the Texan advance. The rangers assumed a hasty defensive line and shattered the charge with blazing revolvers and precision rifle fire. Tobin and his wing then turned back the remainder of the *Tejano* counter-attack. Ford wrote of the deadly impact of Texan weaponry on the rebel cavalry: "Many a charger galloped off, carrying an empty saddle; Cortina's bold riders were left on the ground." Heintzelman's regulars, again slow to advance, arrived in time to skirmish with a Mexican detachment on the defenders' right flank.[116]

Dislodged from the town, Cortina and his remaining fighters retreated down the road towards Roma. After moving several miles they set a blocking position across the road with cannon support. As they attempted to maintain momentum Texans again led the American advance and charged through scattershot to reach Cortina's position. Ford described the attack: "the matter of nationality was decided right there. A furious charge scattered Cortina's bodyguard and left one of his pieces in our possession." The rangers then "mounted the piece and fired a salute." Suffering from a second defeat, Ford recalled how the "enemy attempted no further resistance. They seemed panic-stricken, and abandoning the other cannon, fled."[117]

The Texans feared that Cortina would move on the nearby town of Roma to "rob it" for supplies and launched another rapid pursuit. The fear turned out unfounded; the wily revolutionary had left the road and sought refuge in the wilderness. The rangers continued to Roma where Ford "gave the inhabitants assurance of protection." They then rode east to rejoin Heintzelman and to consolidate their wounded and dead.[118]

The American victory was complete, if only temporary. Ford later assessed Cortina's casualties: "the loss of the enemy was officially reported at sixty killed. We afterwards ascertained it was much greater."[119] Heintzelman likewise boasted of distances marched against the rebels: "We marched yesterday about 20 miles & this morning 20 more & then 9 in pursuit. Near 50 miles & a fight is pretty good business. I hope the matter is ended."[120] Despite the severity of Cortina's defeat and the major hopes for peace, the *Tejano* rebellion survived.

Rangers scoured the Rio Grande on both the American and Mexican sides for the next three months as Cortina shifted to sporadic guerrilla resistance. While the Texas governor discharged Tobin's company, he authorized Ford to raise another. The volunteers supported Heintzelman with patrolling and interdiction to clear the area. The combined state-federal force, known as the Rio Grande Squadron, defeated Cortina at the Battle of La Bolsa on February 4, and again at the Battle of Ranch La Mesa on March 17. The revolutionary survived and suspended his activism, though not for the last time.[121] In the summer of 1861, even as Texas mobilized to fight the Union Army, Ford, along with *Tejano* cavalryman Santos Benavides, would defeat an ever defiant Cortina along the Rio Grande frontier for the last time.[122]

The First Cortina War caused the deaths of an estimated 151 rebel combatants, 80 Hispanic civilians, and 15 Anglo residents. The conflict was characterized by both unconventional and conventional operations, albeit on a far smaller scale than during the Mexican-American War. This mixture of guerrilla fights and linear battles illustrated continued tactical versatility by Texan frontier cavalry, especially when facing troops with inferior armament. As auxiliaries they conducted mounted reconnaissance, infantry-style assaults, and mounted charges in a single campaign. These achievements were similar to Texan actions in the Monterrey Campaign thirteen years prior.[123]

The second consistent Texan military quality highlighted during the Cortina Wars was societal ability to rapidly mobilize and deploy volunteer forces. While the Federal garrison was slow to respond, state horsemen arrived with alacrity and saved Brownsville from another capitulation despite initially suffering defeat. Differences in cavalry mobilization between state and national army further demonstrated Texas's continued cultural fixation with mounted warfare. The U.S. Army found only one company of cavalry to participate while Texas eventually formed and dispatched five mounted companies.

The Cortina War coincided with the ascendency of Sam Houston to the Texas governorship. As with his prior presidency, the new administration resulted in increased, though economized, ranger and militia preparedness. Houston proclaimed the state's security crises, with familiar refrains, in his first address to the Texas Congress: "A considerable portion of our state bordering on the Rio Grande is in a state of turmoil and war, our frontier is unprotected and harassed by Indians ..."[124] This consternation reflected the dual threat scenario that had troubled the frontier polity since the first skirmishes of its 1835 revolution: tribesmen raided along the northwestern frontier while Mexican opponents threatened from the south.

Final Antebellum Years

Texas experienced its largest ranger mobilization since the Mexican-American War, albeit more decentralized and inactive, under Houston's short gubernatorial term. As president he had always preferred minimalist and forward deployed mounted forces. As a U.S. Senator he repeatedly championed constant patrolling by specialized and interested horsemen over regulars and static defenses. Over the next two years, as the state moved towards another rebellion, the aging statesman implemented a familiar and tiered system of pro-active ranger companies and reactive local militia. While the former interdicted with economized benefit, the latter provided localized protection at little cost. State forces would peak at thirty-two companies and detachments just prior to secession.[125]

In December of 1859 and January of 1860, with Ford still commanding two companies along the Rio Grande, Houston activated three additional companies to patrol North and West Texas. Native American raiding had increased with tribal expulsion from the Brazos Reservation and forced deportation to Indian Territory. One angry settler in San Saba County complained in desperation to the governor: "they have never been here in so great numbers, nor have they manifested such hostile depredations as they have been within the last two weeks." Another frontiersman likewise exclaimed that "the Indians" were "stealing and prowling about in almost every direction."[126] With this cry echoing all across frontier counties—whether embellished or not—Houston was politically compelled to take action.

The first of the new companies was led by North Carolinian immigrant William Dalrymple and mobilized on January 14 and patrolled northern Texas until April of 1861. His force eventually counted sixty-five rangers. A second company, led by veteran captain John Conner, served from January to May of 1860 in the counties of San Saba, llano, Mason, McCulloch, and Brown in western Texas. He enlisted sixty men to guard for these localities.

Edward Burleson Jr., now a respected tactical leader, activated the third unit on January 30. He initially led his men along the Nueces River in the south and then shifted north to patrol between the Red and Canadian rivers in May of 1860. The next August and September Burleson once again moved south to protect Coleman and San Saba counties. His company totaled sixty-nine men and reflected another robust complement compared to most ranging companies fielded in Texas between 1822 and 1865. Each of these units maintained its own blacksmith and surgeon since they habitually patrolled beyond support range.[127]

Despite increased patrol saturation, it soon became clear that further defensive measures were required. Civic leader T.H. Espy from Lampasas complained to Houston on February 16 that "the present Ranging Companies of Connor and Dalrymple together with the Frontier Garrisons" were "not near sufficient to keep back these thieving murdering Indians." He then offered his own assessment of the dire situation, writing that even "Six or Eight more companies would not I think suffice." The disgruntled settler finally advocated expeditionary strikes "to carry a devastating war into the Comanche Nation," or failing that, "Militia Companies could be organized in all the frontier counties and Ranging Corps be kept in the field at all times."[128]

Houston chose the latter option in accordance with his preference for inactive military structures. Hoping for tribal conciliation, he declined to massacre domestic populations and instead instigated a localized defense strategy. In February of 1860 he authorized three county detachments of twenty volunteers each. Robert White commanded the first in defense of Hamilton, Comanche, Brown, and Llano counties, and Dixon Walker led the second for Erath and Bosque counties. John Salmon commanded the third company, which also patrolled Erath County.[129]

On February 21 Houston expanded his program of decentralized and localized security by authorizing each county in Texas to form a militia. On March 9 he directed the chief justice of each county to field "minute detachments" of fifteen men to "immediately take the field, and enter upon active scouts, affording protection to the inhabitants of their respective counties." This language and tactical intent emulated the original ranger strategy pioneered by Stephen Austin in 1823. At least fifteen counties formed required units. While Texas could not afford to pay militia for active service, Houston did manage to issue 106 Colt revolvers to empower them.[130]

While county militias organized throughout March the governor authorized another active, and more substantial, ranger force to operate between the Frio River and the Rio Grande. He selected Peter Tumlinson, who had recently fought in the Cortina War, to lead the unit. The forty-eight men of this company rode among the better armed of the period. Each man possessed at least one Colt revolver, and many two, as well as a rifle or shotgun, reflecting the increasing availability of repeating weaponry by this time.[131]

The captain divided his unit into patrols of fifteen men each. Though less powerful, decentralized maneuvering allowed them to clear a greater area while maintaining technological superiority over nearly all native warriors. This tactic proved successful enough for the citizenry of Bandera County to request a continuation of the rangers' term: "We have had no peace for a great while until Capt. Tumlinson came to our relief with his mounted Rangers which for two months he has continually scoured our country—and we have felt safe for the first time."[132]

By early March, Texas maintained over 730 rangers on active and inactive status.[133] Despite the larger distribution—which was actually minute compared to Texas's burgeoning population—tribal raids continued. Houston, under increasing political pressure to act decisively, finally organized an offensive expedition and exclaimed that "our bleeding and suffering fellow citizens on the frontier call for aid!"[134] In addition to deterrence, the governor hoped to retrieve horses that Comanche raiders had stolen and led north of the Red River. To accomplish the campaign he authorized wealthy planter Middleton Johnson, a known political supporter, to recruit a "sufficient number of mounted rangers to repel, pursue and punish the Indians now ravaging the northern and northwestern settlements of Texas."[135] The new battalion comprised five companies.

The rangers rendezvoused at Fort Belknap in North Texas and then rode north to patrol the Red River. They initially based out of Camp Radziminski, an old army station in Indian Territory, but failed to make decisive contact with Comanche or stolen horse herds. Logistical issues, and Johnson's inexcusable absence from the campaign to get married, also degraded tactical potential. The *Austin State Gazette* complained of the battalion's failures on July 21, 1860: "We learn from information derived from the Camp of the Rangers under date of 1st July, that Col. M.T. Johnson has not yet arrived; that the Rangers were sadly complaining of their being forced to stay in camp; and that Gov. Houston was charged by them with the shameful delay which had taken place in giving them not chance to fight the Indians."[136]

Concerned with wasted funds and political criticism, Houston recalled the battalion and dismissed it in August. The dismal execution of the mission reflected the governor's own failure to uphold one of the primary tenets that marked his state's way of war: commanders had to be selected based upon proven tactical experience, interest, bravery, and physical capacity for rigorous campaigning. Though often haphazard, the old tradition of rangers electing their own leadership usually ensured that each new captain already had a reputation as a dauntless and committed fighter. The political appointment of the incompetent Johnson to command such an expensive endeavor proved a costly mistake.

Houston authorized a series of ranger companies for targeted service throughout the fall of 1860 and spring of 1861 as prior mobilizations expired. The most notable of these was Captain Lawrence "Sul" Ross's company, which operated in northern Texas where raids had increased in Parker, Young, Palo Pinto, Wise, and Jack counties. On September 11 the governor authorized Ross, who had led the native contingent in Van Dorn's 1858 Wichita Expedition and later commanded one of Johnson's companies, to "raise a company of mounted volunteers of sixty men rank and file with three Lieutenants, four Sergeants and four Corporals." Houston designated the unit for "service in the neighborhood of Belknap."[137]

Drawing on his own experience as a fighting officer and field general, the governor then provided specific staging guidance: "You will make your Posts or stations twenty miles from Belknap, selecting such positions as you may deem most advantageous for the protection of the people of that vicinity." He also gave instruction intended to restrain the offensive scope of the assignment: "In the execution of this order, you will guard the passes leading into the country, and should Indians get into the settlements, you will attack and if possible destroy them."[138] This order reflected traditionally successful approaches to ranger operations that combined proactive patrolling with ruthless assault.

Ross's most important engagement occurred on December 18, 1860, when he launched a task force to locate and attack a possible Comanche encampment on the Pease River. His surprisingly varied force consisted of forty rangers, twenty Federal cavalrymen, and seventy civilian volunteers. The improvised battalion eventually located the native camp after doggedly riding through a storm, but lost the slower volunteer component while en route. Once in sight, Ross dispatched regulars to envelop the Comanche from the rear while he attacked frontally with rangers.

The assault proved bloodily successful as American regulars and irregulars together routed the surprised natives. Comanche warriors determinedly fought to allow time for their women and children to escape but the rangers swiftly overpowered them with volume of fire. Like most village assaults, combat rapidly devolved into small group and individual fighting. As the battle receded, rangers reportedly cornered the great war chief Peta Nocona and executed him.[139]

Ross's raid held another point of significance that no one anticipated: the repatriation of long-lost captive and now tribal member Cynthia Ann Parker. Captured by Comanche in the devastating raid on Fort Parker in 1836 as a young girl, she had completely assimilated and married Nocona. One of her sons, Quanah Parker, would become the last powerful Comanche war leader to resist westward Anglo-American expansion on the Great Plains. Parker spent her remaining days in Texas as a grieving widow while causing a dramatic sensation for the public as she longed for the tribe and family she had grown to cherish.

Despite tactical success by Ross and his contemporaries, the military value of ranging forces was still offset by controversy over their brutality and depredation. The very strengths of non-doctrinal innovation, specialized mobilization, and volunteer motivation produced unintended consequences of destructive excess and racial hostility. Historian Michael Collins condemned the ranger actions between 1845 and 1861 in his 2008 work, *Texas Devils*, writing that "like apparitions from hell, these Texan devils rode through border history as harbingers of death and destruction." The author also accused them of riding as "soldiers of fortune, not freedom; mercenaries and not missionaries of civilization; privateers rather than patriots."[140] From this perspective, which embraces the plight of conquered peoples, rangers embodied the worst aspects of Anglo imperialism.

Contemporary citizens and officials likewise described the excesses of frontier cavalry in antebellum Texas. One Indian Agent, John Rollins, commented in 1850 that there was "a large class of people here who prefer the wild and indolent life of the volunteer to any other condition." He then criticized that rangers lived only "to fight and exterminate the Indians," and that "hatred of the Indians has been cultivated both by the newspapers and interested individuals."[141]

Settler Moses Cantwell offered another perspective on ranger behavior, internally focused, when he complained in 1860 to Houston that, "those rangers that you sent here are thought to do more harm than good ... they are molesting the people at their private homes and at public worship."[142] With this manner of condemnation, which accused vigilante rangers of brutalizing external opponents while undermining internal civil stability, Texan frontier cavalry offered a double-edged sword to both the Federal government that needed mobility augmentation and the expanding settlements that demanded protection.

Jefferson Davis, in his U.S. Senate rebuttal to Houston's repeated requests for national funding of rangers in 1858, cited critical observations of Texan indiscipline in the Mexican War: "if the General had gone further, and said that irregular cavalry always produce disturbance in the neighborhood of a camp, he would have said no more than my experiences would confirm."[143] The Mississippian then preferred regulars over rangers, asserting that if he "should ever have the fortune to command an army," his "experience in Mexico would tell us that we wanted none but regular cavalry—no irregular mounted men of any kind."[144] This reputation for violent behavior, earned along the contested border zones and during the Mexican War, would follow the Texas Rangers well into the next century.

Houston, ever a proponent of his state's favored way of war, mocked Davis's advocacy for Federal soldiers to secure Texas. Responding to claims of improvement by U.S. Army garrisons in 1858, the Texan mocked: "the Senator from Mississippi has spoken of the achievements performed in Texas by the dragoons. A single company of rangers would have done all that." He then referenced the legendary—and nearly always exaggerated—fighting prowess of rangers of the Texas Republic: "Jack Hays, Ben McCulloch, and Gillespie, achieved more than that; and I believe they never had over seventy-five men, and those for a few days only." Houston finished with an unequivocal and seemingly simple demand: "Give us rangers in Texas."[145]

After decades of constant societal warfare, and despite a fractious relationship with Washington D.C., Texas stood relatively and fleetingly secure in 1860. Even as they ceded military primacy to the U.S. Army, the state retained and furthered its dynamic military tradition. Despite the deceptive calm, thousands of Texan volunteers would soon ride against an enemy of unprecedented scale and might: the Union Army. As the legions of the United States advanced to compel political submission, the Lone Star State would answer the Confederate call to arms with the largest cavalry mobilization by any polity in North American history. To accomplish this it would draw upon its unique martial culture and incorporate every lesson learned in the crucible of frontier combat.

Chapter 8

The War for Confederate Independence, 1861–1865

Texas's way of war culminated in the massive mobilization of its forces under the Confederate banner for the American Civil War. Lasting from 1861 to 1865, subjugation by the Union Army presented the greatest territorial threat since Santa Anna's attempted reconquest in 1836. With such existential peril Texas's horsemen responded *en masse* with enthusiasm. The scope of deployment as light cavalry, mounted riflemen, partisan rangers, and mounted militia was unprecedented in North American history and reflected the pinnacle of mounted warfare on the continent. The resulting quantity of Texan horsemen who fought in the Civil War remained unmatched by any state, Confederate or Union, proving the centrality of mounted arms in their society's unique approach to warfare.[1]

As in Texas's previous conflicts, its frontier communities, towns, and cities embraced rebellion with a distinctive martial fervor. For most Texans the contest reflected a nationalistic crusade to preserve Lone Star freedom and honor as they fought first to protect home territory, then for safety of extended family in threatened states, and lastly to preserve the Confederacy. As articulated by Victor Rose of the 3rd Texas Cavalry Regiment, "To us, Texas was the 'nation'; to her alone we owed allegiance; we were allied with the other Southern States, not indissolubly joined."[2] In this regard, the war was seen by many Texans as the second war for independence where they countered yet another foreign army compelling political subordination through military conquest.

This galvanizing nationalism found ready expression in traditional militarism. From its colonial beginnings Texas had favored, with few exceptions, a martial culture that embraced short-term mobilization by volunteer soldiers. Fighting the Union Army would prove no exception. Recognizing the wellspring of Texan inspiration, Brigadier General Paul Hebert, Commander of the Department of Texas, beseeched them to "remember the days of gone, when your own red right hands achieved your independence." Taking the call further, he exhorted heirs of Edward Burleson and Jack Hays to "keep your soil free from the enemy's touch, and to preserve the unsoiled fame of the Texas Rangers."[3]

The geographical and industrial nature of the war demanded the return to a familiar dual threat environment and a monumental effort to fight along multiple fronts. Francis Lubbock, governor of Texas from 1861 to 1863, proudly described his society's feat in simultaneously deploying dozens of regiments to distant theaters while yet patrolling the expansive Indian Frontier. Confident that Texas would rise to the strategic challenge, he wrote that "she needed no foreign bayonets to protect her soil; that, her sons demonstrated their ability to do; and besides, she had been gallantly represented by regiments, composed of her bravest and best, on every battlefield from New Mexico to Virginia."[4]

By 1861, as the American Union hurtled towards fragmentation, Texan militancy stood ready and willing to confront the threat from the northeast. In November of the previous year the *Austin State Gazette* had praised the state's mounted men with old Texian bravado: "We believe Texas Rangers make the most formidable cavalry in the world ... in addition to their six-shooters and rifles, they should be armed with sabers."[5] This advocacy for the superiority of irregulars reflected the deep patriotic pride the frontier polity placed in martial valor. It also emphasized the ingrained culture of masculinity that yet centered on mastery of horses and firearms.

This mobilization drew on the state's storied, and unquestionably embellished, history where the embattled republican era represented a heroic age defined by invincible captains and their legendary feats. As Texans embraced secession in 1861, Lubbock romanticized his society's militarism in a definitively cavalry context while explicitly associating Civil War participation with past icons: "Such gallant frontiersmen as Hays, Walker, Burleson, Ford, McCulloch, Ross, and Baylor had in times past made famous the Texas Rangers and demonstrated their superiority over the United States regulars for frontier service, and men of this class were now in special demand."[6]

This assessment held degrees of truth despite its obvious exaggeration. Though clearly boastful, the governor recognized that similar to previous involvement in the Mexican-American War, his people joined the Confederacy in possession of the largest and most experienced class of combat veterans amongst the American states. No other polity in the fractured Union had faced such a relentless march of bloody border conflict over the previous half-century and no other single state matched the depth, or galvanizing interest, of Texan volunteerism in the Mexican-American War. Yet unlike prior clashes with tribal and Hispanic opponents, the enemy to the north would present an insurmountable challenge in manpower and industry.

Texan-Confederate Mobilization: A Cavalry Affair

The Lone Star State generated a disproportionately large war effort for the rebellion. It mobilized sixty-one cavalry regiments and thirty-nine cavalry battalions reflecting its historical focus on mounted warfare. It also deployed twenty-eight infantry regiments, thirteen infantry battalions, thirty light artillery batteries, and one heavy artillery regiment due to the combined arms nature of the Trans-Mississippi and Eastern theaters. Texas additionally marshaled two Rebel legions containing cavalry, infantry, and artillery, while Unionist Texans who fought against rebellion formed two cavalry regiments and several partisan companies.[7]

While officials in Richmond eventually assigned the preponderance of Texan horse to serve under Confederate command—totaling forty-five regiments and twelve battalions—the frontier polity retained another five regiments and four battalions of rangers to guard against Indian opportunists. The former group generally consisted of conventionally oriented soldiers who fought as centralized light cavalry in support of larger-scale infantry confrontations. The latter forces, which mostly defended along Texas's Indian Frontier to the northwest, patrolled in a counter-guerrilla context to protect peripheral settlements.

Despite the designation of most Texan horsemen as numbered cavalry in the Confederate Army according to doctrinal organizations, the multiplicity of fielded light cavalry, mounted riflemen, and partisan rangers fielded remained distinctly irregular. Each of these regiments formed specifically for wartime service absent professional continuity and with intent to deactivate after the war. Though some served intact for the duration of the conflict and doubtlessly acquired beginnings of *esprit de corps* inherent to regular army lineage, they nevertheless served as amateur cavalrymen.

The rapid creation of so many volunteer regiments profoundly impacted the Texas populace. The rush to arms from virtually every county, for either home defense or expeditionary assignment, militarized most adult males. Aggregate comparisons of total available service age men versus quantity who served under arms revealed the enormous scope of mobilization that spanned national, state, and local echelons. The Federal Census of 1860 counted 92,145 male Anglo-Germanic residents in Texas between the ages of eighteen and forty-five. It can thus be presumed that, at the rate of immigration in 1860 and 1861, the state potentially held 100,000 to 110,000 eligible recruits at the onset of the Civil War. Of this available reserve, somewhere between 60,000 and 90,000 Texan men, stunningly large proportions in any era, provided military service during the rebellion.[8]

This scale of wartime mobilization—which remains disputed amongst scholars—reflected male participation rates between 55 and 81 percent. While not all served simultaneously and many conducted repeat enlistments as units dissolved and reconstituted, it nevertheless demonstrated a strong societal inclination for military service. These percentiles dwarfed enlistment rates even during the Texas Revolution when roughly 2,000 volunteers served from a population of approximately 30,000 Anglo men, women, and children. Given that men comprised the vast majority of early Anglo-Texan colonists, this would have conservatively placed military enlistment during the 1836 San Jacinto Campaign at less than 10 percent. A decade later, during the Mexican-American War, the state deployed an even lower rate from a much larger male population due to its reliance on the U.S. Army for security.

Differentials between Texas's mobilizations for previous conflicts and the Civil War can be further assessed, in plain military terms, by examining the historical disparity in fielded regiments. In the San Jacinto Campaign, under extraordinary pressure, the revolutionary council deployed two minimalist ranger battalions, one small cavalry battalion, and two infantry regiments over a six-month period.[9] In the Mexican-American War, Texas produced a larger effort to provide auxiliary support to the U.S. Army south of the Rio Grande. Throughout the conflict it contributed one ranger regiment, four mounted rifle regiments, one mounted rifle battalion, and one infantry regiment. Though composition of these six regiments differed according to quantities of companies and men due to *ad hoc* mobilization, the normative baseline of five to ten companies comprising 500 to 1000 soldiers remained standard.

These relatively small wartime deployments from 1835 to 1836 and 1846 to 1848 contrasted starkly with much larger and better organized mustering between 1861 and 1865 of ninety-two regiments, fifty-two battalions, and thirty artillery batteries. Intensified commitment reflected the nationalistic passions of Texan citizenry, militarization that characterized their frontier experience, and modernizing recruitment that exhorted and later compelled enlistment. Most Texas cavalry served at home and in Arkansas, Louisiana, and Indian Territory while a lesser portion fought in New Mexico, Tennessee, Mississippi, Georgia, North Carolina, and South Carolina. Unlike their countrymen in the Lone Star infantry, no Texan mounted regiments rode with the famous Army of Northern Virginia, thus diminishing them in popular Civil War imagination.[10]

The ethnic composition of Texan-Confederate units likewise revealed inculcated militancy across various immigrant communities. As the state formed units in rapid succession, comingling of citizens represented a return to past years when Anglos, *Tejanos*, and Indians fought together. Though enlistment across most formations remained 80 percent English, Welsh, and Scottish in ancestry, the 3rd and 8th Texas Infantries served as examples that enjoyed significant *Tejano* presence. Santos Benavides, a leader from Laredo who joined the rebellion, fought as a captain in the 33rd Texas Cavalry against renewed resistance by Juan Cortina.[11] On the Native American side, the 24th Texas Cavalry included twenty Alabama warriors during operations in Arkansas in 1862. Tribesmen likewise conducted logistical duties in Texas to relieve white recruits for front-line service.[12]

Texan ranks also included German, Jewish, and eastern European immigrants who had populated the state over previous decades. The 3rd Texas Infantry Regiment from South Texas, in particular, contained a significant Teutonic concentration. The regiment's second-in-command, August Buchel, immigrated with experience from the Crimean and Mexican-American Wars. Central European immigration presence was even more prevalent in companies that mustered from specific settlements. Company E of the 1st Texas Cavalry, Company B of the 7th Texas Cavalry, and Companies B and F of the 8th Texas Cavalry each contained heavy Germanic representation.[13]

Throughout the conflict all Texan ethnicities displayed a distinct proclivity for mounted arms enlistment above all other military functions. As the state initiated large-scale mobilization in the spring of 1861, propensity for service as armed horsemen emerged in telling differentials between successful recruitment of cavalrymen and the more challenging mustering of infantrymen. While cavalry enlistment revealed a preexisting inclination for historical ranger functions, the call to march and fight on foot was seen by most cowboys and *rancheros* as lower enlistment status.

The highest officials in Texan government noted this dichotomy. Edward Clark, governor at the beginning of the war, emphasized it to the legislature in November of 1861 when he proclaimed that "the predilection of Texans for cavalry service, founded as it is upon their peerless horsemanship, is so powerful that they are unwilling in many instances to engage in service of any other description unless required by actual necessity." He then boasted with pride that his countrymen's "passion for mounted service is manifest in the fact that no call for cavalry has yet been made which has not been complied with almost instantaneously."[14]

Foreign observers who surveyed the Confederacy also noticed Texas's fixation with mounted warfare. Colonel Arthur Fremantle, a British Coldstream Guards officer who toured the South on behalf of his kingdom, further reported differences in martial proclivities from a European perspective. After personally observing various Confederate military establishments, the Englishman noted that, "at the outbreak of the war it was found very difficult to raise infantry in Texas, as no Texan walks a yard if he can help it."[15]

Volunteers in the ranks were not shy or hesitant to reveal their predilection for fighting on horseback and echoed this sentiment in letters and journals. Robert Bunting, chaplain of the 8th Texas Cavalry Regiment, wrote of his society's cavalry fixation: "It is a burning shame that such horsemen as Texians are, and I may justly add, such fighters, too, should be put in the infantry service." Henry Graber of the same regiment complained of instances when tactical considerations forced him to fight dismounted, explaining that "the average cavalryman feels near half whipped if he has to leave his horse any great distance to fight."[16]

Texan soldiers wore distinctive dress that signified their association with a frontier culture enamored with horsemanship and guns. Fremantle again described the appearance of volunteers patrolling the Rio Grande: "their dress consisted simply of flannel shirts, very ancient trousers, jack boots with enormous spurs, and black felt hats ornamented with the 'Lone Star' of Texas." Another traveler, Thomas North of Illinois, described famed Texan spurs as "generally the immense wheel-spur, and though they were not born with them on, yet they might as well have been, for they not only rode in them, but walked in them, ate in them, and slept in them." [17] By the end of war the rangers' ubiquitous boot accoutrements became symbols of expertise in horsemanship.

Texas society's inclination for cavalry service—along with exceptional weaponry and dress that reflected frontier adaptation—reflected tangible sources of nationalistic pride. On September 18, 1861, the *Bellville Countryman* reported the 8th Texas Cavalry's formation in Houston and echoed prevailing sentiments in towns and cities across the state as they sent young men to war: "The regiment will be the pride of Texas, and will feel that they have an ancient and glorious fame to sustain." The editor then referenced the prized martial culture with shameless exaggeration, explaining that "there is an amount of manliness, chivalry and bravery in the Regiment which cannot be surpassed by any regiment of troops in the word. We feel a pride in them, as the representatives of the State itself."

In addition to stoking patriotic zeal, the paper also described the volunteers' tactical specialization. Beginning with the Colt revolver made famous by rangers and then focusing on dual mastery of horsemanship and marksmanship, the editor emphasized qualities of soldiering on the frontier: "Every man has a six-shooter and a bowie-knife in his belt, as well as a rifle or double-barrel shot-gun to be slung in the saddle bow. Trained as they are to riding from infancy, their skill as marksmen is equal to their feats of horsemanship." He then described how "with the rifle they are all sure shots at any fair shooting distance for any of the game in our forest."

This armament focus indicated awareness of the singular status Texan horsemen achieved amongst North American military traditions by the 1860s. Emphasis on tactical skills gained from equine husbandry, hunting, and traveling armed demonstrated an appreciation of mutually supportive benefits of frontier vocations. Like Comanche connections between mounted buffalo hunting and raiding, Texans gained from functionally reinforcing relationships between ranching and stalking animals and riding and firearm skills required for ranger and cavalry operations. While this background allowed an initial edge over Union counterparts, some Federal cavalry attained parity with Southerners after several years of campaigning.

In addition to frequent association with revolvers, Texans relied upon a variety of weaponry innovated by border communities. In the first years of conflict many augmented traditional rifles and hand-guns with an assortment of improvised firearms and long knives that allowed transition and close fire during attacks. Theophilus Noel, a Texan in the Confederate Army of New Mexico, recorded that they deployed from San Antonio in 1861 "armed with squirrel guns, bear guns, sportsman's guns, shot-guns, both single and double barrels, in fact, guns of all sorts." While often effective, this variety of weapons often made resupply of parts and ammunition challenging.[18]

This multiplicity of Texan firearms illustrated a penchant for military adaptation after decades of countering tribal and Mexican opponents. Rangers had learned through costly lessons on both sides of the Rio Grande that repeating and spread-shot firearms allowed tactical superiority in hand-to-hand combat over the edged weapons often favored by Euro-centric cavalries of the period. Famed preference for "Bowie" knives to allow savage work at close quarters reflected a conscious divergence from the sabers favored by traditional cavalry, lancers, and dragoons. Unlike many eastern horsemen, especially in Union ranks, Texan volunteers—true to their classification as mounted riflemen—generally eschewed long slashing blades throughout the war.[19]

Infatuation with revolvers made Texans particularly adept at the ultimate cavalry maneuver of the era: the mounted shock charge. The militant society's historical proclivity for combining aggressive tactics with repeating firearms found immediate impact in the proving grounds of the Civil War. Dating back to their first use of Paterson Colts in the early 1840s on the Indian Frontier, Texan riders had come to specialize in breaking enemy formations with outsized firepower.[20] The Mexican-American War, where the Walker Colt made its debut, proved the inordinate lethality of audacious Texans armed with advanced weaponry.

Walter Lane, a patriotic Texan who personified his state's martial tradition since the San Jacinto Campaign, recalled how his commands utilized speed and density to shatter defensive lines early in the war. While leading the 3rd Texas Cavalry Regiment at the Battle of Wilson's Creek in Missouri in 1861, he led an audacious flank assault against Union infantry. The former ranger described the attack: "I rode down the line, and, the horses being saddled, ordered the men to mount, and drew them from under fire. We were then ordered up to the right, to attack them there." The battle then culminated: "We formed and charged through them. My horse was shot centrally through, falling dead under me. My men passed on in the charge and I was left alone … after a hard fought battle, we defeated the enemy."[21]

These aggressive tactics demonstrated the potency of Texan audacity when combined with speed and lethality. In a later battle, in which Lane led his men against Unionist Creek Indians at the Battle of Chustenahlah in Oklahoma in December of 1861, he recalled another instance where they broke the enemy with a coordinated charge:

> I gave the order to "Mount!" and told the men that when Charlie Watts blew the bugle, and I gave the order to "Charge!" that the sooner they got on the top of that hill, the fewer empty saddles there would be … The hill was very steep, nearly impracticable for cavalry, so our charge on horseback took the Indians by surprise. We went up the hill like "shot out of a shovel," and in a moment were amongst them, before they had time to reload their guns.

As Texan momentum ruptured the native line, Lane recalled "the order of the day then was, six-shooters and double-barreled guns." Due to the rapidity and weight of the charging horsemen, the warriors were soon "running in all directions."[22]

These attacks could terrify static opponents, especially in 1861 and 1862 when volunteers, and even many regulars, arrived to battlefields unprepared for such fury. A shock charge in December of 1861 by Terry's Texas Rangers near Woodsville, Kentucky, offered a another example where Union defenders recalled the impact of a mounted assault. August Willich, commander of the 32nd Indiana Infantry Regiment, described the action from the receiving end: "With lightning speed, under infernal yelling, great numbers of Texas Rangers rushed upon our whole force."[23]

While the psychological impact of massed horsemen proved unnerving, it was deadly firepower at close range that destroyed enemy cohesion. Remembering the culmination of the thundering charge, the Union colonel grudgingly admitted the Texans shattered his line when they "advanced to fifteen or twenty yards of our lines, some of them even between them, and opened fire with rifles and revolvers." Successful actions like this one, where Confederate horsemen attacked similar to Napoleonic heavy cavalry, gave proven units like Terry's Texas Rangers reputations as "Charging Regiments."

Attacks like those described by Lane and Willich revealed the strengths and weaknesses of mounted combat in the 1860s. On one hand, audacious charges could inflict severe physical and psychological damage on the defenders. Infantry regiments broken by charging horsemen were often shattered beyond repair, requiring reassignment and restructuring. Yet the immediacy of the maneuver also placed cavalry in precarious positions. If they failed to carry the charge, encountered massed and prepared infantry or artillery, or lost momentum in difficult terrain the ride could end in disaster. This dilemma made the mounted charge an all-or-nothing proposition requiring total commitment by men and horses vaulting into the melee. Despite the risk, Antoine-Henri Jomini called the audacious maneuver "a duty for which light cavalry is particularly fitted."[24]

Texan predilection for aggressive tactics earned fierce reputations amongst the general public. *Harper's Weekly*, in addition to publishing a fantastical picture of a heavily armed and unkempt

ranger, offered popular descriptions of Texans and their armaments for readership in eastern states. Referencing the riflemen
then riding the Indian Frontier, the writer colorfully stated that
"Ben McCulloch's Texas Rangers are described as a desperate set of
fellows. They number one thousand half savages, each of whom is
mounted upon a mustang horse." He then wrote that "each is armed
with a pair of Colt's navy revolvers, a rifle, a tomahawk, a Texan
bowie-knife, and a lasso. They are described as being very dexterous
in the use of the latter."[25]

In 1864 and 1865, as charging became problematic due to
improved Union tactics and armaments, many Texans upgraded
and adopted Spencer and Sharps carbines captured from Federal
stores. Though European dragoons had employed carbines since
the advent of single-shot muskets with shortened barrels, some
American versions offered limited repeating capability and water-
proof cartridges. This allowed versatility in both mounted and
dismounted operations but remained difficult for the Rebels to
sustain without reliable ammunition resupply.[26] Confederate inability
to mass-produce or purchase quality firearms impaired the fighting
capacity of many Southern cavalrymen.

Despite the tactical benefits of possessing a martial culture that
prized cavalry prowess, Texas society's lionizing of mounted service
came at a cost. While fascination with armed horsemanship unquestionably catalyzed cavalry recruitment, it correspondingly, and
predictably, hindered rapid formation of foot regiments so critical
in modernizing warfare. As remembered by volunteer Frank Files,
"it was almost impossible to get a Texan to join the infantry."[27] The
state's inability to raise foot soldiers so critical to large-scale campaigns of massed armies resulted in frequent dismounting of cavalry
units for specific battles or permanent removal of horses.

Reassignment from cavalry to infantry duty naturally resulted in
a suspicion of deceptive recruitment by Confederate officers. From his
position in the ranks, Files viewed redirection of Texans from their
historical passion skeptically when he sourly accused that authorities

would purposefully "organize a cavalry troop and then dismount them" in order to meet recruitment quotas. Given the deep cultural appeal of joining mounted units in emulation of famous rangers, the forced transition from cavalry to infantry status often hurt morale.[28]

Proportions of Texans who enlisted specifically for mounted service reflected imbalances in societal martial perceptions. Of the possible 90,000 that fought in the rebellion—as reported by the state executive—58,000 joined as armed horsemen while only 30,000 served in infantry, artillery, or logistics.[29] Even when taking into account the fact that many designated horse regiments actually fought dismounted, vastly disproportionate enlistment rates between mounted and non-mounted arms signaled the culmination of decades of riding and fighting along troubled borders.

The scope of Texan mounted arms preference can be further evaluated by chronologically assessing recruitment during the most intense phases of Confederate mobilization in the first two years of war. By December of 1861 Texas had activated 17,338 cavalrymen in contrast to just 7,100 infantrymen. This disparity resulted in a 2.4 to 1 ratio between horse and foot soldiers. By summer of 1862 approximately 28,500 Texans served as designated cavalry, nearly one-third of the state's male fighting-aged population. The rapid increase in horsemen resulted from conscription laws that prompted Texans to volunteer for cavalry lest they be drafted into infantry. This preference again exacerbated state challenges with fulfilling quotas for Confederate foot regiments.[30]

While Texas's recruitment disparity between combat functions definitively proved martial biases, its unique cavalry focus finds further validation against other states. Civil War mobilization in Arkansas and Louisiana—proximate states which likewise maintained historical militant traditions—created regional contrast. While Arkansas enjoyed a relatively balanced cavalry to infantry ratio of 1 to 1.2, Louisiana produced just one mounted for every 30 foot soldiers. By close of 1862 the former had deployed five regiments and five battalions of cavalry while the latter formed just one horse regiment. The Lone Star State easily surpassed their combined total at that time with sixteen regiments, three battalions, and three independent companies of horsemen.[31]

As Texas surpassed neighboring states in its zeal for cavalry mobilization, the same dynamic proved true for regions farther away. In the embattled state of Virginia—which had cultivated a robust military culture amongst white male residents since before the American Revolution—similar disparity prevailed. According to a governor's report in 1863, by then the Commonwealth had recruited over 52,000 soldiers as infantry to just 14,000 as cavalry. Another 30,000 men enlisted in units of unspecified function, but given the likelihood of allocation similar to specified regiments, only a third of those, at best, would have been mounted.[32]

Under this analysis, the 28,500 Texans enlisted as cavalrymen in 1862 already far surpassed the total mounted quantity Virginia achieved a year later, even when discounting expanded mobilization by 1863. Regimental contrast, which allows admittedly inexact assessment due to roster and composition discrepancies, the western polity likewise proved the largest contributor of mounted forces for the Confederacy. While Virginia produced twenty-one cavalry regiments by 1863 and a total of thirty-one by the end of the war, Texas fielded sixty-one regiments and thirty-nine battalions of the same by 1865.[33]

Despite an inclination to privilege mounted service, Texas produced infantry that fought with distinction in the war. Increasing competence by massed foot soldiers with rifled muskets ensured they dominated major campaigns. Foremost amongst Texan infantry stood John Bell Hood's aggressive brigade in the Army of Northern Virginia. A veteran officer who had served in the 2nd U.S. Cavalry on in antebellum Texas, the stalwart general led the 1st, 4th, and 5th Texas Infantry Regiments to enduring fame at the battles of Second Manassas, Antietam, and Gettysburg.[34] The brigade's performance in the decisive theater of the war under premier Southern field commander Robert E. Lee ensured it received greater historical attention than most cavalry counterparts.

Rising functional pride in the Texan infantry corps—which harkened to the glory of Sam Houston's foot regiments at San Jacinto while contrasting starkly with the lackluster service of Albert Sydney Johnston's riflemen in the Monterrey Campaign—created tensions within Texas's military establishment. With Hood's men accruing enviable victories in the east concurrent to flourishing of traditional cavalry enthusiasm, inter-service competition developed. Ironically, Johnston would serve as the highest ranking Texan in the Confederate Army and die at Shiloh as its highest ranking casualty despite pursuing a military career that mostly diverged from his state's way of war.

This rivalry led to antagonism between branches common to all robust, multi-arm military establishments. As an anonymous Confederate observer wrote, "the cavalry and infantry were generally at daggers' points, and never failed to improve an opportunity for talking very plainly to each other."[35] William Fletcher of Terry's Texas Rangers remembered how they insultingly called the infantry "wagondogs" for their slowness, while the foot soldiers mocked that mounted men "had little to do but to find Yankees for them to fight, and as the Yankees were so plentiful, they had an easy job."[36] Despite the popularity of many Rebel Texan infantry units, cavalry retained its cultural primacy across the state throughout and after the war.

Considering the large-scale nature of Texan mobilization and patriotic fervor that catalyzed widespread volunteerism, predictable order and discipline problems developed. Lack of self-control and respect for chains of command in the ranks, a perennial and sometimes debilitating weakness in past wars, again plagued operational cohesion. A penchant for individualism and initiative, so necessary in decentralized frontier patrolling, often destabilized larger maneuvers that demanded echeloned unity and coordination.

This troublesome behavior manifested most visibly in Texan cavalry subordinated to larger, non-Texan commands. Another member of Terry's Texas Rangers, Leonidas Giles, explained his countrymen's reaction to military control: "If there was any serious attempt to discipline the regiment, the effort was soon disbanded ... volunteers we began, volunteers we remained to the end. If any wished to evade duty, they found a way, and punishment for the occasion was light."[37] Major General Richard Taylor, who commanded the Southern effort in the Red River Campaign of 1864, complained with creative license that Texans "had no more conception of military gradations than of the celestial hierarchy of the poets."[38]

This critique followed many Texan units while marching across the American South. When the 21st, 24th, and 25th Texas Cavalries passed through Shreveport, Louisiana, in 1862 to serve in Arkansas, they drew harsh criticism for destructive behavior. The Bayou State governor, Thomas Moore, complained that the volunteers "seized private property, entered houses of private citizens, brutally practiced extortion and outrage, and with bullying and threatening language and manner spread terror among the people."[39] Texan soldiers caused similar instability in their own state towards the end of war as military discipline atrophied across the exhausted Confederacy.

Criticism of volunteer behavior sometimes began with senior officers. On another occasion when Texans marched through Louisiana, Shreveport's townspeople brought charges against an unnamed cavalry colonel for "continual drunkenness and other improprieties, and for fighting in a grog ship ... with one of his own men." With leadership modeling disorderly conduct and setting toxic examples for behavior, destructive emulation by subordinates was sure to follow. In the end, the enraged governor threatened to use his own "marksmen" to solve the problem.[40]

While avoidance of professional army standards had been a constant quality on the frontier, the military infraction of desertion raised unfamiliar issues for Texas authorities. It was further compounded by Confederate laws which forced unwilling citizens to enlist and catalyzed rates of desertion. Conscription of Unionist Texans then exacerbated the problem and engendered mistrust and dissention. John Ford, who commanded along the Rio Grande, questioned the efficacy of compelling "union men" into Rebel ranks by asking: "In the event we forced men into our ranks who believed we were wrong, would they not desert us at a critical point?"[41]

The veteran ranger further criticized conscription laws that "exempted the rich man and made the poor man a soldier by force of law," another destabilizing social factor. He recalled its negative effect on morale: "Very soon the cry went up from our armies: 'The rich man's war and the poor man's fight.' It did great harm."[42] As the war continued into years three and four and authorities drafted unwilling Texans amongst lower socio-economic classes into military service, elite avoidance of combat duty undermined the legitimacy of the Southern cause. The resulting public mistrust of wealthy Texans contrasted sharply with a cultural memory of shared risk and commitment by all classes supposedly embraced during the Texas Revolution and Indian Wars.

Extreme pressures inflicted by the scope of Texas's militarization eventually fractured its historical strengths of patriotic and communal unity against external threats. Even the cause of protecting Texas, in addition to the necessity of supporting the larger Confederate effort, proved inadequate to galvanize the Texan populace for multiple years. Combinations of Unionist sentiment, conscription, elite avoidance, austere conditions, aversion to centralized authority, and the unexpected duration of the war instigated desertion by at least 4,664 Texans.[43] Many who declined to fight for either side fled to North Texas, specifically around Dallas and along the Red River, where the reduced population allowed avoidance of capture. Other Texans, at least 1,500 men, simply left the state to join the Union Army rather than revolt.

Many of these loyalists formed the 1st and 2nd United States Texas Cavalry regiments, the 2nd Battalion of Texas Cavalry, and the Independent Company of Partisan Rangers to assist the North's planned invasion of Texas in 1864.[44] Formations of Union cavalry from within Texas again emphasized its historical infatuation with mounted arms of all types. The absence of notable Unionist-Texan infantry conversely underscored the state's favored manner of service. Though they chose to fight against neighbors and even family, even loyalists retained strong preference to enlist as horsemen. In that regard, many

Texans were perhaps cavalrymen first and Unionists and Confederates second.

Confederate Cavalry and State Rangers

Texas's strategic participation in the Civil War was similar to its involvement in the 1836 revolution and the Mexican-American War. Simultaneous localized and continental threats compelled it to embrace both conventional and unconventional warfare. While linear operations of mass, scale, and centralization often characterized Confederate-Union confrontations, the state defended home ground against guerrilla-type raiding by both tribesmen and partisan Unionists. In accordance with historical preferences, Texan mobilization as light cavalry, mounted riflemen, and partisan rangers emerged as integral to both efforts.

Unlike previous decades when rangers rode as the primary manifestation of Texas militarism, the more conventional, and less well known, cavalry manifestation of the tradition begun by Houston during the San Jacinto Campaign gained meteoric ascendancy during rebellion. This shift materialized due to the constitutional commitment to fight for the Confederacy in numbered regiments beyond state borders. In popular and historical imagination alike, units like the famed 8th Texas Cavalry attained outsized importance as idealized protectors of Texan freedom and honor. This utilitarian reversal reflected a twelve-to-one disparity between the quantity of Lone Star horsemen mobilized as expeditionary light cavalry and those recruited as rangers and militia for frontier defense.

Texans predominantly campaigned across four theaters that spanned much of North America. Since assessing the scores of thousands of horsemen who fought from the deserts of New Mexico to the forests of Virginia would prove exhaustive, this study will analyze only a selection of illustrative regiments and brigades. These selections include: The 1st Regiment, Texas Mounted Rifles, Frontier Regiment and Border Battalion, and Frontier Organization of State Troops that defended the Indian Frontier; Ross's Texas Cavalry Brigade and the 8th Texas Cavalry Regiment, which supported larger confrontations in the Trans-Mississippi and Eastern Theaters; Sibley's Cavalry Brigade that charged to spectacular failure in the invasion of New Mexico Territory; and the 2nd Texas Cavalry Regiment that brilliantly won the final, though inconsequential, battle of the Civil War near the Gulf Coast.

Defending the Indian Frontier

Texas's initial, and arguably most critical, wartime arena encompassed the traditional orientation along its north and west peripheries of Anglo settlement. The continued threat of frontier attack demanded a renewal of militant ranging methods. Concurrent to involvement in larger Confederate campaigns against the Union Army, Texas deployed three iterations of state-controlled and mostly state-funded mounted organizations throughout the war. These ranger mobilizations, in addition to numerous local militias, successively attempted to protect the South's westernmost borders from tribal warriors, Unionist raiders, and Mexican marauders.[45]

These defenses reflected the tenets of dominant Texan warmaking methodology. They were typified by forward lines of combat outposts supported by ranging patrols with several larger expeditions against Comanche in 1864 and 1865. This strategy emulated the Texas Republic's use of chained forts in 1837, 1839, and 1846 to separate populated counties of Central and East Texas from hostile tribes to the northwest and Mexico to the south. Though it ultimately proved inadequate against intensifying attacks in late 1864 and resulted in the temporary retrenchment of Anglo settlement from the Great Plains, the defense nevertheless called upon the settler militancy begun in the territorial conflicts of colonial *Tejas*.[46]

Establishment of state frontier defense under the Confederate banner began immediately upon Texan secession in spring of 1861 when spontaneously formed Rebel companies seized Federal installations in San Antonio, Austin, and important frontier forts. On February 5, the interim Committee of Public Safety replaced the dismantled U.S. Army system with a new security construct. To facilitate reorganization it assigned the command of border areas to three respected captains from earlier conflicts: Ben McCulloch, his brother Henry McCulloch, and most predictably, John Salmon Ford. The state commissioned the veteran rangers as Colonels of Cavalry in the Provisional Army of Texas.[47]

As state officials pondered a larger mobilization to potentially counter the Union Army in 1861, each frontier commander received responsibility for geographically defined sectors along historically contested zones. Ben McCulloch assumed command of West Texas from Fort McIntosh to Fort Chadbourne, his brother supervised North Texas from Fort Chadbourne to the Red River, and Ford held responsibility for South Texas along the Rio Grande. These assignments reflected traditional reliance upon proven tactical leaders to rapidly form and command event-specific and short-duration volunteer units during crises.[48]

In addition to organizing border defenses, secessionist Texas immediately occupied all Federal installations while seizing all military material. The U.S. Army garrison in 1861 comprised 3,000 soldiers under the command of Bvt. Maj. Gen. David Twiggs. The aging commander peacefully, and controversially, acquiesced with Texan demands to turn over $1,500,000 of military land and property for state use. On February 16 Ben McCulloch triumphantly occupied the Federal headquarters in San Antonio and decapitated any chance for organized Union resistance. [49]

By March 7 the aggressive ranger also controlled Camp Colorado and Fort Chadbourne in West Texas and Camp Cooper on the Clear Fork of the Brazos River. Henry McCulloch likewise led a battalion across the western counties to ensure the Rebel government held a deterring military presence near the plains. In the south Ford established his defenses along the Rio Grande and Gulf Coast, where he had fought Cortina, to complete the strategic perimeter around Central Texas.[50]

Despite rapid progress in militarizing state borders, Texans quickly realized they required a more robust and better organized defense force along the most vulnerable northwest axis of the Indian Frontier. On March 4, 1861, the Confederate War Department authorized Texas, and Ben McCulloch in particular, to form the 1st Regiment of Texas Mounted Rifles for a one-year enlistment. The legendary ranger, who actually desired a more prestigious command against the Union Army in the decisive confrontation unfolding in the East, passed the leadership of the frontier assignment to his able brother.[51]

Texas delegates to the C.S.A. Congress emphasized specialized tactical qualities needed in the regiment's recruits by advising they should "be brave, good horsemen, acquainted with the country, and able to perform the most fatiguing service." Demonstrating familiarity with frontier duty, the officials directed "they must be acquainted with the character and habits of the Indians, and always ready to mount the saddle and start in the pursuit the moment the trail of the enemy is discovered. The volunteer rangers of Texas possess all these requisites, and are better qualified for this service than any others."[52]

The officials, who clearly appreciated differences between irregular riflemen and regular cavalry, suggested a familiar tempo of proactive operations:

> Permanent military posts on this line are wholly useless. The troops should be kept constantly moving and on the lookout for the enemy. They should range the whole of this line of frontier in small detachments, arranged in such a manner that a rapid concentration could be effected whenever necessary. Detachments of sufficient strength should be frequently sent high up the country to hunt out the Indians. We believe that this is the only mode in which this section of our frontier can be successfully defended against depredations.

Henry McCulloch understood and exploited the mounted arms proclivities of his countrymen and emphasized the traditional role of rangers in a recruiting announcement in the Dallas *Herald* on March 20. The canny leader advertised that his volunteers needed "a good horse, a Colt's pistol, and a light rifle or double-barreled shot-gun that can be used on horseback." He also boasted in the poster "the Comanche will know the Ranger is at Home on the Prairie again."

By May 29 most of the regiment had deployed according to detachment assignments across West and North Texas. It comprised 10 companies defending across 400 miles of contested territory from Camp Jackson on the Red River to Fort Mason north of Austin. This posture patterned on much of the old First and Second Federal Lines while clearly orienting against Comanche across the west plains and Indian Territory. It also adopted tactics that had usually allowed success in past conflicts: proactive and constant patrolling by small, but well-armed, detachments. McCulloch's orders for Captain "Buck" James Barry at Camp Cooper to "keep up weekly scouts, in small parties, from the Post to that detachment" illustrated the veteran commander's strategic intent for interlocking patrol sectors.[53]

In South Texas the state officially enlisted Ford's garrisons as the 2nd Regiment, Texas Mounted Rifles, which later reorganized as the 2nd Texas Cavalry Regiment, C.S.A. The famous frontiersman defined his position as "commander of the Military District of the Rio Grande, which extended from the mouth of the river for more than one thousand miles to above El Paso." He also noted "the country between these two points was very sparsely settled."[54] This force would later provide the advance guard for the Confederate invasion of New Mexico, under different leadership, and eventually move east to contest Union designs in Louisiana.[55]

Naming conventions for various mounted regiments in the Civil War indicated appreciation of different cavalry functions in nineteenth-century warfare. Texans initially called its own units mounted rifles, rather than cavalry, as the War Department in Richmond designated later regiments. This description, which revealed intentional classification, contrasted frontier functionality against the Euro-centric inclinations for professional cavalry and dragoons. Lubbock, who supervised all state forces, endorsed the ranger emphasis when he emphasized McCulloch's 1861 regiment "was well officered by men of large frontier experience, good Indian fighters, and brave soldiers."[56]

The improvised state defense capitalized on the strengths of Texan organizational traditions that allowed, and pressured, citizens to enlist in geographical proximity to their communities. Lubbock again described the 1st Regiment: "The entire organization was made up of men already living in the counties to be protected, the law prohibiting the enlistment of men from other localities." He then explained the "intention was to have only hardy, brave men who would be directly interested in giving good protection to their own homes."[57] This localized service ensured geographic familiarity within the ranks and benefited from *esprit de corps* inherent in men serving side by side with family and neighbors.

In December of 1861 the Texas Congress replaced McCulloch's regiment—whose enlistment was due to expire in April of 1862—with legislation designed to "Provide protection of the Frontier of the State of Texas." Intending to better militarize the state's male population while deploying a larger fort system, the governor hoped to "perfect the organization of State troops and place them on a war footing."[58] Though the 1st Regiment engaged in several skirmishes during its tenure it never achieved full authorized strength and was never seriously stressed by Indian attacks.

The legislature defined its new Indian defense as a "regiment of Rangers" comprised of ten companies serving along the "Northern and Western frontier." Called simply the Frontier Regiment, and later designated the 46th Texas Cavalry, it served as a more comprehensive answer to Comanche concerns. In an attempt to address its own historical inability to fund long-term militaries, the state capital naively sought a fiscal reprieve by attaining national funding from Richmond even as the governor demanded to retain operational control. Confederate President Jefferson Davis vetoed the arrangement due to supposed constitutional contradictions.[59]

The Frontier Regiment invoked the martial spirit of its 1839 predecessor of the same name and eventually comprised 1,089 men divided into nine companies across eighteen camps. Under the command of Colonel James Norris, a lawyer with surprisingly little ranging experience, it organized throughout January of 1862 and deployed by April of that year. The regiment occupied many old forts but added more stations to extend the plains line south to the Rio Grande. While centrally commanded like all active regiments, it continued two traditional ranger strengths: assignment to companies near soldiers' homes and subdivision of companies into detachments of twenty-five men each. This organization harnessed the motivation inherent to interested defenders while maximizing breadth of patrolled terrain.[60]

Despite the Frontier Regiment's almost 500-mile perimeter, Texas's far northern reaches remained porous and vulnerable. In the spring of 1863 the state fielded an additional cavalry battalion under command of former ranger, planter, and controversial marshal James Bourland to defend along the Red River. Called the Border Regiment due to its posture along the seam between Texas and the Indian Territory, it countered cross-boundary raids by tribes settled on Federal reservations to the north. The force eventually boasted four officers and 564 soldiers. Unlike state-owned formations like McCulloch's command and the replacement Frontier Regiment, this battalion served as a nationally aligned unit in the Confederate Trans-Mississippi Department.[61]

Officials in Richmond officially designated Bourland's command the 2nd Brigade of the 1st Division and assigned him to the Northern Sub-District of Texas. The cavalry battalion defended 150 miles of open frontier while coordinating with Rebel authorities north of the Red River. Throughout the conflict the Border Regiment regularly confronted both Unionist raiders and Indian warbands while answering both state and national priorities. It served on the Texan periphery in a vital, if underappreciated role, until the close of the war.[62]

As Texas entered the third year of fighting against the United States it again reorganized defense of the Indian Frontier while preserving Ford's command along the Rio Grande and Gulf Coast. The third and final northwestern guard was the more expansive, and ultimately less effective, Frontier Organization of State Troops. On December 15, 1863, the state divided twenty western counties into three military districts under centralized commands. They intended the Frontier Organization to replace the Frontier Regiment since Confederate commanders had ordered it transferred to fight in the East. With so many Texan men now serving in other states, killed, or wounded, state authorities manned the new, and increasingly desperate, territorial defense by compelling all remaining fighting-aged men to enlist in rotational service.[63]

By spring of 1864 Texas enrolled approximately 4,000 men into the Frontier Organization with a quarter of them constantly deployed to assigned forts. More militia than ranger in quality, these companies held little in common with successful Texan fieldings of decades past. Officers complained that the flagging defense was "composed of men from almost every section of the state and even from other states, as well as a considerable number of deserters who have fled from conscription and draft, a great many of whom have neither families, property, nor visible occupation."[64] This debilitation reflected the strained conditions of the male population available after three years of massive mobilization within and outside of the state.

Despite high hopes by state officials, the final wartime expression of the once vaunted ranging tradition largely failed. Its organizational spirit and posture diverged starkly from martial ideals that had often strengthened Lone Star forces in colonial, national, and antebellum years. Compelled enlistment of so many citizens across motivations, ages, vocations, and military experiences diluted specialized qualities of previous rangers and riflemen formations. Taking the divergence further, many who enlisted in state forces did so merely to avoid Confederate conscription. Lieutenant General Edmund Kirby Smith, commanding the Confederate Trans-Mississippi, lamented "the whole male population—the aged and the infirm" had been called "under the acts for local defense."[65]

The Frontier Organization also suffered from a dearth of weaponry, especially repeating firearms, which severely lessened tactical potential. Norris, after commanding the Frontier Regiment, observed of dismal resupply for even old single-shot musketry: "A great part of the powder sent to us would not kill a man ten steps from the muzzle, loaded with all the powder that could be forced into the cylinder."[66] Kirby Smith likewise lamented the lack of effective weaponry for militiamen, attesting that Texas had "in a great measure, been stripped of its shot-guns and rifles, which, early in the struggle were carried east of the Mississippi." He concluded that "the people and the State Troops, which are called out, know they cannot be armed. Despondent and disheartened, they have little hope of the result."[67]

Despite increasing logistical privation and armament shortages, tribal raids against Texan settlements remained mostly sporadic and peripheral between 1861 and 1863. This equilibrium changed dramatically in October of 1864 when a massive allied raiding force of almost 700 Comanche and Kiowa crossed the Red River and attacked into the Brazos River Valley. Though the Border Regiment managed to skirmish with the raiders, Indians devastated several settlements and shocked surrounding regions. Anglo-Texan losses included five cavalrymen and seven civilians killed, seven women and children captured, eleven homesteads burned, and ten thousand head of cattle stolen.[68]

The event became known as the Elm Creek Raid, and when coupled with the Battle of Dove Creek where 600 migrating Kickapoo soundly repulsed a task force of 500 soldiers and militiamen west of Austin in January 1865, demonstrated the strategic inadequacies of the Frontier Organization.[69] The raid also revealed the Border Regiment incapable of sealing off the long northern border against large incursions. Even more ominously, it proclaimed that the Plains Tribes had recovered from the wars of the Texas Republic and could once again generate large-scale attacks to make frontier settlement tenuous. This renewed capability reflected a return to a scope of indigenous military power not seen for a generation on the plains.

Indian attacks killed an estimated 400 Texan settlers during Civil War years with hundreds more captured and wounded. While the 1st Regiment of Texas Mounted Riflemen and the Frontier Regiment proved moderately successful, failures of the Frontier Organization reflected the tremendous duress of wartime commitments. Ford recalled the impact of wartime raiding on Texan settlements: "The Texas frontier suffered greatly from Indian depredations during the war. A tier of counties, at least three deep, was quite depopulated."[70] Captain Barry, who patrolled with the Border Regiment, estimated that "less than two years after these frontier troops had been mustered out, the settlements were pushed back in many places more than one hundred miles."[71] For the Lone Star State, simultaneous demands for home defense and expeditionary deployment proved too much.

Confederate Cavalry in the East

Texas's second and largest combat arena, both in geographical scale and quantity of men involved, centered on the explosion of campaigns between Texas and Virginia. As the scene of decisive confrontation between massive Southern and Northern armies, this contest required the state to deploy a prodigious volume of numbered regiments to fight across the Trans-Mississippi and Eastern Theaters. This conflict was predominantly characterized by combined arms warfare and necessitated extensive use of light cavalry to support larger infantry corps. While Texan horsemen sometimes performed independent, guerrilla-style actions, they typically rode in regiments attached to infantry brigades and divisions and with less frequent service in consolidated cavalry brigades.

Ross's Texas Cavalry Brigade provided an ideal example of effective mounted forces at echelons above regimental level in large-scale contests. Named for its famous commander, Lawrence "Sul" Ross of the antebellum rangers and future Texas governor, it illustrated an ability to serve in multi-functional capacities on both sides of the Mississippi River. First organized in November of 1862, the brigade included the 3rd, 6th, 9th, and 27th Texas Cavalry Regiments. The first three contained ten companies each while the last fielded twelve. The men, who arrived with varied tactical experience, hailed from twenty-three counties across central and northern Texas. After serving as infantry in the Indian Territory, Arkansas, and Missouri, they enthusiastically received horses and moved east of the Mississippi River.[72]

On December 21, 1862, the newly mounted brigade proved integral in Maj. Gen. Earl Van Dorn's Confederate raid on Holly Springs, Mississippi. As a large Union supply depot, the destruction of the town delayed Union commander Ulysses Grant's impending attack on Vicksburg. Lieutenant George Griscom, adjutant for the 9th Texas Cavalry, described how they "charged the town with a long wild yell & took the garrison by surprise." He then recounted how Federal cavalry offered the only resistance and "the 9th being in front of Brig was ord'd to charge them." The Texans won the engagement decisively when they "dismounted & charged them." The audacity of the attack resulted in the capture of "about 75 horses with cavalry equipment."[73]

This action demonstrated a unique contribution by fleet and well-armed cavalry to linear contests: the ability to conduct lightning raids against vulnerable points along enemy lines. As veterans of a volatile frontier and students of the Comanche raiding methods, Texan riders often excelled at audacious maneuvers.[74] Just as in earlier instances when they had transitioned from counter-Indian patrolling to infantry support duty in Mexico, Texas cavalry in the Civil War proved adept at reconnaissance, screen, raid, and attack operations in support of the Confederate Army.

Ross's brigade distinguished itself again on March 5, 1863, after a year of hard fighting in Mississippi. Again working under Van Dorn's direction in a series of raids against Union held Tennessee, it attacked a large U.S. Cavalry force at Thompson's Station. Still with the 9th Texas, Griscom recalled how the Federals repulsed their first assault when the brigade was "compelled to fall back." After reconsolidating behind a set of raised railroad tracks, the unit "reformed and again advanced to the top of the hill in good order." The Texans, who were attacking in the face of well-aimed carbine and musket fire, "had to yield again to a superior force, falling back to the rail road."

The lieutenant then described how a third assault, now completely dismounted and fortuitously synchronized with envelopment forces under famed Tennessean Nathan Bedford Forrest, overwhelmed the out-flanked defenders. Sensing victory, the determined Rebels "reformed under galling fire and again advanced to the hill top when Col Whitfield in the rear of a battery asked if the 9th could go any further, to which the men with one voice replied in the affirmative." The battle culminated as "Forrest by this time coming up in the enemy's rear, they surrendered without resistance."[75] Griscom noted that they captured "five Regts of Infantry with their field and Staff officers numbering about 2,300 prisoners" in the "hard fought battle." The 9th Texas suffered "3 killed, 3 mortally wounded and 15 wounded." In this particular clash bloody persistence had won the day for the South.

These actions again emphasized Texan tactical versatility. Whether raiding mounted or assaulting as shock infantry they had demonstrated an aptitude for multi-functional combat. The brigade's utility at Thomson's Station resembled similar actions of years past, such as Henry Karnes's stand at the Battle at Arroyo Seco in 1838, and Jack Hays's up-hill assaults at Monterrey in 1846. In each of these contests horsemen rode to the point of enemy contact and then dismounted for assault. This dragoon or mounted infantry maneuver maximized approach speed while unleashing repeating and precision fire.

The culmination of the brigade's service occurred in the summer of 1864 in Georgia after five months of rapid tempo raiding throughout the Yazoo River Valley of Tennessee. From May 25 to June 5, Ross's men fought constantly as they harassed the massive Federal army orienting on Atlanta. Throughout this trying period they averaged at least one skirmish per day and participated in several significant battles. Unfortunately for the Texans, larger Union formations defeated them twice during the campaign as their ranks suffered severe attrition and logistical deprivation.[76]

Ross's Cavalry Brigade finished its wartime service once again conducting raids, reconnaissance, and screens in Tennessee. Throughout

November and December of 1864 the Texans lost approximately 100 men, but nevertheless captured over 500 prisoners and 9 Union battle standards. They also destroyed two logistical rail trains and seized almost fifty supply wagons. The outsized impact of these brigaded regiments, which massed horsemen into exceptionally capable strike forces that enjoyed both cavalry speed and an ability to concentrate firepower, revealed the conditional potency of consolidated, well-armed, and aggressive cavalry on nineteeth-century battlefields.[77]

The 8th Texas Cavalry exemplified effective light cavalry at regimental levels during the Civil War. Popularly known as Terry's Texas Rangers, they served as arguably the most lethal, and audacious, mounted force in the conflict. Of all the multiplicity of Texan units that fought for rebellion, this command, more than any other, epitomized Lone Star militancy. As symbolized by its dual names that invoked both ranger and cavalry traditions, it embodied multi-functional fighting capacity to excel in diverse tactical settings. As one of the most famous regiments in Texas history it combined audacity, mobility, and firepower to excel at screening, raiding, reconnaissance, and most importantly, the mounted shock-charge.[78]

Terry's Texas Rangers first organized in Houston in September of 1861 in response to the Confederate call to arms during early mobilization. On August 12 the founders of the organization, Benjamin Terry and Thomas Lubbock, advertised they were "authorized by the Secretary of War of the Confederate States of America to raise a regiment of mounted rangers for service in Virginia." Another announcement stated each company would consist of "not less than 64 nor more than 100 privates" and that "each man must furnish the equipment for his horse, and arm himself either with a short rifle or double barrel shot gun, and a six-shooter."[79]

These advertisements were highly suggestive of the regiment's distinctive frontier character. Intentional selection of mounted rangers for service in Virginia indicated that Richmond fully appreciated the outsized tactical reputations of Texan horsemen. The concurrent requirement for them to equip with both long-range and short-range weaponry also revealed the intended versatility of action. In short, both the Confederate War Department and officials in Austin hoped to capitalize on Texas's long frontier experience by placing a body of aggressive horsemen at the center of the Civil War's decisive theater.

The New Orleans *Picayune* exuberantly agreed as the regiment mobilized: "If this regiment does not make its mark on the Lincolnites, there is no virtue in strength, courage, patriotism and thorough knowledge of the use of horses and arms."[80] Under high expectations it formed ten companies at Houston on September 7, 1861, primarily from McLennan, Brazoria, Matagorda, Gonzales, Bastrop, Fayette, Bexar, Goliad, Fort Bend, Harris, and Montgomery counties. Volunteer James Blackburn, who later commanded a company in the 8th, wrote that "one thousand men were expected to constitute the regiment, but more and more were enlisted until the number reached 1170, an average of 117 to each company."[81]

From the outset of mobilization the 8th Texas Cavalry arrived with high *espirt de corps*. Embracing nationalistic fervor, the volunteers contracted for the duration of the war rather than a three or twelve-month enlistment. This inspiration was rooted in their state's history of willing military service—at least during crises—and reflected typical Southern enthusiasm before privation and conscription afflicted morale across the Confederacy. Generating counties for the regiment predictably represented regions with strong histories of friction with indigenous and Mexican communities and indicated the depth of frontier militancy that the recruits brought to the organization.

The newly formed regiment, which had yet to be numerically designated by Richmond, deployed without horses in September 1861. They traveled by individual company to New Orleans but received orders redirecting them to Kentucky. While en route to Bowling Green, the Texans acquired, or earned, the popular title "Texas Rangers" as Southerners in Louisiana and Tennessee lionized them due to their savage appearance, bristling weaponry, and volatile behavior. In Texas, of course, the press had been referring to them as "Terry's Rangers" and "Terry's Ranging Regiment" since their initial formation.[82]

Upon arriving at the Confederate Army of the West's headquarters in Bowling Green, the rangers, now officially designated the 8th of Texas's numbered light cavalries by Richmond, elected Terry as commanding officer. They also received a full complement of horses and organized themselves along the doctrinal structure of an official regiment. Blackburn remembered companies drew letters "A to K, inclusive, except J." With a fully mobile, unbloodied, and eager regiment at their disposal, the department ordered the rangers to "patrol and picket" from "Bowling Green north as far up as Woodsville on the Green River."[83]

On December 17 the Texans engaged in their first action near Woodsville, Kentucky, and began to establish a reputation for exceptional audacity. Henry Graber, a private in D Company, described how on a reconnaissance for their assigned infantry brigade near the town they "discovered a line of infantry lying down behind a rail fence" while the foot soldiers were "at least a mile behind." The Rebel infantry's commanding general, Thomas Hindman, ordered Terry to "withdraw the regiment and let him bring up the artillery and infantry." Disinclined to wait, the Texan cavalryman reportedly stated impetuously: "General Hindmen, this is no place for you; go back to your infantry."[84]

Unwilling to forgo an opportunity to prove Texan prowess, Terry ordered the regiment to form and charge in two wings against the Federal line. Blackburn, describing the assault, wrote that the commander "immediately ordered a charge, emphasizing the order with an oath not easily forgotten, so we made a rush for those bushes concealing a considerable force of bayonets fixed ready to receive us." As the Rebel horsemen careened into the blue formation he boasted that, "with our shotguns loaded with buckshot we killed, wounded, and scattered that command in short order."[85]

This charge, and the intensity of their first combat with Union soldiers, found the rangers well suited for aggressive fighting. Graber remembered closing violently with the waiting infantry ranks, writing that "in less time than it takes to tell it, we charged them, delivering our fire of double-barreled shotguns, breaking down the fence and getting among them with our six-shooters." He then crowed that "in a few minutes we had run over them."[86] Though not strategically consequential, this action established the template for the infamous shock charge that Terry's Texas Rangers would unleash numerous times throughout the war.

This kind of assault by lines of screaming Texans on horseback often proved a terrifying spectacle for defending troops. Colonel August Willich, commander of the opposing 32nd Indiana Infantry Regiment, described the action from the perspective of men who received thundering attacks: "With lightning speed, under infernal yelling, great numbers of Texas Rangers rushed upon our whole force. They advanced to fifteen or twenty yards of our lines, some of them even between them, and opened fire with rifles and revolvers."[87] The Texans suffered four dead and eight wounded while the Federals lost five missing, eleven killed, and twenty-two wounded.

Like many Texan successes in the Civil War, these close combat tactics were rooted in their state's embattled history. In the case of the 8th Texas Cavalry's shock charges, they emulated aggressive maneuvers pioneered by Houston's horsemen at San Jacinto and Jack Hays and his rangers during the pursuit of Woll's retreating army in 1842 and in the Mexican-American War. Techniques of riding within shotgun or carbine range of the enemy, firing a suppression volley, and then causing panic by crashing with massed horsemen firing revolvers and shotguns demonstrated a continued proclivity for combining firepower with speed and shock. Graber endorsed this mentality when he boasted that "Texas Ranger expected and would fight only in close quarters."[88]

Despite the 8th Texas Cavalry's success at Woodsville, Terry died during the assault. The unit retained the name of its organizer and first leader, at least informally, though it would serve under several other colonels of note in the Confederate officer corps. After several months of reconnaissance and skirmishing activities the Texans moved south to Tennessee while following the withdrawal of the western Confederate line in the spring of 1862.

The clash of armies soon brought the regiment into the heart of the struggle for the Trans-Mississippi region. On April 6 and throughout the next day it participated in the strategic Battle of Shiloh where the Confederate Army of Mississippi with 44,000 men attempted to defeat the 66,000-strong Union Army of the Tennessee. Learning the limitations of horsemen on combined arms battlefields, the rangers conducted two charges against the Federal left, one mounted and another on foot, and failed on both attempts. Blackburn recalled they experienced their "first repulse" in this battle with the Union lines "resisting with great stubbornness."[89]

The following day the Texans rebounded as the stymied Rebel army marched south to the city of Corinth.[90] Blackburn recorded they were "employed in patrolling the space now behind the army and as rear guard." When Maj. Gen. Ulysses S. Grant sent a division to pressure the retreat, cavalry commander Nathan Bedford Forrest included the rangers in a spontaneously formed cavalry brigade to block, or at least slow, the attack. Blackburn remembered the Tennessean's orders that stressed familiar frontier tactics as Federals closed in: "Boys, go in twenty steps of the Yankees before you turn your shotguns loose on them."

The young volunteer then recalled the sequence of attack: "Forrest ordered forward. Without waiting to be formal in the matter, the Texans went like a cyclone, not waiting for Forrest to give his other orders to trot, gallop, charge, as he had drilled his men." As the Rebels advanced on the enemy position the Union infantry stood with "their bayonets ready to lift us fellows off our horses." In response, the Southerners "halted in twenty steps of their two lines of savage bayonets" to fire their first volley.

Blackburn described the chaotic melee that followed after the Texans came to a precarious halt within firing range of the infantrymen: "in the twinkling of an eye almost, both barrels of every shotgun in our line ... was turned into that blue line and lo! What destruction and confusion followed." He then emphasized how they transitioned smoothly from stand-off to close combat engagement: "after the shot-guns fired, the guns were slung on the horns of our saddles and with our six-shooters in hand we pursued those fleeing, either capturing or killing until they reached their reserve force. Just before we reached this force, we quietly withdrew."[91]

This engagement, named for a nearby place called Fallen Timbers, illustrated Texans' penchant for aggressive action. It also signified that successful mounted charges were conditional and greatly depended upon the enemy's preparedness and weaponry and the difficulty of the terrain to be traversed. While the moderately fortified infantry positions and wooded landscape at Shiloh defeated the 8th Texas's attacks, the maneuver at Fallen Timbers benefited from catching a similar enemy while marching on open ground. The additional tactic of pausing to discharge rifles and shotguns before closing also revealed controlled flexibility. Giles called the attack at Fallen Timbers a "brilliant charge."[92]

The regiment next won greater fame, again under Forrest's leader-ship, at the First Battle of Murfreesboro on July 13, 1862. Now attached to a specialized raiding brigade under the aggressive commander, the Texans struck the strategic Union rail center at Murfreesboro, Tennessee. The town garrison comprised approximately 900 cavalry, infantry, and artillery soldiers from Michigan, Minnesota, and Pennsylvania separated into three camps. Blackburn recalled that after an "all night ride," the Rebel force of 1,400 attacked the unsuspecting defenders from the east with "three divisions, sending one to attack the court house, one to attack the enemy at Stone River ... and the balance of the rangers to attack the encampment in the edge of Tennessee."[93]

The dispersed Federal companies initially resisted, but lacking coordination surrendered in detail. At one point Forrest threatened hold-outs that if they did not surrender he would charge with "the Texas Rangers under the black flag."[94] This statement, and the immediate capitulation that followed, indicated the reputation Texans now held amongst Northern and Southern armies. The Confederates captured or killed almost the entire garrison, and most importantly, destroyed the supply depot and rail hubs.[95]

The 8th Texas Cavalry spent the fall of 1862 supporting the great Confederate invasion of Kentucky with reconnaissance and screening. Performing traditional roles of light cavalry in Western nation-state warfare, Blackburn wrote they were "to be the vanguard on this trip in order to clear up the way, and keep the commanding general posted as to what was before him on his line of march." For thirty-eight consecutive days the "regiment in part or as a whole had been under fire ... fighting and skirmishing occurred every day."[96] By October the Southerners were retreating back into Tennessee as Union mass proved irresistible. Giles recounted his regiment's role in the retreat when General Braxton Bragg "now started for the Cumberland Gap, leaving his cavalry to protect his rear, and retard, as best they could, the onward march of the enemy."[97]

By December of 1862 the rangers had received enough reinforcements to increase their strength back to 690 men. Despite the upgrade, populated almost entirely by Texans, the unit was suffering from more than a year of constant combat. On December 31 they participated in the Second Battle of Murfreesboro, which Blackburn called "one of the great battles of the Civil War." Over the next two days, as part of a larger cavalry brigade, the regiment sought to envelop the Union right flank with costly attacks. After the broader Confederate attack failed to displace Northern defenses it conducted the familiar duty of covering the bloodied army's retreat.[98]

A particular engagement at Second Murfreesboro revealed the contrast between opposing cavalries when the Texans clashed with a Union mounted regiment. Tasked to prevent the "Yankee cavalry" from harassing the Confederate main forces, Blackburn attested they "charged them, drove them, and scattered them." The commander ordered them to "Let them come up nearly close enough to strike and then feed them on buckshot." The lopsided outcome indicated the conditional superiority of Texan frontier tactics over conventional eastern methods. According to the young ranger, "One volley from the shotguns into their ranks scattered these saber men into useless fragments of a force." The emphasis on "saber men" contrasted with Texans' reliance on revolvers and large knives for close killing. [99]

The 8th Texas Cavalry spent 1863 raiding throughout Tennessee, Alabama, and Georgia, with significant cavalry actions in September at Chickamauga. In early October they participated in a deep raid against Union rear echelons when they destroyed a logistical depot at McMinnville. By the summer of 1864, after a difficult year of fighting across Tennessee, the regiment moved to harass Maj. Gen. William T. Sherman's devastating march through Georgia and South Carolina. Despite their proven effectiveness, their constant attacks against the Federal expedition's rear proved futile; a single cavalry regiment could not hope to decisively alter the epic Union offensive. Blackburn called Sherman's March to the Sea "fearful to behold" as "none had more of devastation and cruelty and inhumanity than this one."[100]

The Battle of Bentonville in North Carolina witnessed the final charge of Terry's Texas Rangers as the war approached its bitter end. The confrontation unfolded between March 19 and 21, 1865, as a last attempt by the Confederate Army of the South—a consolidation of brigades and regiments from Tennessee, Virginia, South Carolina, Georgia, and Florida—to halt Sherman's march north through the Carolinas. As with recent confrontations, Union mass proved too great for the Rebel assaults. As the outmatched Southerners retreated from the battlefield, General Joseph Johnston ordered the Texans to seize a Union-occupied bridge through which the defeated army had to march to escape intact.

The 8th Texas now numbered fewer than 200 serviceable men. It now comprised more a battalion than regiment. Due to combat attrition or promotion of every colonel, lieutenant colonel, and major who had led and served in the unit throughout the war, command now fell to Captain J.F. Mathews. Graber described their final offensive engagement against two Federal infantry companies holding the bridge. Recalling the attack with pride, he explained "the Rangers went into a thick woods, hardly suited for a cavalry charge, raising their accustomed yell and with their pistols, dashed into the first line of infantry, who on account of the sudden, unexpected onslaught, must have overshot them in their first volley." Relishing the telling, the Texan concluded that "the Rangers were right among them, drove them into the second line, which became demoralized and fell back in confusion."[101]

This final attack by Terry's Texas Rangers at Bentonville represented a fitting end to their experience in the Civil War. Blackburn hyperbolically called it a "charge rarely equaled and never surpassed in impetuosity and daring," while Giles proclaimed: "Like our other brilliant charges, it was the very audacity that brought success."[102] These assessments, professed by admittedly interested participants, nevertheless emphasized intangibles and tactical qualities that set the regiment apart from contemporary mounted forces. For Texans who embraced a distinctive way of war developed over decades of fighting on the periphery, cavalry successes rested upon combining speed and firepower to fracture their enemy's organizational and psychological integrity.

Confederate Cavalry in the West

Sparsely populated territories to the west of Texas emerged as another, albeit lesser, expeditionary theater for its forces in the Civil War. Like eastern campaigns that unfolded from Louisiana to Georgia, projection of Texan combat power to New Mexico Territory required deployment across vast distances with cavalry mobility. Also like the Eastern Theater, the Confederacy accomplished the desert invasion predominantly with conventionally oriented regiments. Though the campaign for a western Confederate Empire seemed to benefit from the audacity and strategic rapidity that only flying columns of mounted forces could hope to achieve, it would end in utter disaster.[103]

The invasion of New Mexico began in July of 1861 when the 2nd Texas Mounted Rifles seized Fort Bliss from its Federal garrison. A larger brigade under Brig. Gen. Henry H. Sibley, a West Point graduate and former army officer in antebellum Texas, followed in October and November of 1861 with the 4th, 5th, and 7th Texas

Volunteer Cavalry regiments. Given the mobile nature of the self-styled Army of New Mexico, it offered immense potential for rapid conquest of isolated Union positions in the New Mexico desert. The plan, which was approved in Richmond by President Davis, emulated strategies pioneered in centuries past by the Comanche who had excelled at combining operational reach with sudden striking power.[104]

The Texans first attempted to defeat the Union garrison of 3,800 regulars and volunteers at Fort Craig on the Rio Grande in lower New Mexico Territory. Sibley hoped the speed of a relatively fleet cavalry brigade supported by fifteen mobile artillery pieces would enable its swift capture. Yet on February 15, when the invaders arrived, they found the fort prepared and impregnable to assault. The Confederates then demonstrated to entice a general engagement, but the Union commander, Colonel Edward Canby, pragmatically refused to be drawn out.[105]

Undaunted, Sibley next enveloped the fort from the north in order to isolate the defenders from outside support. The first and largest battle of the New Mexico Campaign occurred when Union forces emerged and intercepted the Southerners at a crossing site over the Rio Grande. At the Battle of Valverde, named for the fording location, Texans and Unionists each reinforced battle lines with fresh companies throughout the day.[106] Albert Peticolas ofthe 4th Texas Cavalry described his regiment's arrival to the scene: "In high spirits and singing songs, we crossed the valley at the same rapid pace and dismounted among the cotton woods and advanced rapidly (after having hitched our horses) to a slight embankment on our line of defense."[107]

The fight at the river devolved into a stubborn and bloody contest of attrition for both sides. In the late afternoon, as the battle culminated, opposing commanders attempted to outflank each other's lines. This included an ill-advised charge by the 2nd Texas Cavalry while armed with lances in which they "lost so many men," as recorded by Peticolas. The young sergeant also recalled how the Texan left wing had "charged upon horseback and had been repulsed with loss by the heavy lines of infantry, who reserved their fire till our men had gotten about 120 yards of them."[108]

Despite repeated setbacks, the Texans eventually gained a tactical, though strategically limited, victory with an aggressive charge on the Union center. Peticolas exulted how "nothing would stand before our victorious forces ... their own cannon were rapidly drawn down towards the left, where we were driving them back, and fired upon them with telling effect."[109] Tom Green, who had commanded a company under Jack Hays in Mexico and now led the 5th Texas Cavalry, wrote that "never were double barreled shot-guns and rifles used to better effect."[110]

Sibley, who was quick to highlight tactical successes but would ultimately fail to achieve success at the theater-level, concurred and praised the efforts of his versatile cavalrymen. The commander reported with dramatic flair: "For the first time ... batteries were charged and taken at the muzzle of double barrel shotguns, thus illustrating the spirit, valor, and invincible determination of Texas Troops."[111] Once again, as in previous hard-fought fights at San Jacinto, Salado Creek, and Monterrey, devotion to aggressive tactics and firepower had paid dividends.

The Union men retreated towards the fort as the Texans failed to exploit victory with pursuit. One officer lamented that their "men and horses were completely worn out" due to the long desert march followed by a difficult and bloody battle. Sibley recalled the attrition to the mounts of the 4th Texas Cavalry, in particular, reporting "many of their horses were killed, thus leaving them half foot and half mounted."[112] In the end, under "flag of truce," the Federals collected their dead and wounded and retired to the safety of Fort Craig. The Confederates suffered 187 casualties, almost 10 percent of the brigade, while the Unionists sustained 110 killed, 240 wounded, and 35 missing, approximately 16 percent of the garrison.[113]

Understanding the precariousness of his isolated position in the austere New Mexico desert, Sibley bypassed Fort Craig and continue up the Rio Grande Valley towards his next target: Fort Union. The Confederate expedition seized Albuquerque on March 2 and Santa Fe on March 13, but failed to capture critically needed

supply dumps. On March 28 at Glorieta Pass on the Santa Fe Trail
while advancing on Fort Union, most of the Army of New Mexico
again engaged Union soldiers in the battle that decided the campaign. Unlike the previous fight at Fort Craig, this contest unfolded
mostly as an infantry and artillery affair due to rough and constrict-
ing terrain.[114]

After much skirmishing and several advances, the Texans managed to flank the Union position and won the battle, again achieving
a limited tactical victory.[115] Colonel William Scurry, the senior Rebel
officer at Glorieta Pass, praised his soldiers with patriotic exaggeration in an overly optimistic document titled General Order No. 4: "You
have proven your right to stand by the side of those who fought and
conquered on the red field of San Jacinto." Peticolas agreed, noting
that "from all I can hear of San Jacinto, that battle was not near such
a hotly contested fight as the battle of Glorieta or Val Verde either."[116]
Despite the Texan victory, comparison with Sam Houston's 1836
achievement remained problematic; while the 1836 victory secured
the political independence, the 1862 campaign farther west came to
symbolize a failed effort.

Unfortunately for the Army of New Mexico, victory at Glorieta
Pass did not result in strategic advantage. The unexpected loss of the
Confederate logistical train during the battle carried more long-term
impact than the actual clash of main force units. Peticolas recalled
the event that eventually spelled disaster for the expedition when he
recalled that a "detachment of the enemy's Cavalry had passed round
through the mountains and attacked, taken, and burnt our train." The
soldier reminisced that his unit "heard cannonading in our rear about
this time and did not know what to think of it. But it turned out in fact
that they had burned our train and retreated rapidly."[117]

The loss of these supplies soon placed the Rebels in a perilous
position in the desolate and arid desert. It also represented an effective use of Union horsemen, who were actually mounted elements
from the 2nd Colorado and 1st New Mexico Infantry Regiments, as
raiders in a seemingly peripheral operation that inflicted a devastating

impact. The economized effectiveness illustrated how commanders on both sides in the Civil War utilized the strike capacity of individual cavalry companies with their smaller signatures and reduced logistical requirements, to conduct precise attacks at decisive points. Having prevented the loss of Forts Craig and Union, Canby was rewarded with promotion to brigadier general soon after the battle.

Sibley and his army fell into an untenable status without possession of forts that dominated New Mexico Territory. Converging and cumulatively superior Federal reinforcements from California and Colorado, in addition to Canby's original garrisons, then threatened disaster when they moved to envelop the Rebels' position. Without adequate resources in the austere desert environment Sibley retired to Albuquerque, and next retreated ignominiously back to San Antonio by the summer of 1862. The arduous retreat, which featured extreme starvation and physical hardship, debilitated the once vaunted Army of New Mexico. The Texans had begun the campaign with 3,700 proud cavalrymen but finished with fewer than 1,800 traumatized and footsore stragglers.[118]

The Confederate invasion of New Mexico illustrated both the advantages and perils of cavalry mobility over distance. While deep or strategic raids could yield valuable results against unsuspecting outposts and unprepared garrisons—as exemplified by Nathan Bedford Forrest's raid at Murfreesboro—the danger to horsemen operating far beyond support range held the potential for unmitigated disaster. In Sibley's case, his brigade's capacity for extended and rapid movement placed them in a vulnerable position without adequate combined arms support or resupply. The inspired Union strike on his supply column, though seemingly a peripheral action when it occurred, further exacerbated the invaders' logistical difficulties.

The resulting logistical nightmare, placed the Army of New Mexico in an unsustainable position. Its condition worsened in the desert environment where the men, and horses in particular, remained vulnerable to thirst and malnourishment. Equine privation emerged as a critical problem and by April Sibley had lost the majority of his mounts and essentially commanded a struggling infantry brigade. This loss deprived the Texans of their traditional reliance on mobility, and in part, doomed the conquest to failure.

Defending South Texas

The final major region of Texan military efforts comprised the southeast coastline as the state defended against seaborne Union invasion. Throughout the war the U.S. Army and Navy attempted to seize footholds on several occasions. This objective would have allowed a strategic envelopment of the Confederate west as well as providing the Union with immense quantities of war-related resources like cotton and beef that frontier industry provided in abundance. The resulting protection of the Gulf Coast unfolded as a remarkable example of economized defense against overwhelming odds.

The first two serious Union attempts at the penetration of Texan coastal defenses did not involve cavalry actions and emerged predictably from the sea. Once the United States captured New Orleans in 1862, the nearby Texan Gulf Coast became a natural target for invasion by armadas of gunships and amphibious assault infantry. This development corresponded with an intermittent naval blockade of the Texas coast to deprive the region of seaborne commerce.

The Union assault on Texas, even as the state deployed rangers to fight across its Indian Frontier, began on October 4, 1862, when the U.S. Navy attacked the island of Galveston. After a brief cannonade, the inferior Confederate garrison withdrew, thus depriving Texas of a critical commercial port. Five hundred Federal soldiers from Massachusetts then occupied the coastal town while the department command in New Orleans prepared to transport several infantry regiments to reinforce the foothold.

Another important coastal town, Corpus Christi, endured naval bombardment soon after. Despite the attack, the valuable port remained occupied by Texan forces. Francis Lubbock, governor of Texas, sought to galvanize resistance with a dramatic call to arms: "The crisis of this war seems to be at hand in Texas, and we must prepare to defend our homes, or be driven from them with insult and degradation, and all the horrors of rapine and violence." Relying on his state's historical strengths in rapid mobilization, the governor called for 5,000 volunteers to defend the coast.[119]

On New Year's Day of 1863 Maj. Gen. John Magruder, commander of the District of Texas, counter-attacked with a synchronized gunboat and amphibious ground offensive to repossess Galveston. A small fleet of brown-water vessels first engaged the unsuspecting Union fleet with a lightning attack in dark of night. With diversion in effect, remnants of the New Mexico brigade under command of William Scurry, along with local militia, assaulted the island. The attack proved successful and the Confederates captured three Union ships and over 350 prisoners. Texans inflicted 650 Federal casualties, marking the operation as a stunning victory despite suffering 26 killed and 117 wounded.[120]

The next significant Union attempt at invasion occurred in September of 1863. Called the Second Battle of Sabine Pass, the day belonged to a single Rebel artillery battery stationed at Fort Griffin at the mouth of the Sabine River. In an act of notable bravery, the severely outnumbered Texans waited until a large seaborne invasion of 15,000 infantry, cavalry, and artillery, approached to within 1,200 yards of the fort. They then opened a rapid-fire cannonade. After sinking one ship and severely damaging another, the forty-four men under Irish immigrant Lieutenant Dick Dowling forced the armada of fifteen ships to retreat. The battle resulted in an astounding economy-of-force victory for the Confederacy.[121] The *Texas State Gazette* subsequently boasted with poetic appeal: "The ball is again opened in Texas. We have met the enemy and they are again ours."[122]

The third major event occurred in May of 1865 as a cavalry affair when the Union Army made a final attempt to seize Texas territory before the war ended. Unlike previous invasions, the Battle of Palmetto Ranch, named for a nearby horse farm, occurred as a tactically important, yet strategically inconsequential, land engagement by opposing cavalry and infantry regiments. It also allowed Colonel John Ford to once again rise to prominence as a popular military leader. Though

Texas won a resounding victory, General Robert E. Lee and the Army of Northern Virginia had surrendered four weeks prior and collapse of the Confederacy was imminent.

The Palmetto Ranch Campaign began on May 11 when Colonel Theodore Barrett, commander of the Union regiment occupying the island of Brazos Santiago near Brownsville, ordered an incursion onto the Texan mainland. Despite the tacit ceasefire that had existed between Texan and Federal opponents for several months due to a shared understanding that the war would be won or lost elsewhere, he ordered an attack for reasons known only to him. It is possible that Barrett sought to requisition horses for his dismounted cavalry, but it is more likely, as claimed by the quartermaster of the 34th Indiana Infantry Regiment in an accusatory letter published in the *New York Times*, that he hoped to "establish for himself some notoriety before the war closed." Barrett later called it a "foraging expedition" at his court martial over the matter.[123]

The attacking battalion comprised eight companies from the 62nd U.S. Colored Troops and two from the 2nd Texas Cavalry Battalion (U.S.), which was populated by Unionist Texans. The task force totaled approximately 300 soldiers. Furthermore, the cavalry did not possess horses, making the entire force functionally infantry. On the Rebel side, Ford commanded the lower Rio Grande defenses with the 2nd Texas Cavalry and several understrength mounted volunteer battalions. At the time of invasion one of the volunteer cavalries was encamped at Palmetto Ranch near old Fort Brown. The disparity in mounted capacity between the Southern and Northern opponents would prove decisive in days to come.[124]

On the night of May 11 Union companies crossed to the Texas mainland under concealment of darkness. Under the command of Barrett's deputy, Lt. Col. David Branson, they marched against a suspected enemy position at White's Ranch near the Rio Grande. When they found the station abandoned, the Federals spent the night under cover and in the morning skirmished with about 190 cavalrymen from Gidding's Texas cavalry battalion led by Captain William Robinson.

When the fight proved inconclusive the Union soldiers retired to White's Ranch while Barrett reinforced the expedition with 200 additional infantrymen and assumed personal command of the offensive.[125]

The next day, on May 12, the Union force of 500 advanced and again skirmished with Robinson's men near another Rebel station at Palmetto Ranch. The larger infantry battalion pushed the Texans out into open ground and pursued a mile west of the ranch. Uncertain of his next move, Barrett then established a temporary camp on a small hill. Though the massed infantry rifles prevailed in the skirmish, the invaders would soon suffer from their lack of horses and inability to conduct wide-ranging reconnaissance or rapid pursuit actions.[126]

That afternoon Ford arrived at the scene of battle and assumed command of the Confederate counter-attack. When his own 2nd Texas Cavalry combined with elements from several volunteer mounted battalions, the veteran ranger commanded approximately 400 horsemen. He also brought a mobile battery comprising six field guns to offset the lack of infantry.[127]

Skirmishing had continued between the Texan volunteers and Union soldiers while Ford deployed from Fort Brown. Upon arrival he first "made reconnaissance and determined to attack." Barrett had let himself be caught in open and flat terrain that suited cavalry and the Texan chose to maximize his superiority in mobility. He planned to use artillery "in advance of the line" while enveloping with "enfilading fire" on the right and dispatching another wing to "turn the enemy's right flank."[128] Despite the audacious scheme, it held great risk for the horsemen since they would be charging infantry who had conceivably entrenched.

Ford grossly overestimated the size of the Federals. He worried about attacking massed foot soldiers when he wrote that "this may be the last fight of the war and from the number of Union men I see before me, I am going to be whipped." Regardless of his concerns, the Rebels initiated the assault with a battery in the center-front. They then followed the barrage with a charge by the 2nd Texas in the center while simultaneously enveloping Barrett's left and right with volunteer horse. Ford described the decisive action on his left where he intended to deliver the decisive blow: "Very soon Captain Robinson charged with impetuosity. As was expected the Yankee skirmishers were captured and the enemy troops were retreating at a run."[129]

The artillery and flank assaults placed the Union battalion in an untenable position and forced it to retreat towards the coast. The Texans "pursued at the gallop" and harassed the retreat, which proved so unorganized that two infantry columns physically marched into each other and caused further chaos. Barrett eventually deployed, and largely sacrificed, a detachment from the 62nd U.S.C.T. to screen his escape. By day's end the Federals had lost two soldiers missing, four dead, twelve wounded, and 102 captured. Adding a sting to defeat, they also suffered the disgrace of losing two "battle flags" of the 34th Indiana.[130]

Texan maneuvers during the final battle of the Civil War provided a veritable display of cavalry advantages when properly wielded on mid-nineteenth-century battlefields. It first manifested when Ford used speed available to mounted forces to mobilize and reinforce the Texan garrison at Palmetto Ranch. He next utilized mobility unique to cavalry to envelop the Federal position before its slower infantry ranks could react. At the battle's culmination, the same maneuverability facilitated rapid charges, which, along with supportive artillery, compelled the Federal retreat. He finally utilized the traditional cavalry pursuit to complete the victory and degrade the retreating battalion.

These qualities exemplified the most effective tactical aspects of Lone Star military traditions. It also revealed that rapid mobilization by interested volunteers remained relevant, if only conditionally, for the state. Ford, as a veteran of the Texian Army, the Mexican-American War, and numerous ranging assignments, had absorbed these lessons throughout thirty years of frontier fighting. As exemplified by the Battle of Palmetto Ranch, this combat experience had uniquely prepared him to counter Union threats, when appropriate, with superior mounted versatility. Since Texas had begun the war with mobilization under one ranger icon, Ben McCulloch, it was only fitting that it would finish under another, John Salmon Ford.

Transcending the Tradition

The strategic deployment of Texan forces across disparate combat theaters demonstrated strengths and weaknesses of societal reliance upon cavalry-centric methods. While the large mobilization of Texas cavalry regiments in the Trans-Mississippi and Eastern Theaters benefited the Confederate cause, use of over-extended Texan volunteers to invade New Mexico perfectly illustrated the limitations of nineteenth-century mounted forces. If the latter stressed perils of strategic and deep attacks without adequate logistical and combined arms support, the former revealed the effectiveness of unencumbered and audacious horsemen when properly employed.

The wartime defense of Texan territory against frontier raiding likewise revealed structural challenges in its reliance on conscripted citizen-soldiers. Traditional inadequacies with logistical support and long-term service plagued the establishment of robust patrolling networks. Recruitment from less desirable demographics for historically specialized and self-interested ranger service also diluted tactical capabilities. Yet in contrast to struggling northwestern defenses, cavalry responses to Union incursions along the Gulf Coast, specifically around Brownsville, proved successful as local commanders harnessed and unleashed traditional Texan strengths of rapid and limited mobilization, aggressive strikes, and mobile superiority.

The transcending careers of Texan officers who commanded cavalry in the rebellion—which contrasted with the highly successful infantry careers by Johnston and Hood—offers a final consideration of how Texas's way of war culminated in the Civil War. The highly publicized careers of Ben McCulloch, John Ford, Walter Lane, Tom Green, and Sul Ross personified the tradition's continuity as the hardy men embraced forty years of nationalistic conflict. Upon the combat deaths of McCulloch and Green, Lubbock proclaimed that the veterans had stalwartly defended the state "regardless of the character of the foe, whether

Indian, Mexican, or Yankee" while recalling how they had begun as "gunnery-boys for the 'Twin Sisters' at San Jacinto."[131] Each of the four noted rangers except Ross began as privates in the old Texian Army, and each of them but Ford finished as general officers in the Civil War.

Under the collective watch of the men Lubbock romanticized as "incomparable fighters" from "all the wars of Texas," Texas's societal investment in volunteer mounted arms emerged from the colonial period, developed throughout republican and state years, and attained full material expression during the final rebellion. At the ceremonial activation of a ranger company named for Walter Lane in 1861, Sallie Smith of Marshall, Texas, proudly addressed the recruits as "the gallant inheritors of the renown and valor of the Alamo and San Jacinto!" She also lauded "miracles of prowess and valor achieved by Texan heroes" and remembered eras when "the valorous cohorts of Texas went forth under the guidance of that Lone Star which shone so long and so gloriously upon her fortunes."[132] Though their namesake did not actually serve in the company, the men mustered in as F Company, 2nd Texas Mounted Rifles, under Ford's command.

Lane's military career, in particular, illustrated the transcendence of Texas's militancy and how iconic leaders influenced its larger cultural tradition. The Irish immigrant had first learned fighting skills from Erastus Smith in the Corps of Texas Cavalry at the Battle of San Jacinto, and then rode as a ranger under the tutelage of Jack Hays during the wars of the Texas Republic. Rising to battalion command, he next led mounted riflemen in the Mexican-American War while conducting rigorous counter-guerrilla operations in northern Mexico. The officer's patriotic service to Texas peaked during the Civil War when he commanded both the 3rd Texas Cavalry and 1st Texas Partisan Rangers.[133]

Lane's hometown press eulogized his martial contributions to Texas upon his death in 1892. The *Marshal Paper* from his adopted community honored him as "The Hero of Three Wars" and the "Immaculate defender of his country." It also noted, as his remains awaited burial, that family placed with him "battle-scarred flags, rusty sabers, spears, spurs, arrows and other trophies" to "keep silent sentinel and look down upon all that remains of the old hero, who either used them with honor, or wrested them from enemies of war."[134] As befitting a true frontier cavalryman, they laid the old fighter to rest with the accouterments and weaponry of a life spent perilously in the hazards of frontier warfare.

Under veteran officers like Lane and other great captains, Texas symbolically and tangibly deployed four decades of brutal combat experience in the cause of rebellion. Texan commanders frequently invoked their state's embattled history to inspire younger patriots who flocked to Confederate banners. Many of these men had never fought, but all had heard stories of Texas's lost golden age. Henry Sibley, after observing the decisive charge at the Battle of Val Verde, invoked this tradition when he proclaimed of his troops: "Nobly have they emulated the fame of their San Jacinto ancestors."[135] Lubbock likewise lauded countrymen with sentimental praise and recounted that "Texans were of heroic mold; some were soldiers of San Jacinto, some had participated in the storming of Monterrey, while others had repulsed Santa Anna's veterans at Buena Vista."[136]

This belief in Texan exceptionalism—which often manifested as much culturally as militarily between the Texas Revolution and the Civil War—transcended conflicts and generations. Henry Graber of Terry's Texas Rangers represented the new generation of Texan horsemen that came of age during Confederate rebellion when he explicitly connected the nationalistic motivations of his peers to the efforts of past Texan soldiers. Connecting their current revolt to when his society first fought for independence, the young recruit wrote that "the young men composing this regiment would endeavor to emulate the example of the heroes of the Alamo, Goliad and San Jacinto."[137]

In addition to appreciating legacies of previous campaigns, Graber placed Texan militancy in a distinctly cavalry context. Upon observing exhibitions of horsemanship during the 8th Texas Cavalry's stay in Tennessee, the young recruit directly connected mobility and firepower with inherited traditions when he explained that the "extraordinary feat, in connection with their general appearance; being armed with shotguns, six-shooters and Bowie knives, seemed to sustain their idea of the Texas Rangers that fought at the Alamo, Goliad and San Jacinto and served under Jack Hayes, Ben McCulloch and other Indian and Mexican fighters."[138] For Graber and the young Texans who fought for Southern independence, a predilection for mounted warfare had been ingrained by the stories, legends, and examples of their forebears.

Despite the scope of Texas's mobilization for the Civil War, by the summer of 1865 the Confederacy collapsed and tens of thousands of its sons straggled home. The martial culture that had long defended and expanded its borders—even if exaggerated in Texan popular imagination—proved inadequate against Union might. James Blackburn, after he demobilized with Terry's Texas Rangers, excused his society's first large-scale defeat by attesting that, "Overwhelming numbers with inexhaustible supplies had triumphed over a half-fed, scantily supplied army, greatly inferior in numbers." In reality, the loss resulted from a much more nuanced confluence of flawed strategy, missed opportunities, political disunity, and eventual tactical inferiority. Blackburn, like so many Texans, returned home dismayed by "the bloodshed, the deaths, the horrors and devastation of the war."[139]

The scale of the military loss for both Texas and the South proved epic in measures of material and human destruction. The Confederacy suffered 260,000 dead, 226,000 wounded, and 247,769 taken prisoner, while the Texan people endured the loss or incapacitation of a quarter of their productive manpower.[140] Though the eastern focus of the war spared Texas direct territorial devastation experienced by states like Virginia and Georgia, four years of frontier defense, massive mobilization, agricultural atrophy, Union blockades, and financial indebtedness had wrecked the state socially and economically.[141]

This calamity resulted in a heretofore unthinkable condition: occupation and rule by an enemy power. As Lubbock observed with dismay, "the din of war had ceased and the blue had supplanted the gray. Everywhere United States soldiers could be seen moving around with the air of conquerors, and we, the once free citizens of

Texas, could only speak of governmental affairs with bated breath." Speaking to the economic toll that years of privation inflicted against Texan society, he lamented how "the long war with a close blockade had deprived our people of many necessaries of civilized life."[142] The sudden onset of Federal political domination, military occupation, and the abolition of slavery emasculated Anglo-Texan pride and ushered in a contentious, painful period known as Reconstruction.

Epilogue

Texas's way of war achieved its zenith in the summer of 1865 as cavalrymen like those at the Battle of Palmetto Ranch fought through the final engagements of the Civil War. Across four decades of relentless warfare the frontier polity had, in accordance with scholar John Grenier's description of the broader Anglo-Colonial warmaking tradition, "forged two elements—unlimited war and irregular war—into their first way of war."[1] Beginning with settler adaption in *Tejas* and ending in societal mobilization for Confederate rebellion, these efforts ranged from raiding along troubled borders to nation-state contests as far apart as Atlanta and Mexico City. Throughout the march of campaigns the Lone Star people remained committed—with varying and sometimes disproportional degrees of cultural and physical manifestation—to cavalry-centric organization, amateur volunteerism, and event-specific mobilization.

Texas's military evolution thus found dynamic expression across diverse mounted arms expressions as it grappled with tribal warriors, Mexican lancers, and Union soldiers. While most of its horsemen gained tactical experience in town and county mounted militias that proliferated across ever-expanding borders and frontiers, fewer acquired deeper expertise in formally authorized companies and battalions that intermittently pursued state territorial interests. Yet of all those who took up arms for the embattled polity, San Antonio rangers of the late republic and mounted riflemen who fought in the Mexican-American War elevated the tradition to its highest combat effectiveness relative to contemporary militaries.

The iconic Texas Rangers—rising as an elite order during republican and antebellum periods—came to personify Lone Star masculinity, martial prowess, and nationalistic militarism. Best represented by John Coffee Hays's companies of the 1840s, they combined decades of military evolution, hybrid equine breeding, and killing capacity of Colt revolvers to achieve peerless tactical lethality in years just before and during the Mexican-American War. The *Telegraph and Texas Register* emphasized this in 1844 when it described how "well armed" horsemen would "by turns scour the country in every direction." It also noted they had "several full blooded race horses, remarkable for their fleetness" and with them could "attack, pursue, or escape from Indian or Mexican enemies."[2]

This military specialty informed Texan mobilizations as the colony, republic, and state intermittently pursued strategies of annihilation, attrition, and exhaustion. As chief executives implemented vacillating military policies that evolved from Sam Houston's economized defense to Mirabeau Lamar's offensive wars and back again, mounted arms remained the heart of citizen militancy. By the time of the Mexican-American War, this inclination for cavalry service had permeated society beyond the proportionally few rangers that actually saw robust combat. This led the state's first governor to observe of wartime recruitment in 1846 that, "there would be no difficulty in raising forty companies provided they were mounted ... Texians are generally good horsemen and prefer to be employed in that way."[3]

Texas continued to rely upon this martial tradition in the wake of failed rebellion, albeit on a far lesser scale due to re-imposed Federal primacy. Once again Texan horsemen augmented inadequate U.S. Army garrisons on contested frontiers to ride against guerrilla and criminal attacks, both provoked and unprovoked. The fighting ethos begun by John Moore, Erastus Smith, Henry Karnes, Jack Hays, Ben McCulloch, Walter Lane, and Sul Ross lived on in Old West themes and traditions. Yet despite similarities with frontier antecedents, new generations gradually shifted focus to a different tactical dimension: civil security. As the state's population exploded from 818,579 in 1870 to 2,235,527 by 1890 and the Indian Frontier fell before the final march of Anglo settlement expansion, post-Reconstruction rangers increasingly oriented on police actions against outlaws and marauders of all ethnicities.[4]

Despite the impending shift to law enforcement, tribal conflict in Texas peaked again in 1865 and 1866. When the U.S. Army and State Police of Reconstruction years proved unable to forestall tribal retaliation against Anglo encroachment, state officials initiated a series of paramilitary ranger organizations to perform traditional ranging functions. In 1870 it passed an act to "raise and muster into the service of the State, for the protection of the northern and western Frontier, twenty companies of Texas Rangers." The legislature approved each man to receive "breech-loading cavalry arms" at state expense, but relied on traditional requirements for each recruit to "furnish himself with a suitable horse, six-shooting pistol, and all necessary accoutrements."[5]

Known as Frontier Forces, the riflemen patrolled against illegal activities along the Nueces Strip and tribal raiding across the northwest plains. After Texas disbanded the battalion for lack of fiscal support in 1871, it initiated the familiar, wide-spread, and more economized use of inactive "Minutemen for the protection of the frontiers from raids of Indians and other marauding parties."[6] However, when reactive militia proved inadequate for defense the state also activated eleven county-level ranger companies in 1874 for a period of four months.[7] These layered authorizations, inactive and active, were remarkably similar to Houston's defensive postures in 1844 and 1860.

Federal occupation of Texas officially ended in 1874, thereby allowing the newly empowered state greater latitude to establish a more robust frontier guard despite continued U.S. Army presence. In an attempt to return to proven methodologies, it established two paramilitary organizations to provide "protection" against "the invasion of hostile Indians, Mexicans, or other marauding or thieving parties."[8] Emphasis in the legislation on banditry indicated a gradual shift in threat perception towards domestic criminal activities and less against external military incursions. While the congress created the Special State Troops, later called the Special Force, to patrol southern Texas, it mobilized a larger formation called the Frontier Battalion to defend northwestern environs. These organizations renewed the auxiliary roles of antebellum rangers and pursued a range of offensive and civil stability tasks.[9]

Just as early Texan martial traditions found exaggerated personification in famed frontier captains like John Moore, Jack Hays, and John Ford, the newest generation of cavalrymen produced its own culturally influential leaders. Leander McNelly, a former Confederate officer, rose to command the highly lethal Special State Troops. Under his leadership it suppressed criminal ranching activity in DeWitt County in 1874 and interdicted Mexican marauders along the Nueces Strip in 1875 and 1876. Though McNelly left a profound legacy as a founder of the modern ranger institution, his summary execution of captured criminals and cross-border excursions remain controversial to this day.[10]

Murderous behavior by hard-eyed rangers reflected the volatility that yet scarred Texas decades after the Civil War. Like generations of nationalistic fighters before him, McNelly embraced a relentless military intensity that demanded proactive and aggressive tactics. According to Napoleon Jennings, a partisan who rode with the Special Force, the captain justified his methods by arguing Mexican bandits who attacked across the Rio Grande would "continue to do so until the robbers are followed to their fastness in Mexico and taught that there is no refuge."[11] The audacity of this unit proved reminiscent of Hays's San Antonio rangers. In 1881, after seven years of aggressive action predominantly in South Texas, the Special Force reorganized into the Frontier Battalion.

The Frontier Battalion emerged as the longest-serving successor to the ranging corps that intermittently patrolled Texas's borderlands since Stephen Austin first initiated the concept fifty years earlier. Retaining a distinctive military structure, the state congress ordered it to be "a battalion of mounted men, to consist of six companies, of seventy-five men each."[12] As a decentralized network that served from 1874 to 1901 the rangers patrolled as the final expression of Texan frontier militarism while occupying a larger space in modern popular memory. This unit finished as the last to orient significant focus toward external military foes, though later rangers fought Mexicans along the Rio Grande during the Mexican Revolution between 1910 and 1920.[13]

Another former Confederate officer, John Jones, commanded the Frontier Battalion. A man of few words who led by example, the major established the enduring personification for the idealized ranger as much as Hays had prior to the Civil War. From May of 1874 to November of 1889 the paramilitary battalion fought in fifty-six engagements against renegade Indians and violent outlaws while wounding twenty-seven opponents and killing sixty-nine designated criminals.[14] While the U.S. Army, and 4th U.S. Cavalry Regiment in particular, degraded the remaining warlike plains tribes in the decades after the Civil War, the Frontier Battalion's efforts assisted with final pacification of the long-violent frontier.[15]

Similar to McNelly's Special Force, Jones's horsemen routinely countered criminal civilian activity and set the precedent for Texas's modern investigative agency. Under the major's competent leadership, they defeated the popular outlaw Sam Bass in a storied gunfight near Austin and figured prominently in the Salt, Mason, and Red River "wars" of the 1870s. These actions captured the imagination of the American nation as romanticized Texas Rangers emerged as the premier Western lawmen and the concept of Lone Star justice, despite its notoriety for excessive brutality and racial discrimination, attained an indelible place in history.

The resulting popularity of the Frontier Battalion held societal impact in Texan society far beyond the few hundred horsemen who actually joined its ranks. In 1891, after a decade of increased focus on civil stability, Adjutant General Woodford Mabry praised the hardy lawmen: "A Texas Ranger is the synonym for courage and vigilance ... A bold rider, a quick eye, and a steady hand, he is the terror of the criminal."[16] Despite the outsized and pervasive place they had achieved in broader Texan culture by the 1880s, the state, ever mindful of fiscal limitations, demobilized the Frontier Battalion in 1901 due to lack of security need.

The last years of the Frontier Battalion coincided with a final event that harkened back to Texan auxiliary and volunteer involvement in larger nation-state wars. In response to sudden national mobilization for the Spanish-American War in 1898, the 1st Regiment, Texas Volunteer Cavalry, formed to augment the U.S. Army for expeditionary warfare against Spain in her residual colonial territories.

This regiment intended to provide conventional reconnaissance and attack support to combined arms brigades and divisions similar to Houston's Corp of Cavalry at San Jacinto, the Mounted Rifles in the Mexican-American War, and the multiplicity of Texas cavalry regiments that fought in Southern armies in the Civil War.

The formation of a new cavalry regiment in the heart of Texas predictably found no shortage of willing recruits. Colonel J. R. Waites commanded the unit with future World War I general John Hulen serving as brevet lieutenant colonel. The force comprised seven troops in accordance with army regulation. From August to November of 1898 it organized and trained in Austin, but then, in an anticlimactic ending, demobilized due to lack of Federal need for the short Spanish-American War. Though the regiment never deployed for combat, the mobilization at the close of the century continued a long, if intermittent, tradition of Texan horsemen supporting armies in international conflicts.[17]

In the decades that followed the turn of the twentieth century, Texas Rangers shifted increasingly towards internal security and became increasingly less militant. In the 1930s they fully embraced the bureaucracy of government agency and shed the final vestiges of military-oriented patrolling. The advent of new technologies likewise made horse-driven tactical operations problematic and marked the final eclipse of the legacy of Napoleonic mounted warfare. Ultimately, the rise of mechanization relegated frontier cavalrymen to the pages of history and heralded a new era of modernized policing and absolute Federal dominance in interstate and foreign affairs.

Despite these transitions, Texas once held a remarkable status amongst contemporary militaries while achieving a controversial record of combat effectiveness. It developed a dynamic and nationalistic tradition centered on tactical adaptation, mastery of horsemanship, and outsized firepower. This militancy stemmed from the explosion of a martial culture that began in the conflicts of colonial

Tejas, nationalized in the Texas Revolution, matured in the wars of the Texas Republic and American Texas, and culminated in the Civil War. As aggressors and opportunists on contested frontiers, these settlers fought and died for the idea of Texas. As citizen-soldiers of a society on the periphery of Western civilization, these rangers and cavalrymen rode for the Lone Star.

Endnotes

Notes for Introduction

1. See John Grenier, *The First Way of War: American War Making on the Frontier* (New York: Cambridge University Press, 2008) and Thomas Cutrer, *Ben McCulloch and the Frontier Military Tradition* (Chapel Hill: The University of North Carolina Press, 1993) for militant Anglo traditions that informed the Texas Way of War.

2. Robert Wooster, *American Military Frontiers: The United States Army in the West, 1783–1900* (Albuquerque: University of New Mexico Press, 2009), xiv; for edited volumes on Texas military history see Joseph Dawson, ed., *The Texas Military Experience: From the Texas Revolution to World War II* (College Station: Texas A&M University Press, 1995) and Alexander Mendoza, ed., *Texans and War: New Interpretations of the State's Military History* (College Station: Texas A&M University Press, 2012).

3. Russell Weigley, *The American Way of War: A History of United States Military Strategy and Policy* (Bloomington: Indiana University Press, 1973), xxii; see Colin Gray, *War, Peace, and International Relations: An Introduction to Strategic History* (New York: Routledge, 2007), 6, for a more limited definition of warmaking as a Way of Battle and Wayne Lee, "Mind and Matter—A Cultural Analysis in American Military History: A Look at the State of the Field," *The Journal of American History* 93, no. 4 (March 2007): 1116–1142, for thematic analysis.

4. Grenier, *First Way of War*, 23; Wayne Lee, *Barbarians and Brothers: Anglo-American warfare, 1500–1865* (Oxford and New York: Oxford University Press, 2011), 4, 214–215; see Guy Chet, *Conquering the American Wilderness: The Triumph of European Warfare in the Colonial Northeast* (Amherst: University of Massachusetts Press, 2003) for the Anglo martial development that Texans inherited indirectly from New England settlers.

5. Brian Linn, *The Echo of Battle: The Army's Way of War* (Cambridge: Harvard University Press, 2007), 233; see also Brian Linn, "The American Way of War Revisited," *Journal of Military History* 66, no. 2 (2002): 530, for an argument against Wiegley's binary annihilation/attrition assessment in favor of "complex" and "utilitarian" frameworks in which American tactics, strategy, and theory have been repeatedly customized for particular challenges.

6. Much of the Texas Republic's inability to maintain a standing army, and Texas's later tensions with U.S. Army garrisons, stemmed from the historical and cultural American aversion to centralized and standing national armies; see Wooster, *American Military Frontiers*, xii.

7. Amelia Williams and Eugene Barker, *The Writings of Sam Houston, 1813–1863* (Austin: The University of Texas Press, 1938), VI: 376–377.
8. Ibid., 490.
9. See Walter P. Webb, *The Texas Rangers: A Century of Frontier Defense*, 2nd ed. (Austin: University of Texas Press, 1965) for the foundational, if dated, history of the Texas Rangers; see Robert Utley, *Lone Star Justice: The First Century of the Texas Rangers* (New York: Oxford University Press, 2002) and Michael Cox, *The Texas Rangers: Wearing the Cinco Peso, 1821–1900* (New York: Forge, 2008) for updated and detailed histories.
10. Nelson Lee, *Three Years Among the Comanche* (Guilford: Globe Pequot Press, 2004), 7.
11. John Caperton, "Sketch of Colonel John C. Hays, Texas Ranger," The Center for American History, The University of Texas at Austin, 35–36.
12. Dunbar Rowland, ed., *Jefferson Davis Constitutionalist: His Letters, Papers and Speeches* (Jackson: Mississippi Department of Archives and History, 1923), I: 460, 467.
13. Charles Trower, *Hints on Irregular Cavalry* (Calcutta: W. Thacker and Co., 1845), 10–12, 18–26. See Philip Haythornthwaite, *Napoleonic Cavalry* (London: Cassell & Co, 2001) for general description of nineteenth-century European and colonial mounted forces in Europe and Asia.
14. John Ford, *Rip Ford's Texas*, edited by Stephen Oates (Austin: University of Texas Press, 1987), 252–253.
15. Luther Giddings, *Sketches of the Campaign in Mexico by an Officer of the First Ohio Volunteers* (New York: Putnam, 1853), 96–97.
16. For criticism of early Texan militancy see Julian Samora, *Gunpowder Justice: A Reassessment of the Texas Rangers* (Notre Dame: University of Notre Dame Press, 1979); Gary Anderson, *The Conquest of Texas: Ethnic Cleansing in the Promised Land, 1820–1875* (Norman: University of Oklahoma Press, 2005); and Michael Collins, *Texas Devils: Rangers and Regulars on the Lower Rio Grande, 1846–1861* (Norman: University of Oklahoma Press, 2008).
17. Tensions developed between Texas and the U.S. Army since Lone Star society held a typically American aversion to the presence of Federal soldiers and instead preferred Federal funding of Texan volunteers. Sam Houston accordingly proclaimed in the U.S. Senate in 1855 that he "would rather have two hundred and fifty Texas Rangers than five hundred of the best cavalry now in service." Williams, *Writings of Sam Houston*, VI: 124.

Notes for Chapter 1

1. Lee, *Barbarians and Brothers*, 119.
2. Lee, "Mind and Matter," 1120; Gregg Cantrell, *Stephen F. Austin: Empresario of Texas* (New Haven: Yale University Press, 1999), 143–144.
3. *The Texas Democrat*, September 9, 1846.
4. Eugene Barker, ed., *The Austin Papers* (Washington, D.C.: Government Printing Office, 1924–1928), I: 166–167, 242, 255–257; Cantrell, *Stephen F. Austin*, 21.
5. Barker, *Austin Papers*, I: 389–390.
6. Ibid., 432.
7. Ibid., 678.
8. Cantrell, *Stephen F. Austin*, 114–115.
9. Barker, *Austin Papers*: I, 651–653, 673; William Dewees, *Letters from an Early Settler of Texas,* edited by Cara Cardelle (Waco: Texian Press, 1968), 113–115.
10. Andres Tijerina, *Tejanos and Texas under the Mexican Flag, 1821–1836* (College Station: Texas A&M University Press, 1994), 103–105.
11. Barker, *Austin Papers*: I, 678; ibid.: II, 383; ibid.: III, 19.
12. Dewees, *Letters*, 118; John Jenkins, *Recollections of Early Texas: The Memoirs of John Holland Jenkins* (Austin: University of Texas Press, 1958), 3.
13. C.E. Castaneda, *The Mexican Side of the Texas Revolution* (Austin: Graphic Ideas Inc., 1970), 25.
14. Dewees, *Letters*, 142.
15. Ibid., 130; Walter P. Webb, *The Great Plains* (Boston: Houghton Mifflin Company, 1936), 4.
16. Cantrell, *Stephen F. Austin*, 176; *Texas Almanac, 2014–2015* (Denton: Texas State Historical Association, 2014), 52.
17. Dewees, *Letters*, 115.
18. Barker, *Austin Papers*, II: 1440–1442; James Haley, *Passionate Nation: The Epic History of Texas* (New York: Free Press, 2006), 87–94.
19. Randolph Campbell, *Gone to Texas: A History of the Lone Star State* (New York: Oxford University Press, 2003), 98–99.
20. For studies on Native American tribes in Spanish, Mexican, and Anglo Texas see Foster Smith, *From Dominance to Disappearance: The Indians of Texas and the Near Southwest, 1786–1859* (Lincoln: University of Nebraska Press, 2005); David La Vere, *Life Among the Texas Indians: The WPA Narratives* (College Station: Texas A&M University Press, 2006); and W. W. Newcomb, *The Indians of Texas* (Austin: University of Texas Press, 1961).

21. Jean Berlandier, *The Indians of Texas in 1830* (Washington: Smithsonian Institution Press, 1969), 54, 68, 147–149.

22. Stephen F. Austin, "Journal of Austin," *Texas Historical Association Quarterly* 7 (July 1903): 305; Eugene Barker, *The Life of Stephen F. Austin: Founder of Texas, 1793–1836* (Chicago: Lakeside Press, 1925), 104.

23. Berlandier, *Indians of Texas*, 146–147, 143–144, 125–126; Cantrell, *Stephen F. Austin*, 97.

24. Berlandier, *Indians of Texas*, 126.

25. Ibid., 106–108, 111–113, 142, 109.

26. Ibid., 113.

27. Barker, *Austin Papers*, II: 1211.

28. Berlandier, *Indians of Texas*, 119; Pekka Hamalainen, *The Comanche Empire* (New Haven: Yale University Press, 2008), 187.

29. Diana Hadley, Thomas Naylor, and Mardith Schuetz-Miller, eds., *The Presidio and Militia on the Northern Frontier of New Spain: A Documentary History. Volume Two, Part Two: The Central Corridor and the Texas Corridor, 1700–1765* (Tucson: University of Arizona Press, 1997), 511.

30. Ibid., 121; despite relatively low populations, historian Pekka Hamalainen emphasized the plains tribes' outsized impact: "Comanches were superior fighters who had matched and then surpassed Spaniards in mounted combat. Their swift, wide ranging guerrilla attacks, refined during the protracted wars against the Apache, wreaked havoc against Spanish settlers and soldiers who preferred to fight in closed places and in tightly organized formations." Hamalainen, *Comanche Empire*, 65.

31. Mary Austin Holly, *Texas: Observations, Historical, Geographical and Descriptive,* edited by Ray Billington. (New York: Arno Press, 1973), 89.

32. Department of the Army, "Field Manual 3–0 Operations," ed. U.S. Army (Washington, D.C., 2008), 6–15.

33. Richard Dodge, *Our Wild Indians, 33 Years' Personal Experience Among the Redmen of the Great West* (New York: Archer House, 1883), 421; Brian DeLay, *War of a Thousand Deserts: Indian Raids and the U.S.-Mexican War* (New Haven: Yale University Press, 2008), 186.

34. Dewees, *Letters*, 36.

35. Barker, *Austin Papers*: II: 1317.

36. Ibid., I: 560.

37. Allen Hatley, *The Indian Wars in Stephen F. Austin's Texas Colony, 1822–1823* (Austin: Eakin Press, 2001), 9–10.

38. Frederick Wilkins, *The Legend Begins: The Texas Rangers, 1823–1845* (Austin: State House Press, 1996), 59.

39. Antoine-Henri Jomini, *The Art of War* (Philadelphia: J.B. Lippincott & Co., 1862), 306.

40. Charles Sawyer, *Firearms in American History* (Northwood: The Plimpton Press, 1910), 144.

41. Noah Smithwick, *The Evolution of a State* (Austin: University of Texas Press, 1983), 159–160.

42. Wilkins, *Legend Begins*, 63.

43. Barker, *Austin Papers*, I: 838–839.

44. Ibid.

45. Campbell, *Gone to Texas*, 59, 72–73; Max Moorhead, *The Presidio: Bastion of the Spanish Borderland* (Norman: University of Oklahoma Press, 1975), 52–54.

46. Priest quoted in David Weber, *The Spanish Frontier in North America* (New Haven: Yale University Press, 1992), 192.

47. Teodoro de Croix quoted in William A. De Palo, *The Mexican National Army, 1822–1852* (College Station: Texas A&M University Press, 1997), 10.

48. Bexar Archives, Briscoe Center for American History, University of Texas at Austin, Cabello to Croix, Establishment of Militia Corps, April 5, 1779. Hereafter referred to as BA.

49. Smithwick, *Evolution*, 135.

50. Antonio Martinez, *The Letters of Antonio Martinez: The Last Spanish Governor of Texas, 1817–1822*, edited by Virginia Taylor (Austin: Texas State Library, 1957), 217–218.

51. For cattle ranching in Spanish *Tejas* see Jack Jackson, *Los Mestenos: Spanish Ranching in Texas, 1721–1821* (College Station: Texas A&M University Press, 1986).

52. Martinez, *The Letters of Antonio Martinez*, 217–218.

53. Campbell, *Gone to Texas*, 72–73; Hamalainen, *Comanche Empire*,187.

54. BA, Report of Ammunition issued to the Militia Corps for Indian Defense, August 17, 1784.

55. Dewees, *Letters*, 37–40; Jenkins, *Recollections*, 160; James De Shields, *Border Wars of Texas* (Waco: Texian Press, 1976), 19, 20–21; Cantrell, *Stephen F. Austin*, 137.

56. Jesse Burnam, "Reminiscences of Capt. Jesse Burnham," *Texas Historical Association Quarterly* 5 (July 1901): 16.

57. Dewees, *Letters*, 39.

58. Utley, *Frontiersmen in Blue: The United States Army and the Indian, 1848–1865* (New York: The Macmillan Company, 1967), 22.

59. North Ludlow Beamish, ed., *On the Uses and Application of Cavalry in War from the Text of Bismark: With Practical Examples Selected from Ancient and Modern History* (London: T. & W. Boone, 1855), 330–331.

60. Albert Brackett, *History of the U.S. Cavalry* (New York: Harper & Brothers, 1865), 159.
61. Dragoon and riflemen should not to be confused with European doctrinal mounted infantry who carried larger caliber muskets and employed horses exclusively for transportation.
62. Dewees, *Letters*, 41–42.
63. J.W. Wilbarger, *Indian Depredations in Texas* (Austin: Pemberton Press, 1967), 204.
64. Ibid., 204–205.
65. Dewees, *Letters*, 43.
66. Barker, *Austin Papers*, I: 676, 711.
67. Ibid., 678.
68. Marshall Kuykendall, *They Slept Upon their Rifles* (Austin: Nortex Press, 2005), 50.
69. Barker, *Austin Papers*, I: 676.
70. A.G. Bradley, ed., *Travels and Works of Captain John Smith* (Edinburgh: John Grant, 1910), 761, 588; Robert Black, *Ranger Dawn: The American Ranger from the Colonial Era to the Mexican War* (Mechanicsburg: Stackpole Books, 2009), 7.
71. Black, *Ranger Dawn*, 18–21; Chet, *Conquering the American Wilderness*, 50–53.
72. Benjamin Church, *The History of Philip's War*, edited by Samuel Drake (Exeter: J & B Williams, 1829), 108–109, 125–126.
73. William Hening, ed., *The Statutes at Large being a Collection of all the Laws of Virginia, from the First Session of the Legislature in the Year 1619* (Richmond: George Cochran, 1823), II: 438.
74. Black, *Ranger Dawn*, 36.
75. Chet, *Conquering the American Wilderness*, 74, 96.
76. Grenier, *First Way of War*, 204–205, 220; Chet, *Conquering the American Wilderness*, 123–125.
77. Barker, *Austin Papers*, I: 711.
78. Ibid., 838–839.
79. De Shields, *Border Wars*, 21.
80. Ibid., 21–22.
81. Ibid.; Cantrell, *Stephen F. Austin*, 139.
82. Lee, *Barbarians and Brothers*, 230–231; Grenier, *First Way of War*, 204–205.
83. Barker, *Austin Papers*, I: 715.
84. Dewees, *Letters*, 51–52.
85. Burnam, "Reminiscences," 18.
86. Barker, *Austin Papers*, I: 844.
87. J.H. Kuykendall, "Reminiscences of Early Texans," *Quarterly of the Texas State Historical Association* 7 (July 1903): 35.

88. Barker, *Austin Papers*, I: 885.
89. Kuykendall, "Reminiscences," *Texas State Historical Association*, 35.
90. Ibid.
91. Ibid., 37.
92. Wilbarger, *Indian Depredations*, 201.
93. Ibid., 202.
94. Dorman Winfrey, *Indian Tribes of Texas* (Waco: Texian Press, 1917), 73.
95. Barker, *Austin Papers*, II: 1208–1211; Cantrell, *Stephen F. Austin*, 141.
96. Barker, *Austin Papers*, III: 101–102.
97. Cantrell, *Stephen F. Austin*, 190, 344; Austin quoted in Paul Lack, *The Texas Revolutionary Experience: A Political and Social History, 1835–1836* (College Station: Texas A&M University Press, 1992), 14.
98. Barker, *Austin Papers*, II: 1211.
99. Ibid., 1318.
100. Ibid., 1305.
101. Ibid.
102. Ibid.
103. Ibid., 1357; Hatley, *Indian Wars*, 47, 51.
104. Barker, *Austin Papers*, II: 1305.
105. Ibid., 1318.
106. Nicolas Lafora, *The Frontiers of New Spain: Nicolas de Lafora's Description, 1766–1768*, Lawrence Kinnaird, editor (Berkeley: Quivira Society, 1958), 214–216; see also Marilyn Sibley, ed., *Travelers in Texas, 1761–1860* (Austin: University of Texas Press, 1967), 73, and Moorhead, *The Presidio*, 56–58.
107. Teran, *Teran*, 25.
108. Kuykendall, "Reminiscences," *Texas State Historical Association*, 38.
109. Barker, *Austin Papers*, II: 1442.
110. Ibid.
111. Ibid., 1441.
112. Ibid., 1403.
113. Lafora, *Frontiers of New Spain*, 214–215.
114. Sidney Brinckerhoff and Odie Faulk, eds., *Lancers for the King* (Phoenix: Arizona Historical Foundation, 1933), 51, 53, 61–62; Moorhead, *The Presidio*, 190–191.
115. Moorhead, *The Presidio*, 73.
116. Rubi quoted in Sibley, *Travelers*, 84; Campbell, *Gone to Texas*, 72; Moorhead, *The Presidio*, 56–60.
117. Martinez, *Letters*, 20, 23; Moorhead, *The Presidio*, 195–196.
118. Dewees, *Letters*, 58; Moorhead, *The Presidio*, 61, 71–73.
119. Barker, *Austin Papers*, II: 1572, 1586; Cantrell, *Stephen F. Austin*, 185–187.
120. Kuykendall, "Reminiscences," *Texas State Historical Association*, 39.

121. Ibid., 38–39; Barker, *Life of Austin*, 199.

122. Barker, *Austin Papers*, II: 1639–1641; Hatley, *Indian Wars*, 55.

123. Wilbarger, *Indian Depredations*, 206.

124. Ibid., 206–207.

125. Ibid., 207.

126. J.H. Kuykendall, "Reminiscences of Early Texans," *Quarterly of the Texas State Historical Association* 6 (1903): 311.

127. Ibid., 312–313.

128. Ibid., 314.

129. *The Texas Gazette*, September 25, 1829.

130. Ibid.; Barker, *Austin Papers*, Sup.: 160–162.

131. De Shields, *Border Wars*, 53.

132. Ibid., 53–54.

133. Ibid., 54.

134. Ibid.

135. Ibid., 54.

136. Ibid., 53.

137. Dewees, *Letters*, 123.

138. *Texas Almanac*, 52.

139. Jenkins, *Recollections*, 160–161.

140. Wilbarger, *Indian Depredations*, 210.

141. Ibid., 210.

142. Ibid., 211–213.

143. Ibid., 8–10.

144. De Shields, *Border Wars*, 124–130.

145. Barker, *Austin Papers*, Sup.: 161.

146. De Shields, *Border Wars*, 36–41; Dewees, *Letters*, 115–118.

147. Jack Jackson, ed., *Almonte's Texas* (Austin: Texas State Historical Association, 2003), 206.

148. Ibid.; Cantrell, *Stephen F. Austin*, 237–238.

149. Malcolm McLean, *Papers Concerning Robertson's Colony in Texas* (Fort Worth: Texas Christian University Press, 1974–1993), X: 47.

150. Ibid.

151. George Erath, *The Memoirs of Major George B. Erath, 1813–1891* (Waco: The Heritage Society of Waco, 1956), 23.

152. Sam Dixon and Louis Kemp, *The Heroes of San Jacinto* (Houston: The Anson Jones Press, 1932), 125; John Jenkins and Kenneth Kesselus, *Edward Burleson: Texas Frontier Leader* (Austin: Jenkins Publishing Company, 1990), 31–32.

153. Erath, *Memoirs*, 23; for a critical perspective on Coleman's and Moore's 1835 campaigns see Anderson, *Conquest of Texas*, 100–101.

154. Erath, *Memoirs*, 23.

155. Ibid.
156. H.P.N. Gammel, ed., *The Laws of Texas*, 1822–1897 (Austin: Gammel Book Company, 1898), I: 1134.
157. Fay Ward, *The Cowboy at Work* (Norman: University of Oklahoma Press, 1958), 3; Jack Jackson, *Los Mestenos: Spanish Ranching in Texas, 1721–1821* (College Station: Texas A&M University Press, 1986), 588–593; Tijerina, *Tejanos and Texas*, 23, 79–82, 88–89.
158. James Wilson, *Hide and Horn in Texas: The Spread of Cattle Ranching, 1836–1900* (Boston: American Press, 1983), 1–3.
159. Tom Saunders, *The Texas Cowboys* (Helena: World Publishing Services, 1997), 22.
160. C.L. Douglas, *Cattle Kings of Texas* (Dallas: The Book Craft, 1939), 20–21.
161. Terry Jordan, *Trails to Texas: Southern Roots of Western Cattle Ranching* (Lincoln: University of Nebraska Press, 1981), 71, 116.
162. Wilson, *Hide and Horn*, 5.
163. Richard Slatta, *Cowboys of the American West* (New Haven: Yale University Press, 1990), 19, 25.
164. Tijerina, *Tejanos and Texas*, 138.
165. Smithwick, *Memoirs*, 82–83.
166. Joseph Nance, *After San Jacinto: The Texas-Mexican Frontier, 1836–1841* (Austin: University of Texas Press, 1963), 21.
167. *Texas Almanac, 2014–2015* (Denton: Texas State Historical Association, 2014), 53.
168. Cantrell, *Stephen F. Austin*, 21.

Notes for Chapter 2

1. See Stephen Moore, *Eighteen Minutes: The Battle of San Jacinto and the Texas Independence Campaign* (Dallas: Republic of Texas Press, 2004) for the definitive work on the San Jacinto Campaign; see H.W. Brands, *Lone Star Nation* (New York: Doubleday, 2004) for an accessible history and Stephen Hardin, *Texian Iliad: A Military History of the Texas Revolution, 1835–1836* (Austin: University of Texas Press, 1994) for a military study.
2. Price Daniel and James Martin, eds., *Legislative Messages of the Chief Executives of Texas* (Austin: Texas State Library, 1972), I: 76–77.
3. Smithwick, *Evolution*, 72.
4. John Jenkins, ed., *The Papers of the Texas Revolution, 1835–1836* (Austin: Presidial Press, 1973), IV: 460.
5. Barker, *Austin Papers*, II: 1317.
6. Ibid., III: 150.

7. Jenkins, *Papers*, I: 467–469.
8. Barker, *Austin Papers*, III: 144, 146; Dewees, *Letters*, 155–156; Cantrell, *Stephen F. Austin*, 135.
9. Gammel, *Laws of Texas*, I: 513.
10. Wooster, *American Military Frontiers*, 80–81.
11. Barker, Austin Papers, III: 217–218, 225; Dewees, *Letters*, 156–159; Cantrell, *Stephen F. Austin*, 317–318.
12. Barker, Austin Papers, III: 217.
13. Ibid., 227, 229; Jenkins, *Edward Burleson*, 60; Hardin, *Texian Iliad*, 28.
14. Castaneda, *Texas Revolution*, 353, 230–236.
15. Jackson, *Almonte's Texas*, 84–85.
16. I bid., 146; Hardin, *Texian Iliad*, 26.
17. Gammel, *Laws of Texas*, I: 526–527.
18. Ibid.
19. Ibid., 527.
20. Smithwick, *Evolution*, 82.
21. John Ford, "John C. Hays in Texas," The Center for American History, The University of Texas at Austin, 1.
22. Gammel, *Laws of Texas*, I: 526–527; *Telegraph and Texas Register*, October 26 and November 14, 1835.
23. McLean, *Papers*, XII: 31.
24. William Binkley, ed., *Official Correspondence of the Texan Revolution, 1835–1836* (New York: D. Appleton-Century Company Inc., 1936), I: 485.
25. Yoakum, *History of Texas*, I: 352.
26. McLean, *Papers*, XII: 31–32, 103–104.
27. Gammel, *Laws of Texas*, I: 543.
28. Ibid.
29. Gammel, *Laws of Texas*, I: 577.
30. Ibid., 620, 578.
31. Ibid., 600–601.
32. Jenkins, *Recollections*, 31.
33. Ibid., 31–32, 543; Darren Ivey, *The Texas Rangers: A Registry and History* (Jefferson, NC: McFarland & Company, Inc., 1970), 15, 29.
34. Smithwick, *Evolution*, 83.
35. Ibid., 85–86.
36. Ibid.
37. Ibid., 87.
38. Ibid., 82–83, 87–89; Jenkins, *Recollections*, 42–43.
39. *Telegraph and Texas Register*, August 2, 1836; Binkley, *Official Correspondence*, I: 485.Yoakum, *Texas*, II: 180–181.
40. Smithwick, *Evolution*, 82.

41. Dewees, *Letters*, 158; Barker, *Austin Papers*, III: 280; See Hardin, *Texas Iliad*, Chapter 5, for a detailed account of the 1835 assault on Bexar.

42. Jackson, *Almonte's Texas*, 167.

43. Vincente Filisola, *Memoirs for the History of the War in Texas*, translated by Wallace Woolsey (Austin: Eakin Press, 1985–1987), II: 149–152; Jose Pena, *With Santa Anna in Texas: A Personal Narrative of the Revolution,* edited by Carmen Perry (College Station: Texas A&M University Press, 1975), 13, 19–21.

44. Pena, *Santa Anna*, 8.

45. Ibid.

46. Christopher Dishman, *A Perfect Gibraltar: The Battle for Monterrey, Mexico, 1846* (Norman: University of Oklahoma Press, 2010), 21.

47. Filisola, *The History of the War in Texas*, II: 150; Jeff Long, *Duel of Eagles: The Mexican and U.S. Fight for the Alamo* (New York: William Morrow and Company, Inc. 1990), 158.

48. Campbell, *Gone to Texas*, 141–146; see Hardin, *Texian Iliad*, Chapters 7 and 8, for details on the fall of the Alamo.

49. Carlos Sanchez Navarro, *The War in Texas: Memoirs of a Soldier*, 2nd ed. (Mexico: Editorial Jus, S.A., 1960), 86–87.

50. Barker, Austin Papers, III: 332.

51. Filisola, *Memoirs*, II: 208–209.

52. Castaneda, *Texas Revolution*, 15–16, 362–363; Pena, *Santa Anna*, 65, 67–68, 72–77; Dewees, *Letters*, 189–190.

53. Smithwick, *Evolution*, 99.

54. Ibid., 87.

55. Castaneda, *Texas Revolution*, 15.

56. Dewees, *Letters*, 189, 203.

57. Ibid., 172–177.

58. See Bill and Majorie Walraven, "The 'Sabine Chute': The U.S. Army and the Texas Revolution," *Southwestern Historical Quarterly* 107 (July 2003-April 2004): 573–601, for theories on the nature of U.S. Army support for the Texian Army.

59. William Zuber, *My Eighty Years in Texas*, edited by Janis Mayfield (Austin: University of Texas Press, 1971), 73.

60. Zuber, *Eighty Years*, 45–46.

61. Jenkins, *Recollections*, 38–39.

62. Williams, *Sam Houston*, I: 374.

63. Ibid., 367–368, 374; Henry Foote, *Texas and the Texans* (Austin: The Steck Company, 1935), II: 292–294.

64. Jean Roemer, *Cavalry: Its History, Management, and Uses in War* (New York: D. Van Nostrand, 1862), 266.

65. Jomini, *Art of War*, 313.
66. Roemer, *Cavalry*, 183.
67. Smithwick, *Memoirs*, 87.
68. Ibid.
69. Foote, *Texas*, II: 269–270; Jenkins, *Papers*, VI: 152.
70. Williams, *Sam Houston*, I: 379.
71. Foote, *Texas*, II: 269–270.
72. Zuber, *Eighty Years in Texas*, 59–60.
73. Pena, *Santa Anna*, 79–80.
74. Jenkins, *Papers*, V: 234–235.
75. Zuber, *Eighty Years in Texas*, 62–63.
76. Ibid., 73–74.
77. Williams, *Sam Houston*, I: 393.
78. *Telegraph and Texas Register*, April 14, 1836.
79. Williams, *Sam Houston*, I: 413; Moore, *Eighteen Minutes*, 238.
80. Castaneda, *Texas Revolution*, 75.
81. Foote, *Texas*, II: 292–294.
82. Williams, *Sam Houston*, I: 417.
83. P. Lane, *The Adventures and Recollections of Walter P. Lane* (Marshall: News Messenger Pub. Co., 1923), 11.
84. Ibid., 11–12; Moore, *Eighteen Minutes*, 275–280; Jimmy Bryan, *More Zeal than Discretion: The Westward Adventures of Walter P. Lane* (College Station: Texas A&M University Press, 2008), 18.
85. Wells quoted in Foote, *Texas*, II: 301.
86. Ibid.
87. Santa Anna quoted in Frank Tolbert, *The Day of San Jacinto* (Austin: Pemberton Press, 1959), 117.
88. Wells quoted in Foote, *Texas*, II: 302.
89. Lane, *Adventures*, 12.
90. Bryan, *More Zeal than Discretion*, 19.
91. Williams, *Sam Houston*, I: 417.
92. Moore, *Eighteen Minutes*, 290, 294.
93. Cleburne Huston, *Deaf Smith: Incredible Texas Spy* (Waco: Texian Press, 1973), 77.
94. Young Alsbury, "Burning of Vince's Bridge," *Texas Almanac* (1861): 55–58, The Portal to Texas History.
95. Williams, *Sam Houston*, I: 418.
96. Pena, *Santa Anna*, 127, 131.
97. Lane, *Adventures*, 14.
98. Hardin, *Texian Iliad*, 210–211.
99. William Foster Young biographical sketch, Kemp Papers Collection, San Jacinto Museum of History, Houston, Texas.

100. Lawrence quoted in Moore, *Eighteen Minutes*, 349–350; Pena, *Santa Anna*, 127.
101. Williams, *Sam Houston*, I: 419.
102. Robert Stevenson letter of April 23, 1836, Kemp Papers Collection.
103. Moore, *Eighteen Minutes*, 364.
104. Pena, *Santa Anna*, 127, 132.
105. Ibid., 83, 160.
106. Yoakum, *Texas*, II: 163; see also Gregg Dimmick, *Sea of Mud: The Retreat of the Mexican Army after San Jacinto* (Austin: Texas State Historical Association, 2006).
107. Williams, *Sam Houston*, I: 424–425; Jenkins, *Edward Burleson*, 126.
108. Lane, *Adventures*, 19.

Notes for Chapter 3

1. For military studies on the early Texas Republic see Stephen Moore, *Savage Frontier: Rangers, Riflemen and Indian Wars in Texas*, 4 vols. (Denton: University of North Texas Press, 2002–2010), I and II; see also Joseph Nance, *After San Jacinto: The Texas-Mexican Frontier, 1836–1841* (Austin: University of Texas Press, 1963).
2. Williams, *Sam Houston*, VI: 468–469.
3. Gammel, *Laws of Texas*, I: 880.
4. Ibid., 840; *Telegraph and Texas Register*, November 2, 1936.
5. Moore, *Savage Frontier*, I: 96, 126.
6. Binkley, *Texan Revolution*, I: 496.
7. Williams, *Sam Houston*, VII: 412.
8. See Hamalainen, *Comanche Empire*, 214–215, for an account that assigns general provocation of Comanche attacks to the Texian government and settler movements.
9. Wilbarger, *Indian Depredations*, 255–257.
10. McLean, *Papers*, XIV: 72.
11. Rachael Plummer, *Rachael Plummer's Narrative of Twenty-one Months Servitude as a Prisoner among the Comanchee Indians* (Austin: Jenkins Publishing Company, 1977).
12. Barker, *Austin Papers*, III: 384.
13. Juan Seguin, *A Revolution Remembered: The Memoirs and Selected Correspondence of Juan N. Seguin* (Austin: State House Press, 1991), 140.
14. Jerry Thompson, *Vaqueros in Blue and Gray* (Austin: Presidial, 1976), 19–23.
15. Smithwick, *Evolution*, 153.
16. Formal authorizations of the 1832 Mounted Ranger Battalion and the 1845 Regiment of Mounted Riflemen by the U.S. Congress, even as it

retained professional dragoon formations, revealed its understanding of how different cavalry models were required for frontier and conventional conflict settings.

17. Jenkins, *Edward Burleson*, 130–131.
18. *Telegraph and Texas Register*, April 24, 1844.
19. Perry quoted in Jenkins, *Recollections*, 193–194.
20. Ibid.
21. Ibid., 194.
22. *Telegraph and Texas Register*, September 13, 1836.
23. Ibid., November 2, 1836.
24. Smithwick, *Evolution*, 108.
25. Jenkins, *Recollections*, 49–51.
26. McLean, *Papers*, XV: 40.
27. *Telegraph and Texas Register*, August 23, 1836.
28. *Niles Weekly Register*, September 17, 1836.
29. McLean, *Papers*, XV: 42, 147, 231.
30. Smithwick, *Evolution*, 149.
31. Ibid., 108.
32. Jenkins, *Papers*, VIII: 214, 361.
33. Ivey, *Texas Rangers*, 16, 34.
34. Nance, *After San Jacinto*, 12, 18, 35.
35. Binkley, *Official Correspondence*, II: 811.
36. Gerald Pierce, "The Army of the Texas Republic, 1836–1845" (Ph.D. Diss., University of Mississippi, 1963), 53.
37. Williams, *Writings of Sam Houston*, I: 443–445.
38. Pierce, "Army of the Texas Republic," 81–82.
39. Gammel, *Laws of Texas*, I: 932–934, 1114–1128.
40. Ibid., 1113.
41. Nance, *After San Jacinto*, 41.
42. Gammel, *Laws of Texas*, I: 1114.
43. Moore, *Savage Frontier*, I: 203–206.
44. McLean, *Papers*, XVI: 198.
45. Gammel, *Laws of Texas*, I: 1334–1335.
46. Ibid.
47. Ibid.
48. Pierce, "Army of the Texas Republic," 91, 101.
49. Gammel, *Laws of Texas*, I: 1114–1128, 1427–1428.
50. *Telegraph and Texas Register*, April 11, 1837.
51. Williams, *Sam Houston*, II: 77.
52. James Greer, *Colonel Jack Hays: Texas Frontier Leader and California Builder* (New York: E. P. Dutton and Company, Inc., 1952), 18.
53. Ibid., 23–35.
54. Gammel, *Laws of Texas*, I: 513, 526, 577, 840, 1113.

Notes for Chapter 4

1. *Texas Almanac*, 53, 60.
2. Campbell, *Gone to Texas*, ix.
3. Williams, *Sam Houston*, VI: 431.
4. See Moore, *Savage Frontier*, vols. III and IV; and Nance, *Attack and Counter-Attack: The Texas-Mexican Frontier, 1842* (Austin: University of Texas Press, 1964) for military studies on the late Texas Republic.
5. Gammel, *Laws* of Texas, I: 1480–1481.
6. Nance, *After San Jacinto*, 42–43.
7. Jenkins, *Edward Burleson*, 150.
8. Tornel quoted in DePalo, *Mexican National Army*, 48.
9. Almazan quoted in Poyo, *Tejano Origins*, 31.
10. McLean, *Papers*, XII: 36; Ibid., XIII: 60.
11. Washington quoted in Theophilius Rodenbough, *From Everglade to Canyon with the Second United States Cavalry* (Originally published 1875. Reprint, Norman: University of Oklahoma Press, 2000), 78.
12. *Telegraph and Texas Register*, September 1, 1838.
13. John Henry Brown, *Indian Wars and Pioneers of Texas* (Austin: L.E. Daniell, Publisher, 1880), 51; *Telegraph and Texas Register*, September 1, 1838.
14. Brown, *Indian Wars*, 50–51.
15. Ibid.
16. Greer, *Jack Hays*, 28.
17. Nance, *After San Jacinto*, 113, 117–118.
18. Jenkins, *Recollections*, 84–85.
19. Moore, *Savage Frontier*, II: 28–36.
20. *Telegraph and Texas Register*, November 3, 1838.
21. Ibid.
22. Moore, *Savage Frontier*, II: 96–97, 118.
23. *Telegraph and Texas Register*, November 3, 1838.
24. Smithwick, *Evolution*, 174.
25. Ibid.
26. Charles Gulick, ed., *The Papers of Mirabeau Buonaparte Lamar* (Austin: A.C. Baldwin Printers, 1973), II: 346–356; Campbell, *Gone to Texas*, 169–171.
27. Hamalainen, *Comanche Empire*, 215; see Lee, "Mind and Matter," 1121–1122, for Anglo-American annihilation strategies prior to the Civil War.
28. Gammel, *Laws of Texas*, II: 15–20.
29. Ibid.; Dewees, *Letters*, 226–229.
30. Gammel, *Laws of Texas*, II: 29–30, 48; *Telegraph and Texas Register*, January 16, 1839.

31. Gammel, *Laws of Texas*, II: 44, 78, 93.
32. Winfrey, *Indian Papers*, I: 57–59.
33. Smithwick, *Evolution*, 156.
34. Winfrey, *Indian Papers*, I: 57–59.
35. Smithwick, *Evolution*, 156.
36. Ibid.
37. Winfrey, *Indian Papers*, I: 57–59.
38. Lee, *Barbarians and Brothers*, 229–231.
39. Grenier, *First Way of War*, 217.
40. Wooster, *American Military Frontiers*, 45. While the 1814 Battle of Horseshoe Bend offers a similar battle, that event reflected a combined arms attack where mounted elements remained subordinated to larger infantry regiments. In contrast, Coffee's attack at Tallushatchee represented an attack by an entirely mounted force that maximized movement on horseback and dismounted to assault.
41. Winfrey, *Indian Papers*, I: 27–28.
42. Grenier, *First Way of War*, 217.
43. Lee, *Barbarians and Brothers*, 4, 229–231.
44. Jenkins, *Recollections*, 56–60.
45. Ibid.
46. Nance, *After San Jacinto*, 135–137, 139; Winfrey, *Indian Papers*, I: 67–69.
47. Brown, *Indian Wars*, 71; Moore, *Savage Frontier*, II: 221–222.
48. Ibid., 229–232.
49. Winfrey, *Indian Papers*, I: 77; Jenkins, *Edward Burleson*, 202–203.
50. Moore, *Savage Frontier*, II: 267.
51. Winfrey, *Indian Papers*, I: 76–77.
52. Ibid., 80.
53. *Telegraph and Texas Register*, December 18, 1839.
54. Moore, *Savage Frontier*, II: 310.
55. *Telegraph and Texas Register*, October 16, 1839.
56. McLean, *Papers*, VIII: 347–346.
57. Gulick, *Lamar Papers*, IV: 231.
58. DeLay, *War of a Thousand Deserts*, 76.
59. Gulick, *Lamar Papers*, II: 464–465.
60. For an example of Texan atrocity against black Union soldiers see Anne Bailey, "A Texas Cavalry Raid: Reaction to Black Soldiers and Contrabands," *Civil War History* 35, no. 2 (1989): 138–152.
61. *Telegraph and Texas Register*, August 31, 1842.
62. Edward Stiff, *The Texan Emigrant* (Waco: Texian Press, 1968), 42.
63. Ibid., 44.
64. David La Vere, *Life Among the Texas Indians: The WPA Narratives* (College Station: Texas A&M University Press, 2006), 18.

65. Nance, *After San Jacinto*, 85, 92–93.
66. Z. N. Morrell, *Flowers and Fruits in the Wilderness; or Forty-six Years in Texas and Two in Honduras* (Dallas: W. G. Scarff & Co., Publishers, 1886), 124.
67. *Telegraph and Texas Register*, April 8, 1840; Hamalainen, *Comanche Empire*, 216. See also Moore, *Savage Frontier*, III: Chapter 2.
68. *Telegraph and Texas Register*, September 2, 1840; Hamalainen, *Comanche Empire*, 216.
69. Nichols, *Journal*, 58–59.
70. Ibid., 58–59; Cutrer, *Ben McCulloch*, 41–42.
71. De Shields, *Border Wars*, 326–327.
72. Jenkins, *Edward Burleson*, 255–256; Cutrer, *Ben McCulloch*, 43.
73. Nichols, *Journal*, 61.
74. Ibid., 62–65. See also Moore, *Savage Frontier*, III: Chapter 5.
75. De Shields, *Border Wars*, 327.
76. Smithwick, *Evolution*, 184.
77. Winfrey, *Indian Papers*, I: 115.
78. *Telegraph and Texas Register*, November 18, 1840.
79. Ibid.
80. Ibid.; Moore, *Savage Frontier*, III: 152–155.
81. Smithwick, *Evolution of a State*, 184.
82. *Telegraph and Texas Register*, November 18, 1840.
83. Jenkins, *Recollections*, 171–174.
84. Nance, *After San Jacinto*, 95.

Notes for Chapter 5

1. Winfrey, *Indian Papers*, I: 119.
2. Gammel, *Laws of Texas*, II: 475.
3. Caperton, "John C. Hays," 8.
4. Nichols, *Journal*, 76.
5. Moore, Savage Frontier, III: 183–187; Ivey, *Texas Rangers*, 25.
6. Gammel, *Laws of Texas*, II: 646–648.
7. It is difficult to assess how many Texan settlers gained combat experience in town and county militias or during overland ranching and agrarian pursuits, since many Anglo-Indian skirmishes went unrecorded or were recalled anecdotally.
8. *Telegraph and Texas Register*, April 28, 1841; Wilkins, *Legend Begins*, 96, 104, 106.
9. Caperton, "John C. Hays," 10.
10. Hays quoted in Samuel Reid, *The Scouting Expeditions of McCulloch's Texas Rangers; or the Summer and Fall Campaigns of the Army of the United States in Mexico* (Philadelphia: John E. Potter and Company, 1885), 116.

11. Gulick, *Lamar Papers*, IV: 232–233.
12. Caperton, "John C. Hays," 14.
13. *Telegraph and Texas Register*, April 28, 1841.
14. Gulick, *Lamar Papers*, 233.
15. *Austin City Gazette*, July 7, 1841.
16. Gulick, *Lamar Papers*, IV: 234.
17. Ibid., 234–235.
18. Ibid., 235.
19. Ibid.
20. Ibid.
21. Reid, *McCulloch's Texas Rangers*, 111–112.
22. Ford, "Hays in Texas," 7.
23. *Telegraph and Texas Register*, December 8, 1841.
24. Cutrer, *Ben McCulloch*, 48, 53.
25. Caperton, "John C. Hays," 10.
26. Ibid., 11.
27. Smithwick, *Evolution*, 185.
28. Williams, *Sam Houston*, VI: 142.
29. Campbell, *Gone to Texas*, 176–177.
30. Morrell, *Flowers and Fruits*, 157; Campbell, *Gone to Texas*, 174.
31. Lee, *Barbarians and Brothers*, 229–231.
32. Daniel, *Legislative Messages*, II: 110.
33. Gammel, *Laws of Texas*, II: 746.
34. Caperton, "John C. Hays," 38.
35. John Forester quoted in Greer, *Jack Hays*, 65–66.
36. Caperton, "John C. Hays," 10.
37. Nance, *Attack and Counter-Attack*, 30, 39, 41, 45; *Telegraph and Texas Register*, March 16, 1842.
38. Nance, *Attack and Counter-Attack*, 190, 248–251; *Telegraph and Texas Register*, August 31, 1842.
39. Gammel, *Laws of Texas*, II: 816.
40. New Orleans *Bulletin*, September 27, 1842.
41. Nance, *Attack and Counter-Attack*, 318.
42. Morrell, *Flowers and Fruits*, 163.
43. Ibid., 166.
44. Nance, *Attack and Counter-Attack*, 343–346.
45. Morrell, *Flowers and Fruits*, 164.
46. Nichols, *Journal*, 98.
47. Morrell, *Flowers and Fruits*, 168–169.
48. Nichols, *Journal*, 98.
49. D.W. C. Baker, *Texas Scrap-Book* (New York, 1875), 293; Nance, *Attack and Counter-Attack*, 350, 358–360.

50. Morrell, *Flowers and Fruits*, 170.
51. Ibid.
52. Nichols, *Journal*, 99.
53. Jenkins, *Recollections*, 97.
54. Ibid.; see Moore, *Savage Frontier*, IV: Chapter 4, for further discussion of the battle.
55. Nichols, *Journal*, 103.
56. Ibid.
57. Morrell, *Flowers and Fruit*, 176–177.
58. Cutrer, *Ben McCulloch*, 56.
59. Samuel Walker, *Samuel H. Walker's Account of the Mier Expedition*, edited by Marilyn Sibley (Austin: Texas State Historical Association, 1978), 29.
60. Ibid., 5.
61. Williams, *Writings of Sam Houston*, III: 170–171.
62. Ibid.
63. Walker, *Walker's Account*, 33.
64. Jenkins, *Recollections*, 107–108.
65. See Sam Haynes, *Soldiers of Misfortune: The Somervell and Mier Expeditions* (Austin: University of Texas Press, 1990) for more on the failed invasion.
66. Jenkins, *Recollections*, 108–110; Greer, *Jack Hays*, 83, 88.
67. Seguin, *Revolution*, 81,86, 92.
68. Nichols, *Journal*, 87–88.
69. Thompson, *Vaqueros in Blue and Gray*, 19–23, 107–109.
70. Gammel, *Laws of Texas*, II: 846–848.
71. Ibid., 865.
72. Nichols, *Journal*, 122–123.
73. Barker, *Austin Papers*, II: 1442.
74. Caperton, "John C. Hays," 28.
75. Clarksville *Northern Standard*, June 15, 1843.
76. *Telegraph and Texas Register*, July 12, 1843; Clarksville *Northern Standard*, June 15, 1843.
77. Nichols, *Journal*, 123.
78. Ibid.
79. Ibid., 124.
80. Hosley, *Colt*, 54; Chapel, *Guns*, 152, 200.
81. See Wilkins, *The Legend Begins*, Chapter 8; and Moore, *Savage Frontier*, IV: 22–24, for studies on Colt firearms in early Texas.
82. Gammel, *Laws of Texas*, II: 846–848, 943–944.
83. Wilkins, *Legend Begins*, 176; Cutrer, *Ben McCulloch*, 64.
84. Jenkins, *Recollections*, 145.

85. *Journals of the House of Representatives of the Ninth Congress of the Republic of Texas* (Washington: Miller & Cushney, 1845), 32–33.
86. Caperton, "John C. Hays," 22.
87. Jenkins, *Recollections*, 145.
88. Greer, *Jack Hays*, 107.
89. *Texas National Register*, December 14, 1844; see also Moore, *Savage Frontier*, IV: Chapter 8.
90. Gammel, *Laws of Texas*, II: 1125.
91. Ibid.
92. Stephen Moore, *Savage Frontier: Rangers, Riflemen and Indian Wars in Texas* (Denton: University of North Texas Press, 2010), IV: 182.
93. *Texas National Register*, September 4, 1845.
94. Williams, *Sam Houston*, VI: 120.
95. Smithwick, *Evolution*, 248.

Notes for Chapter 6

1. See Justin Smith, *The War with Mexico* (New York: Macmillan, 1919) for the foundational, if dated, study on the Mexican War; see John S.D. Eisenhower, *So Far from God: The U.S. War with Mexico, 1846–1848* (Norman: University of Oklahoma Press, 2000) for an accessible history.
2. House Executive Documents No. 60, 30th Congress, 1st Session, 90. Hereafter cited as HED No. 60.
3. Eisenhower, *So Far from God*, 52.
4. HED No. 60, 134, 138, 140; Eisenhower, *So Far from God*, 65; Dishman, *Perfect Gibraltar*, 9–10, 21.
5. HED No. 60, 141.
6. Eisenhower, *So Far from God*, 66.
7. Cutrer, *Ben McCulloch*, 66.
8. Jomini, *Art of War*, 303.
9. HED No. 60, 106–107, 141; Dishman, *Perfect Gibraltar*, 16–18.
10. William Hunter, ed., *Lord William Bentinck* (London: Oxford University Press, 1892), 198; see also George Paget, *A History of the British Cavalry, 1816–1919* (London: Leo Cooper, 1973), 183.
11. Robert Wilson, "Reviews—Sir Robert Wilson's Works," *The Royal Military Chronicle or British Officers Nonthly Register and Mentor* 5 (1813): 207. See also Haythornthwaite, *Napoleonic Cavalry*, 79.
12. Jomini, *Art of War*, 313.
13. Giddings, *Campaign in Mexico*, 97–97.
14. Henry Barton, "The United States Cavalry and the Texas Rangers," *Southwestern Historical Quarterly* 63 (1960): 506.
15. Albert Brackett, *General Lane's Brigade in Central Mexico* (Cincinnati: H.W. Derby & Co, Publishers, 1854), 196.

16. Compton Smith, *Chile con Carne* (New York: Miller and Curtiss, 1857), 266.
17. Ford, *Rip Ford's Texas*, 92, 97.
18. HED No. 60, 1176; Cutrer, *Ben McCulloch*, 68, 70.
19. Ford, *Rip Ford's Texas*, 140.
20. Abner Doubleday, *My Life in the Old Army: The Reminiscences of Abner Doubleday from the Collections of the New York Historical Society*, edited by Joseph Chance (Fort Worth: Texas Christian University Press, 1998), 55.
21. Napoleon Dana, *Monterrey Is Ours! The Mexican War Letters of Lieutenant Dana, 1845–1847* (Lexington: University Press of Kentucky, 1990), 67, 69; Dishman, *Perfect Gibraltar*, 12–15.
22. William Henry, *Campaign Sketches of the War with Mexico* (New York: Harper and Brothers, 1847), 113.
23. Clarksville *Northern Standard*, May 13, 1846; *Telegraph and Texas Register*, October 7, 1846.
24. Lane, *Adventures*, 42; Reid, *McCulloch's Texas Rangers*, 23; Charles Spurlin, *Texas Volunteers in the Mexican War: Muster Rolls of Texas Military Units* (Austin: Eakin Press, 1998), 17–33.
25. James Holland, "Diary of a Texan Volunteer in the Mexican War," *Southwestern Historical Quarterly* 30 (July 1926): 7–8; Spurlin, *Texas Volunteers*, 1–16, 34–53.
26. Holland, "Texan Volunteer," 14, 19.
27. Reid, *McCulloch's Texas Rangers*, 41–43; HED No. 60, 523, 550.
28. Reid, *McCulloch's Texas Rangers*, 41–44.
29. Ibid., 44, 45–46; Cutrer, *Ben McCulloch*, 70–72; Dishman, *Perfect Gibraltar*, 54–55.
30. HED No. 60, 408.
31. HED No. 60, 412–413; Holland, "Texan volunteer," 18–21.
32. HED No. 60, 413; Reid, *McCulloch's Texas Rangers*, 105–107.
33. Holland, "Texan volunteer," 20.
34. Reid, *McCulloch's Texas Rangers*, 117–119; Frederick Wilkins, *The Highly Irregular Irregulars: The Texas Rangers in the Mexican War* (Austin: Eakin Press, 1990), 42–43.
35. Holland, "Texan volunteer," 23.
36. Dishman, *Perfect Gibraltar*, 67–69.
37. Reid, *McCulloch's Texas Rangers*, 126–128, 132–134; Cutrer, *Ben McCulloch*, 76–77.
38. Dana, *Monterrey Is Ours!*, 125.
39. HED No. 60, 506; Reid, *McCulloch's Texas Rangers*, 141; Dishman, *Perfect Gibraltar*, 87–88.
40. Reid, *McCulloch's Texas Rangers*, 141–143.
41. Brackett, *Lane's Brigade*, 196.

42. Dana, *Monterrey Is Ours*, 122; Doubleday, *Old Army*, 79.
43. Doubleday, *Old Army*, 79–80.
44. Lane, *Adventures*, 44.
45. Ibid.; Reid, *McCulloch's Texas Rangers*, 154; Cutrer, *Ben McCulloch*, 82–83; Dishman, *Perfect Gibraltar*, 144–146.
46. Reid, *McCulloch's Texas Rangers*, 161–162.
47. Dana, *Monterrey Is Ours*, 132; Reid, *McCulloch's Texas Rangers*, 163; Dishman, *Perfect Gibraltar*, 150–153.
48. Reid, *McCulloch's Texas Rangers*, 167–168.
49. Holland, "Texan volunteer," 25–26.
50. Lane, *Adventures*, 47; Dishman, *Perfect Gibraltar*, 159–161,165, 169.
51. Dishman, *Perfect Gibraltar*, 175. See Jonathan A. Beall, "Urban Combat in the Nineteenth Century," *War in History* 16 (2009) 157–188, for urban combat in the American capture of Monterrey.
52. T.B. Thorp, *Our Army at Monterey* (Philadelphia: Carey & Hart, 1848), 76–77.
53. Lane, *Adventures*, 47–48; Dishman, *Perfect Gibraltar*, 178–180, 189–191, 197.
54. Dana, *Monterrey Is Ours*, 138.
55. HED No. 60, 1143.
56. Reid, *McCulloch's Texas Rangers*, 233–236.
57. Giddings, *Ohio Volunteers*, 287; Cutrer, *Ben McCulloch*, 94–95; Dishman, *Perfect Gibraltar*, 203.
58. Roemer, *Cavalry*, 264–265.
59. Smith, *Chile con Carne*, 358–359.
60. Lane, *Adventures*, 49.
61. Bryan, *More Zeal than Discretion*, 63–64.
62. Ibid., 52–55.
63. Smith, *Chile con Carne*, 359.
64. HED No. 60, 1178.
65. Ibid.
66. Smith, *Chile con Carne*, 294.
67. Ibid., 281.
68. Ibid., 1067.
69. Lane, *Adventures*, 69.
70. Ibid., 73–74.
71. Wilkins, *Irregular Irregulars*, 152.
72. Timothy Johnson, *A Gallant Little Army: The Mexico City Campaign* (Lawrence: University Press of Kansas, 2007), 85–93; this is the definitive account of the American invasion of Central Mexico in 1847.
73. HED No. 60, 1171–1172.
74. Santa Anna quoted in DePalo, *Mexican National Army*, 124.

75. Irving Levinson, *Wars within War: Mexican Guerillas, Domestic Elites, and the United States of America, 1846–1848* (Fort Worth: TCU Press, 2005), 34–35; this work assesses the American invasion and occupation of Central Mexico in 1847–1848 from the Mexican perspective; see also DePalo, *Mexican National Army*, Chapters 5 and 6.

76. Jacob Oswandel, *Notes of the Mexican War, 1846–1848*, edited by Timothy Johnson and Nathaniel Hughes (Knoxville: University of Tennessee, 2010), 78.

77. Johnson, *A Gallant Little Army*, 246, 252–253.

78. Caperton, "John C. Hays," 62.

79. Ford, *Rip Ford's Texas*, 146–147.

80. HED No. 60, 1185.

81. DeLay, *War of a Thousand Deserts*, 264–266.

82. HED No. 60, 1194.

83. Spurlin, *Texas Volunteers*, 88–111.

84. Ford, *Rip Ford's Texas*, 65.

85. Ibid., 61–63.

86. *Daily Picayune*, October 29, 1847.

87. Ford, *Rip Ford's Texas*, 66.

88. Caperton, "John C. Hays," 62.

89. Ford, *Rip Ford's Texas*, 66.

90. Ibid., 66–67.

91. Ibid., 68.

92. Ibid., 68.

93. Johnson, *Gallant Little Army*, 16–17, 293–295.

94. HED No. 60, 1049.

95. Caperton, "John C. Hays," 65.

96. Winfield Scott, *Memoirs of Lieut.-General Scott, LL.D* (New York: Sheldon & Company, Publishers, 1864), II: 392.

97. Wilkins, *Irregular Irregulars*, 161.

98. Chapel, *Guns*, 153, 157–159; Ford, *Rip Ford's Texas*, 75, 105.

99. Walker quoted in Utley, *Lone Star Justice*, 81.

100. Brackett, *Lane's Brigade*, 174.

101. Ibid., 75–66; Oswandel, *Mexican War*, 217.

102. Daniel H. Hill, *A Fighter from Way Back: The Mexican War Diary of Lt. Daniel Harvey Hill, 4th Artillery, USA*, edited by Nathaniel Hughes and Timothy Johnson (Kent: Kent State University Press, 2002), 141.

103. Brackett, *Lane's Brigade*, 66; Ibid., 90–94.

104. Hill to parents, Oct. 29, 1847, Hill Papers.

105. Brackett, *Lane's Brigade*, 174.

106. Ibid., 189.

107. Ibid.
108. Ford, *Rip Ford's Texas*, 78.
109. Brackett, *Lane's Brigade*, 189.
110. Ibid., 190.
111. Ford, *Rip Ford's Texas*, 79.
112. Brackett, *Lane's Brigade*, 190–192.
113. House Executive Documents No. 1, 30th Congress, 2nd Session, 88.
114. Ford, "Jack Hays," 92.
115. Editorial reprinted in Caperton, "John C. Hays," 56.
116. Ibid., 56, 58.
117. Ford, *Rip Ford's Texas*, 80, 81–82; *Democratic Telegraph and Texas Register*, February 24, 1848.
118. Ibid., 83–85; see Collins, *Texas Devils*, 33–35, for a critical account of Texas Ranger actions in Mexico City.
119. Brackett, *Lane's Brigade*, 220–221.
120. Ford, *Rip Ford's Texas*, 87–88.
121. HED No. 60, 1067.
122. Caperton, "John C. Hays," 66.
123. Ford, *Rip Ford's Texas*, 91–92.
124. Ibid., 91–92.
125. Brackett, *Lane's Brigade*, 288.
126. Ibid., 289–240, 245.
127. Ibid., 263; Ford, *Rip Ford's Texas*, 92–93.
128. Brackett, *Lane's Brigade*, 264.
129. Ibid., 264–265.
130. Ford, *Rip Ford's Texas*, 96; See Ronnie Tyler, "The Rangers at Zacualtipan," *Texana* 4 (1966): 341–350, for another account of this battle.
131. Greer, *Jack Hays*, 203.
132. John Kenly, *Memoirs of a Maryland Volunteer: War with Mexico, in the Years 1846–7–8* (Philadelphia: J.B. Lippincott & Co, 1873), 395.
133. Ford, *Rip Ford's Texas*, 103–104.
134. Caperton, "John C. Hays," 66.
135. Ibid., 35–36.
136. Giddings, *Ohio Volunteers*, 96–97.
137. *Hartford Daily Times* reprinted in Hosley, *Colt*, 83.
138. Holland, "Texan Volunteer," 24–25.
139. Caperton, "John C. Hays," 45.
140. Giddings, *Ohio Volunteers*, 221–222.
141. Hill, *Fighter from Way Back*, 19, 28.
142. HED, No. 60, 430; DeLay, *War of a Thousand Deserts*, 280–281.
143. Ford, *Rip Ford's Texas*, 82, 84–85; see Samara, *Gunpowder Justice*, Chapter 3; and Collins, *Texas Devils*, Chapter 1, for critical assessments of Texas Ranger actions in Mexico.

144. See Bailey, "Texas Cavalry Raid," 138–152, for an example of massacres of black Union soldiers by Texan Confederate cavalrymen.
145. Mark Nackman, "The Making of the Texan Citizen Soldier, 1835–1860," *Southwestern Historical Quarterly* 78 (1975): 239.

Notes for Chapter 7

1. See Wooster, *American Military Frontiers*, for a leading study on the U.S. Army in the West during antebellum years; see Utley, *Frontiersmen in Blue*, for a more dated work.
2. Ford, "Hays in Texas," 4; see Rupert Richardson, *The Frontier of Northwest Texas, 1846 to 1876* (Glendale: Arthur H. Clark Company, 1963) for a pertinent, but dated, study.
3. *Texas Almanac*, 60–61; see Campbell, *Gone to Texas*, 207 for comparable population statistics.
4. Thomas Smith, *The U.S. Army and the Texas Frontier Economy, 1845–1900* (College Station: Texas A&M University Press, 1999), 12.
5. Williams, *Sam Houston*, VI: 506.
6. *Texas State Gazette*, October 27, 1849.
7. George Brooke, Report of the Secretary of War, March 7, 1850, 27; Persifor Smith, Report of the Secretary of War, May 25, 1850, 78.
8. Winfield Scott, Report of the Secretary of War, November 30, 1850, 114.
9. George Brooke, HED, 31st Congress, First Session, August 31, 1849, 143.
10. Report by Herbert Enos, "Condition of the Indian Tribes," 39th Congress, 2nd Session, No. 156, 340–341.
11. Utley, Frontiersmen in Blue, 20.
12. Smith, *Texas Frontier Economy*, 13.
13. Ibid., 12–13.
14. Sam Houston, the final governor before secession, bitterly criticized the U.S. Army, arguing that it was "well known that the Federal troops now in Texas, engaged in the Indian service, are inefficient and not calculated to afford protection." He also warned that "until means are adopted to bring the guerrilla bands that infest that country under subjection of law, and they are taught that no boundary line intervenes between them and punishment, that border can feel no security." Williams, *Sam Houston*, VII: 539.
15. Ibid., VI: 523.
16. Wooster, *American Military Frontiers*, 125; Brooke, Report of the Secretary of War, July 28, 1850, 52.
17. Report printed in Martin Crimmins, "Colonel Robert E. Lee's Report on Indian Combats in Texas," *Southwestern Historical Quarterly* 39

(July 1935): 25; James Arnold, *Jeff Davis's Own: Cavalry, Comanches, and the Battle for the Texas Frontier* (New York: John Wiley & Sons, Inc., 2000, 22–23, 326.

18. See Henry Barton, "Five Texas Frontier Companies during the Mexican War," *Southwestern Historical Quarterly* 66 (1962) for Texas's wartime frontier defense.
19. Ivey, *Texas Rangers*, 61.
20. Winfrey, *Texas Indian Papers*, III: 63–64.
21. Ibid., 77–79.
22. Ibid., 64.
23. Ibid.
24. Ibid., 65.
25. Ibid., 60.
26. Barton, "Frontier Companies," 22–23.
27. Winfrey, *Texas Indian Papers*, III: 72.
28. House Executive Documents No. 119, 29th Congress, 2nd Session, 128; Barton, "Frontier Companies," 23.
29. Ibid., 23–25.
30. *The Texas Democrat*, September 9, 1846.
31. Ford, "Hays in Texas," 56.
32. Highsmith quoted in Michael Cox, *The Texas Rangers: Wearing the Cinco Peso, 1821–1900* (New York: Forge, 2008), 123–124.
33. Ibid., 124.
34. Victoria *Advocate*, November 16, 1848.
35. John Brown, *Heroes of Texas* (Houston: Union National Bank, 1934), 9.
36. Winfrey, *Texas Indian Papers*, III: 43–49.
37. Ibid., 72.
38. Anderson, *Conquest of Texas*, 224.
39. Ibid., 240.
40. Ivey, *Texas Rangers*, 74; Utley, *Frontiersmen in Blue*, 70–71.
41. Richardson, *Frontier of Northwest Texas*, 56–57; see Utley, *Frontiersmen in Blue*, 42–43, for discussion of the roles and implications of U.S. Army frontier forts.
42. Thomas Smith, *The Old Army in Texas: A Research Guide to the U.S. Army in Nineteenth-Century Texas* (Austin: Texas State Historical Association, 2000), 15, 17; see also Wooster, *American Military Frontiers*, 124–125 and Utley, *Frontiersmen in Blue*, 71.
43. *The Nueces Valley*, May 25, 1849.
44. Brooke to Governor P. H. Bell, San Antonio, January 30, 1850, 301–19-Bell5, Archives Division, Texas State Library.
45. *Texas Gazette*, August 25, 1849.
46. Ford, *Rip Ford's Texas*, 150.
47. Ibid., 152.

48. Ibid., 153.
49. Ibid.
50. *The Nueces Valley*, May 25, 1850.
51. Smith, *Old Army in Texas*, 17.
52. Ford, *Rip Ford's Texas*, 188–189.
53. Ibid., 188.
54. Williams, *Sam Houston*, VI: 522.
55. Report of the Secretary of War, November 25, 1832.
56. Davis, Report of the Secretary of War, December 4, 1854; Cooper, Report of the Secretary of War, November 28, 1857, 84; N. Townsend, Report of the Secretary of War, March 6, 1838, 86–87.
57. Smith, *Old Army in Texas*, 15–16; Rupert, *Frontier of Northwest Texas*, 67–73.
58. Smith, *Texas Frontier Economy*, 12.
59. Ivey, *Texas Rangers*, 77.
60. Ibid.
61. Smith, *Old Army in Texas*, 17.
62. *Texas State Gazette*, January 12, 1850.
63. Utley, *Frontiersmen in Blue*, 74–75.
64. Campbell, *Gone to Texas*, 202–203.
65. Frederick Wilkins, *Defending the Borders: The Texas Rangers, 1848–1861* (Austin: State House Press, 2001), 43–45.
66. Smith, *Old Army in Texas*, 17.
67. E.M. Pease to J.H. Callahan, July 5, 1855, Governors Letters, Texas State Archives; see also Earnest Shearer, "The Callahan Expedition, 1855," *Southwestern Historical Quarterly* 54 (1951), 432.
68. Smith, *Texas Frontier Economy*, 12.
69. Shearer, "Callahan Expedition," 437.
70. John Sansom, "Captain Callahan's Raid into Mexico," *Hunter's Magazine*, April-May, 1911.
71. Ibid.
72. Ibid.
73. *Texas State Gazette*, October 20, 1855.
74. Winfrey, *Texas Indian Papers*, III: 256.
75. Ivey, *Texas Rangers*, 80.
76. Smith, *Old Army in Texas*, 17; the 2nd U.S. Cavalry Regiment of antebellum Texas reflagged as the 5th U.S. Cavalry in 1861.
77. Ford, *Rip Ford's Texas*, 223.
78. Ibid.
79. Winfrey, *Texas Indian Papers*, III: 271.
80. Gammel, *Laws of Texas*, IV: 77–78.
81. *Texas State Gazette*, January 30, 1858.
82. Winfrey, *Texas Indian Papers*, III: 272–273.

83. Jenkins, *Edward Burleson*, 380–381; Ford, *Rip Ford's Texas*, 224.
84. Winfrey, *Texas Indian Papers*, III: 275.
85. Chapel, *Guns of the Old West*, 162–164.
86. Winfrey, *Texas Indian Papers*, III: 280.
87. Ford, *Rip Ford's Texas*, 233.
88. Report, Secretary of War, House Executive Documents No. 27, 35th Congress, 2nd Session, 19; hereafter cited as HED No. 27; Wilkins, *Defending the Borders*, 80–85.
89. Ford, *Rip Ford's Texas*, 234.
90. Ibid., 235.
91. Ibid., 236.
92. Ibid.
93. Ibid., 238; Wooster, *American Military Frontiers*, 156.
94. Harold Simpson, *Cry Comanche: The 2nd U.S. Cavalry in Texas, 1855–1861* (Hillsboro, TX: Hill Jr. College Press, 1979), 109.
95. Report, Secretary of War, HED No. 27, 52; Anderson, *Conquest of Texas*, 311; Arnold, *Jeff Davis's Own*, 201–206.
96. Smith, *Old Army in Texas*, 17.
97. Simpson, *Cry Comanche*, 125–126; Wooster, *American Military Frontiers*, 157.
98. Ibid., 128.
99. Williams, *Sam Houston*, 501; Arnold, *Jeff Davis's Own*, 22–23; Anderson, *Conquest of Texas*, 317.
100. Twiggs to L. Thomas, July 6, 1858, Governor's Papers, Texas State Library.
101. Winfrey, *Texas Indian Papers*, III: 304.
102. Ibid., 305.
103. Ford, *Rip Ford's Texas*, 252–253.
104. Ibid., 259; *Telegraph and Texas Register*, July 12, 1843.
105. Ford, *Rip Ford's Texas*, 261–262; Jerry Thompson, *Cortina: Defending the Mexican Name in Texas* (College Station: Texas A&M University Press, 2007), 15–16, 37–39.
106. Ford, *Rip Ford's Texas*, 264; Thompson, *Cortina*, 37–39.
107. Wilkins, *Defending the Borders*, 106–107.
108. Samuel Heintzelman, *Fifty Miles and a Fight: Major Samuel Peter Heintzelman's Journal of Texas and the Cortina War,* edited by Jerry Thompson (Austin: Texas State Historical Association, 1998), 136, 138.
109. Ibid., 138–141.
110. Ibid., 140–141.
111. Ford, *Rip Ford's Texas*, 267.
112. Thompson, *Cortina*, 77.
113. Ford, *Rip Ford's Texas*, 270.

114. Ibid., 271.
115. Ibid., 270.
116. Ibid., 273; Heintzelman, *Fifty Miles*, 155; Thompson, *Cortina*, 78–80.
117. Ford, *Rip Ford's Texas*, 273; Thompson, *Cortina*, 81–82.
118. Ford, *Rip Ford's Texas*, 274.
119. Ibid., 274–275.
120. Heintzelman, *Fifty Miles*, 155.
121. Thompson, *Cortina*, 83–85; these engagements were closer to skirmishes than actual battles.
122. Thompson, *Vaqueros in Blue and Gray*, 19–23.
123. Ivey, *Texas Rangers*, 84.
124. Williams, *Sam Houston*, VII: 408.
125. Wilkins, *Defending the Borders*, 136; Ivey, *Texas Rangers*, 84.
126. Winfrey, *Texas Indian Papers*, IV: 8, 19.
127. Williams, *Sam Houston*, VII: 391, 402–403, 398, 423.
128. Winfrey, *Texas Indian Papers*, IV: 10.
129. Ivey, *Texas Rangers*, 84, 94.
130. Williams, *Sam Houston*, VII: 412–413, 503, 507.
131. Wilkins, *Defending the Borders*, 140–141.
132. Citizens of Sabinal Canyon to Governor Houston, May 30, 1860, Correspondence 1854–1861, Ranger Papers, Texas State Library.
133. Wilkins, *Defending the Borders*, 139.
134. Williams, *Sam Houston*, VII: 526.
135. Ibid., 525.
136. *Austin State Gazette*, July 21, 1860.
137. Williams, *Sam Houston*, VIII: 139–140.
138. Ibid., 140.
139. Smith, *The Old Army in Texas*, 147.
140. Collins, *Texas Devils*, 4, 257.
141. Anderson, *Conquest of Texas*, 238.
142. Winfrey, *Texas Indian Papers*, IV: 36.
143. Rowland, *Jefferson Davis*, I: 460.
144. Ibid., 467; Cutrer, *Ben McCulloch*, 150.
145. Williams, *Sam Houston*, VIII: 506; Cutrer, *Ben McCulloch*, 149.

Notes for Chapter 8

1. See Ralph Wooster, *Texas and Texans in the Civil War* (Austin: Eakin Press, 1995) for a general history of Texas in the Civil War; see Charles Grear, *Why Texans Fought in the Civil War* (College Station: Texas A&M University Press, 2010) for a culturally oriented study.
2. Grear, *Why Texans Fought*, 5–6; Rose quoted on 34.

3. *Neu-Braunfelser Zeitung*, January 11, 1861.
4. Francis Lubbock, *Six Decades in Texas; or Memoirs of Francis Richard Lubbock: Governor of Texas in Wartime, 1861–1863* (Austin: Ben C. Jones & CO. Printers, 1900), 514.
5. *Austin State Gazette*, November 17, 1860.
6. Lubbock, *Six Decades in Texas*, 356.
7. For a comprehensive listing see Lester Fitzhugh, *Texas Batteries, Battalions, Regiments, Commanders and Field Officers Confederate States Army 1861–1865* (Midlothian: Mirror Press, 1959); for unit histories see Ralph Wooster, *Lone Star Regiments in Gray* (Austin: Eakin Press, 2002).
8. Stephen Oates, "Texas Under the Secessionists," *Southwestern Historical Quarterly* 67 (1963): 187; Harry Henderson, *Texas in the Confederacy* (San Antonio: The Naylor Company, 1955), vii; Richard Current, ed., *Encyclopedia of the Confederacy* (New York: Simon and Schuster, 1993), IV: 1583; for arguments for lower enlistment rates see Wooster, Texas and Texans, 32, and Robert F. Felgar, "Texas in the War for Southern Independence, 1861–1865" (Ph.D Diss., University of Texas at Austin, 1935), 106, and Randolph Campbell, "Fighting for the Confederacy: The White Male Population of Harrison County in the Civil War," *Southwest Historical Quarterly* 104 (July 2000): 22–39.
9. See Moore, *Eighteen Minutes*, Appendixes C-E, for unit listings from the Texas Revolution.
10. Fitzhugh, *Texas Batteries, Battalions, Regiments*, entire book; Anne Bailey, *Texans in the Confederate Cavalry* (Fort Worth: Ryan Place Publishers, 1995), 17–19.
11. For examples see Thompson, *Vaqueros in Blue and Gray*, 11–12, 21–23.
12. Robert Wooster, "'Rarin' for a Fight': Texans in the Confederate Army," *Southwestern Historical Quarterly* 84 (1981): 396–397; for more on the demographics of Texan recruits see Grear, *Why Texans Fought*, Chapter 6; for more on Hispanic involvement in the Civil War see Jerry Thompson, *Vaqueros in Blue and Gray* (Austin: Presidial, 1976).
13. Wooster, "Rarin' for a Fight," 396–397.
14. *Governor's Message to the Senators and Representatives of the Ninth Legislature of the State of Texas*: Executive Office, Austin, November 1, 1861, p. 10.
15. Arthur James Fremantle, *The Fremantle Diary; Being the Journal of Lieutenant Colonel James Arthur Lyon Fremantle, Coldstream Guards, on His Three Months in the Southern States*, edited by Walter Lord (Boston, 1954), 58.
16. Thomas Cutrer, ed., *Terry Texas Ranger Trilogy* (Austin: State House Press, 1996), ix.

17. Thomas North, *Five Years in Texas: Or, What You Did Not Hear during the War from January 1861 to January 1866* (Cincinnati, 1871), 104.
18. Theophilus Noel, *A Campaign from Santa Fe to the Mississippi* (Shreveport, 1865), 8.
19. Stephen Oates, *Confederate Cavalry West of the River* (Austin: University of Texas Press, 1961), 67–70.
20. *Texas National Register*, December 14, 1844.
21. Lane, *Adventures*, 83–84; see Douglas Hale, *The Third Texas Cavalry in the Civil War* (Norman: University of Oklahoma Press, 1992) for a pertinent regimental history.
22. Lane, *Adventures*, 87; Bryan, *More Zeal than Discretion*, 112–113; Wooster, *Lone Star Regiments*, 64.
23. Robert N. Scott, ed., *War of the Rebellion: A Compilation of the Official Records of the Union and Confederate Armies* (Washington: Government Printing Office, 1882), Series I, Volume VII: 17.
24. Jomini, *Art of War*, 305.
25. *Harper's Weekly*, July 6, 1861.
26. David Butler, *United States Firearms: The First Century, 1776–1875* (New York: Winchester Press, 1971), 226–227, 148–149; Thomas Thiele, "The Evolution of Cavalry in the American Civil War; 1861–1863" (PhD Diss., University of Michigan, 1951), 148–149.
27. Files quoted in *Itasca Item*, April 25, 1924.
28. Ibid.
29. Oates, "Texas Under the Secessionists," 187; Oates's estimate of 90,000 Texan-Confederate soldiers based on official state reports reflects the high-end of scholarly assessment. Historians Ralph Wooster and Robert Falgar estimate significantly lower participation. Randolph Campbell's study of Harrison County demographics during the war, when expanded proportionally, would likewise suggest a figure closer to 60,000; Randolph Campbell, "Fighting for the Confederacy: The White Male Population of Harrison County in the Civil War," *Southwestern Historical Quarterly* 104 (July 2000): 22–39.
30. Oates, *Confederate Cavalry*, 26, 47.
31. Ibid., 26–27.
32. Executive Department, "Virginia's Contribution to the Confederacy," *The William and Mary Quarterly* 13 (1904): 141.
33. Ibid.; Oates, *Confederate Cavalry*, 26, 47.
34. See Wooster, *Lone Star Regiments*, Chapter 2, for more on Hood's brigade.
35. Confederate Soldier, *The Grayjackets: And How They Lived Fought and Died, for Dixie* (Richmond: Jones Brothers & CO., 1867), 175.
36. William Fletcher, *Rebel Private Front and Rear: Experiences from the Early Fifties and through the Civil War* (Beaumont: The Greer Print, 1908), 99.

37. Leonidas B. Giles, *Terry's Texas Rangers* (Austin, 1911), 100.
38. Richard Taylor, *Destruction and Reconstruction: Personal Experiences in the Late War* (New York, 1879), 150.
39. *Official Records*, Series I, Volume XV: 774.
40. Ibid.
41. Ford, *Rip Ford's Texas*, 333.
42. Ibid., 332.
43. Wooster, "Rarin' for a Fight," 405.
44. Oates, "Texas Under the Secessionists," 201.
45. Gammel, *Laws of Texas*, V: 452–454, 677–678, 700–702.
46. David Smith, *Frontier Defense in the Civil War: Texas' Rangers and Rebels* (College Station: Texas A&M University Press, 1992), 30, 88, 169–170.
47. Ivey, *Texas Rangers*, 101; Cutrer, *Ben McCulloch*, 179.
48. Smith, *Frontier Defense*, 23–24; *Official Records*: Series I, Volume I: 618.
49. Cutrer, *Ben McCulloch*, 181–185.
50. Richardson, *The Frontier*, 227, 230.
51. Cutrer, *Ben McCulloch*, 188.
52. *Official Records*: Series I, Volume I: 618–619.
53. Special Orders Number 40, June 18, 1861, Burleson Papers, Eugene C. Barker Texas History Center, Austin; Smith, *Frontier Defense*, 35–37.
54. Ford, *Rip Ford's Texas*, 324, 326.
55. Wooster, *Lone Star Regiments*, 205–210.
56. Lubbock, *Six Decades in Texas*, 358.
57. Ibid.
58. Ibid., 359.
59. Gammel, *Laws of Texas*, V: 452–454.
60. Cox, *Texas Rangers*, 175.
61. Smith, *Frontier Defense*, 64–65.
62. Ibid; Wooster, *Lone Star Regiments*, 219.
63. Richardson, *The Frontier*, 242.
64. Petition, January 21, 1864, Governor Pendleton Murrah Records, Texas State Library, Austin; Smith, *Frontier Defense*, 92–94.
65. *Official Records*, Series I, Volume XXII, Part II: 993; issues with wartime recruitment suggest that though most Texans maintained cultural pride in their frontier traditions, some remained disinclined to physically serve militarily when called.
66. Norris quoted in Richardson, *The Frontier*, 239.
67. *Official Records*, Series I, Volume XXII, Part II: 993.
68. Smith, *Frontier Defense*, 131–134.
69. Wooster, *American Military Frontiers*, 177.

70. Ford, *Rip Ford's Texas*, 349.

71. James Barry, *A Texas Ranger and Frontiersman: The Days of Buck Barry in Texas, 1845–1906*, edited by James Greer (Dallas: Southwest Press, 1932), 202; Campbell, *Gone to Texas*, 266–267.

72. Henderson, *Texas in the Confederacy*, 89; see Stephen Kirk, *Line of Battle: 3rd Texas Cavalry, 6th Texas Cavalry, 9th Texas Cavalry, 27th Texas Cavalry* (Harrisonville: Burnt District Press, 2012) for more on Ross's brigade; see Anne Bailey, *Between the Enemy and Texas: Parson's Texas Cavalry in the Civil War* (Fort Worth: Texas Christian University Press, 2005) for a similar brigade-level study of Texan-Confederate cavalry.

73. George Griscom, *Fighting with Ross' Texas Cavalry Brigade, C.S.A.: The Diary of George L. Griscom, Adjutant, 9th Texas Cavalry Regiment*, edited by Homer Kerr (Hillsboro: Hill Jr. College Press, 1976), 51.

74. Henderson, *Texas in the Confederacy*, 89–90.

75. Griscom, *Ross' Brigade*, 60.

76. Henderson, *Texas in the Confederacy*, 91–92.

77. Allen Ashcraft, *Texas in the Civil War: A Resume History* (Austin: Texas Civil War Centennial Commission, 1962), 26–27.

78. See Jeffery Murrah, *None but Texians: A History of Terry's Texas Rangers* (Austin: Eakin Press, 2001) and Bryan Bush, *Terry's Texas Rangers: A History of the Eighth Texas Cavalry* (New York: Turner Publishing, 2002) for studies on a single regiment; see Stanley McGowen, *Horse Sweat and Powder Smoke: The First Texas Cavalry in the Civil War* (Collage Station: Texas A&M University Press, 1999) for a regimental-level study about a similar unit.

79. C.C. Jeffries, *Terry's Rangers* (New York: Vantage Press, 1961), 13; Murrah, *None But Texians*, 17–18.

80. New Orleans *Picayune*, September 16, 1861.

81. Cutrer, *Texas Ranger Trilogy*, 96.

82. Jeffries, *Terry's Rangers*, 20–21; Murrah, *None But Texians*, 22–23.

83. Cutrer, *Texas Ranger Trilogy*, 104.

84. Graber, *Terry Texas Ranger*, 44–45; Wooster, *Lone Star Regiments*, 50.

85. Cutrer, *Texas Ranger Trilogy*, 105; Murrah, *None But Texian*, 30–31.

86. Graber, *Terry Texas Ranger*, 45.

87. Cutrer, *Texas Ranger Trilogy*, 16.

88. Graber, *Terry Texas Ranger*, 36.

89. Cutrer, *Texas Ranger Trilogy*, 117; Wooster, *Lone Star Regiments*, 53; Murrah, *None But Texian*, 42–43.

90. The Battle of Shiloh also resulted in the death of Texas's highest ranking officer in the Civil War, Albert Sydney Johnston, whose military career ironically diverged from his state's way of war.

91. Cutrer, *Texas Ranger Trilogy*, 118–119; Murrah, *None But Texians*, 45–46.

92. Cutrer, *Texas Ranger Trilogy*, 126.

93. Ibid.

94. Ibid.

95. Murrah, *None But Texians*, 53.

96. Cutrer, *Texas Ranger Trilogy*, 128.

97. Ibid., 35.

98. Wooster, *Lone Star Regiments*, 56.

99. Cutrer, *Texas Ranger Trilogy*, 136–137.

100. Ibid., 166.

101. Graber, *Terry Texas Ranger*, 227; Wooster, *Lone Star Regiments*, 62; Murrah, *None But Texians*,110–111.

102. Cutrer, *Texas Ranger Trilogy*, 170, 77.

103. See Donald Frazier, *Blood and Treasure: Confederate Empire in the Southwest* (College Station: Texas A&M University Press, 1995); Jerry Thompson, *Henry Hopkins Sibley: Confederate General of the West* (Natchitoches: Northwestern State University Press, 1987); and Flint Whitlock, *Distant Bugles, Distant Drums: The Union Response to the Confederate Invasion of New Mexico* (Boulder: University of Colorado Press, 2006) for studies of the 1861 New Mexico Campaign.

104. Walter Pittman, *New Mexico and the Civil War* (Charleston: The History Press, 2011), 20–21; see Frazier, *Blood and Treasure*, 50, 75 for the Texans' campaign planning and 80–81, 92–94, 97 for their recruitment and training.

105. Frazier, *Blood and Treasure*, 151–152; Whitlock, *Distant Bugles, Distant Drums*, 99–100, 104–105.

106. Frazier, *Blood and Treasure*, 160.

107. Albert Peticolas, *Rebels on the Rio Grande: The Civil War Journal of A. B. Peticolas*, edited by Don Alberts (Albuquerque: University of New Mexico Press, 1884), 42; John Taylor, *Bloody Valverde: A Civil War Battle on the Rio Grande, February 21, 1862* (Albuquerque: University of New Mexico Press, 1995), 44–53.

108. Peticolas, *Rebels on the Rio Grande*, 48–49; Taylor, *Bloody Valverde*, 67–69; Frazier, *Blood and Treasure*, 162–169.

109. Peticolas, *Rebels on the Rio Grande*, 49.

110. *Official Record*, Series I, Volume IV: 520; Taylor, *Bloody Valverde*, 86–91, 93–94.

111. *Official Record*, Series I, Volume IV: 506.

112. Ibid., 509; Frazier, *Blood and Treasure*, 180.

113. Peticolas, *Rebels on the Rio Grande*, 49; Frazier, *Blood and Treasure*, 180; Whitlock, *Distant Bugles, Distant Drums*, 107–108, 136.
114. Don Alberts, *The Battle of Glorieta: Union Victory in the West* (College Station: Texas A&M University Press, 1998), 14–15.
115. Ibid., 122–123, 146–147.
116. Quoted in Peticolas, *Rebels on the Rio Grande*, 90.
117. Peticolas, *Rebels on the Rio Grande*, 85; Alberts, *Battle of Glorieta*, 134–135; Whitlock, *Distant Bugles, Distant Drums*, 206–207.
118. Oates, *Confederate Cavalry*, 21; W.H. Watford, "Confederate Western Ambitions," *Southwestern Historical Quarterly* 44 (1940): 184–185l; Frazier, *Blood and Treasure*, 264.
119. Lubbock quoted in Ashcraft, *Texas in the Civil War*, 13.
120. Ibid., 13–14.
121. Henderson, *Texas in the Confederacy*, 117–118; Wooster, *Lone Star Regiments*, 286.
122. *Texas State Gazette*, September 16, 1863.
123. *New York Times*, June 18, 1865; Jeffrey Hunt, *The Last Battle of the Civil War: Palmetto Ranch* (Austin: University of Texas Press, 2002), 56–57.
124. Ibid., 58; Ford, *Rip Ford's Texas*, 389.
125. Hunt, *Last Battle*, 58–61.
126. Ibid., 61–62.
127. Ford, *Rip Ford's Texas*, 390.
128. Ibid., 390.
129. Ibid., 391.
130. Ibid., 391, 392; Hunt, *Palmetto Ranch*, 112, 128.
131. Lubbock, *Six Decades in Texas*, 536–537.
132. Reprinted in Lane, *Adventures*, 152–153, 155.
133. Bryan, *More Zeal than Discretion*, 180–181.
134. Reprinted in Lane, *Adventures*, 145–148.
135. *Official Record*, Series I, Volume IX: 506.
136. Lubbock, *Six Decades in Texas*,403.
137. Graber, *Terry Texas Ranger*, 34.
138. Ibid., 36.
139. Cutrer, *Texas Ranger Trilogy*, 178–179, 181. See Gabor Boritt, ed., *Why the Confederacy Lost* (New York: Oxford University Press, 1992), for a compilation of essays that explore causes of the South's defeat.
140. Current, *Encyclopedia of the Confederacy*, I: 338; Ibid, III: 1264.
141. Campbell, *Gone to Texas*, 259–262; See also Carl Moneyhon, *Texas after the Civil War: The Struggle of Reconstruction* (College Station: Texas A&M University Press, 2004), a post-war study.
142. Lubbock, *Six Decades in Texas*, 398.

Notes for Epilogue

1. Granier, *First Way of War*, 23.
2. *Telegraph and Texas Register*, April 17, 1844.
3. Henderson to Taylor, Austin, May 3, 1846, 301–17–3, Archives Division, Texas State Library.
4. Campbell, *Gone to Texas*, 290.
5. Gammel, *Laws of Texas*, VI: 179–182; Utley, *Lone Star Justice*, 138–142; Hamalainen, *Comanche Empire*, 314.
6. Gammel, *Laws of Texas*, VII: 36–38.
7. Ivey, *Texas Rangers*, 138–139; Utley, *Lone Star Justice*, 144.
8. Gammel, *Laws of Texas*, VIII: 86.
9. Richardson, *The Northwest Frontier*, 287–288.
10. Campbell, *Gone to Texas*, 304–305.
11. N.A. Jennings, *A Texas Ranger* (Dallas: Turner Company, 1930), 99.
12. Gammel, *Laws of Texas*, VIII: 86–91.
13. See Rick Miller, *John B. Jones and the Frontier Battalion, 1874–1881* (Denton: University of North Texas Press, 2012) for more on how this unit continued the Texas Way of War.
14. Ivey, *Texas Rangers*, 164.
15. Wooster, *American Military Frontiers*, 194.
16. *Report of the Adjutant General*, 1891, 8.
17. "Texas Military Forces Historical Sketch: Spanish American War," Texas Military Forces Museum.

Bibliography

Primary Sources

Alsbury, Young. "Burning of Vince's Bridge." *Texas Almanac* (1861): 55–58. The Portal to Texas History.

Ambrose Powell Hill Papers, Virginia Historical Society, Richmond.

Ashcraft. Allan C. *Texas in the Civil War: A Resume History*. Austin: Texas Civil War Centennial Commission, 1962.

Austin, Stephen F. "Journal of Austin." *Texas Historical Association Quarterly* 7 (July 1903): 286–307.

Baker, D.W.C. *Texas Scrap-Book*. New York, 1875.

Barker, Eugene C., ed. *The Austin Papers*. 4 vols. Washington: Government Printing Office, 1924–1928.

Barry, James. *A Texas Ranger and Frontiersman: The Days of Buck Barry in Texas, 1845–1906*. Edited by James Greer. Dallas: Southwest Press, 1932.

Berlandier, Jean. *The Indians of Texas in 1830*. Washington: Smithsonian Institution Press, 1969.

Bexar Archives, Briscoe Center for American History, University of Texas at Austin.

Binkley, William C., ed. *Official Correspondence of the Texan Revolution, 1835–1836*. 2 vols. New York: D. Appleton-Century Company Inc., 1936.

Beamish, North Ludlow, ed. *On the Uses and Application of Cavalry in War from the Text of Bismark: With Practical Examples Selected from Ancient and Modern History*. London: T. & W. Boone, 1855.

Blackburn, J.K.P. *Terry's Texas Rangers: Reminiscences of J. K. P. Blackburn*. Austin: Ranger Press, 1979.

Brackett, Albert. *General Lane's Brigade in Central Mexico*. Cincinnati: H.W. Derby & Co, Publishers, 1854.

———. *History of the U.S. Cavalry*. New York: Harper & Brothers, 1865.

Brinckerhoff, Sidney, and Odie Faulk, eds. *Lancers for the King*. Phoenix: Arizona Historical Foundation, 1933.

Brown, John Duff. *Heroes of Texas*. Houston: Union National Bank, 1934.

Brown, John Henry. *Indian Wars and Pioneers of Texas*. Austin: L.E. Daniell, Publisher, 1880.

Bradley, A.G., ed. *Travels and Works of Captain John Smith*. Edinburgh: John Grant, 1910.

Burleson Papers, Eugene C. Barker Texas History Center, Austin.

Burnam, Jesse. "Reminiscences of Capt. Jesse Burnham." *Texas Historical Association Quarterly* 5 (July 1901): 12–18.

Caperton, John. "Sketch of Colonel John C. Hays, Texas Ranger." Center for American History, University of Texas at Austin.

Castaneda, C.E., ed. *The Mexican Side of the Texas Revolution*. Austin: Graphic Ideas Inc., 1970.

Church, Benjamin. *The History of Philip's War*. Edited by Samuel Drake. Exeter: J & B Williams, 1829.

Clarksville *Northern Standard*, Portal to Texas History, University of North Texas Libraries.

Confederate Soldier. *The Grayjackets: And How They Lived Fought and Died, for Dixie*. Richmond: Jones Brothers & CO., 1867.

Crimmins, Martin L. "Colonel Robert E. Lee's Report on Indian Combats in Texas." *Southwestern Historical Quarterly* 39 (July 1935): 21–32.

Cutrer, Thomas, ed. *Terry Texas Ranger Trilogy*. Austin: State House Press, 1996.

Dana, Napoleon. *Monterrey Is Ours! The Mexican War Letters of Lieutenant Dana, 1845–1847*. Lexington: University Press of Kentucky, 1990.

Daniel, Price, and James Martin, eds. *Legislative Messages of the Chief Executives of Texas*. 3 vols. Austin: Texas State Library, 1972.

Dewees, W.B. *Letters from an Early Settler of Texas*. Edited by Cara Cardelle. Waco: Texian Press, 1968.

Dodge, Richard. *Our Wild Indians, 33 Years' Personal Experience Among the Redmen of the Great West*. New York: Archer House, 1883.

Doubleday, Abner. *My Life in the Old Army: The Reminiscences of Abner Doubleday from the Collections of the New York Historical Society*. Edited by Joseph Chance. Fort Worth: Texas Christian University Press, 1998.

Filisola, Vincente. *Memoirs for the History of the War in Texas*. Translated by Wallace Woolsey. 2 vols. Translated by Wallace Woolsey. Austin: Eakin Press, 1985–1987.

Fletcher, William. *Rebel Private Front and Rear: Experiences from the Early Fifties and through the Civil War*. Beaumont: The Greer Print, 1908.

Ford, John. *Rip Ford's Texas*. Edited by Stephen Oates. Austin: University of Austin Texas Press, 1987.

———. "John C. Hays in Texas." Center for American History, University of Texas at Austin.

Erath, George B. *The Memoirs of Major George B. Erath, 1813–1891*. Waco: Heritage Society of Waco, 1956.

Gammel, H.P.N., ed. *The Laws of Texas, 1822–1897*. 10 vols. Austin: Gammel Book Company, 1898.

Giddings, Luther. *Sketches of the Campaign in Mexico by an Officer of the First Ohio Volunteers*. New York: Putnam, 1853.

Graber, Henry. *A Terry Texas Ranger: The Life Record of H.W. Graber*. Austin: State House Press, 1987.

Griscom, George. *Fighting with Ross' Texas Cavalry Brigade, C.S.A.: The Diary of George L. Griscom, Adjutant, 9th Texas Cavalry Regiment*. Edited by Homer Kerr. Hillsboro: Hill Jr. College Press, 1976.

Gulick, Charles, ed. *The Papers of Mirabeau Buonaparte Lamar*. 6 vols. Austin: A. C. Baldwin, Printers, 1973.

Harper's Weekly.

Hening, William, ed. *The Statutes at Large being a Collection of all the Laws of Virginia, from the First Session of the Legislature in the Year 1619*. 13 vols. Richmond: George Cochran, 1823.

Henry, William. *Campaign Sketches of the War with Mexico*. New York: Harper and Brothers, 1847.

Heintzelman, Samuel. *Fifty Miles and a Fight: Major Samuel Peter Heintzelman's Journal of Texas and the Cortina War*. Edited by Jerry Thompson. Austin: Texas State Historical Association, 1998.

Hill, Daniel. *A Fighter from Way Back: The Mexican War Diary of Lt. Daniel Harvey Hill, 4th Artillery, USA*. Edited by Nathaniel Hughes and Timothy Johnson. Kent: Kent State University Press, 2002.

Holland, James K. "Diary of a Texan Volunteer in the Mexican War." *Southwestern Historical Quarterly* 30 (July 1926): 1–33.

Holley, Mary Austin. *Texas: Observations, Historical, Geographical and Descriptive*. Edited by Ray Billington. New York: Arno Press, 1973.

Hunter, William, ed. *Lord William Bentinck*. London: Oxford University Press, 1892.

Itasca Item.

Jackson, Jack, ed. *Almonte's Texas*. Austin: Texas State Historical Association, 2003.

Jenkins, John Holmes. *The Papers of the Texas Revolution, 1835–1836*. 10 vols. Austin: Presidial Press, 1973.

Jenkins, John Holland. *Recollections of Early Texas: The Memoirs of John Holland Jenkins*. Austin: University of Texas Press, 1958.

Jennings, N. A. *A Texas Ranger*. Dallas: Turner Company, 1930.

Jomini, Antoine-Henri. *The Art of War*. Philadelphia: J.B. Lippincott & Co., 1862.

Journals of the House of Representatives of the Ninth Congress of the Republic of Texas. Washington: Miller & Cushney, 1845.

Kemp Papers Collection. San Jacinto Museum of History, Houston, Texas.

Kenly, John. *Memoirs of a Maryland Volunteer: War with Mexico, in the Years 1846-7–8*. Philadelphia: J.B. Lippincott & Co, 1873.

Knopf, Richard, ed. *Anthony Wayne: A Name in Arms*. Pittsburgh: University of Pittsburgh Press, 1960.

Kuykendall, J.H. "Reminiscences of Early Texans." *Quarterly of the Texas State Historical Association* 7 (July 1903): 29–64.

Kuykendall, Marshall. *They Slept Upon their Rifles*. Austin: Nortex Press, 2005.

Lafora, Nicolas. *The Frontiers of New Spain: Nicolas de Lafora's Description, 1766–1768*. Edited by Lawrence Kinnaird. Berkeley, CA: Quivira Society, 1958.

Lane, Walter P. *The Adventures and Recollections of Walter P. Lane*. Marshall: News Messenger Pub. Co., 1923.

Lee, Nelson. *Three Years Among the Comanche*. Guilford: Globe Pequot Press, 2004.

Lubbock, Francis. *Six Decades in Texas; or Memoirs of Francis Richard Lubbock: Governor of Texas in Wartime, 1861–1863*. Austin: Ben C. Jones & Co. Printers, 1900.

Martinez, Antonio. *The Letters of Antonio Martinez: The Last Spanish Governor of Texas, 1817–1822*. Edited by Virginia Taylor. Austin: Texas State Library, 1957.

McLean, Malcolm D. *Papers Concerning Robertson's Colony in Texas*. 19 vols. Fort Worth: Texas Christian University Press, 1974–1993.

Morrell, Z. N. *Flowers and Fruits in the Wilderness; or Forty-six Years in Texas and Two in Honduras*. Dallas: W. G. Scarff & Co., Publishers, 1886.

New Orleans *Bulletin*.

New Orleans *Picayune*.

New York Times.

Nichols, James W. *Now You Hear My Horn: The Journal of James Wilson Nichols, 1820–1887*. Edited by Catherine McDowell. Austin: University of Texas Press, 1967.

Niles Weekly Register.

Noel, Theophilus. *A Campaign from Santa Fe to the Mississippi*. Shreveport, 1865.

Oswandel, Jacob. *Notes of the Mexican War, 1846–1848*. Edited by Timothy Johnson and Nathaniel Hughes. Knoxville: University of Tennessee Press, 2010.

Pena, Jose Enrique *With Santa Anna in Texas: A Personal Narrative of the Revolution*. Edited by Carmen Perry. College Station: Texas A&M University Press, 1975.

Peticolas, Albert. *Rebels on the Rio Grande: The Civil War Journal of A. B. Peticolas*. Edited by Don Alberts. Albuquerque: University of New Mexico Press, 1884.

Plummer, Rachael. *Rachael Plummer's Narrative of Twenty-one Months Servitude as a Prisoner among the Comanchee Indians*. Austin: Jenkins Publishing Company, 1977.

Reid, Samuel Chester. *The Scouting Expeditions of McCulloch's Texas Rangers; or theSummer and Fall Campaigns of the Army of the United States in Mexico*. Philadelphia: John E. Potter and Company, 1885.

Rodenbough, Theophilius. *From Everglade to Canyon with the Second United States Cavalry*. Originally published 1875. Reprint. Norman: University of Oklahoma Press, 2000.

Roemer, Jean. *Cavalry: Its History, Management, and Uses in War*. New York: D. Van Nostrand, 1862.

Rowland, Dunbar, ed. *Jefferson Davis Constitutionalist: His Letters, Papers and Speeches*. 10 vols. Jackson: Mississippi Department of Archives and History, 1923.

Ruiz, Jose Francisco. *Report on the Indian Tribes of Texas in 1828*. Edited by John Ewers. New Haven: Yale University Library, 1972.

Sanchez Navarro, Carlos. *The War in Texas: Memoirs of a Soldier*. 2nd ed. Mexico: Editorial Jus, S.A., 1960.

Sansom, John. "Captain Callahan's Raid into Mexico." *Hunter's Magazine*, April-May, 1911.

Scott, Winfield. *Memoirs of Lieut.-General Scott, LL.D.* 2 vols. New York: Sheldon & Company, Publishers, 1864.

Seguin, Juan. *A Revolution Remembered: The Memoirs and Selected Correspondence of Juan N. Seguin*. Austin: State House Press, 1991.

Sibley, Marilyn S., ed. *Travelers in Texas, 1761–1860*. Austin: University of Texas Press, 1967.

Smith, Compton. *Chile con Carne*. New York: Miller and Curtiss, 1857.

Smithwick, Noah. *The Evolution of a State*. Austin: University of Texas Press, 1983.

Sowell, A.J. *Rangers and Pioneers of Texas*. San Antonio: Shepard Bros. & Co., 1884.

Stiff, Edward. *The Texan Emigrant*. Waco: Texian Press, 1968.

Taylor, Richard. *Destruction and Reconstruction: Personal Experiences in the Late War*. New York, 1879.

Telegraph and Texas Register. The Portal to Texas History. University of North Texas Libraries.

Texas Adjutant General. *Annual Reports*.

Texas National Register. The Portal to Texas History, University of North Texas Libraries.

The Bellville Countryman. The Portal to Texas History, University of North Texas Libraries.

The Nueces Valley. The Portal to Texas History, University of North Texas Libraries.

The Texas Democrat. The Portal to Texas History, University of North Texas Libraries.

The Texas Gazette. The Portal to Texas History, University of North Texas Libraries.

Thorp, T. B. *Our Army at Monterey*. Philadelphia: Carey & Hart, 1848.

Trower, Charles. *Hints on Irregular Cavalry*. Calcutta: W. Thacker and Co., 1845.

Walker, Samuel. *Samuel H. Walker's Account of the Mier Expedition*. Edited by Marilyn Sibley. Austin: Texas State Historical Association, 1978.

Wallace, Ernest, ed. *Documents of Texas History*. Lubbock: Texas Tech Press, 1960.

War of the Rebellion: A Compilation of the Official Records of the Union and Confederate Armies. 128 vols. Washington, D.C.: Government Printing Office, 1880–1901.

Wilbarger, J.W. *Indian Depredations in Texas.* 1889. Rpt., Austin: Pemberton Press, 1967.

Williams, Amelia and Eugene Barker, eds. *The Writings of Sam Houston, 1813–1863.* 8 vols. Austin: The University of Texas Press, 1938.

Wilson, Robert. "Reviews—Sir Robert Wilson's Works." *The Royal Military Chronicle or British Officers Monthly Register and Mentor* 5 (1813): 207.

Winfrey, Dorman H., ed. *Texas Indian Papers.* 5 vols. Austin: Texas State Library, 1959.

Zuber, William. *My Eighty Years in Texas.* Edited by Janis Mayfield. Austin: University of Texas Press, 1971.

Secondary Sources

Alberts, Don. *The Battle of Glorieta: Union Victory in the West.* College Station: Texas A&M University Press, 1998.

Anderson, Gary C. *The Conquest of Texas: Ethnic Cleansing in the Promised Land, 1820–1875.* Norman: University of Oklahoma Press, 2005.

Army, Department of the. "Field Manual 3-0 Operations," ed. U. S. Army. Washington, DC., 2008.

Arnold, James. *Jeff Davis's Own: Cavalry, Comanches, and the Battle for the Texas Frontier.* New York: John Wiley & Sons, Inc., 2000.

Ashcraft, Allan C. *Texas in the Civil War: A Resume History.* Austin: Texas Civil War Centennial Commission, 1962.

Autrey, Russell. *Austin's Old Three Hundred: The First Anglo Colony in Texas.* Austin: Eakin Press, 1999.

Bailey, Anne J. "A Texas Cavalry Raid: Reaction to Black Soldiers and Contrabands." *Civil War History* 35, no. 2 (1989): 138–152.

———. *Between the Enemy and Texas: Parson's Texas Cavalry in the Civil War.* Fort Worth: Texas Christian University Press, 2005.

———. *Texans in the Confederate Cavalry.* Fort Worth: Ryan Place Publishers, 1995.

Barker, Eugene C. *The Life of Stephen F. Austin: Founder of Texas, 1793–1836.* Chicago: Lakeside Press, 1925.

Barton, Henry W. *Texas Volunteers in the Mexican War.* Waco: Texian Press, 1970.

———. "The United States Cavalry and the Texas Rangers." *Southwestern Historical Quarterly* 63 (1960): 495–510.

———. "Five Texas Frontier Companies during the Mexican War." *Southwestern Historical Quarterly* 66 (1962): 17–30.

Black, Robert. *Ranger Dawn: The American Ranger from the Colonial Era to the Mexican War.* Mechanicsburg: Stackpole Books, 2009.

Boritt, Gabor, ed. *Why the Confederacy Lost.* New York: Oxford University Press, 1992.

Brands, H.W. *Lone Star Nation.* New York: Doubleday, 2004.

Bryan, Jimmy. *More Zeal Than Discretion: The Westward Adventures of Walter P. Lane.* College Station: Texas A&M University, 2008.

Bush, Bryan. *Terry's Texas Rangers: A History of the Eighth Texas Cavalry.* New York: Turner Publishing, 2002.

Butler, David F. *United States Firearms: The First Century, 1776–1875.* New York: Winchester Press, 1971.

Campbell, Randolph. "Fighting for the Confederacy: The White Male Population of Harrison County in the Civil War." *Southwestern Historical Quarterly* 104 (July 2000): 22–39.

———. *Gone to Texas: A History of the Lone Star State.* Oxford and New York: Oxford University Press, 2003.

Cantrell, Gregg. *Stephen F. Austin: Empresario of Texas.* New Haven and London: Yale University Press, 1999.

Chapel, Charles E. *Guns of the Old West.* New York: Coward-McCann, Inc., 1961.

Chet, Guy. *Conquering the American Wilderness: The Triumph of European Warfare in the Colonial Northeast.* Amherst: University of Massachusetts Press, 2003.

Chipman, Donald E. *Spanish Texas, 1519–1821.* Austin: University of Texas Press, 1992.

Christian, Asa. *Mirabeau Buonaparte Lamar.* Austin: Von Boeckmann-Jones Co., Printers, 1922.

Collins, Michael. *Texas Devils: Rangers and Regulars on the Lower Rio Grande, 1846–1861.* Norman: University of Oklahoma Press, 2008.

Cox, Michael. *The Texas Rangers: Wearing the Cinco Peso, 1821–1900.* New York: Forge, 2008.

Current, Richard, ed. *Encyclopedia of the Confederacy.* 4 vols. New York: Simon and Schuster, 1993.

Cutrer, Thomas. *Ben McCulloch and the Frontier Military Tradition.* Chapel Hill: University of North Carolina Press, 1993.

Davis, William C. *Lone Star Rising: The Revolutionary Birth of the Texas Republic.* New York: Free Press, 2004 .

Dawson, Joseph G., ed. *The Texas Military Experience: From the Texas Revolution to World War II.* College Station: Texas A&M University Press, 1995.

DeLay, Brian. *War of a Thousand Deserts: Indian Raids and the U.S.-Mexican War.* New Haven and London: Yale Universtity Press, 2008.

De Shields, James T. *Border Wars of Texas.* Waco: Texian Press, 1976.

Depalo, William. *The Mexican National Army, 1822–1852*. College Station: Texas A&M University Press, 1997.

Dimmick, Gregg. *Sea of Mud: The Retreat of the Mexican Army after San Jacinto*. Austin: Texas State Historical Association, 2006.

Dishman, Christopher. *A Perfect Gibraltar: The Battle for Monterrey, Mexico, 1846*. Norman: University of Oklahoma Press, 2010.

Drewry, P. H. "Fort Henry." *William and Mary Quarterly* (January 1923).

Dixon, Sam, and Louis Kemp. *The Heroes of San Jacinto*. Houston: The Anson Jones Press, 1932.

Eisenhower, John S.D. *So Far from God: The U.S. War with Mexico, 1846–1848*. Norman: University of Oklahoma Press, 2000.

Ellis, John. *Cavalry: The History of Mounted Warfare*. New York: G.P. Putnam's Sons, 1978.

Elting, John R. *Amateurs, To Arms: A Military History of the War of 1812*. New York: Da Capo Press, 1995.

Farber, James. *Texas, C.S.A.: A Spotlight on Disaster*. New York: The Jackson Co., 1947.

Fehrenbach, T.R. *Lone Star: A History of Texas and Texans*. New York: Collier Books, 1968.

———. *Comanches: The Destruction of a People*. New York: Alfred A. Knopf, 1974.

Felgar, Robert F. "Texas in the War for Southern Independence, 1861–1865." Ph.D Diss., University of Texas at Austin, 1935.

Fitzhugh, Lester. *Terry's Texas Rangers: 8th Texas Cavalry, CSA*. Houston: Civil War Round Table, 1958.

———. *Texas Batteries, Battalions, Regiments, Commanders and Field Officers Confederate States Army 1861–1865*. Midlothian: Mirror Press, 1959.

Foote, Henry S. *Texas and the Texans*. 2 vols. Austin: Steck Company, 1935.

Frazier, Donald. *Blood and Treasure: Confederate Empire in the Southwest*. College Station: Texas A&M University Press, 1995.

Gambrell, Herbert. *Mirabeau Buonaparte Lamar*. Dallas: Southwest Press, 1934.

Glasscock, Sallie. *Dreams of an Empire: The Story of Stephen Austin and His Colony in Texas*. San Antonio: Naylor Company, 1951.

Gray, Colin. *War, Peace, and International Relations: An Introduction to Strategic History*. New York: Rutledge, 2007.

Grear, Charles. *Why Texans Fought in the Civil War*. College Station: Texas A&M University Press, 2010.

Greer, James K. *Texas Ranger: Jack Hays in the Frontier Southwest*. College Station: Texas A&M University Press, 1993.

Grenier, John. *The First Way of War: American War Making on the Frontier*. New York: Cambridge University Press, 2008.

Gwynne, S.C. *Empire of the Summer Moon: Quanah Parker and the Rise and Fall of the Comanches, the Most Powerful Indian Tribe in American History*. New York: Scribner, 2010.

Hadley, Diana, Thomas Naylor, and Mardith Schuetz-Miller, eds. *The Presidio and Militia on the Northern Frontier of New Spain: A Documentary History. Volume Two, Part Two: The Central Corridor and the Texas Corridor, 1700–1765*. Tucson: University of Arizona Press, 1997.

Hale, Douglas. *The Third Texas Cavalry in the Civil War* (Norman: University of Oklahoma Press, 1992.

Haley, James L. *Sam Houston*. Norman: University of Oklahoma Press, 2002.

———. *Passionate Nation. The Epic History of Texas*. New York: Free Press, 2006.

Hamalainen, Pekka. *The Comanche Empire*. New Haven and London: Yale University Press, 2008.

Hardin, Stephen L. *Texian Iliad: A Military History of the Texas Revolution, 1835–1836*. Austin: University of Austin Press, 1994.

Hatley, Allen G. *The Indian Wars in Stephen F. Austin's Texas Colony, 1822–1823*. Austin: Eakin Press, 2001.

Haynes, Sam. *Soldiers of Misfortune: The Somervell and Mier Expeditions*. Austin: University of Texas Press, 1990.

Haythornthwaite, Philip. *Napoleonic Cavalry*. London: Cassell & Co, 2001.

Henderson, Harry M. *Texas in the Confederacy*. San Antonio: The Naylor Company, 1955.

Higginbotham, Don. *The War of American Independence*. New York: Macmillan Company, 1971.

Hooper, Frederick. *The Military Horse*. New York: A.S. Barnes and Company, 1976.

Hosley, William. *Colt: The Making of an American Legend*. Amherst: University of Massachusetts Press, 1996.

Howell, Kenneth, ed. *The Seventh Star of the Confederacy: Texas during the Civil War*. Denton: University of North Texas Press, 2009.

Hunt, Jeffrey. *The Last Battle of the Civil War: Palmetto Ranch*. Austin: University of Texas Press, 2002.

Huston, Cleburne. *Deaf Smith: Incredible Texas Spy*. Waco: Texian Press, 1973.

Hyde, Anne F. *Empires, Nations and Families: A History of the American West, 1800–1860*. Lincoln: University of Nebraska Press, 2011.

Ivey, Darren L. *The Texas Rangers: A Registry and History*. Jefferson: McFarland & Company, Inc., 1970.

Jackson, Jack. *Los Mestenos: Spanish Ranching in Texas, 1721–1821*. College Station: Texas A&M University Press, 1986.

Jarymowycz, Roman. *Cavalry from Hoof to Track*. Westport: Stackpole Books, 2009.

Jeffries, C.C. *Terry's Rangers*. New York: Vantage Press, 1961.

Jenkins, John, and Kenneth Kesselus. *Edward Burleson: Texas Frontier Leader*. Austin: Jenkins Publishing Company, 1990.

Jewett, Clayton. *Texas in the Confederacy: An Experiment in Nation Building*. Columbia: University of Missouri Press, 2002.

Johnson, Swafford. *History of the U.S. Cavalry*. Greenwhich: Bison Books Corps, 1985.

Johnson, Timothy D. *A Gallant Little Army: The Mexico City Campaign*. Lawrence: University Press of Kansas, 2007.

Kessell, John L. *Spain and the Southwest*. Norman: University of Oklahoma Press, 2002.

Kirk, Stephen. *Line of Battle: 3rd Texas Cavalry, 6th Texas Cavalry, 9th Texas Cavalry, 27th Texas Cavalry*. Harrisonville: Burnt District Press, 2012.

Kopel, Hal. *Today in the Republic of Texas*. Waco: Texian Press, 1968.

Koury, Michael J. *Arms for Texas*. Fort Collins: Old Arms Press, 1973.

Knowles, Thomas W. *They Rode for the Lone Star: The Saga of the Texas Rangers*. Dallas: Taylor Publishing Company, 1999.

La Vere, David. *Life Among the Texas Indians: The WPA Narratives*. College Station: Texas A&M University Press, 2006.

Lack, Paul D. *The Texas Revolutionary Experience: A Political and Social History, 1835–1836*. College Station: Texas A&M Press, 1992.

Lang, Andrew. "'Victory is Our Only Road to Peace': Texas, Wartime Morale, and Confederate Nationalism, 1860–1865." Thesis, University of North Texas, 2008.

Lee, Wayne. *Barbarians and Brothers: Anglo-American Warfare, 1500–1865*. Oxford and New York: Oxford University Press, 2011.

———. "Mind and Matter—A Cultural Analysis in American Military History: A Look at the State of the Field." *The Journal of American History* 93, no. 4 (2007): 1116–1142.

Levinson, Irving, W. *Wars within War: Mexican Guerrillas, Domestic Elites, and the United States of America, 1846–1848*. Fort Worth: TCU Press, 2005.

Brian Linn, "The American Way of War Revisited." *Journal of Military History* 66, no. 2 (2002): 501–530.

———. *The Echo of Battle: The Army's Way of War*. Cambridge: Harvard University Press, 2007.

Long, Jeff. *Duel of Eagles: The Mexican and U.S. Fight for the Alamo*. New York: William Morrow and Company, Inc. 1990.

Lozano, Ruben R. *Viva Tejas: The Story of the Tejanos, the Mexican-born Patriots of the Texas Revolution*. San Antonio: Alamo Press, 1936.

Lyles, Ian B. "*Mixed Blessing: The Role of the Texas Rangers in the Mexican War, 1846–1848.*" Thesis, University of Texas at Austin, 2001.

Mahon, John K. *The War of 1812*. Gainesville: University of Florida Press, 1972.

McCaslin, Richard. *Fighting Stock: John S. "Rip" Ford of Texas*. Fort Worth: Texas Christian University Press, 2011.

McGowen, Stanley. *Horse Sweat and Powder Smoke: The First Texas Cavalry in the Civil War*. Collage Station: Texas A&M University Press, 1999.

Mendoza, Alexander, ed. *Texans and War: New Interpretations of the State's Military History*. College Station: Texas A&M University Press, 2012.

Miller, Rick. *John B. Jones and the Frontier Battalion, 1874–1881*. Denton: University of North Texas Press, 2012.

Moneyhon, Carl. *Texas after the Civil War: The Struggle of Reconstruction*. College Station: Texas A&M University Press, 2004.

Moore, Stephen L. *Eighteen Minutes: The Battle of San Jacinto and the Texas Independence Campaign*. Dallas: Republic of Texas Press, 2004.

———. *Savage Frontier: Rangers, Riflemen and Indian Wars in Texas*. Volume I. Denton: University of North Texas Press, 2002.

———. *Savage Frontier: Rangers, Riflemen and Indian Wars in Texas*. Volume II. Denton: University of North Texas Press, 2006.

———. *Savage Frontier: Rangers, Riflemen and Indian Wars in Texas*. Volume III. Denton: University of North Texas Press, 2007.

———. *Savage Frontier: Rangers, Riflemen and Indian Wars in Texas*. Volume IV. Denton: University of North Texas Press, 2010.

Moorhead, *Max. Presidio: Bastion of the Spanish Borderlands*. Norman: University of Oklahoma Press, 1979.

Murrah, Jeffery. *None but Texians: A History of Terry's Texas Rangers*. Austin: Eakin Press, 2001.

Nackman, Mark. "The Making of the Texan Citizen Soldier, 1835–1860." *Southwestern Historical Quarterly* 78 (1975): 231–253.

Nance, Joseph M. *After San Jacinto: The Texas-Mexican Frontier, 1836–1841*. Austin: University of Texas Press, 1963.

———. *Attack and Counter-Attack: The Texas-Mexican Frontier, 1842*. Austin: University of Texas Press, 1964.

Nevin, David. *The Texans*. New York: Time Life Books, 1975.

Newcomb, W.W. *The Indians of Texas*. Austin: University of Texas Press, 1961.

Nunnally, Michael L. *American Indian Wars*. Jefferson: McFarland & Company, Inc. 2007.

Oates, Stephen B. *Confederate Cavalry West of the River*. Austin: University of Texas Press, 1961.

———. "Texas Under the Secessionists." *Southwestern Historical Quarterly* 67 (1963): 167–212.

Paget, George. *A History of the British Cavalry, 1816–1919.* London: Leo Cooper, 1973.

Pickering, David. *Brush Men and Vigilantes: Civil War Dissent in Texas.* College Station: Texas A&M University Press, 2004.

Pierce, Gerald S. "*The Army of the Texas Republic, 1836–1845.*" Ph.D. Diss., University of Mississippi, 1963.

Pittman, Walter. *New Mexico and the Civil War.* Charleston: History Press, 2011.

Poyo, Gerald, and Gilberto Hinojosa, eds. *Tejano Origins in Eighteenth-Century San Antonio.* Austin: University of Texas Press, 1991.

Prucha, Francis. *The Sword of the Republic: The United States Army on the Frontier, 1783–1846.* Bloomington & London: Indiana University Press, 1969.

Purcell, Allen Robert. "*History of the Texan Militia, 1835–1903.*" Ph.D. Diss., University of Texas at Austin, 1981.

Radding, Cynthia. "The Presidio and Militia on the Northern Frontier of New Spain: A Documentary History." *Ethnohistory* 47 (Summer-Fall 2000): 767–775.

Richardson, Rupert. *Texas: The Lone Star State.* Englewood Cliffs: Prentice-Hall, Inc, 1958.

———. *The Frontier of Northwest Texas, 1846 to 1876.* Glendale: Arthur H. Clark Company, 1963.

Robinson, Charles M. *The Men Who Wear the Star.* New York: Random House, 2000.

Rosebush, Waldo E. *American Firearms and the Changing Frontier.* Spokane: Litho-Art Printers, 1962.

Ross, John F. *War on the Run: The Epic Story of Robert Rogers and the Conquest of America's First Frontier.* New York: Bantam Books, 2009.

Ross, Steven T. *From Flintlock to Rifle: Infantry Tactics, 1740–1866.* London: Frank Cass, 1996.

Samora, Julian. *Gunpowder Justice: A Reassessment of the Texas Rangers.* Notre Dame: University of Notre Dame Press, 1979.

Sawyer, Charles W. *Firearms in American History.* Northwood: The Plimpton Press, 1910.

Shearer, Earnest. "The Callahan Expedition, 1855." *Southwestern Historical Quarterly* 54 (1951): 430–451.

Simpson, Harold. *Cry Comanche : The 2nd U.S. Cavalry in Texas, 1855–1861.* Hillsboro: Hill Jr. College Press, 1979.

Smith, David P. *Frontier Defense in the Civil War: Texas' Rangers and Rebels.* College Station: Texas A&M University Press, 1992.

Smith, Digby. *Charge! Great Cavalry Charges of the Napoleonic Wars.* London: Greenhill Books, 2003.

Smith, Foster T. *From Dominance to Disappearance: The Indians of Texas and the Near Southwest, 1786–1859*. Lincoln: University of Nebraska Press, 2005.

Smith, Gene. *Mounted Warriors: From Alexander the Great and Cromwell to Stuart, Sheridan, and Custer*. Hoboken: John Wiley & Sons, Inc, 2009.

Smith, Justin. *The War with Mexico*. 2 vols. New York: Macmillan, 1919.

Smith, Thomas T. *The Old Army in Texas: A Research Guide to the U.S. Army in Nineteenth-Century Texas*. Austin: Texas State Historical Association, 2000.

———. *The U.S. Army and the Texas Frontier Economy, 1845–1900*. College Station: Texas A&M University Press, 1999.

Spurlin, Charles D. *Texas Volunteers in the Mexican War: Muster Rolls of Texas Military Units*. Austin: Eakin Press, 1998.

Starr, Stephen. *The Union Cavalry in the Civil War*. 3 vols. Baton Rouge: Louisiana State University Press, 1979.

Steffen, Randy. *The Horse Soldier, 1776–1943: The United States Cavalryman: His Uniforms, Arms, Accoutrements, and Equipments*. 4 vols. Norman: University of Oklahoma Press, 1977.

Taylor, John. *Bloody Valverde: A Civil War Battle on the Rio Grande, February 21, 1862*. Albuquerque: University of New Mexico Press, 1995.

Tebbel, John. *The Compact History of the Indian Wars*. New York: Hawthorn Books, Inc. 1966.

Texas Almanac, 2014–2015. Denton: Texas State Historical Association, 2014.

"Texas Military Forces Historical Sketch: Spanish American War." Texas Military Forces Museum Web Site.

Thiele, Thomas F. "The Evolution of Cavalry in the American Civil War; 1861–1863." Ph.D. Diss., University of Michigan, 1951.

Thompson, Jerry. *Cortina: Defending the Mexican Name in Texas*. College Station: Texas A&M University Press, 2007.

———. *Henry Hopkins Sibley: Confederate General of the West*. Natchitoches: Northwestern State University Press, 1987.

———. *Vaqueros in Blue and Gray*. Austin: Presidial, 1976.

Tierney, John. *Chasing Ghosts: Unconventional Warfare in American History*. Washington, D.C.: Potomac Books, Inc., 2006.

Tijerina, Andrés. *Tejanos and Texas under the Mexican flag, 1821–1836*. College Station: Texas A&M University Press, 1994.

Tolbert, Frank. *The Day of San Jacinto*. Austin: Pemberton Press, 1959.

Tyler, Ronnie. "The Rangers at Zacualtipan." *Texana* 4 (1966): 341–350.

Utley, Robert. *Frontiersmen in Blue: The United States Army and the Indian, 1848–1865*. New York: The Macmillan Company, 1967.

———. *Lone Star Justice. The First Century of the Texas Rangers*. New York: Oxford University Press, 2002.

Wahgelstein, John D. "Preparing for the Wrong War: United States and Low Intensity Conflict, 1775–1890." Ph.D. Diss., Temple University, 1990.

Walraven, Bill, and Marjorie Walraven. "The 'Sabine Chute': The U.S. Army and the Texas Revolution." *Southwestern Historical Quarterly* 107 (July 2003–April 2004): 573–601.

Ward, Fay E. *The Cowboy at Work*. Norman: University of Oklahoma Press, 1958.

Watford, W. H. "Confederate Western Ambitions." *Southwestern Historical Quarterly* 44 (1940): 161–187.

Webb, Walter P. *The Great Plains*. Boston: Houghton Mifflin Company, 1936.

———. *The Texas Rangers: A Century of Frontier Defense*. 2nd ed. Austin: University of Texas Press, 1965.

Weber, David. *The Spanish Frontier in North America*. New Haven: Yale University Press, 1992.

Weigley, Russell. *The American Way of War: A History of United States Military Strategy and Policy*. Bloomington: Indiana University Press, 1973.

Whitlock, Flint. *Distant Bugles, Distant Drums: The Union Response to the Confederate Invasion of New Mexico*. Boulder: University of Colorado Press, 2006.

Wilkins, Frederick. *The Highly Irregular Irregulars: The Texas Rangers in the Mexican War*. Austin: Eakin Press, 1990.

———. *The Legend Begins: The Texas Rangers, 1823–1845*. Austin: State House Press, 1996.

———. *Defending the Borders: The Texas Rangers, 1848–1861*. Austin: State House Press, 2001.

Wilson, James A. *Hide and Horn in Texas: The Spread of Cattle Ranching, 1836–1900*. Boston: American Press, 1983.

Winfrey, Dorman H. *Indian Tribes of Texas*. Waco: Texian Press, 1917.

Wooster, Ralph. *Lone Star Regiments in Gray*. Austin: Eakin Press, 2002.

———. *Texas and Texans in the Civil War*. Texas and Texans in the Civil War. Eakin Press, 1995.

Wooster, Ralph, and Robert Wooster. "'Rarin' for a Fight': Texans in the Confederate Army." *Southwestern Historical Quarterly* 84 (1981): 387–426.

Wooster, Robert. *The American Military Frontiers: The United States Army and the West, 1783–1900*. Albuquerque: University of New Mexico Press, 2009.

Wormser, Richard. *The Yellowlegs: The Story of the United States Cavalry*. New York: Doubleday & Co., 1966.

Yoakum, H. *History of Texas from Its First Settlement in 1685 to Its Annexation to the United States in 1846*. 2 vols. New York: Redfield, 1855.

Yoder, Randy L. "Rackensackers and Rangers: Brutality in the Conquest of Northern Mexico, 1846–1848." Thesis, Eastern Mennonite University, 1992.

INDEX

A

B

L

M